I BELIEVE
IN THE HOLY SPIRIT

III

The River of the Water of Life
flows in the East and in the West

Principal works by Yves Congar

Chrétiens désunis (1937): *Divided Christendom* (1939)

Esquisses du Mystère de l'Eglise (1941; 2nd ed. 1953): in *The Mystery of the Church* (1960)

Vraie et fausse réforme dans l'Eglise (1950)

Le Christ, Marie et l'Eglise (1952): *Christ, Our Lady and the Church* (1957)

Jalons pour une théologie du laïcat (1953): *Lay People in the Church* (1957)

Le Mystère du Temple (*Lectio divina* series; 1958): *The Mystery of the Temple* (1962)

Vaste monde, ma paroisse (1959): *The Wide World my Parish* (1961)

La Tradition et les traditions (2 vols, 1960, 1963): *Tradition and Traditions* (1966)

Les Voies du Dieu vivant (1962): *The Revelation of God* (1968) and *Faith and Spiritual Life* (1969)

La Foi et la Théologie (*Le mystère chrétien*, 1; 1962)

Sacerdoce et laïcat (1963): *Priest and Layman* (1967)/*A Gospel Priesthood* (1967) and *Christians Active in the World* (1968)

Sainte Eglise (1963)

La Tradition et la vie de l'Eglise (1963): *Tradition and the Life of the Church/The Meaning of Tradition* (1964)

Pour une Eglise servante et pauvre (1963): *Power and Poverty in the Church* (1964)

Chrétiens en dialogue (1964): *Dialogue between Christians* (1966)

Jésus-Christ, notre Médiateur, notre Seigneur (1965): *Jesus Christ* (1966)

Situation et tâches présentes de la théologie (1967)

L'Ecclésiologie du haut Moyen Age (1968)

L'Eglise de S. Augustin à l'époque moderne (*Histoire des Dogmes* series; 1970)

L'Eglise une, sainte, catholique, apostolique (*Mysterium Salutis*, 15; 1970)

Ministères et communion ecclésiale (1971)

Un peuple messianique. Salut et libération (1975)

Eglise catholique et France moderne (1978)

Je crois en l'Esprit Saint (3 vols, 1979, 1980): *I Believe in the Holy Spirit* (3 vols, 1983)

YVES M. J. CONGAR

I BELIEVE IN
THE HOLY SPIRIT

VOLUME III

The River of the Water of Life (Rev 22:1)
flows in the East and in the West

TRANSLATED BY
DAVID SMITH

THE SEABURY PRESS
New York

●

GEOFFREY CHAPMAN
London

A Geoffrey Chapman book published by
Cassell Ltd.
1 Vincent Square, London SW1P 2PN

The Seabury Press
815 Second Avenue, New York, NY 10017

First published in French as *Je crois en l'Esprit Saint*, III: *Le Fleuve de Vie coule en Orient et en Occident*
© Les Editions du Cerf, 1980

English translation first published 1983

English translation © Geoffrey Chapman, a division of Cassell Ltd. 1983

Typeset in VIP Times by
D. P. Media Limited, Hitchin, Hertfordshire

Printed and bound in Hungary

Library of Congress Cataloging in Publication Data

Congar, Yves, 1904–
  I believe in the Holy Spirit.

  Translation of: Je crois en l'Esprit Saint.
  Contents: v. 1. The Holy Spirit in the 'economy'—v. 2. 'He is Lord and giver of life'—v.3. The river of the water of life (Rev 22:1) flows in the East and in the West.
  1. Holy Spirit. I. Title.
BT121.2.C59713 1983   231′.3   82–19420

Geoffrey Chapman:
ISBN 0 225 66355 4 (this volume)
      0 225 66352 X (three-volume set)

The Seabury Press:
ISBN 0-8164-0537-9 (this volume)
      0-8164-0540-9 (three-volume set)

In memory of Patrice Kučela
who was perhaps the most gifted of my students
and who was killed by the Gestapo in Prague,
when his country was subjected to tyranny.

'Arise, O Jerusalem, stand upon the height . . .
and see your children gathered from west and east
at the word of the Holy One!'

(Bar 5:5)

CONTENTS

CONTENTS

ABBREVIATIONS
USED IN THIS BOOK

AAS Acta Apostolicae Sedis
Acta Acad. Velehrad. Acta Academiae Velehradensis
Anal. Greg. Analecta Gregoriana
Année théol. august. Année théologique augustinienne
Arch. Franc. Hist. Archivum Franciscanum historicum
Arch. Fr. Praed. Archivum Fratrum Praedicatorum
Arch. hist. doctr. litt. M.A. Archives d'histoire doctrinale et littéraire du Moyen Age
Arch. Hist. Pont. Archivum historiae pontificiae
Bibl. August. Bibliothèque augustinienne
Bibl. Byzant. Brux. Bibliotheca Byzantina Bruxellensis
Bibl. de philos. contemp. Bibliothèque de philosophie contemporaine
Bibl. ETL Bibliotheca Ephemeridum Theologicarum Lovaniensium
Bibl. Œcum. Bibliothèque Œcuménique
BLE Bulletin de littérature ecclésiastique
BullThom Bulletin thomiste
CNRS Centre National de la Recherche Scientifique
CSEL Corpus Scriptorum Ecclesiasticorum Latinorum
DACL Dictionnaire d'archéologie chrétienne et de liturgie
Dict. Hist. Geó. Eccl. Dictionnaire d'histoire et de géographie ecclésiastiques
Doc. cath. La documentation catholique
DS Enchiridion Symbolorum, ed. H. Denzinger, rev. A. Schönmetzer
DTC Dictionnaire de théologie catholique
ECQ Eastern Churches Quarterly
ETL Ephemerides Theologicae Lovanienses
GCS Griechische christliche Schriftsteller
Greg Gregorianum
JTS Journal of Theological Studies
Mansi *Sacrorum Conciliorum nova et amplissima Collectio*, ed. J. D. Mansi
M-D La Maison-Dieu
MGH Monumenta Germaniae historica
MScRel Mélanges de science religieuse
NRT Nouvelle Revue théologique
Or. Chr. Oriens Christianus
Or. Chr. Anal. Orientalia christiana analecta
Or. Chr. Period. Orientalia christiana periodica
Patr. Or. Patrologia Orientalis
Patr. Syr. Patrologia Syriaca
PG Migne, *Patrologia Graeca*
PL Migne, *Patrologia Latina*

RAM   *Revue d'ascétique et de mystique*
RB   *Revue biblique*
RBén   *Revue bénédictine*
Rev. Et. byz.   *Revue des études byzantines*
Rev. M.A. latin   *Revue du Moyen Age latin*
RHE   *Revue d'histoire ecclésiastique*
RHPR   *Revue d'histoire et de philosophie religieuses*
RSPT   *Revue des sciences philosophiques et théologiques*
RSR   *Recherches de science religieuse*
RTAM   *Recherches de théologie ancienne et médiévale*
RThom   *Revue thomiste*
RTL   *Revue théologique de Louvain*
SC   *Sources chrétiennes*
Spicil. Sacr. Lovan.   *Spicilegium Sacrum Lovaniense*
ST   *Summa Theologica*
TDNT   G. Kittel and G. Friedrich (eds), *Theological Dictionary of the New Testament* (Eng. tr.)
ThSt   *Theological Studies*
TQ   *Theologische Quartalschrift*
VS   *La Vie spirituelle*
ZAW   *Zeitschrift für die alttestamentliche Wissenschaft*
ZKT   *Zeitschrift für katholische Theologie*
ZTK   *Zeitschrift für Theologie und Kirche*

INTRODUCTION

1

THE PRESENTATION OF THIS VOLUME

I must begin this book by explaining its nature and contents and how it came to be written. Chamfort said that 'theology is to religion what casuistry is to justice', but I am not very impressed by this observation, because I know that it is not true. Theology is the cultivation of faith by the honest use of the cultural means available at the time. Bonhoeffer's remark that the only choice for the Church is between concrete statement and silence, and that the Church is lying if it only utters principles, touches me more nearly, though not to the extent that I feel his disapproval of my own work. He spoke in this way, after all, at a time when Christians were required to resist Nazism. He also criticized Karl Barth in a more general way for 'positivism of Revelation', and here I would think the reference more closely applied to me, although I would point out that there is also a positivism of experience and the here and now. To each his own positivism!

One question seems to me to be very important for everyone and also for the theologian and his special task. It is the question of the country he lives in, the frame of reference within which he works and the language he speaks. As a theologian, I live in the Church of the Scriptures, the Fathers and the Councils. I am a teacher and my task is to teach. This task is reflected in my language, which is didactic. My way of life is marked by—I could almost say that it bears the stigmata of—difficulties that have for years now made it more sedentary than it once was, more restricted to papers, books and texts. This present work is the fruit of labours commenced a long time ago. Over the years, a great deal of documentation, perhaps too much, has accumulated. The work has been accompanied by love and prayer, and the sometimes too ponderous elements of scholarship have been transformed every day into praise and worship.

I have been told that my language is not the language of today and will not be understood by contemporary readers. A friend asked me if I could not go on to publish an outline of the whole which would be accessible to people like him, ordinary people of the kind described by Chesterton—if God had not loved them he would not have made so many of them. I would like to satisfy him and I may try to do so, though I cannot be sure that I shall succeed. However true these comments may be, they have not prevented me from writing, nor have they convinced me that my task is vain. After all, the suggestion that I should 'speak the language of today' raises the immediate question: Which language of today? And would it be more easily understood? All language is related to man and to whatever relationships he has, and that of the Fathers of the Church is related to God and his mystery. It not only calls for a great intellectual effort to move into the country inhabited by the Fathers—it even requires a religious conversion. And is their language really so remote from the language of today? Their writings are certainly being widely read, questioned and heeded again today. In this volume, however, I have had in mind above all the theological dialogue between Orthodox Christianity and Roman Catholicism.

This dialogue is, fortunately, to begin with the subject of the sacraments and of the Church as a 'mystery', that is, as the great sacrament. These realities of grace have remained common to Orthodox and Western Catholics at a deep level. Sooner or later, however, and probably sooner, we shall again come up against difficulties concerning the theology of the Holy Spirit as such and the theology of the part that he plays in the sacraments that have not been overcome in a thousand years of confrontation. I shall try to deal with some of them in the present volume and I have, for this purpose, divided it into two parts. In the course of his meeting with Pope John Paul II on 29 November 1980 in Istanbul, the Ecumenical Patriarch Dimitrios I spoke of the 'serious theological problems contained in essential chapters of the Christian faith'. He was probably thinking here of the problems with which I deal in this volume. The Bishop of Rome, on the other hand, spoke of 'disagreement not so much at the level of faith as at the level of expression', and in so doing confirmed the conclusion reached in several very serious studies and even in my own modest efforts.

Before proceeding to this Volume III, I should like to express my gratitude to those who have helped me so much, either by obtaining the books that I needed or by typing the manuscript. I would like to thank especially Fr Nicolas Walty and Mme Nicole Legrain, without whom this book would never have appeared, any more than Volumes I and II.

2
GREEK AND LATIN
TRINITARIAN THEOLOGY

The mystery of the Trinity only came to be suitably formulated after many tentative expressions, errors and half-truths, a large number of them running into dead-ends, had been hazarded by some of the most clear-thinking and most Christian authors in each successive period in the early history of the Church. This history has been fully written[1] and I shall not attempt to rewrite it here. I am more concerned with pneumatology, but this is, of course, inseparable from the mystery of the Tri-unity of God himself.

These very imperfect and tentative expressions conceal an intention that is much firmer than the expressions themselves. Justin Martyr made no distinction between the Logos and the Spirit, yet he gave his life for the Christian faith. It took at least two further centuries of more or less successful attemps for a satisfactory vocabulary to emerge, that of one substance and three hypostases or persons. Even such a heroic defender of orthodox faith as Athanasius did not distinguish between *ousia* (essence) and *hypostasis*.[2] Basil the Great was still hesitant on this point. This very vocabulary itself was also a source of difficulties between the Greek East and the Latin West. The literal translation of *hypostasis* into Latin was *substantia*, but the problem arose as to whether one should speak of 'three substances' in the way that the Greeks spoke, quite rightly, of 'three hypostases'. This difficulty troubled Jerome and it appeared again in the Middle Ages.[3]

The faith that was not only professed in the doxology but also lived was, however, fundamentally the same both in the East and in the West. There were, of course, differences in approach, in the theological articulation of the mystery, even at the level of its dogmatic expression, and in intellectual categories and vocabulary. However deep these differences were, however, I am convinced that the Trinitarian faith of the eastern part of the Church was the same as that of the western part.[4] I knew, liked and admired Vladimir Lossky (†1958), who had outstanding ability as a dogmatic theologian in the highest sense of the word, but I told him again and again that I could not agree with his conviction that the *Filioque* was not only the origin of all the differences between the Greek Orthodox and the Roman Catholic Church, but also an article causing an insurmountable opposition between the two branches of the Church and an unbridgeable distance between them. Lossky became less obstinate on this point as he got older, but he had in the meantime, unfortunately, won over a large number of followers.[5]

As I have indicated, there are differences between the East and the West. Their approach and their way of articulating the mystery of the Tri-unity of God are different. It is a precondition of any effort to make manifest the deep community of faith that exists between the two parts of the Church and to express that community in a satisfactory way that this different approach should be recognized and accepted. My own personal experience, both from reading and from contact with individuals and communities, leads me to agree with several experts, including Mgr Szepticky, the Metropolitan of Lwow: 'the East differs from the West even in questions in which they do not differ at all';[6] or T. de Régnon: 'we ought to regard the Greek and the Latin Churches as two sisters who love and visit each other, but who have a different way of keeping house and who therefore live apart'.[7]

It was above all de Régnon († 26 December 1893) who gave a new impetus to Trinitarian studies, more precisely to studies devoted to an improved understanding of the Greek Fathers compared with the Latin Fathers.[8] We all owe a great deal to this scholar, who came to the extremely valuable conclusion that the dogmatic structures of the East and the West are different, but express the same intention in faith. The East and the West agree in faith. At the same time, however, de Régnon simplified the difference between the theologies, with the result that many theologians, especially Orthodox scholars, have since taken his most clear-cut formulae as they stand. It is interesting to quote some of these here:

> Latin philosophers focused first on nature in itself and then traced it back to the supposit, whereas the Greeks first focused on the supposit and then entered into it in order to find nature. The Latins regarded the personality as the way in which nature was expressed, while the Greeks thought of nature as the content of the person. These are contrary ways of viewing things, throwing two concepts of the same reality on to different grounds.
>
> The Latin theologian therefore says: 'three persons in God', whereas the Greek says: 'one God in three persons'. In both cases, the faith and the dogma are the same, but the mystery is presented in two different forms.
>
> If we think first of the concept of nature and the concept of personality is then added to it, the concrete reality has to be defined as a 'personified nature'. This is seeing nature *in recto* and the person *in obliquo*. If, on the other hand, we think first of the concept of the person and the concept of nature comes later, then the concrete reality must be defined as 'a person possessing a nature'. This is seeing the person *in recto* and nature *in obliquo*. The two *definitions* are true and complete and both are adequate to the object in mind, but they are the result of two different views, and that is why the logical deductions from them follow opposite paths.
>
> The Scholastic theology of the Latin Church followed one of these ways, while the dogmatic theology of the Greek Church continued on the other path. The consequence is that the two theologies express the same truth, just as two symmetrical triangles may be equal, but cannot be placed one on top of the other.[9]

De Régnon had clearly perceived an authentic and fundamental truth here, and we shall see later how closely it corresponds to the reality. Similar comments were made more recently by the historian of doctrine J. N. D. Kelly, whose conclusions are closer to the original texts and at the same time less systematic.[10] De Régnon's insights have unfortunately often been even further simplified and hardened to the point of becoming misleading caricatures. A few examples will illustrate this:

> What characterizes all these constructions is their initial impersonalism. This is present at the very birth of the hypostases and it points to the ontological primacy of the ousia over the hypostasis. It is not characteristic of the Cappadocian Fathers, for whom the hypostases existed as such, but it is characteristic of Augustine's teaching and that of all Catholic theologians, with their initial *deitas* in which the hypostases exist as relationships of origin, through mutual opposition. This Catholic doctrine of the procession is simply an impersonal subordinationism, in which the *deitas* or deity is the primordial metaphysical basis and, in this sense, the sufficient foundation or the cause of the hypostases.[11]

> For Augustine, on the other hand, the processions can be reduced to attributes of the one essence of God.[12]

> Latin theology has yielded to this influence and has abandoned the level of theological personalism, becoming a philosophy of the essence.[13]

> The doctrine of the *Filioque* . . . confines the Trinity of the persons within the unity of nature by making them relations based on essence. . . . (If the Father and the Son are a single principle of spiration) there are no longer two distinct hypostases, but impersonal substance instead.[14]

It is important first of all to understand the logic by which the Greeks on the one hand and the Latins on the other theologically (or dogmatically) elaborated their common faith in the mystery of the Trinity, and then to consider the attempts that have been made to resolve this irritating difference between their ideas concerning the procession of the Holy Spirit. Before going on to this question, however, I propose to conclude this Introduction by commenting, however schematically, on the different approach and development of theology in the East and the West and then recalling the history of the whole teaching about the Spirit. This mere reminder will enable me to discuss in a synthetic form the significance of each theology.

The contrast or at least the differences between these two theologies of the Trinity are the consequence of two different ways of approaching the mystery and of 'doing theology'. The Greeks inherited two rules from the Fathers and attempted to synthesize them. On the one hand, they made use of the resources of human reason. In opposition to Julian the Apostate, who had forbidden Christians to teach in the schools of grammar and rhetoric and to send their children to the public schools, the three 'hierarchs', Basil of Caesarea, Gregory Nazianzen and John Chrysostom, had insisted on and practised the use of rational resources. These resources were employed in the training of theologians rather than in the elaboration of revealed data. On the other hand, they had actively combated the wretched heresy of Eunomius and the Anomoeans [see below, p. 29], which proposed an entirely homogeneous and easy knowledge of God who, it claimed, could be known in the same way as other objects of our human reason. In opposition to this teaching, the Cappadocian Fathers affirmed that God was unknowable. We are able, they taught, to know something of him on the basis of his activity, but he himself always transcends every representation, which is always confined to the created order. John Chrysostom wrote a treatise on the unknowability of God (*SC* 28 (1951)) and Gregory of Nyssa's writings on the inaccessibility of God to the created mind, even when that is illuminated by faith, are classical.[15]

Reason, then, was put to good use in the theology of the Trinity—this is abundantly clear from the writings of Athanasius, Basil the Great and the two Gregorys. It was employed above all to refute heresies and to expose their errors of interpretation. In the positive treatment of the mystery, however, one simply had to follow Scripture, the Fathers and the Councils. The practice followed in the East is well summarized in the nineteenth canon of the Council 'in Trullo' (692), which is usually regarded as belonging to the Sixth Ecumenical Council (the Third Council of Constantinople): 'The Church's pastors must explain Scripture in accordance with the commentaries of the Fathers'.[16]

The situation changed with regard to our subject, the procession of the Holy Spirit, when the Patriarch Photius published his *Mystagogic Discourse on the Holy Spirit* (*PG* 102, 280–392) about 886. Photius did not confine himself to scriptural arguments and references to patristic or papal texts—he also made extensive use of his critical reason. Since his time, the debate between Orthodox and Catholic Christians over the dogmatic construction of the mystery has at least partly consisted of rational theological argument. The Greek theologians could on occasion be as competent and as subtle in their reasoning as their Latin counterparts. Their theological attitude and temperament, however, remained different. The Catholic dogma of the *Filioque* is based on dogmatic reasoning, but in the first place it goes back to scriptural data. Augustine, for example, spoke of the *Filioque* because the New Testament attributes the Spirit both to the Father and to the Son. At the same time, he also made it a rule in Latin theology that an *intellectus fidei* or an 'understanding of faith' should be sought through reasoning and meditation and therefore, if necessary, outside Scripture. Anselm and Thomas Aquinas devoted their metaphysical brilliance to developing this theology.

In the fourteenth century, therefore, in the face of the predominant Scholastic theology of the West and the humanistic attitude of, for example, Barlaam, and then when translations of the great Latin theological writings began to appear in Greece, intense discussions took place about the theological method and the place and structure of the syllogism, as well as whether it should consist of two premises of faith, or one of faith and one of reason.[17] Over and against these views, Gregory Palamas (1296–1359) defended both the unknowability of the divine essence and the reality of a supernatural and mystical knowledge of God that was quite different from a rational or intellectual knowledge. The Greek theologians of this tradition found the rationality of the Latin Scholastics an unacceptable intrusion on the part of created reason into the mysteries of God. The best example of a serious criticism of Latin theology by the Greeks who accused their Western counterparts of rationalizing the mystery of God's being by a mistaken use of the syllogism will be found in the treatise written by Nilus Cabasilas, the Archbishop of Thessalonica (†1363). This was edited some years ago by Emmanuel Candal.[18] Nilus discussed (and believed that he had refuted) fifteen syllogisms on which the theology of the *Filioque* was supposedly based. This is the impression that many Greek theologians still had at the Council of Ferrara (Florence) in 1438–1439.[19] The Latin theologians, on the other hand, thought that the Greeks' opposition to their arguments was attributable to a lack of intellectual power.[20]

I should like to make my own the testimony of Pope Paul VI in support of the position that the above observations have a significance for us today, even though they are concerned with past history; that I have a very high regard for the Eastern way of doing theology, and that I should like to place myself in a tradition common to both East and West. What Pope Paul VI said on his return from a journey—or pilgrimage—to Turkey, where he visited Istanbul (Constantinople) and Ephesus among other places, was as follows:

The East is a master, teaching us that we, as believers, are not only called to reflect about the revealed truth, that is, to formulate a theology which may rightly be described as scientific (see *DS* 3135ff.), but also obliged to recognize the supernatural character of that revealed truth. That character does not entitle us to interpret that truth in terms of pure natural rationality and it requires us to respect, in the texts, the very terminology in which that truth was stated with authority (*DS* 824 [442], 2831 [1658]). The East provides us with an example of faithfulness to our doctrinal inheritance and reminds us of a rule which is also our own and which we have often reaffirmed recently, at a time when so many attempts are being made—many of them full of good intentions, but not always with happy results— to express a new theology that is in accordance with present-day attitudes. This rule was expressed by the First Vatican Council, which looked for progress in 'understanding, knowledge and wisdom' in the Church's teaching, on condition that that teaching remained what it had always been (see *De fide* IV; Vincent of Lérins, *Commonitorium*, 28: *PL* 50, 668).

During our journey, we wanted to assure the East that the faith of the Councils that were celebrated on this blessed soil and that are recognized by the Latin Church as ecumenical is still our faith. That faith forms a very wide and solid basis for studies destined to restore perfect Christian communion between the

Orthodox and the Catholic Churches in that single and firm teaching that the Church's magisterium, guided by the Holy Spirit, proclaims as authentic.[21]

NOTES

1. J. Lebreton, *Histoire du dogme de la Trinité*, I and II (as far as Irenaeus), 6th ed. (Paris, 1927–1928); G.-L. Prestige, *God in Patristic Thought*, 2nd ed. (London, 1952); J. N. D. Kelly, *Early Christian Doctrines*, 5th ed. (London, 1977); G. Kretschmar, 'Le développement de la doctrine du Saint-Esprit du Nouveau Testament à Nicée', *Verbum Caro*, 88 (1968), 555. In addition to these works, the following may also be mentioned: H. B. Swete, *On the History of the Doctrine of the Procession of the Holy Spirit from the Apostolic Age to the Death of Charlemagne* (Cambridge, 1876); *idem*, *The Holy Spirit in the Ancient Church* (London, 1912); T. Reusch, *Die Entstehung der Lehre von Heiligen Geiste* (Zürich, 1953); H. Opitz, *Ursprünge frühchristlicher Pneumatologie* (Berlin, 1960).

2. See G. Bardy, *DTC*, XV, cols 1666–1667. See also Epiphanius of Salamis, *Haer.* 69, 72.

3. Volume I, pp. 75–76, 82 note 23; Prestige, *op. cit.*, pp. 187ff., 235ff.; T. de Régnon, *op. cit.* below (note 8), I, p. 216, with Faustus of Riez' excellent text of 480. For Anselm, see below, pp. 101–102, note 8; Thomas Aquinas, *Contra Err. Graec.*, I, prol.

4. Richard of Saint-Victor, confirming that some in fact spoke of three substances and one essence, while others spoke of three subsistences and one substance, wrote in his *De Trin*. IV, 20 (*PL* 196, 943C): 'Sed absit ab eis (Graeci et Latini) diversa credere, et hos vel illos in fide errare! In hac ergo verborum varietate intelligenda est veritas una, quamvis apud diversos sit nominum acceptio diversa.' Alexander of Hales said in this context: 'idem credunt (Graeci et Latini) sed non eodem modo proferunt': see below, pp. 174ff.

5. See H.-M. Legrand's article in *RSPT*, 56 (1972), 697–700.

6. Quoted by G. Tsébricov, *L'esprit de l'Orthodoxie* (*Irénikon*, Collection No. 7) (1927), p. 9.

7. T. de Régnon, *op. cit.* below (note 8), III, p. 412.

8. T. de Régnon, *Etudes de théologie positive sur la Sainte Trinité*, 4 vols (Paris, I and II 1892, III and IV 1898).

9. *Ibid.*, I, pp. 433–434 and 251–252 respectively. See also I, pp. 276, 305, 309, 387–388, 428ff.; IV, pp. 128, 143.

10. Kelly, *op. cit.* (note 1), says, for example (p. 136): 'Western Trinitarianism . . . had long been marked by a monarchian bias. What was luminously clear to the theologians representing it was the divine unity; so mysterious did they find the distinctions within the unity that, though fully convinced of their reality, they were only beginning, haltingly and timidly, to think of them as "Persons". In the East, where the intellectual climate was impregnated with Neo-Platonic ideas about the hierarchy of being, an altogether different, confessedly pluralistic approach had established itself.' He is referring to the third century, that is, before Athanasius and the Cappadocian Fathers on the one hand and Augustine on the other.

11. S. Bulgakov, *Le Paraclet*, Fr. tr. C. Andronikof (Paris, 1946), pp. 67–68; see also pp. 118 ff.

12. J. Meyendorff, *Russie et Chrétienté*, 4th series, 2nd year (1950), 160.

13. S. Verkhovsky, *ibid.*, 195.

14. V. Lossky, quoted by O. Clément, 'Vladimir Lossky, un théologien de la personne et du Saint-Esprit', *Messager de l'Exarchat du Patriarche russe en Europe occidentale*, 8th year, 30–31 (April–September 1959), 137–206, especially 194. This number of the journal was devoted to Vladimir Lossky and appeared one year after his death.

15. See Gregory of Nyssa, *Life of Moses*, II, 163–164 (*SC* 1, 1955 ed., pp. 81–82). For the apophatism of the Fathers, see J. Hochstaffl, *Negative Theologie, Ein Versuch des patristischen Begriffs* (Munich, 1976). Examples of apophatism among the Latin Fathers and even among the Scholastic theologians can, however, also be found in dozens of texts.

16. C. J. Hefele and H. Leclercq, *Histoire des Conciles*, III/1 (Paris, 1913), p. 566.

17. The history of this movement will be found, exhaustively documented, in G. Podskalsky, *Theologie und Philosophie in Byzanz. Der Streit um die theologische Methodik in der spätbyzantinischen Geistesgeschichte (14./15. Jh.); seine systematischen Grundlagen und seine historische Entwicklung (Byzantinisches Archiv, 15)* (Munich, 1977), pp. 124 ff.

18. E. Candal, *Nilus Cabasilas et theologia S. Thomae de Processione Spiritus Sancti. Novum e Vaticanis codicibus subsidium ad historiam theologiae Byzantinae saeculi XIV plenius elucidandam (Studi e Testi*, 116) (Vatican, 1945).

19. J. Gill, *The Council of Florence* (Cambridge, 1959), p. 223, writes: 'One noteworthy difference can be remarked between the Greek and Latin methods as illustrated by Mark Eugenicus and Montenero. Though Mark showed that he understood and was at home in the philosophical explanation of the mystery of the Blessed Trinity, he did not bring that into his arguments except when pressed by an opponent. When he was putting forward his own proofs he was content to quote his scriptural or patristic authority and add comments which amounted to little more than a repetition of the words of his texts. The Latin orator on the other hand almost invariably argued from the passages that he quoted to the conclusion that he claimed must follow from an acceptance of the truth enunciated in the quotation.'

20. See, for example, this text by the former Master General of the Order of Preachers in his famous report to the Council of Lyons in 1274: 'Perit apud eos pro magna parte scientia cum studio, et ideo non intelligunt quae dicuntur eis per rationes, sed adhaerent semper quibusdam conciliis et quibusdam quae tradita sunt eis a praedecessoribus suis, sicut faciunt quidam haeretici idiotae, ad quos ratio nihil valet': Humbert of Romans, *Opus tripartitum*, Pars II, col. 11, in Edward Brown, *Appendix ad Fasciculum rerum expectandarum et fugiendarum* (London, 1690), II, p. 216.

21. Paul VI, audience of 2 August 1967: see *Doc. cath.*, 64, No. 1500, 1580.

PART ONE

THE HOLY SPIRIT
IN THE DIVINE TRI-UNITY

I
KNOWLEDGE OF THE TRINITARIAN MYSTERY

1
THE SOURCES OF OUR KNOWLEDGE OF THE HOLY SPIRIT NECESSITY AND CONDITIONS FOR A DOGMATIC AND THEOLOGICAL EXPRESSION

Our first source of knowledge is obviously Revelation itself, of which the conciliar document *Dei Verbum* had this to say: 'This plan of revelation is realized by deeds and words having an inner unity: the deeds wrought by God in the history of salvation manifest and confirm the teaching and realities signified by the words, while the words proclaim the deeds and clarify the mystery contained in them'.[1] There are, in other words, certain data with a revelatory value and, together with them, inspired words which disclose their meaning.

These data are those of the whole economy of grace, in the first place those contained in the Old and New Testaments, and then those of the whole history of salvation, including the modern period. I have drawn attention to a great number of these in the first two volumes of this work, as I have also to the corresponding texts. The texts in question are pre-eminently those of Scripture, but also those of the witnesses to Tradition, texts which are of secondary importance, but nonetheless very rich: the writings of the Fathers, the saints and the theologians of the Church and the Church's liturgy, all bearing witness to the Holy Spirit in different ways. I have already quoted many such witnesses and shall quote others in this volume. Together they constitute the great Christian family of which we acknowledge that we are members.

There are numerous statements in Scripture, some of them remarkably dogmatic in character and others substantially theological. Scripture often speaks of the Spirit and even of 'God', however, in images, and these were

3

taken up again by the Fathers, who frequently commented on them. It is worth recalling some of the principal ones here:

Breath, air, wind: this is the very name of the Spirit.

Water, and especially living water.[2]

Fire, tongues of fire (Acts 2:3; Is 6:6): 'The great symbols of the Spirit—water, fire, air and wind—belong to the world of nature and do not have definite shapes; above all they call to mind the idea of being invaded by a presence and of a deep and irresistible expansion'.[3]

Dove: see especially Volume I, pp. 16–17.

Anointing, chrism.[4]

Finger of God: especially in Lk 11:20, the parallel text, Mt 12:28, having 'Spirit'.[5] In the Old Testament, the finger of God is the instrument and the sign of God's power (Ex 8:15) and even of his creative power (Ps 8:3; in 33:6, it is the 'breath of his mouth'). It is also the sign of the authority employed by God in his initiative—the tablets of the Law were, for example, written by his finger (Ex 31:18; Deut 9:10). In Christianity, God's law is written by his Spirit in our hearts.[6] God's power, then, is expressed by his arm and his hand, the extremity of which touches man. This touch is clearly both strong and delicate: in his great painting of the creation of Adam in the Sistine Chapel, Michelangelo provides a wonderful representation of this. In the gospel, this is, it has been suggested, the expression of a participation in God's holiness through a powerful, yet delicate touch.[7]

There are also other names given to the Holy Spirit which are less graphic, but more open to speculation. They include:

Seal: the Spirit with whom the Father anointed Christ at his baptism (Jn 6:27; Acts 10:38) and who has since then anointed and marked Christians (2 Cor 1:22; Eph 1:13; 4:30). This 'seal' represents something final and definitive. The Spirit is the Promised One, the eschatological Gift. In God, he is the fulfilment of the communication of the deity. Athanasius said that the seal that marks us can only be the Spirit, God himself.[8]

Love: see Thomas Aquinas (*C. Gent.* IV, 19; *ST* Ia, q. 37 and parallel texts).

Gift: see below, the chapter on St Augustine; see also Thomas Aquinas, *ST* Ia, q. 38 and parallel texts. This title is so important that a whole chapter will be devoted to it in this volume (see below, pp. 144–151).

Peace: see Jn 20:19, 21; cf. verses 22–23; see also Rom 14:17: 'peace and joy in the Holy Spirit'.

To these images can be added those used in the liturgy. In this context, the section in Volume I, pp. 104–111 should be re-read; the hymn *Veni Creator* and the sequence *Veni, Sancte Spiritus* are there translated. A number of texts of the Fathers and the spiritual writers can also be added, as, for example, when St Simeon the New Theologian compares the Holy Spirit to the key which opens the door (Volume I, pp. 97–98) or when St Bernard compares him to a kiss exchanged between the Father and the Son (Volume I, pp. 90, 92 note 16).

The fact that the mystery of God has often and even preferentially been revealed in images of this kind can be justified in many different ways. The Alexandrian theologians (Origen and others), Pseudo-Dionysius and even Thomas[9] saw in it less a value of revelation than a veil concealing it, an *occultatio*. In that case, I would go so far as to speak of the 'kenotic' conditions of God's self-revelation and self-communication. (I shall discuss this later.) It is in any case worth recalling that the crudest comparisons are often the best, because they preclude any idea of reaching the mystery itself. In my view, however, the fact that God is revealed above all in images has a much deeper reason. It is this: the most material images are metaphors which do not in any sense claim to express being in itself, that is, the quiddity of what they are speaking about; they only express behaviour and what that represents for us. God is a rock, Christ is a lamb, the Spirit is living water. This does not mean that God is a mineral, Christ is an animal, or the Spirit is a liquid with a known chemical formula. It does, however, mean that God is, for us, firmness, Christ is a victim offered for us, and the Spirit is a dynamic bearer of life. Revelation, in other words, by being expressed in images, is essentially an expression of what God is *for us*. It also, of course, discloses something of what God is in himself, but it only does this secondarily and imperfectly. What he is is his secret. 'I know what God is for me', St Bernard said, 'but *quod ad se, ipse novit*—what he is for himself, he knows.'[10]

This fact of a revelation of a 'theology', that is, of the eternal and intimate mystery of God, in the 'economy', that is, in what God has done for us in his work of creation and grace, forms the basis of the thesis that I shall examine later [pp. 11–17] in connection with the question of the identity of the economic Trinity and the immanent Trinity.

This is particularly true in the case of the Holy Spirit. He is affirmed as the subject of certain actions in the New Testament, but not, as some exegetes have insisted, to the extent that he is no more than an impersonal power. At the same time, however, subject of actions as he is, he is certainly revealed without a personal face. The incarnate Word has a face—he has expressed his personality in our human history in the way persons do, and the Father has revealed himself in him. The Spirit does not present such personal characteristics. He is, as it were, buried in the work of the Father and the Son, which he completes. 'We do not usually spend too much time thinking about the breath that supports the word.'[11]

Vladimir Lossky and Paul Evdokimov have spoken of the Spirit's kenosis as a person. He has, as it were, emptied himself of the characteristics of a private or particular person. This is why those who have written about the Holy Spirit have frequently called him the 'unknown' or the 'half-known' one.[12] Already in his own time, Augustine noted that the Holy Spirit had hardly ever been discussed and his mystery had not been examined.[13]

However many theological difficulties there may still be surrounding our knowledge of the third Person, we are now, thank God, in a position to provide a more balanced account. These difficulties have often been discussed by theologians of the Western Church. They include a lack of words and concepts to express the term, in us, of the act of love, whereas for the act of understanding we have the expression 'mental word'.[14] There is also the fact that 'spiration' does not really express the relation that is constitutive of the Person (of the Holy Spirit) as 'fatherhood' and 'sonship' do for the first two persons.[15] 'Holy Spirit' is not, in itself, a relative, but an absolute name. In itself, it would be equally suitable for the Father or the Son, or even for the divine essence.[16] In other words, it is only by virtue of an 'accommodation' authorized by Scripture that it has come to be used as the name of the third Person.[17] In short, our knowledge of the Person known as the 'Holy Spirit' is limited and beset with difficulties.

It is clear, then, that we moved straightaway to a certain level of conceptualization and intellectual construction in our understanding of the Spirit. One is bound to ask whether this is legitimate or even possible. Did theologians themselves not confess that when speaking of God himself they ought to follow the rule of remaining as closely as possible to the scriptural ways of speaking? This was a rule in theology even before theologians knew of Pseudo-Dionysius, who formulated it very decisively: 'It is important to avoid applying rashly any word or any idea at all to the super-essential and mysterious Deity apart from those divinely revealed to us in the holy Scriptures'.[18] This was certainly one of the reasons why those advocates of the divinity of the Holy Spirit, Athanasius and Basil, and even the First Council of Constantinople of 381, avoided giving the title 'God' to the Spirit. Cyril of Jerusalem had this to say about the Spirit: 'In the matter of the Holy Spirit, let us say only those things that have been written. If anything has not been written, let us not stop to investigate the fact. It is the Holy Spirit himself who dictated the Scriptures, he who has also said of himself everything that he wanted to say or everything which we are capable of grasping. Let us therefore say what he has said and let us not be so bold as to say what he has not said.'[19]

Cyril, who was a pastor and a catechist, was quite faithful to the rule which he himself professed. Later theologians, however, who were likewise saints, did not hesitate to go beyond the scriptural texts, at least materially. Thomas Aquinas, who often quoted the text of Pseudo-Dionysius, sometimes in objection to the term *Filioque*, commented that it was Pseudo-Dionysius himself who broke his own rule most frequently.[20] The rest of this present volume will be full of terms and concepts that are not found as such in Scripture. I would therefore ask once again: is it legitimate to use them and, if so, why?

It is justified in the first place by the fact that the scriptural statements and even the images that I have mentioned above have a very full dogmatic content. There is no need for speculation. All that is required is to consider and weigh the meaning of the words, and one is at once involved in theology. Examples of this are: 'The Spirit of truth, who proceeds from the Father' (Jn 15:26); 'He will take what is mine. . . . All that the Father has is mine; therefore I said that he will take what is mine and declare it to you' (16:14–15); 'All mine are thine and thine are mine' (17:10). The whole of Christian experience in the world over nineteen centuries points to the fact that there is something to be intellectually penetrated in the profession of one's faith, that there is coherence and substance in the faith, and that these can be understood, that there is great benefit and joy in looking for these elements, and that faith itself emerges from the search nourished and strengthened.[21]

We have to try to establish a coherence between the images that are found in Scripture. Each term may have several meanings and needs to be interpreted. What is not expressed by one image or idea has to be completed by another image.[22]

It would be impossible to confine ourselves exclusively to Scripture. The Arian and Semi-Arian creeds, the Antiochian creed of 341 and others were composed only of scriptural terms as far as the article on the Holy Spirit is concerned.[23] The Arians' objection to the *homoousios* of Nicaea was that it could not be found in Scripture, and it was for the same reason that the Macedonians rejected the attribution of the title of God to the third Person. However, it was these interpretations, which were held with great stubbornness and therefore became 'heretical', which obliged the Catholic theologians to evolve formulae and expressions sufficiently precise to exclude error. Hilary of Poitiers, who bore witness to and championed the Trinitarian faith (†367), greatly lamented the need for this: 'We are forced . . . to express things that cannot be expressed, . . . we are driven to extend the weakness of our discourse to things that cannot be said, we are constrained to do what is deplorable because the others have also done what is deplorable—what should have been kept in the inner sanctuary has to be exposed to the danger of a human formulation'.[24]

The greatest theologians of the Western tradition may not have had such a strong feeling as Hilary did of being forced to do the impossible, but it is clear that they had to discuss matters of faith and to develop an adequate vocabulary precisely because of the existence of heresies.[25] We have inherited the results of their thought and debate. In this sense, we are what Maurice Blondel called the 'adults of Christianity'. We are bound to use the language that they have evolved and express ourselves in the concepts that they have developed. I shall try to do this in this volume, while at the same time preserving the sense of the mystery that exists far beyond our hesitant efforts. It is possible to outline the mystery and to mark out its contours, but it is not possible to penetrate into it.

The ardent professions of 'apophatism' that we have inherited from the

Greek Fathers are well known, but it is sometimes forgotten that many comparable testimonies can also be found in the writings of the Latins. I have personally compiled a list that could fill several pages. Let me give only one example—a verse written by Adam of Saint-Victor (†1192) that was sung by our forebears in the Middle Ages:

Digne loqui de personis	To speak worthily of the Persons
vim transcendit rationis,	transcends the power of reason
excedit ingenia.	and goes beyond our understanding.
Quid sit gigni, quid processus	What is 'being begotten'? What
me nescire sum professus:[26]	is 'processing'?
	I profess that I do not know.

*   *   *

Faith in the mystery of the Trinity, then, goes beyond any theological terms and constructions that can be formulated by man. It is therefore clear that it is possible for several different Trinitarian theologies to exist, and even several dogmatic formulae and constructions dependent on these theologies. T. de Régnon studied the writings of the Greek and the Latin authors on the Trinity with a close attention that has proved extremely valuable to those who have come after him. His conclusion was that the Western and the Eastern Church share the same faith, although they have approached the mystery from different points and along different ways. This is also what I believe. I go so far as to think that the difference between the two great cultures—the East and the West—forms part of a historical structure of humanity that can be regarded as providential.[27] It is true, of course, that this whole matter cannot be divided neatly into two, in the way that the continent and the islands of the New World were divided between Portugal and Spain, by Alexander VI's Bull *Inter caetera divinae* (1493), according to whether they were situated to the east or the west of a certain meridian. No, there is rather a different attitude of the spirit between Eastern and Western Christians, the first being more symbolic and the second more analytical in their thinking, and this different spirituality has manifested itself in the thought, liturgy and art of the East and the West and in the entire theological approach to the same Christian mysteries. Those who are familiar with the situation will not disagree with me here. This present volume will illustrate yet again the fact that there is both a duality in the unity and also, I believe, a unity within the duality. We can conclude this chapter by quoting Goethe:

Gottes ist der Orient,	The East is God's,
Gottes ist der Okzident;	The West is God's;
Nord und südliches Gelände	Both North and South
Ruht im Frieden Seiner Hände.[28]	Rest in the peace of his hands.

8

NOTES

1. Dogmatic Constitution on Revelation, *Dei Verbum* (1965), 2.
2. See Is 44:3–4; Jn 4:10; 7:37–39; Volume I, pp. 49–51; Volume II, p. 108. T. de Régnon, *Etudes de théologie positive sur la Sainte Trinité*, IV (Paris, 1898), pp. 389ff., quotes the following patristic texts: Irenaeus, *Adv. haer.* III, 17, 2–3; IV, 14, 2; Athanasius, *Ad Ser.* I, 19; Cyril of Jerusalem, *Cat.* XVI, 11 and 12; Didymus, *De Trin.* II, 6, 22 (*PG* 39, 553).
3. J. Guillet, 'Esprit de Dieu', *Vocabulaire biblique*, 2nd ed. (1971), col. 391.
4. See Is 61:1 (Lk 4:18); Acts 10:38; Volume I, pp. 19–21; T. de Régnon, *op. cit.*, pp. 401–406, has quoted several excellent texts: Irenaeus, *Adv. haer.* III, 18, 3; Athanasius, *Ad Ser.* I, 23; Basil the Great, *De spir. sanct.* 12; Gregory of Nyssa, *Adv. Mac.* 15 and 16 (*PG* 45, 1320). See also de Régnon, *op. cit.*, pp. 413–421, on 'perfume, aroma and quality'.
5. The Fathers frequently made this compelling comparison: see Augustine, *Contra Faustum* 30 (*PL* 42, 270); *Ep.* 55, 16 (*PL* 33, 218ff.); *Serm.* 156, 13; etc.; Cyril of Alexandria, *Comm. in Luc.* XI, 20; Martin of Leon, *Serm.* 32 (*PL* 208, 1203); Gregory the Great, *In Ezech.* I, 10, 26 (*PL* 76, 891), made a comparison with Mt 7:33.
6. 2 Cor 3:2–3. See also Augustine, *De spir. et litt.* 16, 28; 17, 29–30; 21, 36 (*PL* 44, 218–219, 222).
7. J. Leclercq, 'Le doigt de Dieu', *VS*, 78 (May 1948), 492–507, who quotes a large number of patristic texts.
8. Athanasius, *Ad Ser.* I, 23 (*PG* 26, 584C–585B; *SC* 15 (1947), pp. 124ff.).
9. Thomas Aquinas, *ST* Ia, q. 1, a. 9, ad 2; IIIa, q. 42, a. 3.
10. St Bernard, *De consid.* V, 11, 24 (*PL* 182, 802B); *Serm. 88 de diversis* 1 (*PL* 183, 706), in which this is applied to the Holy Spirit; *In die Pent., Serm.* 1, 1 (*PL* 183, 323).
11. J. R. Villalón, *Sacrements dans l'Esprit* (Paris, 1977), p. 424.
12. Mgr Gaume (†1879) subtitled his book on the Holy Spirit 'Ignoto Deo'; in 1921, Mgr M. Landrieux published his *Le divin Méconnu* (Eng. tr.: *The Forgotten Paraclete*, London, 1924); Victor Dillard wrote a book on the Holy Spirit in 1938 entitled *Au Dieu inconnu*; in 1965, Pastor A. Granier wrote *Le Saint-Esprit, ce méconnu*; E. H. Palmer began his *The Holy Spirit* (Grand Rapids, 1958) with the words 'The Unknown God' (p. 11) and L. Wunderlich published (St Louis, 1963) *The Half-known God: The Lord and Giver of Life*.
13. Augustine, *De fid et symb.* 9, 19 (*PL* 40, 191).
14. Thomas Aquinas, *ST* Ia, q. 37, a. 1.
15. *Comp.* I, 59; *In I Sent.* d. 10, q. 1, a. 4 ad 1; *ST* Ia, q. 40, a. 4.
16. *ST* Ia, q. 36, a. 1 ad 2.
17. *ST* Ia, q. 36, a. 1, c and ad 1; see also Augustine, *De Trin.* V, 14; XV, 19.
18. Pseudo-Dionysius, *On the Divine Names*, 1 (*PG* 3, 585; Fr. tr. M. de Gandillac (Paris, 1943)). Before Pseudo-Dionysius was translated into Latin, this rule was already observed in the Western Church: see, for example, Bede, *Super par. Salom.* II, 23 (*PL* 91, 1006A–B); Alcuin, *Ad Fel.* VII, 17 (*PL* 101, 230B); *Adv. Elipand.* IV, 11 (*PL* 101, 295A).
19. Cyril of Jerusalem, *Cat.* XVI, 2 (*PG* 33, 920A; quoted and Fr. tr. J. Lebon, *SC* 15, p. 70, note 1); cf. XVI, 24 (*PG* 33, 952). References to other Fathers will be found in H. de Lubac, *La Foi chrétienne* (Paris, 1969), p. 117, note 2. See also Hugh of Saint-Victor, *De sacr.* III, pars 1, c. 4 (*PL* 176, 376A).
20. Thomas Aquinas, commentary on the text of Pseudo-Dionysius: see J. Kuhlmann, *Die Taten des einfachen Gottes* (Würzburg, 1968), p. 21. Thomas quotes Pseudo-Dionysius (in support of an objection) in *In III Sent.* d. 25, q. 1, q. 3, ad 2, 3, 4; *De ver.* q. 14, a. 6; *De pot.* q. 9, a. 9, ad 7; q. 10, a. 4, obj. 12; *Contra Err. Graec.* c. 1; *ST* Ia, q. 29, a. 3, ad 1; q. 32, a. 2, ad 1; q. 36, a. 2, obj. 1; q. 39, a. 2, ad 2; IIa IIae, q. 4, a. 1; IIIa, q. 60, a. 8, ad 1. Quotations of this rule in early Scholastic writings will be found in A. Landgraf, *Dogmengeschichte der Frühscholastik*, I (Regensburg, 1952), p. 20.
21. Thomas Aquinas often quoted the words of Augustine: 'huic scientiae attribuitur illud

tantummodo quo fides saluberrima gignitur, nutritur, defenditur, roboratur': *De Trin*. XIV, 1, 3 (*PL* 42, 1037); see his *ST* Ia, q. 1, a. 2; IIa IIae, q. 6, a. 1, ad 1.

22. Thomas Aquinas, *ST* Ia, q. 42, a. 2, ad 1, in reaction to Arius, who developed twelve senses or modes of 'begetting'.
23. H. B. Swete, *The Holy Spirit in the Ancient Church* (London, 1912), pp. 166ff.
24. Hilary, *De Trin*. II, 2 (*PL* 10, 51).
25. See Augustine, *De Trin*. VII, 9 (*PL* 42, 941–942); Thomas Aquinas, *Contra Err. Graec*. prol.; *De pot*. q. 9, a. 8; q. 10, a. 2.
26. Adam of Saint-Victor, *Seq. XI de sancta Trin*. (*PL* 196, 1459).
27. On the basis of the understanding that the ancient world had of things, it is possible to ask whether God's work did not often follow a pattern of unity within duality: see my *Ecclésiologie du Haut Moyen Age* (Paris, 1968), pp. 262ff.
28. Goethe, 'Talisman', *West-östliche Divan*, 3.

2
THE 'ECONOMIC' TRINITY AND THE 'IMMANENT' TRINITY

Karl Rahner has provided the most original contemporary contribution to the theology of the Trinity.[1] In it, he deals with several aspects of the question and especially with the idea of 'person'—I shall be returning to this later—but his essential argument, which he calls his *Grundaxiom*, is that the 'economic' Trinity *is* the 'immanent' Trinity and vice versa.

By 'economy' is meant the carrying out of God's plan in creation and the redemption of man or the covenant of grace. In it, God commits and reveals himself. One of Rahner's intentions and one of his main concerns in his Trinitarian theology is to establish a relationship, and even a unity, between the treatises which the analytical genius of Scholasticism and modern teaching present successively, but without showing their mutual coherence. We attribute 'creation' to 'God', for example, but at the same time we continue to have a fundamentally pre-Trinitarian notion of that 'God'. We obviously attribute 'redemption' to Jesus Christ, but he is 'God' and we do not place the Word as such into that 'God'. In addition, despite the exegetical studies that have been written about this question, the relationship between creation and redemption, which is a relationship that is closely connected with the Word made flesh, is seldom developed. The eschatological end of that relationship has also to be taken into account. What part does the Holy Spirit play in all this? The treatise on grace was written without reference to the treatise on the Tri-unity of God. Was that grace not a participation in the divine *nature*? Where, then, was the reference to the Persons? Was there also a reference to the uncreated grace which is the Holy Spirit?

It is, however, true to say that Scripture, the Creed and the ante-Nicene Fathers spoke the language of the Economy.[2] The Creed is Trinitarian only within this framework. Rahner brings them together when he affirms his 'fundamental axiom' that the *Trinity that is manifested in the economy of salvation is the immanent Trinity and vice versa*.

Three reasons justify and throw light on that fundamental principle:

(a) The Trinity is a mystery of salvation. If it were not, it would not have been revealed to us. Our recognition of this fact enables us to establish a relationship and even a unity between the treatises which have to a great extent lacked this. This implies, however, that the Trinity in itself is also the Trinity of the economy.

11

(b) There is at least one case of fundamental importance in which this affirmation must be made—the incarnation. 'So there is at least one "sending", one presence in the world, one reality in the economy of salvation which is not merely appropriated to a certain divine person, but is proper to him. Thus it is not a matter of saying something "about" this particular divine person in the world. Here something takes place in the world itself, outside the immanent divine life, which is not simply the result of the efficient causality of the triune God working as one nature in the world. It is an event proper to the Logos alone, the history of one divine person in contrast to the others.'[3]

(c) The history of salvation is not simply the history of God's revelation of himself. It is also the history of his communication of himself. God himself is the content of that self-communication. The economic Trinity (the revealed and communicated Trinity) and the immanent Trinity are identical because God's communication of himself to men in the Son and the Spirit would not be a self-communication of God if what God is for us in the Son and the Spirit was not peculiar to God in himself. In this, there is an echo of an anti-Arian argument concerned with our deification that calls for the communication of God himself in the economy. At the same time, a reality is ascribed to the 'appropriations', since the three ways in which the economy manifests that God is with us and communicates himself to us correspond to the three modes of relationship in which God subsists in himself.

There has been a wide measure of agreement with Rahner's positions, which were already those of Karl Barth in Protestant theology. If it is merely a question of the knowledge that we have of the Tri-unity of God, there is no real problem, since that knowledge is measured by the economy within which it is given to us.

On the other hand, we also know that the 'divine missions' of the Word and the Spirit are the processions of those Persons insofar as they result in an effect in the creature. In their case, then, the economic Trinity *is* in fact the immanent Trinity. This is what brings about an absolutely supernatural, theologal and even divine effect in the spiritual life of true believers and in the Church as such. The Church lives, in the conditions of the flesh, from communication with God. It is one and holy because of God's oneness and holiness. The Fathers did not hesitate to say this[4] and I have discussed this question already in Volume II of this work. The Father does not himself 'proceed' and thus he is not 'sent'. He is communicated in the economy as the absolute source of all procession, mission and work *ad extra*. 'The Father is the incomprehensible origin and the original unity, the "Word" his utterance into history, and the "Spirit" the opening up of history into the immediacy of its fatherly origin and end'.[5] 'There is only one outward activity of God, exerted and possessed as one and the same by Father, Son and Spirit, according to the peculiar way in which each possesses the God-head'.[6]

I accept Rahner's teaching, but would like to add two comments which limit its absolute character.

(A) 'The economic Trinity is the immanent Trinity and vice versa [*umgekehrt*].' The first half of this statement by Rahner is beyond dispute, but the second half has to be clarified. Can the free mystery of the economy and the necessary mystery of the Tri-unity of God be identified? As the Fathers who combated Arianism said, even if God's creatures did not exist, God would still be a Trinity of Father, Son and Spirit, since creation is an act of free will, whereas the procession of the Persons takes place in accordance with nature, *kata phusin*.[7] In addition to this, is it true to say that God commits the whole of his mystery to and reveals it in his communication of himself?[8] It seems to me to be obvious that we cannot simply affirm the reciprocity of Rahner's fundamental axiom when we read the statements that result from a purely logical proposal to develop and affirm this reciprocity. This is precisely what Piet Schoonenberg has done in his presentation of a number of theses as an extension of Rahner's. But these are the conclusions he comes to:[9]

(11) In the theology of the Trinity too, the Father should not be seen simply as the 'first Person' or as the origin and source of divinity; he should also and above all be seen as our Father in Christ. The economic fatherhood of the history of salvation is the intra-divine fatherhood and vice versa.

(12) The Son should be seen not only as intra-divine, but also and above all as the man Jesus Christ. The Logos is not simply the intra-divine Word—he is never presented in Scripture as the intra-divine response—but also and above all as the Word which reveals and which gives life in the history of salvation, the Word which became flesh and fully man in Jesus Christ. The economic sonship of the history of salvation is the intra-divine sonship and vice versa.

(13) The Holy Spirit is not only the intra-divine link between the Father and the Son, but also and above all 'gift' and 'power of sanctification' in the history of salvation. These titles were given to him by the Fathers in order to characterize his being as a Person. The Spirit of God who is active in the history of salvation is the intra-divine (Spirit) and vice versa.

(14) The communications or 'missions' of the Son and the Spirit are revealed as intra-divine 'processions'. These intra-divine 'processions' are known to us only as missions. The missions are processions and vice versa.

(15) The relations between the Father, the Son and the Spirit are accessible to us only in their relations with us. The economic relations of the history of salvation are intra-divine and vice versa. That is why the Father, the Son and the Spirit must be characterized first by their relationships with us and then by their relationships with each other.

These theses are classical insofar as we remain at the level of knowledge derived from revelation, that is, from the manifestation of God. The problem, however, is concerned precisely with the 'vice versa' or the 'reciprocity', the *umgekehrt*, in other words, to the extent to which the latter implies a transition from knowledge to ontology. He does not in fact do this formally, but he does profess an apophatism, that is, the impossibility of affirming or denying anything, where the intra-divine life is concerned.

(7) The immanent Trinity, vice versa, is the economic Trinity. It is accessible for us only as the economic Trinity. The fact that God is, apart from his communication of himself in the history of salvation, Trinitarian, can neither be presupposed as a matter of course nor denied.

(24) The fact remains that Jesus Christ and the Father personally face each other and that the Holy Spirit prays to the Father in us and calls to the Son and therefore also personally faces them. According to Scripture, then, the Father, the Son and the Holy Spirit face each other as Persons *in* the history of salvation. It follows from thesis 23 that this is possible only *through* the history of salvation. The immanent Trinity is a Trinity of Persons through the fact that it is an economic Trinity.

In God himself, the Father, the Son and the Spirit are only modes of the Deity. There are 'Persons' or personal relationships only in the economy (see thesis 28). For us at least, God is three-personal only in the economy. 'Through the history of salvation', Schoonenberg insists, 'there is a Trinity in God himself; through his own saving action, God himself becomes three-personal [*driepersoonlijk*], that is, three Persons.'[10]

This depends on the fact that Schoonenberg's understanding of the word 'person' is quite contemporary and therefore includes the person's human mode of existence and contains the ideas of consciousness, freedom and interpersonal relationships (see thesis 18). Applying this understanding of 'person' to Christ, Schoonenberg attributes a pure human personality to him and points out with insistence that speaking about Christ's pre-existent divine Person runs the risk of damaging the reality of the human personality. Because our knowledge is limited by the economy of salvation, which is its only source, we cannot know what that is in God himself. Schoonenberg therefore leaves the mystery of the immanent Trinity open, but unknown and even unknowable. This clause is a saving one and it leaves the author's orthodoxy intact.

Is it, however, permissible to act as Schoonenberg has done here and place oneself outside the whole Christian tradition of reflection based on the inspired evidence of Revelation? Jesus himself pointed to the distance between being a son through grace and a Son by nature: 'My Father and your Father, my God and your God' (Jn 20:17). And how can there be a communication of the three Persons if they are not three Persons to begin with? Rahner does not overlook this. He says, for example: 'The "immanent" actual possibility of this threefold way of being given is, despite God's free gratuitous trinitarian self-communication, forever given in God, belonging therefore necessarily and "essentially" to him'.[11]

14

(B) God's communication of himself, as Father, Son and Holy Spirit, will not be a full self-communication until the end of time, in what we call the beatific vision. Thomas Aquinas' thesis on this matter is well known—he describes it as a vision without created *species*, that is, God himself as the objective form of our understanding. This is, however, an heroic, an almost untenable thesis, and it has been widely disputed. The Eastern Church does not accept it as it is, although there have been many Orthodox statements about the beatific vision of God. Almost all of these, however, insist that the divine essence is unknowable and make a distinction between what cannot and what can be communicated (the 'energies' that emanate from the divine essence).

On the other hand, no Western theologian has ever maintained that we can know or understand God as he understands himself. John of the Cross, for example, applied the image of the 'distant islands' to the beatific vision. There is no participation in the aseity, the *Ipsum esse* or what makes God God. There is a very great difference between Eastern and Western theological constructions of the reality, but it would be a mistake to regard the two as dogmatically incompatible. Here, however, we are above all concerned with the perception that God's communication of himself will be complete only in the eschatological era.

This self-communication takes place in the economy in accordance with a rule of 'condescendence', humiliation, ministry and 'kenosis'. We have therefore to recognize that there is a distance between the economic, revealed Trinity and the eternal Trinity. The Trinity is the same in each case and God is really communicated, but this takes place in a mode that is not connatural with the being of the divine Persons. The Father is 'omnipotent', but what are we to think of him in a world filled with the scandal of evil? The Son, who is 'shining with his glory and the likeness of his substance', is the Wisdom of God, but he is above all the wisdom of the cross and so difficult to recognize that blasphemy against him will be pardoned. Finally, the Spirit has no face and has often been called the unknown one.

It is important in this context to recall certain essential elements in Christian thought and especially the theme of 'condescendence' and the theology of the cross. Before Luther, the latter is found above all in the writings of Maximus the Confessor, who declared: 'The Lord, who wanted us to understand that we should not look for natural necessity in what is above nature, wanted to bring about his work by means of opposites. He therefore fulfilled his life by his death and accomplished his glory by means of dishonour.'[12] It was, however, Luther who originated the term *theologia crucis*. He taught that God is not accessible to us through human logic. He reveals himself by hiding himself.[13] He does his own work under the species or by means of the opposite: justice, grace and life by a way of judgement and death. True knowledge of God is that which approaches him in this way and which finds its *opus proprium* in an *opus alienum*.

Salvation, in other words, is in the cross, on which Jesus was treated as accursed.[14]

There is nothing in anything that has been said above that contradicts Rahner's 'fundamental axiom'. Rahner also says : 'What Jesus is and does as man reveals the Logos himself; it is the reality of the Logos as our salvation amidst us'.[15] All these things—condescendence, humiliation, kenosis, the cross and the fact that life is stronger than death, but that love is manifested in accepting death[16]—reveal who the Word is, and the Word himself reveals who the Father is: 'He who has seen me has seen the Father' (Jn 14:9).[17]

There is powerful evidence that this 'economy' does not in any way conceal the 'theology' in the manner in which the episode of the washing of the feet is introduced in the fourth gospel: 'Jesus, knowing that the Father had given all things into his hands and that he had come from God and was going to God' (Jn 13:3). It was because he was conscious of being the expression of the Father that Jesus performed this act of humble love and service. This act was typical of God himself. The economic trinity thus reveals the immanent Trinity—but does it reveal it entirely? There is always a limit to this revelation, and the incarnation imposes its own conditions, which go back to its nature as a created work.

If all the data of the incarnation were transposed into the eternity of the Logos, it would be necessary to say that the Son proceeds from the Father and the Holy Spirit—a Patre Spirituque.[18] In addition, the forma servi belongs to what God is, but so does the forma Dei. At the same time, however, that latter form and the infinite and divine manner in which the perfections that we attribute to God are accomplished elude us to a very great extent. This should make us cautious in saying, as Rahner does, 'and vice versa'.

I shall be speaking later about Palamism and pointing, at the level of a theologoumenon, to a possible construction of faith. For this reason, it is possible to ask what Gregory Palamas' reaction to Rahner's thesis would have been. The first thing that strikes me is that the idea that the Trinity is a mystery of salvation would have been acceptable to Palamite theology, in which that salvation would have been interpreted in the Eastern tradition as a deification or theōsis. The idea of God's communication of himself would also have been accepted, so long as that self-communication was situated within the order of uncreated energies. As those energies manifest the Persons of the Trinity, there would be a revelation of the Tri-unity of God through them.

It was undoubtedly in such conditions that the Archimandrite Kallistos Ware, in his defence of the difference between essence and energies when criticized by R. Williams (who had criticized V. Lossky and Gregory Palamas for having left our level of knowledge and moved to the plane of intra-divine ontology), replied: 'This self-revelation is a real sign of the eternal being of God. If we did not believe it, how would we be able to move from the "economic" level of the Trinity to that of the eternal distinctions in the Trinity?'[19] Only a few pages earlier on in the same journal, however, Amphilokios Radovic had observed that the distinction between the essence and the energies implied a distinction, and even a radical difference, between the existential origins of the Persons and the economic manifestation of those Persons: 'On the basis of the manifestation of the Trinity in the world, we cannot come to any conclusions about God's mode of eternal existence'. The identification of the order of eternal existence of the hypostases with the order of the economy is fundamental to the Latin position.[20] What is clear is that this identification between the two calls for the *Filioque* or at least for an equivalent *per Filium* at the level of the eternal procession. This was one of the reasons why Karl Barth thought that it was necessary to preserve the *Filioque*, in the name of scriptural evidence. According to Palamite thinking, however, God may be partly revealed in the economy by his activity, but he remains absolutely hidden in his essential being.

NOTES

1. K. Rahner, 'Remarks on the Dogmatic Treatise "De Trinitate" ', *Theological Investigations*, 4 (Eng. tr.; London and Baltimore, 1966), pp. 77–102; *idem*, *The Trinity* (Eng. tr.; London, 1970), first pub. in German as part of *Mysterium Salutis* (Einsiedeln, 1967). To this should be added the preface (untranslated) to the book by Mario de França Miranda, *O Mistério de Deus em nossa vida* (São Paulo, 1975), pp. 7–13. This book is a study of Rahner's thesis discussed in this chapter.
2. In ante-Nicene writings, this is often balanced by a subordinationism, the Word being regarded, because of the influence of Stoicism, as the one through whom God carried out his creation and therefore as a mediator of that creation. This idea was systematized in Arianism, according to which the Son had a beginning, in the same way that a creature has a beginning. Athanasius and the Cappadocian Fathers affirmed, against this thesis, that if the Son was a creature in this way, he could not deify us, and that he could be our Saviour in the full sense only if he was God and communicated the life of God to us, in other words, if he was consubstantial with the Father. The same idea was also applied to the Spirit. By insisting in this way on consubstantiality, in other words, on the intra-divine aspect, the anti-Arian writers and the First Council of Nicaea to some extent diverted men's minds from the question of the economic Trinity.
3. K. Rahner, 'Remarks', *op. cit.*, pp. 88–89. Rahner has developed the idea that God is the subject of a history, namely the history of salvation, in the incarnate Word: 'Current Problems in Christology', *Theological Investigations*, 1 (Eng. tr.; London and Baltimore, 1961), pp. 149–200; and in *Problèmes actuels de christologie*, ed. H. Bouëssé (Bruges and Paris, 1965), pp. 15–33, 401–409.
4. See Cyprian, *De cath. Eccl. unit.* 7; *De orat. dom.* 23 (*PL* 4, 553; ed. W. von Hartel, p. 285); Origen, *In Jesu Nave, Hom.* VII, 6; Epiphanius of Salamis, *Anc.* 118, 3: 'One is the unity of the Father, the Son and the Holy Spirit, one substance, one lordship, one will, one Church, one baptism, one faith' (*GCS*, Epiph. 1, p. 146); Augustine, *Sermo* 71, 20, 33 (*PL* 38, 463ff.); John Damascene, *Adv. Icon.* 12 (*PG* 96, 1358D); see also the Dogmatic Constitution on the Church, *Lumen Gentium*, 4.

5. K. Rahner, *The Trinity, op. cit.* (note 1), p. 47.
6. *Ibid.*, p. 76.
7. Athanasius, *Contra Arian*. I, 18 (*PG* 26, 49); II, 31: 'Even if God had not decided to create, he would nonetheless have had his Son' (*PG* 26, 212B); John Damascene, *De fide orthod*. I, 8 (*PG* 94, 812–813).
8. My criticism has also been made, for example, by G. Lafont, *Peut-on connaître Dieu en Jésus-Christ?* (Paris, 1969), pp. 220, 226; B. Rey, *RSPT* (1970), 645.
9. P. Schoonenberg, 'Trinität—der vollendete Bund. Thesen zur Lehre von dreipersönlichem Gott', *Orientierung*, 37 (Zürich, 1973, fascicle of 31 May), 115–117, especially 115. Schoonenberg presented these theses as a continuation and a justification of his book *Hij is een God van Mensen*; Eng. tr., *The Christ* (London and Sydney, 1972).
10. This formula is taken from an article, in Dutch, on 'Jesus Christ, the same today', in *Mélanges W. H. van der Pol* (Roermond and Maaseik, 1967) and analysed and criticized by J. Coppens in *ETL*, 45 (1969), 127–137. The following statement also appears in the same article: 'The presence of God as the Word becomes the personal Son of the Father because, from the beginning, it includes the whole human existence of Jesus Christ and constitutes that existence (and not because it fills the already existing man). The presence of God as the Spirit becomes the personal Paraclete because, in a parallel manner, it bears and constitutes the community of believers. God becomes the Father, the first Person of the Trinity, because he produces in Jesus a Son of the same nature and spreads a Spirit in the Church of the same being (*wezensgelijk*).'
11. K. Rahner, *The Trinity, op. cit.* (note 1), p. 74. This transposition means that we have to speak more precisely, because of the need to respect the absolute consubstantiality of the 'Persons' in the immanent Trinity. Similarly, both Rahner and Schoonenberg speak personally in the case of the economy and modally in the case of the eternal Trinity.
12. See Maximus' 'Questions and Difficulties' (*PG* 94, 793); quoted in Fr. tr. by J.-M. Garrigues, *Maxime le Confesseur. La charité avenir divin de l'homme* (Paris, 1976), p. 160.
13. Luther, *Commentary on Galatians*, 1525: *Works*, XV (Geneva, 1969), pp. 282–295.
14. Writings of 1518: *Asterici*; marginal gloss on Heb.; Resolutions and especially the Heidelberg Disputation, 22 and 24: *Works*, I (Geneva, 1957), pp. 121ff. See also J. E. Vercruysse, 'Luther's Theology of the Cross in the Time of the Heidelberg Disputation', *Greg*, 57 (1976), 523–548.
15. K. Rahner, *The Trinity, op. cit.*, p. 33; 'Remarks', *op. cit.*, p. 94.
16. This aspect was emphasized by E. Jüngel, 'Das Verhältnis von "ökonomischer" und "immanenter" Trinität', *ZTK*, 72 (1975), 353–364.
17. See my 'Dum visibiliter Deum cognoscimus', *M-D*, 59 (1959/3), 132–161; Eng. tr. in *The Revelation of God* (London and New York, 1968), pp. 67–96.
18. See K. Barth, *Church Dogmatics*, I. 1 (Eng. tr.; Edinburgh and New York, 1936), pp. 554–556.
19. K. Ware, 'Dieu caché et révélé. La voie apophatique et la distinction essence–énergie', *Le Messager de l'Exarchat du patriarche russe en Europe occidentale*, 89–90 (1975), 45–59, especially 56.
20. This was the explicit reaction of A. Radovic: see his 'Le "Filioque" et l'énergie incréée de la Sainte Trinité selon la doctrine de S. Grégoire Palamas', *ibid.*, 11–44, especially 15–17 and 19. This can also be compared with what the monk Hilarion says, *ibid.*, 81–82 (1973), 19–25, namely that the Roman Catholic view is, in his opinion, tied to an identification of the temporal missions with the eternal processions; Hilarion rejects this idea in the name of the distinction between the procession of the hypostases and the uncreated energies.

II
THE STAGES IN THE DEVELOPMENT OF A THEOLOGY OF THE THIRD PERSON

Three great stages in this development can be distinguished: the period before the Arian crisis, the period of the crisis itself and the period of systematic constructions.

BEFORE THE ARIAN CRISIS

This was a time of slow and difficult gestation. We who are so used to firm dogma and authoritative interpretation of biblical texts have difficulty in understanding why there was such a long period of hesitation and why such apparently strange paths were followed. The theological question of the Spirit was only really approached in good conditions when light had been thrown on the relationship between the Son, the Word, and the Father.[1]

First came the Christian apologists, using the philosophical data fairly widely accepted in their times and therefore more inclined to speak about the Word than about the Spirit. They confessed the Trinitarian faith and the fact that the Logos and the Spirit (Wisdom) were eternally in God before he projected them into creation and time in order to manifest himself there. They believed that the Spirit spoke in the prophets, that he was united with the souls of those who lived in justice and that he came or flowed from God.[2] No other more precise definition of the procession of the one who, as Justin claimed, was revered by Christians in the third place[3] is to be found in the early apologetic writings.

Irenaeus was less an apologist than a man, a Doctor, of the Church. Conscious of the fact that the Spirit of God flowed constantly from the divine being,[4] he acknowledged the existence of the immanent Trinity. At the same time, however, he developed above all the part played by the Trinity in the economy, calling the Word and the Spirit (Wisdom) the two hands of God (cf. Volume II, p. 9) working together to fashion his creatures. According to Irenaeus, the Word, having become visible, revealed the Father, and the

Spirit was the one 'through whom the prophets spoke and the Fathers learned what concerns God, the righteous were led in the way of justice, and who was poured out at the end of time in a new way . . . in order to renew man over the whole of the earth with God in mind'.[5]

Tertullian (*c*. 160–*c*. 220) believed that the Spirit came *a Patre per Filium*, 'from the Father through the Son',[6] and that he 'came third from the Father and the Son (*a Deo et Filio*), just as the fruit from the branch comes third from the root, the channel led from the river comes third from the source, and the glowing point of light at the end of the ray comes third from the sun'.[7]

Is there a lowering in rank in the fact that, according to Tertullian, there is a passage from one Person to another in the economic existence of the Trinity? Does this imply subordinationism? The question has often been considered, but no certain answer has been provided.[8] The Spirit is the 'vicar' of the Son who, from his seat at the right hand of the Father, sent *vicariam vim Spiritus Sancti, qui credentes agat*.[9] At the same time, however, Tertullian also believed that the Son and the Spirit were *consortes substantiae Patris*.[10] The Three are one in *status, substantia* and *potestas*,[11] but they are not one individual or one person (*unus*), but rather the same reality: *unum . . . ad substantiae unitatem, non ad numeri singularitatem*.[12]

Tertullian wrote this, of course, long before the Council of Nicaea, and his idea of the economy led him to make certain statements that could easily be misunderstood. He was moving in the direction of an orthodox theology in the Trinity, but lacked the means to express it properly. He was, however, responsible for 'those well-known formulae: *Trinitas, tres personae, una substantia*, which he coined and which have become commonplaces in the Trinitarian doctrine, together with the other, more imaginative terms: *Deum de Deo, lumen de lumine*, which we still use when we profess our faith'.[13]

Origen (*c*. 185–254) was one of the greatest geniuses in the history of Christian thought, and a better metaphysician than Tertullian. His cultural climate was that of Middle Platonism, with the result that it is possible to find two kinds of statements in his writings. On the one hand, he teaches a theology of the three co-eternal hypostases and the eternal procession of the Spirit from the Father through the Son.[14] On the other hand, in connection with the Platonic idea of a graduated hierarchy, his work contains a number of subordinationist themes and formulae.[15] These subordinationist ideas can be found especially in his teaching that only the Father is *ho theos* or *autotheos*, whereas the Son is *deuteros theos* or God in second place.[16] The Son and the Spirit are connected with the Father, who is the 'source of divinity', but they are not alone in being co-eternal with him—a great

20

number of spiritual beings are also co-eternal with the Father. On the other hand, however, Origen used the term *homoousios* at least with the meaning of a community of nature and affirmed the eternal existence of three *hypostases*,[17] the eternal begetting of the Son and the eternal procession of the Spirit[18] through the Son.[19] In this way, he anticipates the ideas that can be found later in the great classical Greek patristic and other writings. It must be admitted, however, that the Arians also found support in the writings of Origen, whom Prestige called 'the common father of Arianism and of Cappadocian orthodoxy'.[20]

The confession of faith under the name of Origen's disciple Gregory Thaumaturgus (†between 260 and 270) is fundamentally orthodox; it contains the following words about the Holy Spirit: 'And one Holy Spirit, who takes his subsistence from God (*ek Theou tēn huparxin echōn*) and who appeared (was revealed) to men by the Son; image of the Son; perfect (image) of the perfect one, life, cause of the living, holy source, holiness leading to satisfaction, in whom God the Father, who is above all and in all, is manifested and God the Son who is through all'.[21] This elaborate vocabulary has led other scholars to doubt whether this text should be attributed to Gregory Thaumaturgus, and Abramowski has suggested that it is the work of Gregory of Nyssa.

Pope Dionysius of Rome suspected that the teaching of his namesake Dionysius of Alexandria, another of Origen's disciples, contained a danger of tritheism ('three hypostases') and in 262 reacted strongly in favour of the monarchy of the Father. We owe to him this excellent statement:

> It is necessary for the divine Word to be united to the God of the universe and for the Holy Spirit to have his dwelling-place and his habitation in God. And it is above all necessary for the Holy Trinity to be recapitulated and brought back to one as to its peak; by this I mean that one all-powerful God of the universe. It is necessary to believe in God the Father almighty and in Christ Jesus his Son and in the Holy Spirit (quotations from Jn 10:30 and 14:10 follow here). It is in this way that we may be sure of the divine Trinity and at the same time of the holy preaching of the monarchy.[22]

NOTES

1. The most recent analysis has been written by F. Bolgiani, 'La théologie de l'Esprit-Saint. De la fin du Ier siècle après Jésus-Christ au concile de Constantinople (381)', *Les quatre fleuves*, 9 (1979), 33–72.

2. Athenagoras, *Supplicatio* (in 177), X (see *SC* 3 (1943), p. 94), who uses the word *aporroia*

for 'flowing from': cf. Wis 7:25. He also says (*SC* 3, pp. 92–93): 'The Son being in the Father and the Father being in the Son through the unity and power of Spirit', although the last word is without the article, so that it does not refer to the third Person, but rather to the divine nature.

3. Justin, *I Apol*. 4, 1; Athenagoras, *op. cit*., speaks of a 'distinction in rank' in this context.

4. Irenaeus, *Adv. haer*. V, 12, 2; the quotation is from Is 57:16 (*SC* 153 (1969), pp. 145ff.). For the Holy Spirit in Irenaeus, see A. d'Alès, 'La doctrine de l'Esprit-Saint chez S. Irénée', *RSR*, 14 (1924), 426–538; A. Benoît, 'Le Saint Esprit et l'Eglise dans la théologie patristique des quatre premiers siècles', *L'Esprit Saint et l'Eglise* (Paris, 1969), pp. 131–136; H.-J. Jaschke, *Der Heilige Geist im Bekenntnis der Kirche. Eine Studie zur Pneumatologie bei Irenäus von Lyon im Ausgang vom altchristlichen Glaubensbekenntnis* (Münster, 1977).

5. *Dem*. 6 (*SC* 62, p. 40). A little further on, *Dem*. 7 (*SC* 62, pp. 41–42), Irenaeus enlarges on the revelatory function of the Spirit, saying that he reveals the Son, who in turn reveals the Father. The 'from the Father through the Son in the Spirit' is the principle of a return 'in the Spirit through the Son to the Father'.

6. Tertullian, *Adv. Prax*. 4 (*PL* 2, 159; *CSEL* 47, p. 232). According to J. Moingt, this *per Filium* concerns not the intra-divine procession, but the order of the economy, the Spirit being sent and poured out by the Son: *Théologie trinitaire de Tertullien*, III (*Théologie*, 70) (Paris, 1966), p. 1057.

7. *Adv. Prax*. 8 (*PL* 2, 163; *CSEL* 47, p. 238). According to P.-T. Camelot, 'Spiritus a Patre et Filio', *RSPT*, 30 (1946), 31–33, the idea of the *Filioque* is not present in this text of Tertullian's. Other scholars have, however, thought differently, especially B. de Margerie.

8. B. Piault, 'Tertullien a-t-il été subordinatien?', *RSPT*, 47 (1963), 337–369. J. Moingt, *op. cit*. (note 6), pp. 1071–1074, banished the idea of subordinationism by recalling that Tertullian made no distinction between God in himself and God as he exists for us.

9. *De praescr*. 13, 5 (*PL* 2, 26).

10. *Adv. Prax*. 3 (*PL* 2, 158; *CSEL* 47, p. 231).

11. *ibid*., 2 (*PL* 2, 156; *CSEL* 47, p. 229).

12. *ibid*., 25 (*PL* 2, 188; *CSEL* 47, p. 276).

13. Piault, *op. cit*. (note 8), p. 204.

14. H. B. Swete, *The Holy Spirit in the Ancient Church* (London, 1912), pp. 61–65.

15. See S. Bulgakov, *Le Paraclet* (Paris, 1946), pp. 22–23; J. N. D. Kelly, *Early Christian Doctrines*, 5th ed. (London, 1977), pp. 132–136, gives a more balanced and more fully documented account.

16. Origen, *Contra Cels*. V, 39 (*SC* 147 (1969), p. 118, including the long footnote 2); *Comm. in Ioan*. VI, XXXIX, 202 (*SC* 157 (1970), p. 280). Later on, Thomas Aquinas said: 'The Arians, of whom Origen was the source': *ST* Ia, q. 34, q. 1, ad 1.

17. *Comm. in Ioan*. II, X, 75 (*SC* 120, p. 257). According to G. L. Prestige, *God in Patristic Thought*, 2nd ed. (London, 1952), p. 179, Origen was the first Father to define the Persons of the Trinity using the term *hypostasis*: see *Contra Cels*. 8, 12.

18. *De Prin*. II, 1 (*PG* 11, 186).

19. Swete found this in Origen's commentary on Rom 8:9–11 (*PG* 14, 1098)—the Spirit proceeds from the Father and receives from the Son; he is also the Spirit of the Father or of Christ. Or in the commentary on Jn 1:2, 'nothing was done without him'. The Spirit has a *genesis* depending on the Word: see *Comm. in Ioan*. II, 75 and 79 (*SC* 120, pp. 254ff.; *PG* 14, 128).

20. G. L. Prestige, *op. cit*. (note 17 above), p. xiv.

21. *PG* 10, 985. According to M. Jugie, there is here a dependence on the part of the Spirit with regard to the Son: *De processione Spiritus Sancti* (Rome, 1936), pp. 104–106. See also L. Abramowski, *Zeitschrift für Kirchengeschichte*, 87 (1976), 145–166; A. Arunde, 'El Espíritu Santo en la Exposición de fe de S. Gregorio Taumaturgo', *Scripta Teol*. (Pamplona), 10 (1978), 373–407.

22. *DS* 115. In his reply defending himself against the suspicion of tritheism, of which he was accused by his namesake Dionysius of Rome, Dionysius of Alexandria formulated the well-known statement: 'We extend the unity into a trinity and summarize the trinity in a unity'; this is quoted by Athanasius in *Sent. Dionys*. (*PG* 25, 505A).

(A) IN THE GREEK PART OF THE CHURCH

1

THE CRITICISM OF ARIANISM ADVANCES IN THE THEOLOGY OF THE TRINITY

In these chapters, I shall first discuss, in a perhaps over-simplified form, the contribution made to the Trinitarian doctrine by the great doctors of the Church Athanasius, Epiphanius of Salamis, Basil the Great, Gregory Nazianzen and Gregory of Nyssa, and Cyril of Alexandria. I shall then examine John Damascene's theology of the Trinity and after that look at the intervention of the Patriarch Photius. This should place me in a position where I can survey the whole Greek approach to the mystery of the Tri-unity of God. I shall also include at the end [Chapter 5] a brief account of the theology of Gregory Palamas.

It would have been desirable to discuss the work of the Latin doctors and the Councils and pontifical pronouncements of the Western branch of the Church in parallel with that of the East, and in its chronological place. I have, however, chosen to follow a theological rather than a historical course and shall therefore consider the contribution made by the Latin Church afterwards, when I shall try to identify the points at which the same faith is expressed by both East and West, but explained in ways that are at least partly different.

Arius[1] was a priest in charge of the church of Baucalis in Alexandria. In 318 he began to preach a doctrine denying the divinity of Christ in a very radical way. His systematic teaching was largely based on subordinationism of a kind that formed part of the inheritance of Origen, Dionysius of Alexandria and Eusebius of Nicomedia. The mystery of the divine being was realized only in the Father, who alone was 'God'. The Son was a creature (no distinction was made in Arian teaching between being begotten and being created); he therefore had a beginning and there was therefore a time when he did not exist. He was, admittedly, the first among creatures and God had created the other, inferior creatures through him. In support of these arguments, Arius used a certain number of biblical texts in which such expressions as 'God has created me (Wisdom)' and 'he (Christ) was made' occur.

24

Athanasius (†373) is identified, in the history of Christian doctrine, with the Nicaean cause. He was a simple priest when he went with his bishop to the council (325). He became Bishop of Alexandria in 326 and carried on a tireless combat against Arianism. This struggle led to as many as five periods of exile from Alexandria: 335–337, to Trier; 339–346, to Rome; 356–362, in the desert, where he wrote his four letters to Serapion, probably in 359; 362–364, also in the desert; and for the last time for a few months in 365–366.

When he accepted Serapion's request to defend the divinity of the Spirit,[2] Athanasius had already actively championed the divinity of the Son and the *homoousios* of Nicaea, as a formula that affirmed the identity of substance between the Son and the Father. In that defence, he made use of the following arguments: God (the Father) can never be without his Word. As he is eternal, the Word also belongs eternally to him. We are called to be sons and to be deified. That is only possible if Christ, the incarnate Son, is truly and fully God: 'The Word would never have been able to deify us if he had only been divine by participation and had not himself been the deity by essence, the true image of the Father'.[3]

Athanasius applied to the Spirit what he had said of the Son. Although he quotes the text of Jn 15:26, he speaks of the relationship between the Spirit and the Father only through his relationship with the Son. He defends the divinity of the Spirit entirely on the basis of his Christology.[4] There is, he teaches, a relationship between the Spirit and the Son similar to that between the Son and the Father, 'because the state that we have recognized (as that) of the Son with regard to the Father is, we shall find, precisely that which the Spirit has with regard to the Son'.[5] Applying the linear and dynamic idea of 'from the Father through the Son in the Spirit' to this relationship, Athanasius says: 'the Father is light, the Son is its brilliance and the Spirit is the one through whom we are illuminated' and 'the Father is the source and the Son is the river, so that we can say that we drink the Spirit'. He applies that to everything that is concerned with the communication of the divine life.[6] The Spirit does this because he is consubstantial with the Father and the Son.[7]

What relationship of origin does this teaching presuppose between the Spirit and the Son? Athanasius does not speculate about the eternal and intra-divine relationships, but only speaks about them in the context of the activities of the divine Persons within the economy of salvation. All the same, however, J. Lebon has, with as much discretion as precision, drawn attention to three texts which might constitute a statement about the dependence in origination of the Spirit in the Son. It is particularly the use of the preposition *para* which gives force to these texts:

Everything that the Spirit has, he has from the Son (*para tou Logou*).[8]

. . . his gift (the Spirit), who is said to proceed from the Father because, from the

Son (*para tou Logou*) who is confessed (as coming) from the Father, he shines out and is sent and is given.[9]

For the Father creates all things through the Word in the Spirit, since where the Word is, there is also the Spirit, and the things created by the intermediary of the Word have from the Spirit through the Word (*para tou Logou*) the power of being.[10]

There are many indications and even formal evidence of the fact that the Greek Fathers thought that the Son, the Word, played a part in the eternal being of the Spirit. They kept to Scripture and never applied to the role of the Son the verb *ekporeuomai* which is employed in Jn 15:26 to speak of the procession of the Spirit from the Father. In fact, they did not ask this question in the polemical form in which it has been asked in the controversy between Greek and Latin theologians from the time of Charlemagne, and especially from the time of the Patriarch Photius onwards. Sergey Bulgakov was right in this matter, although the path that he chose to follow in his attempt to bypass the contentious posing of the question has not found much favour. It is, however, impossible to deny that there are numerous indications in the writings of the fourth- and fifth-century Greek Fathers of the Church of a dependence on the part of the Spirit with regard to the Son in the life of the eternal Trinity.

Didymus the Blind, who was head of the catechetical school at Alexandria from 340 until 395, continued Athanasius' struggle on behalf of the divinity of the Holy Spirit. His treatise *De Spiritu Sancto*, which influenced Ambrose of Milan, has come down to us only in Jerome's Latin translation. There can be little doubt that Jerome left his mark on the text and was probably responsible for such expressions as 'a Patre et me, hoc enim ipsum quod subsistit et loquitur, a Patre et me illi est' and 'procedens a Veritate' or 'neque alia substantia est Spiritus Sancti praeter id quod datur ei a Filio'.[11] These expressions have, however, been integrated into the context, which is entirely devoted to a commentary on biblical texts.

The almost complete Greek text of his treatise on the Trinity, *Peri Triados*, has, however, been preserved, Showing that the Spirit is from God (the Father), Didymus quotes the text of Tit 3:4–6: 'he has poured out that Spirit on us' and asks when God did that. It was, he replies to his own question, when Christ said 'Receive the Holy Spirit'. He then adds: 'It is right to say "he has poured out", since he in fact poured it out like water coming substantially from him'.[12] Once again, then, the context is that of the 'economic' Trinity, but the statement is general. It is also quite isolated, since Didymus only speaks of the procession *a Patre* in the rest of the chapter.[13]

Epiphanius, who began life as a monk, but later became Bishop of Salamis (367–403), was hardly a genius, but he has handed down to us an abundance of writings. In his *Ancoratus* of 374 he sometimes simply quotes Jn 15:26 on the Paraclete who proceeds from the Father and receives from the Son,[14] and at others says that he is (which means 'has consubstantial being') from the Father and the Son.[15] He is clearly referring here to the intra-divine being that is eternal, but he neither speculates nor suggests any explanation concerning the 'procession' of the Spirit. This dependence of the Spirit on the Son is identified with the fact that he receives from him. Epiphanius also says: 'the Spirit who (is) from the two, as Christ himself bears witness to this by saying: "who proceeds from the Father" (Jn 15:26) and "he will take (receive) from me" (Jn 16:14, 15)'.[16]

NOTES

1. G. L. Prestige, *God in Patristic Thought*, 2nd ed. (London, 1952), pp. 129–156: chapter VII, 'Subordinationism'; J. N. D. Kelly, *Early Christian Doctrines* (London, 1977), pp. 226–231; E. Boularand, *L'hérésie d'Arius et la foi de Nicée*, 2 vols (Paris, 1972).
2. P. Galtier, *Le Saint-Esprit en nous d'après les Pères grecs* (Rome, 1946), pp. 117–133; J. N. D. Kelly, *op. cit.*, pp. 231–237, 240–247; J. Meyendorff, 'La Procession du Saint-Esprit chez les Pères orientaux', *Russie et Chrétienté* (1950), pp. 158–178. The fundamental text here is Athanasius, *Lettres à Sérapion sur la divinité du Saint-Esprit,* Fr. tr. J. Lebon, *SC* 15 (1947).
3. *De Syn*. 51. The one who sanctifies is not the same nature as those whom he sanctifies; he is holy in himself: see *Ad Ser*. I, 23 (*PG* 26, 584B) and 25 (*PG* 26, 589). The same argument can also be found in Basil the Great, *De spir. sanct.* 26 (*PG* 32, 185; *SC* 17, pp. 230ff.), etc.
4. Sergey Bulgakov criticized Athanasius for his dyadic rather than triadic doctrine: see *Le Paraclet* (Paris, 1946), pp. 29–34.
5. *Ad Ser*. III, 1 (*PG* 26, 625B; *SC* 15, p. 164); see also *Ad Ser*. I, 21 (*PG* 26, 580B; *SC* 15, p. 120).
6. *Ad Ser*. I, 19 (*PG* 26, 573Cff.; *SC* 15, pp. 116ff.).
7. *ibid*., 27 (*PG* 26, 593C; *SC* 15, p. 133ff.): 'He has nothing that is common or proper in his nature or substance, to the creatures, but he is proper to the substance and divinity of the Son, through which, belonging also to the Trinity . . .'; I, 25 (*PG* 26, 589A; *SC* 15, p. 128): 'But if the Son, because he comes from the Father, is proper to the substance of the latter, then the Spirit, because he is said to come from God, must be proper to the Son according to the substance'.
8. *Contra Arian*. III, 24 (*PG* 26, 376A); see J. Lebon, *SC* 15, p. 74, note.
9. *Ad Ser*. I, 20 (*PG* 26, 580A: *SC* 15, p. 120). H. B. Swete, *The Holy Spirit in the Ancient Church* (London, 1912), p. 92, thought that this *eklampsis (resplendit)* that the Spirit has from (*para*) the Word could not be regarded as implying anything less than an essential dependence.
10. *Ad Ser*. III, 5 (*PG* 26, 632C; *SC* 15, p. 169).
11. Didymus, *De spir. sanct.* 34, 36 and 37 (*PG* 39, 1064A, 1064–1065, 1065–1066) respectively.
12. 'Eu de kai to *execheen*, hate hudōr ex autou homoousiōs ekporeuthen': II, 2 (*PG* 39, 456).
13. See *PG* 39, 460B: 'apo tou henos Patros kath' enōsin tēs heautou theotētos esti gennēsis kai ekporeusis'.

14. Epiphanius, *Anc.* 6 (*PG* 43, 25C), 7 (*PG* 43, 28A), 11 (*PG* 43, 36C), 67 (*PG* 43, 137B), 73 (*PG* 43, 153A), 120 (*PG* 43, 236B); *Panarion, Haer.* LXII (*PG* 41, 1056). Epiphanius said of the 'procession' of the Son: *ek Patros proelthōn*: *Anc.* 19 (*PG* 43, 52B), 43 (*PG* 43, 93C).

15. *Anc.* 8 (*PG* 43, 29C), 9 (*PG* 43, 32C), 67 (*PG* 43, 137B), 70 (*PG* 43, 148A), 71 (*PG* 43, 148B), 72 (*PG* 43, 152B), 75 (*PG* 43, 157A); *Panarion, Haer.* LXIX, 54 (*PG* 42, 285D).

16. *Anc.* 67 (*PG* 43, 137B); *Panarion, Haer.* LXII, 4 (*PG* 41, 1053D).

2

THE CAPPADOCIAN FATHERS
THE FIRST COUNCIL OF
CONSTANTINOPLE
(381)
JOHN DAMASCENE

It proved very difficult to formulate faith in the consubstantial divinity of the Son, the incarnate Word in Jesus, and the Spirit. A multiplicity of errors and deviations arose. Sabellius, who came to Rome shortly before 220, believed that what was involved was merely two projections or modes of action of 'God' (that is, the Father). His teaching was therefore a form of 'modalism'. Aetius and Eunomius thought that only the Father was *agennētos* and that the Son and the Spirit were not the same substance or even of a similar substance. These two Arians and their followers were known as Anomoeans. Eunomius (*c*. 335–393), a disciple of Aetius, regarded the Spirit as a creature of the Son and the Son as a creature of the Father, who was *agennētos*. The Spirit was the third, not only in rank and dignity, but also in nature. Treatises attacking this teaching (*Contra Eunomium*) were written by Basil the Great and by his brother, Gregory of Nyssa. The divinity of the Spirit was called into question by Christians of various parties during these dramatic years. The so-called Pneumatomachi or 'fighters against the Spirit', together with Macedonius and Eustathius of Sebaste (*c*. 361 onwards), based their teaching on the fact that the Spirit is not called 'God' in Scripture, which refers to the Spirit quite often as a power subordinate to God, and consequently placed the Spirit between God and the creatures.

The orthodox teachers of the Church opposed these deviations from the truth. They included Athanasius, who wrote his letters to Serapion (357 onwards), and, when he returned to Alexandria, held a council there in 362. The faith of Nicaea implied that the Spirit belonged fully to the holy Triad and had the same divinity as the Father and the Son.[1] There were also interventions from Hilary of Poitiers, Epiphanius, Didymus and Cyril of Jerusalem. In Rome, Pope Damasus proclaimed the Spirit 'increatum atque unius maiestatis, unius usiae, unius virtutis cum Deo Patre et Domino nostro Jesu Christo'.[2] A council held at Iconium (*c*. 375) extended the faith of Nicaea to the Holy Spirit in terms that were employed at the same time by Basil, the Bishop of Caesarea, who was a friend of Amphilochius, the Bishop of Iconium.[3]

It was at this time that Basil wrote his treatise on the Holy Spirit. We have already considered the circumstances in which this treatise was written (see Volume I, p. 74). Basil continued in the direction indicated by Athanasius, insisting that the Spirit belonged, both in equality and in dignity, to the holy Triad. He took as his point of departure two data that no one could seriously refute. The first was baptism in the name of the Father, the Son and the Holy Spirit. Faith should be confessed in the form in which one was baptized, and one should praise as one confesses one's faith.[4] On the other hand, as Athanasius had already said, if the Spirit is not consubstantial with the Father and the Son, he cannot make us conform to the Son and therefore cannot unite us to the Father. He cannot, in other words, deify us.[5] The Spirit, who is the image and the reflection of the Son, reveals the Son to us and incorporates us into him. It is in this context that Basil uses this formula, which is so difficult to interpret:

> He is called the 'Spirit of Christ' because he is intimately united to him by nature. Also: 'Anyone who does not have the Spirit of Christ does not belong to Christ' (Rom 8:9). Because of this, only the Holy Spirit can worthily glorify the Lord, since 'he will glorify me' as Christ himself has said (Jn 16:14), not as creation, but as Spirit of truth, who makes the truth shine in him, and as Spirit of wisdom, who reveals Christ in his own majesty as Power of God and Wisdom of God. As the Paraclete, he expresses in him the goodness of the Paraclete who sent him and in his own dignity reveals the greatness of the One from whom he came (*tēn megalosunēn emphainei tēn tou hothen proēlthen*).[6]

Note the important part played in this text by 'manifestation'. Basil repeats Athanasius' statement that the Spirit has a relationship with the Son similar to that which the Son has with the Father[7]—he is the image or the expression (*rēma*) of the Son.[8] This manifestation and assimilation clearly place us within the order of the economy and God's action in and for his creatures, but the word used—*proēlthen*—points to intra-divine relationships between the Persons. The Spirit proceeds from the Father: in chapter 16 of his treatise (*PG* 32, 136C; *SC* 17, p. 177), Basil goes back to the *para tou Patros ekporeuetai* of Jn 15:26, although a little later, in chapter 18 (*PG* 32, 152B; *SC* 17, p. 195), he also uses *proelthon* for the procession *a Patre*, as does Epiphanius (see above [p. 28, note 14]). Basil does not give the exact place occupied by the Son in the intra-divine 'coming from' of the third Person. A passage in his *Adversus Eunomium* would seem to situate it in the sense of the *Filioque*. This text was vehemently discussed at the Council of Florence.[9] In a critical study of the original text, one scholar has concluded that an explanatory scholion, reproduced in the margin by a copyist but originally borrowed from Eunomius, must have been introduced into the text of Basil's treatise and handed down in certain manuscripts. Basil must have been criticizing this scholion, which read: the Spirit is third, that is, subordinate and inferior to the Word in nature. This is a Neo-Platonic idea that was combated by the Cappadocian Fathers.[10]

Basil was not very philosophically minded. He made use of the already accepted distinction between *ousia* and *hypostasis*, which he explained in the following way: '*Ousia* and *hypostasis* can be differentiated in the same way as common (*koinon*) and the particular (*to kath' ekaston*), as, for example, in the case of "animal" and a "particular man" '.[11] Each hypostasis is the *ousia*, and so Basil attached the unity of the hypostases to the identity of nature, but at the same time taught that each hypostasis was distinguished by a special characteristic or *idiazon*.[12] This characteristic consisted of the fact that two of the Persons came from a first Person who did not come from any other. Or, put better, each hypostasis was marked by a special property or *idiotēs*—that of fatherhood, sonship or the power of sanctification.[13] This last *gnoristikē idiotēs* corresponds to what Thomas Aquinas called 'notion'. It marked the Spirit as the one who sanctified and who fulfilled in the perfection of communion with the deity.

Basil died on 1 January 379. The struggle that he had been conducting was taken up by his brother Gregory, Bishop of Nyssa (†394 or later).[14] Like Athanasius and Basil, Gregory also based his thesis on the Trinitarian baptismal formula[15] and concluded, as they had done, from the fact of our deification that the Spirit was fully divine. He went further than they had, however, and developed this classical argument into a theologal anthropology, teaching that the formation (*morphōsis*) of the Christian and his perfection (*teleiōsis*), of which Christ was the model, were the work of the sanctifying Spirit.[16] The Spirit was therefore consubstantial with the Son and the Father; he was of the same nature (against Macedonius and Eunomius); a unity of nature (*phusis, ousia*), but a distinction between hypostases.[17] The action attributed to the Spirit by Scripture required him to be God, Gregory argued on the eve of the First Council of Constantinople in May 381, and as such to receive the same honour as the Father and the Son.[18] The progress of the Council and the text of its creed were both guided by this thought. Jaeger has shown clearly that Gregory played a decisive part in the Council.[19] He brought together the various statements that insisted on the unity of nature in the Trinity and the conviction, so strong in the East, of the monarchy of the Father, saying: 'of one and the same Person of the Father (*prosōpon*), by whom the Son was begotten and from whom the Spirit proceeds. That is why we speak strictly of only one God and of only one cause of those who depend on him as on their cause.'[20] He also illustrated this theology by various meaningful images. He spoke, for example, of a lamp which communicates its light to another lamp and through that lamp to a third. The Spirit shone in this way, Gregory taught, eternally through the Son.[21] He also used the comparison of a source of power, of that power itself and of the spirit of that power.[22]

The Word therefore appears as the intermediary between the Father and the Spirit in Gregory's teaching, in which he clearly has biblical formulae in mind: the Spirit proceeds (comes) from the Father and receives from the Son, with the result that he is from God and he is from Christ.[23] This implies a certain dependence on the part of the Spirit, in his being, with regard to the Son. What Gregory does not say, however, is *ek tou Huiou* or *apo tou Huiou*—Jaeger has shown that the *ek* in certain manuscripts of *De Orat. Dom.* 3 is an interpolation.[24] At the end of Book I of his *Contra Eunomium*, however, he wrote (in 380) that the Son was always with the Father and that he, Gregory, taught the same thing about the Spirit, the only difference being in the order (*taxis*), 'since, just as the Son is united to the Father, having his being from him (*ex autou*), but is not after him (in time) in his hypostasis, the Spirit is also united to the monogenous one, for, in the hypostasis, the Son is conceived before the Spirit only in respect of the cause (*kata ton tēs aitias logon*)'.[25] Does this word *aitia*, 'cause', apply in this text to the monogenous Son or to the Father? This might be implied in such a passage.[26] A very valuable statement is made, however, at the end of his *Quod non sint tres dii*:

> If we should be accused, by not making a difference with regard to nature (*phusis*), of confusing the hypostases, we would reply: In confessing a divine nature without difference or variation, we are not denying a difference with regard to the situation of cause and caused (*kata ton aition kai aitiaton*). It is only in this way that we can understand that the one is distinguished from the other—being the cause is quite different from being caused. And we perceive in what is caused a new distinction between what comes immediately (*prosechōs*) from the first, and what comes through the intermediary of what comes immediately from the first. In this way, the property of being monogenous remains unambiguously with the Son, and there can be no doubt that the Spirit is from the Father, the middle position of the Son preserving for him the property of being monogenous, and the Spirit not being deprived of his natural relationship with the Father.[27]

This is not, of course, the same as the *Filioque* of the Latin Church, since the Eastern Christians have never spoken of the Father and the Son as forming a single principle of active spiration, even if it has been emphasized, as Augustine and Christians in the West did, that this goes back *principaliter* to the Father. The Greeks did not like speculating or arriving at greater precision on the basis of deductions. It is, however, hardly possible to deny that the Son played a part in the intra-divine existence of the Spirit, although that part was not of a causal nature. Gregory of Nyssa, however, uses the formula, either literally or with the same meaning, *ek tou Patros dia tou Huiou ekporeuetai*: the Spirit comes from the Father through the Son.[28]

Gregory's namesake of Nazianzus was born about 330 and was consecrated Archbishop of Constantinople on 27 November 380. He resigned from that office in June 381, however, and retired to his birthplace, where he died in

389 or 390.[29] He is called 'the Theologian' by the Eastern Church. Like his friend Basil, he showed that the Spirit had all the qualities of God and that his activities were those of God.[30] Unlike Basil, who did not in fact say the word, Gregory Nazianzen explicitly stated that the Spirit *is* God.[31] In his affirmation of consubstantiality, he insisted on the monarchy of the Father, who was, according to Gregory, 'without a beginning', *anarchos*:

> The name of the one who is without a beginning is Father; the name of the beginning is Son; the name of the one who is with the beginning is Holy Spirit.[32]

> Each is God by reason of consubstantiality; the Three are God by reason of monarchy.[33]

> Nature is one in the Three; it is God. What makes their unity, however, is the Father, on whom the others depend, not in order to be confused or mixed, but in order to be united.[34]

Gregory Nazianzen also makes use of comparisons. These include the source, the stream and the river on the one hand, and the sun, the ray and the light on the other.[35] He points out, however, that every comparison is insufficient. He also stresses our (his) inability to penetrate into and define precisely the nature of the processions and the difference between them, although we are acquainted with that difference through the very terms used by the sovereign theologian, Christ himself.[36] It is enough to affirm, as mysteriously different, the begetting by and the procession from the one who alone is *agennētos*.[37] Gregory ventures, however, to provide a comparison here. Eve, he says, was taken from Adam by means of an immediate coming out and that is the way in which the Spirit proceeded. Seth, on the other hand, came from Adam (and Eve!) by means of begetting (see Gen 4:35).[38] This is certainly a strange comparison—if it is taken further, then it would have to be said that the Son was begotten *a Patre Spirituque*, which would contradict the idea of the *taxis*, the order of the three Persons in their perfect consubstantiality.

The Cappadocian Fathers definitively established the distinction between the common *ousia* (substance or nature) and the hypostases, which they also sometimes called 'persons', *prosōpa*. The hypostasis is what has distinctive consistency and a concrete existence; it is what Aristotle called the *protē ousia*, the concrete being in which alone a concrete substance can exist. It is characterized by its *idiotēs*, which is known by its *gnōrismata*. Kelly has pointed out that 'for Basil these particularizing characteristics are respectively "paternity" (*patrotēs*), "sonship" (*huiotēs*) and "sanctifying power" or "sanctification" (*hagiastikē dunamis*; *hagiasmos*). The other Cappadocians define them more precisely as "ingenerateness" (*agennēsia*), "generateness" (*gennēsis*) and "mission" or "procession" (*ekpempsis*;

ekporeusis). . . . Thus the distinction of the Persons is grounded in their origin and mutual relation . . . and hence they come to be termed "modes of coming to be" (*tropoi huparxeōs*).'[39] The hypostatic characters are in this way 'derived from relationships of origin'.[40]

All the Greek Fathers, however, believed that this 'mode of coming to be' of the Word and the Spirit is inexpressible.[41] All that man can do, they insisted, is recognize, respect and affirm it. The Son, the Father's Word, was begotten *huiokōs*, filially, and the Spirit was begotten *pneumatikōs*, as Spirit, according to Didymus of Alexandria.[42] The analyses made by the Latin Fathers, which are fundamentally in agreement with the teaching of the Greeks, seemed to the latter to be a rational elaboration which lacked discretion and went beyond what could properly be said about the inexpressible mystery of the divine processions.

The struggle and the work of the Cappadocian Fathers resulted in the article on the Holy Spirit in the creed which the Council of Chalcedon attributed to the First Council of Constantinople.[43] In this creed, the Holy Spirit was not called 'God' or said to be 'consubstantial with the Father'; he was, however, said to be 'Lord, who gives life, who proceeds from the Father (*ekporeuomenon*), who is adored and glorified with the Father and the Son, who has spoken through the prophets'. To these words were added the words: 'in the one, holy, catholic and apostolic Church'. The Council followed the example of the Greek Fathers and used the words employed by Jesus in Jn 15:26, but replaced *para* with *ek*, assuming that the two prepositions were equivalent. At the same time, the Council said nothing about the part played by the Son in the Spirit's coming to be. It could have used the formula taken from Jn 16:14 and so frequently cited by the Fathers: *kai ek tou Huiou lambanon*, 'and receiving from the Son'. On the other hand, it could also have followed the example of, for example, Epiphanius, Pseudo-Cyril (*PG* 77, 1140B), John Damascene (*PG* 94, 821B) and Pope Zacharias (†752), and spoken of *en Huiō anapauomenon*, 'reposing in the Son'.

Fifty years later, nothing was said about the question by the Council of Ephesus, even though the opportunity presented itself in the Council's condemnation of the teaching of Nestorius, who limited the part played by the Spirit in the fact of Christ to a sanctificaton of his pure humanity. Against this, Cyril of Alexandria showed that the Spirit was not unrelated to the incarnate Son at the level of essence. In his ninth anathema, written before the Council, he condemned anyone who should say that the Lord Jesus Christ was glorified by the Spirit as though by an alien power, instead of acknowledging the Spirit by whom he accomplished the signs of his divinity (*theosēmeias*) as being proper to him (*idion*).[44]

This brings us to Cyril (†444), who was Bishop of Alexandria for more than thirty years. His leading part in the Christological debate has been extensively studied. In pneumatology, he merits particular attention as regards the indwelling of the Holy Spirit in the righteous and the fact that, in his being as the third Person, the Spirit depends on the Son.

I have discussed the first of these questions in Volume II (pp. 85–90, and 95–98 notes 24–45) and have provided a bibliography there. The Greek Fathers insisted not only on the community of action *ad extra* of the divine Persons, but also on the mark, in this action, of what is the property of each hypostasis in the Tri-unity of God. The Spirit, as the image of the Son, brings about our sonship by grace and, as the virtue of sanctification of the deity, he also brings about our sanctification.

With regard to the second question, there can be no doubt that the most impressive statements are to be found in the writings of Cyril.[45] His first intention was to oppose Nestorius and to show that the Spirit rightly belonged to the incarnate Word. Within this perspective of the incarnation, he from time to time had the 'economy' in mind,[46] but what is remarkable is that he based that economy on the eternal Tri-unity—the evidence is abundant.[47] The same applies to the formulae relating to the Spirit as proper to the Son (*idion*),[48] coming from him (*ek*),[49] the Spirit as proceeding from the Son (*proïenai* or *procheitai*)[50] and proceeding from the two (*ex amphoin*), that is, from the Father and the Son[51] or from the Father through the Son.[52]

All these statements point to the same context. The latter can be expressed in a precise form in Thomistic categories in the following way: the Spirit is sent by the Father and by the Son and this 'mission' is based on the eternal processions, of which it is the term in the creature, by bringing about the 'economy'. This economy is that of the incarnation of the Word and is therefore Christological. The mission of the Spirit is to bring about the (mystical) Body of Christ. The sanctification of the humanity of Christ by the Spirit is the beginning of our sanctification and it is extended to his (mystical) body.[53] In this action, which makes us into the body of Christ, making us 'con-corporeal' with Christ, the Eucharist or 'mystical eulogy' brings about a corporeal unity, just as the Spirit brings about a spiritual unity.

I have already referred to Cyril's ninth anathema against Nestorius. Theodoret of Cyrrhus came to the rescue of Nestorius and, in a pitiless criticism of Cyril's statements, had this to say about the relationship between the Spirit and the Son: 'If he says that the Spirit is proper to the Son insofar as he is consubstantial and proceeds from the Father (*kai ek Patros ekporeuomenon*), we would agree with him and regard that pronouncement as orthodox. But if he claims that this is so because the Spirit has his existence either from the Son or through the Son (*hōs ex Huiou ē di' Huiou*), then we reject that sentence as blasphemous and impious, since we believe the Lord, who said: "the Spirit of truth who proceeds from the Father".'[54]

Cyril did not deal with the question to which later controversies gave such prominence, but simply reaffirmed that 'the Spirit is the Spirit of the Son just as he is the Spirit of the Father. . . . The Holy Spirit proceeds from God the Father, as the Lord said, but he is not alien to the Son, since the latter has everything (in common) with the Father, as he said himself when he spoke of the Holy Spirit' (here Cyril quotes Jn 16:14).[55] J. Meyendorff said: 'It is interesting to note that, after that incident, which took place about 430, Cyril did not give up either his theology or his vocabulary. In his later works, expressions such as "coming from the two" (*ex amphoin*) are still to be found. This makes it possible for us to say that these expressions had for him a quite different meaning from the one they had for Augustine.'[56] To say 'different' is probably correct, but to say '*quite* different' is, I think, too much. Cyril was dealing with the Nestorian heresy and developed his own, relatively simply, uncomplicated vocabulary. Augustine used his own concepts. It is certainly not possible to misunderstand Cyril's repeated statements about the Spirit's dependence on the Son with regard to being, but he did not develop this theology as Augustine did, because he was not preoccupied with it. As G. M. de Durand has pointed out recently: 'Cyril's principal preoccupation was to draw attention to the unfailing link between the Spirit and the divine essence. Flowing physically from the Father through the Son (*De Trin. Dial.*, ed. J. Aubert, 423a) or poured out by the Father from his own nature (634b–c), the Spirit is at the same level as they are and cannot be a creature. The Son who distributes such a gift as his own (492a and d; 494c) also cannot be a creature. It was probably because of this limited and quite narrow intention in most of the texts, that of determining the nature of the Spirit and not his precise relationship with the other Persons, that Photians and Latinophrones were able to refer almost endlessly to such passages.'[57]

*   *   *

John was born about 700 at Damascus and was therefore known as John Damascene or John of Damascus. He was a monk at St Sabas, between Jerusalem and the Dead Sea, from 726 until he died in 749.[58] His main work, *Pēgē gnōseōs*, the 'Fount of Wisdom', consists of three parts, dealing with philosophy, heresies and orthodox faith respectively. The third part, translated into Latin as *De fide orthodoxa* in the twelfth century, was widely read during the Scholastic period in the West. In the East, it was used as a handbook of theology in the Byzantine schools and universities. It can certainly be regarded as a faithful expression of the faith of the Church, since John Damascene was not a very original writer. In his Trinitarian teaching, he virtually repeats two-thirds of a treatise *De Sacrosancta Trinitate* by an unknown author writing at the end of the seventh or the beginning of the eighth century. This treatise was printed at the end of the works of Cyril of Alexandria, and the author is, for that reason, called Pseudo-Cyril.[59] This author was also influenced by Basil of Caesarea and Gregory Nazianzen. John Damascene owned his use of the idea of *perichōrēsis* in the theology of the Trinity to Pseudo-Cyril especially.[60] The following is an example of his writing on the Trinity:

> These hypostases are within each other, not so that they are confused, but so that they contain one another, in accordance with the word of the Lord: I am in the Father and the Father is in me. . . . We do not say three gods, the Father, the Son and the Holy Spirit. On the contrary, we say only one God, the Holy Trinity, the Son and the Spirit going back to only one Principle, without composition or confusion, quite unlike the heresy of Sabellius. These Persons are united, not so that they are confused with each other, but so that they are contained within each other. There is between them a circumincession without mixture or confusion, by virtue of which they are neither separated nor divided in substance, unlike the heresy of Arius. In fact, in a word, the divinity is undivided in the individuals, just as there is only one light in three suns contained within each other, by means of an intimate interpenetration.[61]

The opportunity clearly presents itself at this point to say a few words about this reality which is so difficult to define. The fourth gospel frequently speaks of the existence of the Father in the Son and of the Son in the Father[62] and such an important factor as this 'in-existence' was bound to have a deep effect on the minds of Christians. Although the words *perichōrēsis* and circumincession may not occur as such in the writings of the earliest Fathers of the Church, the idea certainly does.[63] It was first applied in Christology[64] and Maximus the Confessor was the first to use the word *perichōrēsis* to express the oneness of action and effect resulting from the union of the two natures in Christ.[65] It was first employed in Trinitarian theology by Pseudo-Cyril, who was followed by John Damascene.

Perichōrēsis in the theology of the Trinity points to the in-existence of the Persons within each other, the fact that they are present to each other, that they contain one another and that they manifest each other. This in-existence is based on the unity and identity of substance between the three, even in the teaching of the Greek Fathers.[66] If this teaching were to go no further than this, however, it would simply indicate the identity of God with himself, and no more than this. This is reflected in the very differences that exist within God himself, that is, in the Persons who hypostatize the same substance. They are in or within each other—in Greek *en* and in Latin *circuminsessio*; John Damascene speaks of it in this way—and each one is turned towards the other and is open and given to the other (*eis*; *circuminsessio*). They are inconceivable without each other. Sergey Bulgakov insisted that the hypostases were always Trinitarian.[67] An interesting datum with a bearing on the delicate problem of consciousness in God can be derived from the concept of circumincession, and I shall touch on this question when we come to consider the idea of 'person'.

To return to John Damascene, it is clear that he begins by speaking of

'God' (*De fide orthod*. I, 3, 4 and 8) and, though it is not long before he is speaking of the Father, the Son and the Holy Spirit, he is still concerned primarily, to begin with at least, with 'God' as the absolute being. There is a certain ambivalence about this name, and Bulgakov criticizes John for this.[68] It is quite possible that his procedure may have strengthened Thomas Aquinas in his own approach to the question, which Orthodox theologians have seen as a perfect example of the Latin tendency to stress the essence rather than the hypostases. It is certainly true that we know, in faith, that God is Father, Son and Spirit, but is it not legitimate, if we follow the economy of revelation, to speak first of all of 'God' as the one who is and who will be what he will be (Ex 3:14)?

The one 'God' is also the Father, and John soon goes on to discuss the monarchy of that Father as the Father by nature (and not by a free decision) of his monogenous Son and the *proboleus*[69] or 'producer' of the very Holy Spirit (*De fide orthod*. I, 8; *PG* 94, 809B). The Spirit is not another Son—he does not proceed by begetting, but *ekporeutōs* or by 'procession' (*PG* 94, 816C). which is another mode of coming to be or mode of subsistence, *tropos tēs huparxeōs*.[70] Both are beyond our understanding and neither can be explained. John ventures a fairly common comparison, however, that of Eve coming from the side of Adam (the Spirit) and of Seth, who was born through being begotten (see above, p. 33 and below, note 38). The three hypostases have everything in common except their 'hypostatic properties' (*De fide orthod*. I, 8; *PG* 94, 824B, 828D) of being *agennētos, gennētos* and *ekporeuomenon*. This teaching became classical in Eastern triadology. It would be wrong to regard this teaching as diametrically opposed to what was worked out in the Western Church, even if precise concepts and logical connections were much further developed in Latin theology, where they were so developed in terms of relationships of origin. John Damascene spoke of *pros allēla scheseōs* and wrote: 'We have learnt through faith that there is a difference between begetting and proceeding, but faith tells us nothing about the nature of that difference'.[71] Many of the Western theologians said the same.[72] John Damascene, on the other hand, thought of the modes of subsistence of the one who was begotten and the one who proceeds only with reference to the unbegotten one, the Father, and his monarchy (see *De fide orthod*. I, 8, 12; *PG* 94, 824A-B, 829A and C, 849A).

It is at this point that the question concerning the relationship between the Spirit and the Son arises. Here John Damascene reproduces Pseudo-Cyril's text (*PG* 77, 1145A) and says: 'We do not say that the Son is the cause, nor do we say that he is Father. . . . We do not say that the Spirit comes from the Son (*ek tou Huiou*), but we do say that he is Spirit of the Son.'[73] 'The Spirit is Spirit of the Father . . . but he is also the Spirit of the Son, not because he comes from him (*ouch hōs ex autou*), but because he comes through him (*all' hōs di' autou*) from the Father, since the Father is the only cause (*monos*

38

aitios ho Patēr)'.[74] The Spirit is united to the Father by the Son.[75] He is called Spirit of the Son because he is manifested and given by him.[76] This, of course, is an economic aspect of the Spirit, but it becomes clear at the end of chapter 12 of the treatise that this is based on the immanent reality of the Tri-unity: 'Through the Word, the Father produces the Spirit, who manifests him (*dia logou proboleus ekphantorikou Pneumatos*). . . . The Holy Spirit is the power of the Father making the secrets of the deity known and proceeding from the Father through the Son in a way that he knows, but which is not begetting. . . . The Father is the source of the Son and the Holy Spirit. . . . The Spirit is not Son of the Father, he is the Spirit of the Father, as proceeding from him (*ekporeuomenon*), . . . but he is also Spirit of the Son, not as (proceeding) from him, but proceeding through him from the Father. Only the Father is cause (*aitios*).'[77]

The *per Filium* of John Damascene is not the *Filioque*. In the material sense, John's texts are a denial of the procession of the Spirit 'from the Father and from the Son as from a single principle'. They do, however, give the Son a certain place in the eternal state of the Spirit. J. Grégoire has vigorously analysed John's terms and formulae within their original doctrinal context, trying to make clear in this way what they aimed to establish, and against whom. He has in this way been able to define quite precisely the meaning of the procession of the Spirit from the Father in the sense of John's 'through the Son'. He has said, for example, that 'His hypostatic property, the procession, is only accessible and understandable—insofar as it can be made intelligible—by reference to the Son, just as the breath can only be accessible by reference to the word. The Spirit can therefore reveal the Father, his cause, by the procession, only through the Son and our understanding cannot pass directly from the Spirit to the Father' (*op. cit.* (note 58 below), pp. 750–751).

J. Grégoire also says, a little later in his article: 'If the Spirit comes from the Father by procession and remains in him, unlike our breath which disappears into the air, this must be by "penetrating" the Son until he remains and dwells in him at the same time as he does in the Father. The procession must therefore be *dia Huiou* (as John Damascene claims) or else the Spirit must rest *in* the Son (as the Pseudo-Cyril says). This *dia Huiou* is the dynamic expression—one is almost tempted to say the "genetic" expression—of the *perichōrēsis*, the interpenetration and the dwelling of the hypostases in each other being the static expression, the eternal "result" of the procession *dia Huiou*' (*op. cit.*, p. 753).

The subject-matter and the quality of Grégoire's work is in my opinion so important that I would like to summarize it here in his own words, given at the conclusion of his article (*op. cit.*, pp. 754–755):

1. The Father is the only cause in the Trinity; this causality cannot be divided or shared. The category of 'secondary cause' is completely absent in the teaching of John Damascene.

2. John's theology of the Trinity is dominated by the ideas of *nous, logos* and *pneuma*. It expresses in a single movement the fact that the Spirit reveals the Word and the Word reveals the Father.

3. The procession is not begetting and the Spirit is not the son of the Son.

4. The Spirit rests in the Word and accompanies him, that is, he participates indissolubly in his activity by making him manifest. He is the revelation and the image of the Son.

5. The procession of the Spirit goes back to the begetting of the Son; at the level of the *perichōrēsis*, the Spirit comes from the Father through the Son and is poured out in him.

6. In the divine activity, the Son provides the basis of the work that is wanted by the Father and the Spirit perfects it.

In John's teaching, then, there is no separation between economy and theology; these are completely integrated into a single vision. There is also no polemical element in his writing except possibly against Arianism and Manichaeanism (and perhaps against Islam). There is certainly no argument directed against the *Filioque* or the theology of Cyril of Alexandria or Theodoret of Cyrrhus. He is neither a filioquist nor a monopatrist. He is not a filioquist because, in his teaching, the causal category does not and cannot apply to the eternal relationship between the Spirit and the Son. He is not a monopatrist because, in his theology, an essential presupposition for the procession is the begetting of the Word and the procession refers entirely to that begetting.

The synthetic treatment of this subject by John Damascene on the basis of the contribution made by Athanasius and the Cappadocian Fathers provided Greek theologians with their basic concepts. These included the distinction between substance and hypostasis, the monarchy of the Father and the distinction between the begetting of the Son and the *ekporeusis* of the Spirit, as by two modes of coming into being and of subsistence establishing themselves as such in their difference. They also included the relationship between the Spirit and the Word, the Son (of whom he is the Spirit), either in the form of coming from the Father through the Son, or in the form of a resting of the Spirit in the Son, or by the fact that the Spirit expresses the Son and is the image of the Son, or, finally, at the level of the 'economy', by the fact that the Spirit is communicated by the Son and makes him known.

This is a suitable point, in view of the fact that the term plays such an important part in the triadology of the Eastern Church, to say a few words about *ekporeusis*, which is the noun derived from the verb used in Jn 15:26: 'Hotan de elthē ho paraklētos hon egō pempsō humin para tou patros, to pneuma tēs alētheias ho para tou patros ekporeuetai'—'When the Paraclete comes, whom I shall send to you from the Father, the Spirit of truth who proceeds from the Father, he will bear witness to me'. The verb *ekporeuomenai* appears in the present tense in this text, but, in view of the context, it has to be interpreted in the sense of a *futurum instans*.[78] The verb is derived from a root *poros*, which means a 'crossing' or a 'ford', and from the verb *poreuō*, to cause to cross or pass over. It means 'to come or go out' and examples of its use are: to come or go out like a word from a man's mouth, like water from the temple (Ezek 47:12), to go out of a town (Mt 20:29; Mk 10:46; 11:19), to come out of tombs (Jn 5:29); demons come out of those who are possessed and judgement comes out of the mouth of God (Rev); flashes of lightning come out of God's throne (Rev 4:5) and water comes out of the throne of God and the Lamb (Rev 22:1). In the text in question (Jn 15:26), the verb is in the middle voice, suggesting a reference to the subject of the action: 'the Spirit himself comes out of the Father'.[79]

According to the text, the Spirit 'comes out from near the Father' (*para*), as in the first half of the verse. The context is not that of a statement about the inner being of the Triad. It is rather a pronouncement about the sending by the Son to bear witness. As A. Wenger pointed out, 'the Son sends the Spirit on behalf of the Father and the Spirit will leave from near the Father—that is the meaning which should be given to the repetition of *para*, which should not be understood in the first case as meaning the temporal mission and in the second as pointing to the eternal procession'.[80] If this interpretation is correct, all that we have here is the eternal procession as the prerequisite for the economic mission. But, as J. Giblet has said, 'the two aspects are reached conjointly and understood together'.[81]

It is therefore not possible to say with certainty that the text of Jn 15:26 is as dogmatically significant as the Greek theologians have claimed, especially since there are other equivalent Greek verbs which also express the idea of procession and which can in fact be found in Greek patristic writings. Examples are: *proerchesthai, proïenai, procheisthai* and *pephēnenai*.[82] In this case, Tradition clearly accompanies Scripture. Both the Greek Fathers, most of whom read *ek* instead of *para*, and the Council of 381 regarded the text of Jn 15:26 as expressing the procession of the Spirit *a Patre*.[83] Both Augustine and Thomas Aquinas also saw the text in the same light and Augustine came very close to the Greeks with his *principaliter*. As V. Rodziensko has observed, he would never have said that the Spirit proceeds from the Father and the Son as from a single source *principaliter*. This term was reserved for the Father, with the result that it is necessary to distinguish the titles of origin in 'as from a single source'. It is a pity that the verb *procedere* was used indiscriminately here. A distinction should have been made in the terms themselves.

*   *   *

John Damascene was born in Syria. If we go back several centuries in the history of the Church in that country, we see that a very lyrical form of liturgy was developed there in continuity with the Semitic origins of Christianity, at least until the Eastern Church's liturgy as a whole came strongly under

Byzantine influence. The Syrian office was composed not only of psalms, which did not play such a dominant part as in the West, but also of hymns (*madrashē*), responses and *sedrē* (long prayers). The theology which is contained in this liturgy and can be deduced from it and the sacramental celebrations of the Syrian Church is made explicit in homilies, catechetical instructions and commentaries on Scripture, produced in considerable quantities between the fourth and the eighth centuries.[84] The principal authors are, in the fourth century, Aphraates, a Persian (†345), Ephraem Syrus of Nisibis (†373), Cyril of Jerusalem (†386), John Chrysostom (†407), Theodore of Mopsuestia (†428); a little later, Isaac of Antioch (fourth to fifth century), Narsai (†507), Philoxenus of Mabbug (fifth to sixth century), Jacob of Sarug (†521) and Severus of Antioch (†538).

As in the case of the Greek Church, to which John Chrysostom also belonged, both liturgical celebrations and theology in Syrian Christianity are full of Trinitarian evocations and doxologies. These are characterized by a deeply paschal or rather pentecostal spirituality: what the Holy Spirit has done for Christ in his conception, baptism and resurrection, he causes to function in the Church and the lives of Christians. He is life itself and he is life-giving. He is invoked especially in the celebration of the sacraments of initiation—baptism, the Eucharist and the *myron* or anointing with holy oils. In all three cases, the epicleses are very similar.[85] One special feature of the liturgy in the ancient patriarchate of Antioch is that baptism by water was preceded by anointing with oil. This was to indicate that faith had to precede reception into the Church, and the New Testament attributes this to a spiritual anointing by the Spirit.[86] Later an anointing with the *myron* was added after baptism; this has sometimes been interpreted as a form of the sacrament of confirmation.

The Holy Spirit was regarded as active in the Eucharist, not only through the epiclesis, but also in communion, of which he was seen to be the *res*. It is interesting in this context to consider some of the remarkably powerful formulae of Ephraem Syrus: 'The Fire and the Spirit are in our baptism; in the bread and the cup are also the Fire and the Spirit',[87] Isaac of Antioch: 'Come and drink, eat the flame which will make you angels of fire and taste the flavour of the Holy Spirit', or Matins of the second Sunday after Pentecost: 'Here is the body and blood which are a furnace in which the Holy Spirit is the fire'.[88]

According to the Syrian Church, the whole life of the Church, including that of its ordained ministers and its faithful, came from a Pentecost that was extended in time,[89] and even the order of the Church was attributed to the Spirit: 'It was he who said to the apostles at Pentecost: "Go and teach and baptize in the name of the Father, of the Son and of the Holy Spirit and lo, I am with you until the end" (Mt 28:19–20)'.[90]

The theology of the third Person was not developed speculatively to any great extent. The dynamic pattern of the 'economy' was fairly closely followed. 'The truth', Ephraem Syrus declared, 'comes from the Father through the Son and gives life to all through the Spirit.'[91] In other words, the Spirit was seen as life and as life-giving. In the case of the intra-divine life, the formula that was so much used by the Eastern Fathers was also popular in the Syrian Church: 'Father who begets and is not begotten, Son who is begotten and who does not beget, Spirit who proceeds from the Father and receives from the Son. They are three holy Persons and three distinct properties.'[92]

This theology was developed by Bar Hebraeus (†1286). According to E. P. Siman, 'The Spirit, who was caused by the Father by means of procession and not by means of begetting, is a Person who is consubstantial with the Father and the Son by the fact that the three Persons are a single essence and a single nature. That Person, Life, proceeding from the Father, also receives from the Son (Jn 16:14–15) the mode of revelation to creatures. Thus for Bar Hebraeus, who was the greatest witness to the theological tradition in the Syrian Church, the Holy Spirit is life. All life exists through that life. It proceeds from the Father and comes through the Son into the world, animating all things and giving life and deifying men and, through them, the whole cosmos.'[93]

NOTES

1. Athanasius, *Tomus ad Antioch*. 3 (*PG* 26, 797); cf. his letter to Jovianus (*PG* 26, 816 and 820).
2. See Damasus' letter *Ea gratia* to the Eastern Christians, c. 374 (*PL* 13, 351; *DS* 145 and 147); see also the very detailed text of 375, *Fides Damasi* (*PL* 13, 358ff.).
3. *PG* 39, 95ff.
4. Basil, *De spir. sanct*. 10 (*PG* 32, 112ff.); Fr. tr., ed. with intro. and notes by B. Pruche, *Traité du Saint-Esprit* (*SC* 17, pp. 149ff.). See also *Ep*. 159 (*PG* 32, 621A). The following monographs and articles are also valuable: H. Dörries, *De Spiritu Sancto. Der Beitrag des Basilius zum Abschluss des trinitarischen Dogmas* (Göttingen, 1956); B. Pruche, 'L'originalité du Traité de S. Basile sur le Saint-Esprit', *RSPT*, 32 (1948), 207–224; *idem*, 'Autour du Traité sur le Saint-Esprit de Basile de Césarée', *RSR*, 52 (1964), 204–232. Finally, the whole of *Verbum Caro*, 89 (1968). For Eunomius, see M. Spanneut's article in *Dict. Hist. Géo. Eccl.*, XV (1963), cols 1499–1504.
5. Athanasius, *Ad Ser*. I, 25 (*PG* 26, 589; *SC* 15, pp. 128ff.); Basil, *De spir. sanct*. 26 (*SC* 17, pp. 230ff.); see also B. Pruche's Introduction, pp. 64–77; *PG* 32, 185).
6. Basil, *De spir. sanct*. 18 (*PG* 32, 152C; *SC* 17, pp. 195–196). The question of the interpretation of this passage is discussed by B. Pruche on pp. 82ff. This aspect of manifestation makes it, in my opinion, difficult to translate as 'by the means of whom the Holy Spirit *proceeds*' the phrase which forms the transition from the Son to the Spirit in Basil's anaphora: 'par' hou to Pneuma to hagion *exephanē*', as B. Capelle has it in 'La procession du Saint-Esprit d'après la liturgie grecque de Basile', *L'Orient syrien*, 7 (1962), 69–76.
7. *De spir. sanct*. 17 (*PG* 32, 148A; *SC* 17, p. 188), which goes back to Athanasius, *Ad Ser*. I, 21; III, 1 (*PG* 26, 580B and 625B; *SC* 15, pp. 120 and 164).
8. *Adv. Eunom*. V (*PG* 29, 723 and 731). According to J. Lebon, *Le Muséon*, 50 (1937),

61–84, however, Books IV and V of the *Adv. Eunom.* were written by Didymus of Alexandria.

9. This is the text in the *Adv. Eunom.* III, beginning, which was disputed at Florence: see J. Gill, *The Council of Florence* (Cambridge, 1959), p. 199:

TEXT UPHELD BY THE LATINS	TEXT UPHELD BY THE GREEKS
Even if the Holy Spirit is third in dignity and order, why need he be third also in nature? For that he is second to the Son, *having his being from him and receiving from him and announcing to us and being completely dependent on him,* pious tradition recounts; but that his nature is third we are not taught by the Saints nor can we conclude logically from what has been said.	Even if the Holy Spirit is third in dignity and order, why need he be third also in nature? For that he is second pious tradition *perhaps* recounts; but that his nature is third we are not taught by Scripture nor can we conclude from what has been said.

10. M. van Parys, 'Quelques remarques à propos d'un texte controversé de Basile au concile de Florence', *Irénikon*, 40 (1967), 6–14. L. Lohn has written the history of this controversial text in his 'Doctrina S. Basilii de processionibus divinarum Personarum', *Greg*, 10 (1929), 329–364, 461–500. Lohn is in favour of the Latin text.

11. *Ep.* 214, 4 and 236, 6 to Amphilochius (in 376) (*PG* 32, 789 and 884). See also *Ep.* 38, written to Gregory of Nyssa, his brother, in 369–370 (*PG* 32, 325ff.).

12. *De Spir. sanct.* 18 (*PG* 32, 149B; *SC* 17, pp. 192–193).

13. *De Spir. sanct.* 25 (*PG* 32, 177B; *SC* 17, p. 222); *Ep.* 214, 4 and 236, 6 (*PG* 32, 789 and 884); *Adv. Eunom.* II, 28 (*PG* 29, 637).

14. W. Jaeger, *Gregor von Nyssa's Lehre vom Heiligen Geist* (Leiden, 1966; published posthumously, ed. H. Dörries). More general works are: H. U. von Balthasar, *Présence et Pensée. Essai sur la philosophie religieuse de G. de Nysse* (Fr. tr.; Paris, 1942); J. Daniélou, *Platonisme et théologie mystique. Essai sur la doctrine spirituelle de Grégoire de Nysse* (Paris, 1944); J. Quasten, *Initiation aux Pères de l'Eglise*, III (Paris, 1963), pp. 365–420; M. Canavet, *Dictionnaire de Spiritualité*, VI (1967), cols 971–1011.

15. Gregory of Nyssa, *Refutatio Confessionis Eunomii: Opera*, ed. W. Jaeger, II, pp. 312ff,; *Ep.* V: *Opera*, VIII/2, pp. 32ff.

16. This theme has been developed by W. Jaeger in 'Paideia Christi', *Humanistische Reden und Vorträge* (Berlin, 1960), pp. 250–265; *Early Christianity and Greek Paideia* (Cambridge, Mass., 1961); *op. cit.* (note 14), chapter V, pp. 101ff. See also the studies by M. Lot-Borodine (1932–1933) and J. Gross (1938).

17. *Orat. cat.* c. 3ff. (*PG* 45, 17ff.); *De comm. not.* 176ff.

18. *Adv. Maced.* (*PG* 45, 1301ff.); *Opera*, III/1, pp. 89ff.

19. W. Jaeger, *op. cit.* (note 14), pp. 70ff. For the council and the creed attributed to it by the Council of Chalcedon, see A. M. Ritter, *Das Konzil von Konstantinopel und sein Symbol. Studien zur Geschichte und Theologie des II. ökumenischen Konzils* (Göttingen, 1965); G. I. Dossetti, *Il Simbolo di Nicea e di Costantinopoli* (Rome, 1967); see also the introduction to *Conciliorum Œcumenicorum Decreta*, ed. J. Alberigo *et al.*, 3rd ed. (Bologna, 1973).

20. *De comm. not.* (*PG* 45, 180C).

21. *Adv. Maced.* 6 (*PG* 45, 1308); see also his *Contra Eunom.* I (*PG* 45, 416C, 396D). The same image will be found in Gregory Nazianzen, *Orat. theol.* V (*PG* 36, 136).

22. *Adv. Maced.* 13 (*PG* 45, 1317).

23. *Adv. Maced.* 2 and 10 (*PG* 45, 1304, 1313B). These include the classical references to Jn 15:26 and Rom 8:9.

24. W. Jaeger, *op. cit.* (note 14), pp. 122–153.

25. *Contra Eunom.* I (*PG* 45, 464).

26. See his *Contra Eunom.* I (*PG* 45, 416).

27. *PG* 45, 133. In this context, it is worth noting that Basil had already spoken of the distinction between the Father and the Son in terms of *aition* and *to ek tou aitiou*: see his *Ep.* 52 (*PG* 32, 393C); *Contra Eunom.* II, 22 (*PG* 29, 621B).

28. H. Dörries, in W. Jaeger, *op. cit.* (note 14), p. 149, refers back to Gregory of Nyssa, *Opera*, ed. W. Jaeger, III/1, p. 56; VIII/2, p. 76.

29. Gregory Nazianzen's works will be found in *PG* 35–38. His *Theological Orations* (*Orat. theol.*) have appeared in a Fr. tr. by P. Gallay, published as *Discours théologiques* in the series *Les grands écrivains chrétiens* (Lyons, 1942) and then, in collaboration with M. Jourjon, in *SC* 250 (1978); *Orat.* 1–3 repub. in new Fr. tr. by J. Bernardi in *SC* 247 (1978). See also J. Plagnieux, *S. Grégoire de Nazianze, théologien* (Paris, 1952); J. Rousse, *Dictionnaire de Spiritualité*, VI (1967), cols 932–971; S. Harkianekis, 'Die Trinitätslehre Gregors von Nazianz', *Klēronomia* (Thessalonica) (January 1969), 83–102.

30. *Orat.* 31 (= *Orat. theol.* V), 29 (*PG* 36, 165B–168B); 41, 9 (*PG* 36, 441).

31. *Orat.* 31 (= *Orat. theol.* V), 10 (*PG* 36, 144A).

32. *Orat.* 42, 15 (*PG* 36, 476B). This is the farewell oration to the Council.

33. *Orat.* 40, 41 (*PG* 36, 417); cf. *Orat.* 31, 14 (*PG* 36, 148D–149A).

34. *Orat.* 42, 15 (*PG* 36, 476B).

35. *Orat.* 31 (= *Orat. theol.* V), 32 (*PG* 36, 169; *SC* 250, p. 398).

36. We should not try to find how the Spirit proceeds from the Father: *Orat.* 20 (*PG* 35, 1077). It is no more possible to explain what 'proceed' (*ekporeuetai*; Jn 15:26) means than it is possible to explain the *agennēsia* of the Father or the begetting of the Son: *Orat.* 31, 7ff. (*PG* 36, 140ff.). For the inexpressible nature of the begetting of the Son and the use of Is 53:8b in this sense, see G. M. de Durand, *RSPT*, 53 (1969), 638–657.

37. *Orat.* 30 (= *Orat. theol.* IV), 19 (*PG* 36, 127C); 31 (= *Orat. theol.* V), 7–8 (*PG* 36, 140ff.); 39, 12 (*PG* 36, 348); Sermon at Epiphany, 381 (*PG* 35, 347). It was Gregory Nazianzen who made the terms *ekporeuton, ekporeusis* acceptable.

38. *Orat.* 31 (= *Orat. theol.* V), 11 (*PG* 36, 144–145), 35 (*PG* 36, 348C); *Carmen dogm.* III (*PG* 37, 408). This comparison was also used by Gregory of Nyssa (*PG* 44, 1329C), Pseudo-Basil, *Adv. Eunom.* IV (*PG* 29, 681B), Didymus, *De Trin.* II, 5 (*PG* 39, 504C–505A), Pseudo-Cyril, *De sanct. Trin.* 8 (*PG* 77, 1136D), John Damascene, *De fide orthod.* I, 8 (*PG* 94, 816C–817A) and Photius, *Q. Amphil.* 28 (*PG* 101, 208C).

39. J. N. D. Kelly, *Early Christian Doctrines*, 5th ed. (London, 1977), pp. 265–266. For *tropos tēs huparxeōs*, see Gregory of Nyssa (*PG* 45, 404C); 'Father' is the name for a relation: see Gregory Nazianzen, *Orat.* 29 (= *Orat. theol.* II), 16 (*PG* 36, 96); 31 (= *Orat. theol.* V), 9 (*PG* 36, 292 and 293). 'Between the three, everything is identical, except the relationship of origin': *Orat.* 41 (*PG* 36, 441C).

40. S. Bulgakov, *Le Paraclet* (Paris, 1946), p. 37.

41. A. Malet, *Personne et amour dans la théologie trinitaire de S. Thomas d'Aquin* (Paris, 1956), p. 18, quotes Basil, *De spir. sanct.* 18, 46 (*PG* 32, 152B), Gregory Nazianzen, *Orat.* 31, 8 (*PG* 36, 141), Cyril of Alexandria, *Contra Iulian.* IV (*PG* 76, 725) and John Damascene, *De fide orthod.* I, 8 (*PG* 94, 820A and 824A). Together with B. Pruche, *Traité, op. cit.* (note 4), p. 195, it is also possible to add Athanasius, *Ad Ser.* I and IV (*PG* 26), Didymus, *De Trin.* 2, 1 (*PG* 39, 438C) and to compare them with Augustine, *De Trin.* XV, 27, 48, 50 and 45 (*PL* 42, 1080A, 1095B, 1097A and 1092B).

42. Didymus, *De Trin.* II, 2 (*PG* 39, 464C).

43. *DS* 150 or *Conciliorum Œcumenicorum Decreta, op. cit.* (note 19).

44. *DS* 260. See also P. Galtier, 'Le Saint-Esprit dans l'Incarnation du Verbe d'après S. Cyrille d'Alexandrie', *Problemi scelti di Teologia contemporanea* (Rome, 1954), pp. 383–392.

45. H. B. Swete, *On the History of the Doctrine of the Procession of the Holy Spirit* (Cambridge, 1876), pp. 148–152; M. Jugie, *De Processione Spiritus Sancti ex Fontibus Revelationis et secundum Orientales dissidentes* (Rome, 1936), pp. 138–143; J. Meyendorff, 'La Procession du Saint-Esprit chez les pères orientaux', *Russie et Chrétienté* (1950), 159–178,

especially 163–165; H. du Manoir, *Dogme et spiritualité chez S. Cyrille d'Alexandrie* (Paris, 1944), pp. 221–256.

46. Cyril of Alexandria, *Adv. Nest.* IV, 1 (*PG* 76, 173).

47. See Cyril's *Thes.* (*PG* 75, 585A): 'Jesus breathed on his disciples, saying: "Receive the Holy Spirit", so that we shall be formed again in the first image and shall appear conformed to the Creator through participating in the Spirit. Thus, as the Spirit who is sent to us makes us conformed to God and as he proceeds from the Father and the Son, it is clear that he is of the divine *ousia*, proceeding essentially (by essence) in it and from it.' See also *Thes.* (*PG* 75, 608A–B), in which Cyril says (after quoting 2 Cor 5:17), 'Since when Christ renews us and makes us enter a new life, it is the Spirit who is said to renew us, as the psalmist says: "Send forth thy Spirit and they will be created and thou wilt renew the face of the earth" (Ps 104:30), we are bound to confess that the Spirit is of the *ousia* of the Son. It is by having his being from him according to nature and by having been sent from him to the creature that he brings about the renewal, being the fullness of the holy Triad.'

48. *Comm. in Ioel.* XXXV (*PG* 71, 377D): 'idion autou te, kai en autō, kai ex autou to Pneuma esti kathaper amelei kai ep' autou noeitai tou Theou kai Patros'; *De recta fide ad Theod.* XXXVII (*PG* 76, 1189A); *De SS. Trin. Dial.* VII (*PG* 75, 1093A): 'to Pneuma labōn, alla to ex autou te kai en autō, kai idion autou'; *Comm. in Ioan.* II (*PG* 71, 212B): 'pros ton idion autou kai par autou kata phusin procheomenon Pneuma'. See also *PG* 74, 301, 444, 608; 75, 600, 608, 1120. The Spirit *proeisi* from the Son; see *PG* 75, 585A, 608B, 612B–C; 76, 1408B, 308D.

49. See the texts listed in note 48 above. Cyril also says *dia* or *ek*: see Swete, *op. cit.* (note 45), p. 150; Meyendorff, *op. cit.* (*ibid.*), p. 163, note 7.

50. *Adv. Nest.* IV, 1 (*PG* 76, 173A–B).

51. *De recta fide ad Reg. Or. alt.* LI (*PG* 76, 1408B); *De ador.* I (*PG* 68, 148A); see also *PG* 74, 585; 76, 1408.

52. *De ador.* I (*PG* 68, 148A); *Adv. Nest.* IV, 3 (*PG* 76, 184D); see also *PG* 74, 449, 709 (the commentary on St John).

53. See his *Comm. in Ioan.* XI, 11 (*PG* 74, 557). See also H. du Manoir, *op. cit.* (note 45), pp. 290ff., 315.

54. Reproduced by Cyril in his *Apol. contra Theod. pro XII cap.* (*PG* 76, 432C–D).

55. *Apol. contra Theod*, (*PG* 76, 433B–C).

56. J. Meyendorff, *op. cit.* (note 45), 165. Jugie, *op. cit.* (*ibid.*), p. 142, and du Manoir, *op. cit.* (*ibid.*), p. 224, give these references, apart from the preceding one: *Explic. XII cap.* (*PG* 76, 308D): 'idion echōn to ex autou'; *Apol. XII cap. contra Or.* (*PG* 77, 356–368).

57. G. M. de Durand, Introduction to Cyril, *Dialogues sur la Trinité*, I (*SC* 231) (1976), p. 66.

58. For a good bibliography, see J. Nasrallah, *Saint Jean de Damas, son époque, sa vie, son œuvre* (Harissa, Lebanon, 1950). Studies include J. Bilz, *Die Trinitätslehre des Johannes von Damaskus* (Paderborn, 1909) and especially J. Grégoire, 'La relation éternelle de l'Esprit au Fils d'aprés les écrits de Jean de Damas', *RHE*, 64 (1969), 713–755.

59. G. L. Prestige, *God in Patristic Thought*, 2nd ed. (London, 1952), pp. 263–264 and 280; see also B. Fraigneau–Julien, 'Un traité anonyme de la Sainte Trinité attribué à S. Cyrille d'Alexandrie', *RSR*, 49 (1961), 188–211, 386–405.

60. For the term *perichōrēsis*, see T. de Régnon, *Etudes sur la Sainte Trinité*, I (Paris, 1892), pp. 409–427; Chollet, *DTC*, II (1905), cols 2527–2532; A. Deneffe, 'Perichōrēsis, circuminsessio, circumincessio', *ZKT*, 47 (1923), 497–532; G. L. Prestige, '*Perichōreō* and *perichōrēsis* in the Fathers',*JTS*, 29 (1928), 242–252; *idem*, *op. cit.*, pp. 290–299; B. de la Margerie, *La Trinité chrétienne dans l'histoire* (Paris, 1975), pp. 244ff.

61. *De fide orthod.* I, 8 (*PG* 94, 829; de Régnon's translation, p. 417); see also I, 14 (*PG* 94, 860). The comparison with the three suns can also be found in Gregory Nazianzen and Pseudo-Cyril: see Fraigneau–Julien, *op. cit.* (note 59), p. 200.

62. See Jn 10:30 and 38; 14:11 and 20; 17:21; see also, less clearly expressed, 8:29. This mutual in-existence forms the basis of the unity of purpose between the Father and the Son

and between the Father and the Spirit (see Rom 8:27; 1 Cor 2:10–11). Jesus will send the Spirit, but he will send the Father's Promised one (Lk 24:49; Acts 2:33); the Father will send the Paraclete, but only at the request and in the name of the Son (Jn 14:16, 26).

63. There are only a few texts: Athenagoras, *Supplication* X, 5: 'Father and Son are one; the Son is in the Father and the Father is in the Son'; Hilary of Poitiers, *De Trin*. IX, 69; Gregory of Nyssa and Cyril of Alexandria, quoted by Prestige, *op. cit.* (note 59), pp. 287–288, 289–290; Augustine, *De Trin*. VI, 10, 12 (*PL* 42, 932): 'Each (of the divine Persons) is in each one and they are all in each one, and each one is in all, and all make only one'; Fulgentius of Ruspe, *De fide ad Petrum*, c. 1, n. 4 (*PL* 65, 674A–B; c. 508), who is quoted in the Decree *Pro Iacobitis* of 1442 (*DS* 1331). The German mystic Gertrude (†1302) also expressed her experience of the Trinity in these terms: 'The three Persons together radiated an excellent light, each appearing to send its flame through the other, and yet they were all with each other': see W. Oehl, *Deutsche Mystiker*, II, p. 90.

64. See Gregory Nazianzen, *Ep.* 101 (*PG* 37, 141C).

65. Maximus, *PG* 91, 88A and 85C–D.

66. T. de Régnon, pursuing his excessively simple idea of the difference between the Greeks and the Latins, was convinced that this was a Latin and not a Greek concept. But the very texts that he quotes—Cyril of Alexandria, Pseudo-Cyril and John Damascene—all speak of a unity and identity of substance or essence!

67. In *Le Paraclet, op. cit.* (note 40), p. 134, Bulgakov says: 'They should be conceived not on the basis of themselves alone, but on the basis of their Trinitarian unity; they are defined and radiated not only thanks to their own light, but also thanks to the light that they reflect and that comes from the other hypostases'.

68. S. Bulgakov devotes pp. 50–58 of *Le Paraclet* to John Damascene. This section of his book is precise and well-documented, but critical.

69. The term *proboleus* is not biblical and was relatively new when John Damascene used it. It can be found in Pseudo-Cyril, c. 7 (*PG* 77, 1132C) whom John copied, and it originated with Gregory Nazianzen, *Orat*. 23, 7; 29, 2 (*PG* 35, 1169A and 36, 76B).

70. *De fide orthod*. I, 8 (*PG* 94, 811A and 828D); I, 10 (*PG* 94, 837C); here, in an attempt to define more precisely what expresses what is different rather than the common nature, John says that the fact of being without a cause or unbegotten, of being begotten or of proceeding 'expresses the mutual relationship between the persons and their mode of subsistence'.

71. *De fide orthod*. I, 8 (*PG* 94, 824A; cf. 820A).

72. See Augustine, *Contra Maxim*. II, 14, 1; Anselm of Havelberg, *Dial*. II, 5. See also P. Vignaux, *Luther commentateur des Sentences* (*liv.* I, *dist*, XVII) (Paris, 1935), pp. 95ff.: he quotes first the hymn of Adam of Saint-Victor, *Sequentia XI de S. Trinitate* (*PL* 196, 1459): 'Quid sit gigni, quid processus, me nescire sum professus'—'What is "being begotten"? What is "processing"? I profess that I do not know'; see above, p. 8. Robert Holcot, Gregory of Rimini and Gabriel Biel all held the same position.

73. *De fide orthod*. I, 8 (*PG* 94, 832–833, with the long note, no. 28, by J. Aubert); *De hymno Tris*. (*PG* 95, 60); *In sab. sanct*. (*PG* 96, 605); see also J. Meyendorff, *op. cit.* (note 45), 171.

74. *De fide orthod*. I, 12 (*PG*, 94, 849B).

75. *De fide orthod*. I, 13 (*PG* 94, 856B). The *dia* was also taken up by Tarasius at the Seventh Oecumenical Council (Nicaea II): *PG* 98, 1461. A list of the *dia tou Huiou* will be found in J. Grégoire, *op. cit.* (note 58), 753–754, note 1.

76. Quotations from Rom 8:9 and Jn 20:29 in *De fide orthod*. I, 5, 8 (*PG* 94, 833A); see also his *In sab. sanct*. 4 (*PG* 96, 605B). John also uses the classical formula of Athanasius and says that the Spirit is the image (*eikōn*) of the Son as the Son is the image of the Father: *De fide orthod*. I, 13 (*PG* 94, 855B).

77. *De fide orthod*. I, 12, end (*PG* 94, 849). This chapter 12 of the treatise on orthodox faith, Migne observes (*PG* 94, 845–846), is missing from several early manuscripts, but it is in

accordance with the teaching of undisputed texts and those who oppose the *Filioque* do not hesitate to quote it as authoritative.

78. F. Hauck and S. Schulz, '*Poreuomai, eisporeuomai, ekporeuomai*', *TDNT*, VI, pp. 566–579, although the authors devote hardly two lines to our verse. See also F. Porsch, *Pneuma und Wort. Ein exegetischer Beitrag zur Pneumatologie des Johannesevangeliums* (Frankfurt, 1974), pp. 273–274.

79. V. Rodziensko insists on this aspect to such an extent that he lets it bear an almost excessive theological weight of freedom of action; he says, for example, that the Pneuma 'makes himself to go out from the only Father': ' "Filioque" in Patristic Thought', *Studia Patristica*, II (Berlin, 1957), pp. 295–308.

80. A. Wenger, 'Bulletin de spiritualité et de théologie byzantine', *Rev. Et. Byz.*, 10 (1953), 162; see also F. Porsch, *op. cit.* (note 78). Wenger finds it possible to say: '*para* usually denotes a relationship between two persons already existing', but is this strictly true?

81. J. Giblet, 'La Sainte Trinité selon l'Evangile de S. Jean', *Lumière et Vie*, 29 (1956), 95–126; 671–702, especially 673.

82. This comment is by M. Jugie, *op. cit.* (note 45), p. 139. Cyril of Alexandria used *procheitai* and *ekporeuesthai* as equivalents; see his *Ep.* 55 (*PG* 77, 316D–317A). He used *ekporeuetai* only once for the procession of the Son *a Patre: Comm. in Ioan.* V, 26 (*PG* 74, 420A).

83. The difference that they stressed from the term 'begetting' was, they felt, sufficient to distinguish the second from the third Persons; this difference to a great extent came from the response that they had to make to the objection that, if there was a second procession, there would be two Sons and the Word would have a brother. See Athanasius, *Ad Ser*. I, 15 (*SC* 15, pp. 109ff.).

84. See the bibliography in Emmanuel-Pataq Siman, *L'expérience de l'Esprit d'après la tradition syrienne d'Antioche* (*Théologie historique*, 15) (Paris, 1971). See also P. Rancillac, *L'Eglise, manifestation de l'Esprit chez S. Jean Chrysostome* (Dar-el-Kalima, Lebanon, 1970); F. Heiler, *Die katholische Kirche des Ostens und Westens*, I: *Urkirche und Ostkirche* (Munich, 1937).

85. E. P. Siman, *op. cit.*, pp. 227–229, has made a synopsis of these texts.

86. See I. de la Potterie, 'L'onction du chrétien par la foi', *Bib*, 40 (1959), 12–69, reproduced in *La vie selon l'Esprit, condition du chrétien* (Paris, 1965), pp. 107–167; E. P. Siman, *op. cit.*, pp. 74ff., 131ff.

87. Ephraem's 'Hymn of faith'; quoted by E. P. Siman, *op. cit.*, pp. 105, 223.

88. Isaac of Antioch, quoted by E. P. Siman, *op. cit.*, pp. 107, 224.

89. I will confine myself to only two texts out of the great number. They are quoted by E. P. Siman, *op. cit.*, pp. 56 and 57: 'We worship you, Lord God, Holy Spirit Paraclete, you who console us and pray in us. . . . It is you who have sealed the covenant with the Church, the spouse of the Word, the Son of God, and who have placed in her the treasures of your graces and your virtues. It is you who have taught the world the mystery of the adorable and very holy Trinity and who have led us to worship it in Spirit and truth' (*sedrē* of Terce; First Sunday after Pentecost); 'It was on Sunday that your spouse, the holy Church, triumphed and became majestic, since the covenant of her nuptials was concluded by the coming of the Holy Spirit Paraclete over her and by her spread in every region and every country, thanks to the twelve Stewards (of the Spirit)' (Sixth Sunday after Pentecost).

90. Quoted by E. P. Siman, *op. cit.* (note 84), p. 204.

91. Ephraem's 'Hymn on faith', quoted by E. P. Siman, *op. cit.*, p. 188.

92. Quoted by E. P. Siman, *op. cit.*, p. 275.

93. See E. P. Siman, *op. cit.*, p. 276.

3

THE FILIOQUE
AS PROFESSED BY THE LATIN FATHERS
AND THE COUNCILS BEFORE IT BECAME
A SUBJECT OF DISUNITY

In this question, it is important to do what Pope Leo III took care to do when he received Charlemagne's envoys, that is, to make a distinction between two things—the teaching itself and its inclusion as a formula in the creed.

THE TEACHING

All the New Testament texts that speak of a relationship between the Spirit and the Son are concerned with the economy. This includes even Jn 15:26: 'But when the Paraclete comes, whom I shall send you from the Father, even the Spirit of truth, who proceeds from the Father, he will bear witness to me', which is, of course, the reference *par excellence* in favour of the procession from the Father alone. Apart from the fact that the word 'alone' is not found in this text and that the creed refers to it only by making two small changes,[1] what is involved here in an immediate and explicit way is the temporal mission of the Paraclete.

The passages in the New Testament which speak of the relationship between the Spirit and the Son are concerned with the *incarnate* Word and the economy of grace. What is more, they also speak of a very close relationship that is concerned with the essential element. If we are indeed sons and are able to call God 'Father', that is because we have received the 'Spirit of *his Son*'.[2] Christ's sonship is eternal and the Spirit must be eternally from the *Son*. The texts to which the Latin Fathers appealed again and again are Jn 16:14–15 and 20:22,[3] which are directly concerned with the economy of grace. At the same time, as Swete has observed, it is not unreasonable to make an extrapolation. Since the Spirit belongs eternally to the divine essence, it is normal for the only Son, who has, as the Word, been with God from the beginning, to be in a relationship that is outside time with the Spirit of God.[4] It is not possible to say any more from the exegetical point of view. We have already seen that the Greek Fathers, and especially the

49

Alexandrians, believed that there was a connection and even a dependence that was eternal, but that they did not define this very precisely.

We should note one other text, namely Rev 22:1: 'Then he (the angel) showed me the river of the water of life, bright as crystal, flowing from the throne of God and of the Lamb (*ekporeuomenon ek tou thronou tou Theou kai tou Arniou*)'. This living water is the Spirit (Jn 4:10ff.; 7:37–39; Rev 21:6), proceeding from the throne of God and from the Lamb. The Lamb points to the Son in his commitment to our salvation. We are clearly still concerned with the economy here, although now at the stage of its eternal fulfilment. Scripture, as strictly limited to New Testament texts, does not therefore do away with our problem. As we shall see, it is extremely important to note that the West professed the *Filioque*, through its Fathers and its councils, at a time when it was in communion with the East and the East was in communion with the West.

The Latin Fathers[5]

Of the cloud of witnesses to this conviction, I will deal mainly with those mentioned by the Fifth Ecumenical Council, the Second Council of Constantinople (553), and called by that Council, together with the Greek Fathers, holy Fathers and doctors of the Church, whose teaching as a whole should be followed: Hilary. Ambrose, Augustine and Leo.[6]

Hilary of Poitiers (†366) said that the Spirit was *Patre et Filio auctoribus confitendus* (*De Trin*. II, 29; *PL* 10, 69), which clearly points, not to a procession, but to the witness borne by the Father and the Son. Hilary did, however, think that the *de meo accipiet* of Jn 16:14 might have a meaning equivalent to 'receiving—and therefore proceeding—from the Father' (see below, note 3), although his most certain position on the Spirit was *a Patre per Filium*.

In 381, the year of the First Council of Constantinople, Ambrose materially formulated the statement: 'Spiritus quoque Sanctus, cum procedit a Patre et Filio',[7] but, as the Benedictine editor acknowledged, before Swete and Jugie, this referred to the temporal mission of the Spirit. Ambrose seems to include the communication of the divine life itself, however, in the *de meo accipiet*.[8]

Ambrose was not a speculative thinker. In the case of Augustine, however, we are no longer left in any doubt. He not only unequivocally affirms the *Filioque* on several occasions, but also justifies, on the basis of the New Testament evidence, that the Spirit is both Spirit of the Father and Spirit of the Son and, from 393 onwards, provides a theological foundation for this in the idea of 'communio quaedam consubstantialis Patris et Filii, dilectionem in se invicem amborum caritatemque'.[9] The treatises on this subject that followed are works both of laborious scholarly research and of rich and fervent contemplation. The main works are the *De Trinitate*, Books IV and

V, the *Tractatus XCIX in Ioannem*, reproduced at the end of *De Trinitate* XV, 27, and, in 427–428, the *Contra Maximinum*, Maximinus being the bishop of an Arian community. Augustine's teaching, written in a full and eloquent Latin, had a decisive influence on thinking in the Western Church, whether it was read in his own texts or in the versions of Fulgentius of Ruspe (†533), who wrote in a more pedagogic and almost scholarly style (*PL* 65).

The evidence provided by Leo the Great is clear, but brief, and contains no further theoretical development.[10] This is not much, but numerous holy and learned bishops of the Church should be added: Eucherius of Lyons (†454), Faustus of Riez (†485), Avitus of Vienne (†523) and Fulgentius of Ruspe, whom I have mentioned above; likewise several priests, such as Gennadius of Marseilles (†495) and Julian Pomerius of Arles (†498), the Roman deacon Paschasius (†512), and highly educated laymen, such as Boethius (†c. 525) and Cassiodorus (†c. 570). At a slightly later period, the question was discussed by various doctors of the Church such as Gregory the Great, who was revered by the Greeks (†604), and Isidore of Seville (†636). Texts by all these authors and many others can be read in the works listed in note 5 below.

Texts by the Greek authors who assumed or stated that the Spirit was dependent in his eternal subsistence on the Son can also be found in the same works as well as in other books. The most important of these Greek Fathers were, of course, Epiphanius and Cyril of Alexandria. I have already discussed their contribution to this debate as well as that provided by those Fathers, notably Gregory of Nyssa, Maximus and John Damascene, who spoke of a procession from the Father through the Son.

The Councils and the Creeds[11]

A place of honour must be given here to the Councils of Toledo. Their insistence on the need to profess a Trinitarian faith and especially on the importance of the procession of the Holy Spirit *a Patre et a Filio* can be explained by the situation that had been brought about, first by the heresy of Priscillianism at the end of the fourth century, and then by the arrival of Arian invaders at the beginning of the fifth century. The Priscillianists combined the figures of the Trinity in a single Person, and the Arians regarded the Spirit as a creature of the Son, who, they believed, was himself created. The First Council of Toledo (440 and 447) is itself disputed and has therefore to be left out of account.[12] We begin on firm ground with the Third Council of Toledo in 589, at which King Recared renounced Arianism, in the name of his people, and professed the Catholic faith. Although it is doubtful whether the Niceno-Constantinopolitan creed with the addition of *et Filio* was recited there, it is certain that Recared professed 'Spiritus aeque Sanctus confitendus a nobis et praedicandus est a Patre et a Filio procedere et cum Patre et Filio unius esse substantiae',[13] in other words, 'We must equally confess and preach that the Spirit proceeds from the Father and the Son and that he is of one and the same substance with them'. The Council therefore was opposed to any form of Priscillianism or Arianism and declared that the Son was in no way inferior to the Father. The intention was to affirm the consubstantiality of the Spirit with the Father and the Son.

It is also possible in this context to quote the Fourth Council of Toledo (633), for which Isidore of Seville, who presided over it, composed the beautiful prayer *Adsumus*, with which all the assemblies of the Second Vatican Council began.[14] The Sixth Council (638) also produced an excellent and well-developed text.[15] Developed texts were also formulated at the Eighth Council (653) and the Eleventh (675). Fulgentius of Ruspe played a part in the formulation of these latter texts, and Vladimir Lossky declared that he was able to accept them.[16] At the Sixteenth Council of Toledo in 693, the Spirit was professed to be 'ex Patre Filioque absque aliquo initio procedentem' and was especially called a 'Gift'.[17]

Similar professions of faith were also made during the same period of a hundred years in other parts of the Christian world. An excellent documentation was provided by J. A. de Aldama (*op. cit.* (note 12 below), pp. 124–131) and more recently by J. Vivès (*ibid.*). The creed *Quicumque vult*, which was at one time attributed to Athanasius, was in fact composed between 440 and 500 in Augustinian circles in the south of Gaul.[18] In England, the Synod of Hatfield confessed in 680 'Spiritum Sanctum procedentem ex Patre et Filio inenarrabiliter'.[19] At the same time, however, nothing was added, in Rome, to the Niceno-Constantinopolitan text, even though the Popes were personally in favour of the *Filioque*.

It should not be forgotten that the East was in communion with the West at the time when the latter professed that the Spirit proceeded from the Father and the Son, although it is true that some people in Byzantium were unhappy about this. There is evidence of this in a letter written by Maximus the Confessor to the Cypriot priest Marinus in 655. Pope Martin I had apparently said in his synodic letter that the Spirit also proceeded from the Son, and this scandalized those who had been condemned in Rome for their Monothelitism, so that they were not slow to take revenge. This was Maximus' response:

> Those of the Queen of cities (Constantinople) have attacked the synodic letter of the present very holy Pope, not in the case of all the chapters that he has written in it, but only in the case of two of them. One relates to the theology (of the Trinity) and, according to them, says: 'The Holy Spirit also has his *ekporeusis (ekporeuesthai)* from the Son'. The other deals with the divine incarnation.
>
> With regard to the first matter, they (the Romans) have produced the unanimous evidence of the Latin Fathers, and also of Cyril of Alexandria, from the study he made of the gospel of St John. On the basis of these texts, they have shown that they have not made the Son the cause (*aitian*) of the Spirit—they know in fact that the Father is the only cause of the Son and the Spirit, the one by begetting and the

other by *ekporeusis* (procession)—but that they have manifested the procession through him (*to dia autou proïenai*) and have thus shown the unity and identity of the essence. . . .

They (the Romans) have therefore been accused of precisely those things of which it would be wrong to accuse them, whereas the former (the Byzantines) have been accused of those things of which it has been quite correct to accuse them (Monothelitism). They have up till now produced no defence, although they have not yet rejected the things that they have themselves so wrongly introduced.

In accordance with your request, I have asked the Romans to translate what is peculiar to them (the 'also from the Son') in such a way that any obscurities that may result from it will be avoided. But since the practice of writing and sending (the synodic letter) has been observed, I wonder whether they will possibly agree to do this. It is true, of course, that they cannot reproduce their idea in a language and in words that are foreign to them as they can in their mother-tongue, just as we too cannot. In any case, having been accused, they will certainly take some care about this.[20]

Maximus the Confessor's explanation throws a good deal of light on the situation. He himself believed that the Spirit proceeded from the Father *dia mesou tou Logou*, 'by means of the Logos'.[21] The Spirit proceeded, in his view, ineffably from the Father and consubstantially through the Son.[22] It will be necessary to return to this question later, or rather to recognize, with all due explanation, that there was never any intention to say anything else.

THE ADDITION OF THE *FILIOQUE* TO THE CREED

The history of this addition is so well known that all that I need to do here is summarize the principal points.[23] The teaching was widely accepted, but it would seem that the text of the creed was not changed in any way, even at the Third Council of Toledo in 589. The addition did not, in any case, come from Spain, but from England, through the offices of Alcuin, who went from York in 782 to the court of Charlemagne.[24] There can be little doubt, however, that he himself received it from Spain. At that time, the creed was recited during Mass in Gaul and in Spain. The *Filioque* was probably added during the last decade of the sixth century in those places and it was accepted in good faith that it came from Nicaea-Constantinople—so much so that even before the time of the fiery Humbert of Silva Candida in 1054, the *Libri Carolini* of 790 or thereabouts were able to accuse the Greeks of having suppressed it there![25]

The Second Council of Nicaea (787), which canonized the cult of images, also received the confession of faith of the Patriarch Tarasius, who professed that he believed 'in the Holy Spirit, Lord and giver of life, proceeding from the Father through the Son'.[26] Charlemagne protested through a capitulary which he sent to Pope Hadrian I, who replied by guaranteeing that Tarasius' formula was in conformity with the teaching of the holy Fathers.

Charlemagne, however, persisted, maintaining that *per* did not have the same meaning as *ex*.[27] In 794, he convoked a council at Frankfurt, which was to condemn the teachings of the Council of Nicaea of 787 with its cult of images and to proclaim the *Filioque*. Frankfurt—the ford of the Franks—became a line of demarcation and division. The addition to the creed was justified at a synod held in Friuli (Venezia Giulia) in 796 by the argument that it was necessary to affirm full consubstantiality in opposition to heretics. Pope Leo III, who succeeded Hadrian I, however, defended the Council of Nicaea and denounced the Council of Frankfurt.

Frankish monks of the Mount of Olives at Jerusalem had introduced the singing of the creed into the Mass, with the addition of the *Filioque*, in the form in which they had heard it in the palace at Aix-la-Chapelle. They were, as a result of this, accused of heresy by a Greek monk of Mar Sabas at Christmas 808. They consequently appealed to the Pope, who in turn wrote to the emperor. The latter called on the theologians to justify the Western teaching and practice in opposition to the Greeks and, at a council convoked at Aix-la-Chapelle in November 809, decreed that the *Filioque* was a doctrine of the Catholic Church and had to be retained in the creed that was sung at Mass. He also sent two trusted prelates to Pope Leo III to win his support for these decisions. We have the account of this audience.[28] The Pope agreed about the doctrine, but refused to change or add anything to the creed. In confirmation of his position, the text of the creed, engraved in Greek and Latin without the addition, was hung up in St Peter's [see next chapter].

Rome, a city in which traditions are carefully preserved, remained faithful to this practice for a long time. That is why Photius did not criticize Rome for making the addition and appealed to the example of Nicholas I and John VIII, the Popes who were his contemporaries. The controversy about the addition of the *Filioque* clause was unleashed when Cardinal Humbert accused the Greeks in 1054 of having suppressed the clause.[29]

The creed was not in fact introduced into the Mass in Rome until 1014, during the pontificate of Benedict VIII, and it certainly included the Latin interpolation then. Henry II was to be crowned emperor and he was astonished that the creed was not chanted at Mass. The explanation he was given was that the Roman Church had no need to express its faith because it had never fallen into heresy! Henry insisted on the creed, however, and had his way.[30] A new tradition was created.

The question of the insertion of the *Filioque* into the creed was raised with some determination by the Greeks at the Council of Ferrara-Florence in 1438–1439. If communion was to be re-established betweeen East and West, they insisted, the clause had to be suppressed. The question is still with us, and its importance should not be underestimated. I shall deal with it when I come to discuss the attempts made to reach an understanding from Florence to the present.

NOTES

1 The text of Jn 15:26 has 'ho para tou Patros ekporeuetai', with the verb in the present, whereas the creed has 'to ek tou Patros ekporeuomenon', thus replacing *para* with *ek* and placing the verb in the form of a participle, which makes it express the eternal procession. See H. B. Swete, *The Holy Spirit in the New Testament* (London, 1909), p. 304, note 2. I do not in any sense criticize this approach. A.-M. Dubarle has shown that the Greek Fathers established the eternal relationship of the incarnate Word with the Father (God) from his part in the economy and has concluded from this that a similar approach is legitimate in the case of the Spirit: 'Les fondements bibliques du "Filioque" ', *Russie et Chrétienté* (1950), pp. 229–244. In the same volume, pp. 125–150, Mgr Cassien discusses the biblical teaching regarding the procession: 'L'enseignement dans la Bible sur la procession du Saint-Esprit'.

2. Gal 4:6; 'Ex hoc ergo Spiritus Sanctus nos facit filios Dei in quantum est Spiritus Filii Dei': Thomas Aquinas, *Contra Gent*. IV, 24.

3. Hilary of Poitiers thought that *de meo accipiet* (Jn 16:14) might possibly have the same meaning as *a Patre procedere*: *De Trin*. VIII, 20 (*PL* 10, 250–251). As we shall see, Augustine and later Anselm believed that the breathing on the disciples in Jn 20:22 implied the procession of the Spirit *a Filio*.

4. H. B. Swete, *op. cit.*, pp. 304–305.

5. H. B. Swete, *On the History of the Doctrine of the Procession of the Holy Spirit* (Cambridge, 1876); A. Palmieri, 'Filioque', *DTC*, V (1913), cols 2309–2343; see also cols 762–829; M. Jugie, *De Processione Spiritus Sancti* (Rome, 1936), pp. 196–232; P. T. Camelot, 'La tradition latine sur la procession du Saint-Esprit "a Filio" ou "ab utroque" ', *Russie et Chrétienté* (1950), pp. 179–192.

6. Mansi, 9, 201–202.

7. Ambrose, *De Spir. Sanct*. I, 11 (*PL* 16, 762).

8. See the passages in *De Spir. Sanct*. II, 5 and 11; III. 1 (*PL* 16, 783, 800, 810), and in *Comm. in Luc*. VIII (*PL* 15, 1876); these are quoted by Swete, *op. cit.* (note 5), p. 121.

9. Augustine, *De fid. et symb*. IX, 19 (*PL* 40, 191), in which he alludes to certain predecessors, especially Marius Victorinus in his hymn to the Trinity (*PL* 8, 1146; *SC* 68, p. 620): see Volume I of this work, p. 77.

10. In his sermon at Pentecost 442, Leo says: 'Spiritus Sanctus Patris Filiique . . . Spiritus . . . cum utroque vivens et potens, et sempiterne ex eo quod est Pater Filiusque subsistens' (*PL* 54, 402; *SC* 74 (1961), p. 150; sermo 63). The letter to the Bishop of Astorga, Turibius, which says 'ab utroque processit' (*PL* 54, 680; *DS* 284) is, at least according to K. Künstle, *Antipriscilliana* (Freiburg, 1905), pp. 118 and 126, a forgery made after the Council of Braga in 563. According to J. A. de Aldama, *op. cit.* (below, note 12), p. 54, note 34, it is authentic. De Aldama quotes several authors who are in favour of it.

11. H. B. Swete, *op. cit.* (note 5), pp. 160–176; Jugie, *op. cit.* (note 5), pp. 115–120; F. Cavallera, *Thesaurus Doctrinae catholicae ex documentis Magisterii ecclesiastici* (Paris, 1920), pp. 284ff.

12. F. Cavallera, No. 533 and 560, according to the *Libellus Pastoris* (Mansi, 3, 1003–1004); K. Künstle, *op. cit.*, pp. 43ff.: 'Paraclitus a Patre Filioque procedens'. J. A. de Aldama, *El simbolo Toledano I. Su texto, su origen, su posición en la historia de los símbolos* (*Anal. Greg.*, VII) (Rome, 1934), concluded that there were two editions. The first was a shorter version, made by the Council of 400; the second and longer edition was the work of Bishop Pastor, in 447, and contained two references to the term *Filioque*. See J. Vivès, ed., in collab. with T. Marín and G. Martínez. *Concilios Visigóticos e Hispano-Romanos* (Barcelona and Madrid, 1963); for this first creed, see p. 26.

13. *DS* 470; this reference is not found in Denz.; see also Vivès, *op. cit.*, p. 109.

14. Mansi, 10, 615–616; *DS* 458; Vivès, p. 187. For the *Filioque* in Isidore of Seville, see H. B. Swete, *op. cit.* (note 5), pp. 172–173.

15. Mansi, 10, 661ff.; *DS* 490; Vivès, p. 234.

16. Mansi, 11, 131ff.; *DS* 525–541 (for the Spirit, see 527); Vivès, *op. cit* (note 12), p. 348; see also J. Madoz, *Le symbole du XIe Concile de Tolède* (Louvain, 1938).
17. Mansi, 12, 67; *DS* 568–570; Vivès, p. 489; see also J. Madoz, *El símbolo del concilio XVI de Toledo (Estudios Onienses*, I, vol. 3) (Madrid, 1946).
18. *DS* 75–76, with the introduction; J. N. D. Kelly, *The Athanasian Creed 'Quicumque vult'* (London, 1964).
19. Mansi, 11, 177B.
20. Maximus, letter to Marinus, *PG* 91, 136; Mansi, 10, 695ff.; Swete, *op. cit.* (note 5), pp. 183–186; Jugie, *op. cit.* (note 5), pp. 182–186; Fr. tr., apart from one or two words, by J. M. Garrigues, *Istina* (1972), 363–364. There is evidence of the fact that the procession of the Holy Spirit continued to be a controversial point between the Greeks and the Latins in what we know of the Synod held at Gentilly in 767: see Swete, *op. cit.*, pp. 198ff.
21. Maximus, *Quaestiones et dubia, Interr.* XXXIV (*PG* 90, 813B).
22. *Quaestiones ad Thalassium*, LXIII (*PG* 90, 672C).
23. Swete, *op. cit.*, (note 5), pp. 196–226 with the texts in an appendix, pp. 227–237; Jugie, *op. cit.* (note 5), pp. 234–258; *idem*, 'Origine de la controverse sur l'addition du Filioque au Symbole. Photius en a-t-il parlé?' *RSPT*, 28 (1939), 369–385; see also below, note 29; E. Amann, *L'époque carolingienne (Histoire de l'Eglise, VI)* (Paris, 1947); B. Capelle, 'Le pape Léon III et le Filioque', *L'Eglise et les Eglises, Mélanges Dom Lambert Beauduin* (Chevetogne, 1954), I, pp. 309–322; R. G. Heath, 'The Schism of the Franks and the Filioque', *Journal of Ecclesiastical History*, 23 (1972), 97–113; R. Haugh, *Photius and the Carolingians. The Trinitarian Controversy* (Belmont, Mass., 1975).
24. B. Capelle, 'Alcuin et l'histoire du Symbole de la Messe', *Travaux liturgiques de Doctrine et d'Histoire* (Louvain, 1962), II, pp. 211–221.
25. See Jugie, *op. cit.* (note 5), p. 238, note 2. H. Sieben, *Die Konzilsidee der Alten Kirche* (Paderborn, 1979), pp. 306–343, has examined the basis on which the Second Council of Nicaea in 787 was received in the East and in Rome and has suggested the reasons why the Frankish Church rejected it (the *Libri Carolini* and the Council of Frankfurt in 794).
26. Mansi, 12, 1122; reception by the Council, col. 1154.
27. *Libri Carolini* III, 3 (*PL* 98, 1117).
28. See *PL* 102, 971ff.; *MGH, Concilia* II/1, pp. 239ff. Swete has reproduced this text, *op. cit.* (note 5), pp. 233ff. See also B. Capelle, *op. cit* (note 23).
29. See M. Jugie, *op. cit.* (note 23). V. Grumel has critically examined point by point Jugie's argument eliminating Photius from the controversy about the addition: 'Photius et l'addition du Filioque au symbole de Nicée-Constantinople', *Rev. Et. Byz.*, 5 (1947), 218–234.
30. This is according to an eye-witness, Berno: *De officio missae*, 2 (*PL* 142, 1061–1062).

4

THE PATRIARCH PHOTIUS
THE ERA OF CONFRONTATION
AND POLEMICS

The age of confrontation between East and West began before Photius. The letter written to the Second Council of Nicaea in 787 (which approved the cult of images) by the Patriarch Tarasius, who professed the procession of the Spirit *ek tou Patros di' Huiou*,[1] had caused great scandal at the court of Charlemagne. The emperor had sent a capitulary to Pope Hadrian I, as we have already seen, protesting against this teaching. He had also criticized it in the *Libri Carolini* and had finally had it condemned by the Council of Frankfurt in 794.[2] The *Filioque* was by this time included in the creed and chanted in the churches of the Empire. A few years later, at the end of 808, this practice gave rise to a serious incident, when a Greek monk in the monastery of Mar Sabas noticed that the liturgical books used in a Frankish monastery on the Mount of Olives included the *Filioque*. The monk, John, proclaimed the heresy of the books and conducted a campaign against the Frankish monks, who, as we have seen, appealed to the Pope, who, in his turn, wrote to the emperor.[3] Charlemagne convoked a synod at Aix-la-Chapelle in 809, with the aim of approving and justifying, through his own bishops, the practice already accepted in his own chapel and in his empire. He sent a delegation to the Pope to win him over not only to the doctrine—of which the Pope was already convinced—but also to the inclusion of the *Filioque* in the text of the creed. Leo III, however, refused to comply with the second request and insisted on retaining the pure text. In order to make his own position public, he had the text without the *Filioque* engraved in Greek and Latin on two silver scrolls and these were hung on each side of the entrance to the high altar or Confessio in St Peter's.[4] This took place in 810.

Ten years after Leo III had defined his position as being in favour of the teaching, but against the addition of the *Filioque* to the text of the creed, Photius was born.[5] This extremely gifted man led a life full of tensions and dramatic episodes. He was enthroned as Patriarch of Constantinople on 25 December 858, throught the favour of Bardas, the uncle of the Emperor Michael III. He was, however, twice deposed and relegated to a monastery, in 868–878 and in 886–897. (He died on 6 February 897). He was

57

excommunicated and deposed by Pope Nicholas I in 863 and he himself excommunicated the Pope in 867. He was condemned by a council which was regarded in Bellarmine's accredited list of councils as the Eighth Ecumenical Council (869–870), but this same council was condemned to oblivion by Pope John VIII.[6] Another council, over which the legates of the same Pope John VIII presided and which our Orthodox friends would like the Western Church to call the Eighth Ecumenical Council, solemnly annulled the measures taken against Photius. It is probable and even almost certain that the creed was proclaimed at that council without the *Filioque*,[7] which was at that time the practice in Rome. Photius himself died in communion with the Roman See. He was canonized by the Orthodox Church at a time when that Church was also in communion with Rome and the West.[8]

Nevertheless, from 867 onwards Photius condemned the *Filioque* in a series of texts and formulated the doctrine of the procession of the Holy Spirit from the Father alone: *ek monou tou Patros*.[9] He did not understand the homogeneity of the Latin idea of the mystery of the Trinity, according to which the distinction between the Persons in their perfect consubstantiality is derived from their relationship and the opposition of their relationship— the Father and the Son are relative to one another—and that relationship is one of origin and procession. Photius, however, believed that the Persons were distinguished by personal properties that could not be communicated. Their properties were, in his opinion, sufficient to characterize them. The Father was *anarchos*, without principle or beginning. The Son was begotten, and this referred him to the Father as such. The Spirit proceeds from the Father as *aitia*, the cause and the only cause both of the Spirit and of the Son.[10]

Photius regarded the monarchy of the Father as the principle both of the Spirit and of the monogenous one, and as the principle of their consubstantiality.[11] Whereas the Greek Fathers saw this monarchy as moving dynamically in a straight line, from the Father through the Son in the Spirit, however, Photius adopted a scheme consisting of two branches: Father $\Big\langle{\text{Son} \atop \text{Spirit}}$.[12] He also either passed over in silence or eliminated numerous patristic texts which were open to the idea that the Son played a part in the eternal coming of the Spirit to consubstantial being.[13] In his view, there were only two possibilities—an activity that is common to the three Persons and goes back to their nature, or one that is strictly personal.[14] To admit, as the Latins did, that the procession of the Spirit came both from the Father and from the Son, as from a single principle, was to withdraw that procession from the hypostases and to attribute it to their common nature. In those conditions, it would be wrong to dissociate the Spirit from that common nature, because he also possesses the same nature as the Father and the Son—thus he would proceed from himself, which would be clearly absurd.[15]

The Latin construction is only tenable if the Persons are distinguished by an opposition in relationship, but the spiration does not allow for such an opposition in relationship between the Father and the Son. It can therefore be common to them. We do not, for that reason, do an injustice to the hypostatic order and favour the divine nature, because that nature is hypostatic in its existence and the hypostases are constituted by their *subsistent* relationships—the Father *is* fatherhood and the Son *is* sonship or begottenness. What is more, in that unity of the principle of active spiration, the Father is the first principle (*principaliter*). It is necessary to admit that this is not sufficiently apparent—the word 'procession' is not clear. The Father and the Son seem to be at the same level, whereas they are in fact not, since 'the Father is greater than I'. The Father is the absolute and primordial origin.[16]

It cannot be denied that the teaching of the Fathers and of John Damascene was narrowed down and hardened in the theology of Photius. Although, as Sergey Bulgakov has pointed out, 'there is no unanimous and homogeneous patristic doctrine of the procession of the Holy Spirit',[17] and there are openings in the direction of a procession *per Filium* and even *Filioque*, Photius enshrined pneumatology in a form of expression which put out of the question an agreement with the West or even with those Latin Fathers whom the Orthodox Christians accept as their own. As a result of this, confrontation and polemics have all too often prevailed over an attempt to reach agreement. But—as I shall be happy to show—the victory of confrontation has not been total, nor is it definitive. We must, however, take Photius' arguments seriously—the more so because the Greek Church has taken over his theology—without at the same time losing sight of those Fathers whose work Photius himself tended to leave aside.

NOTES

1. Mansi, 12, 1122 D.
2. The *Libri Carolini*, which were composed *c.* 790, are attributed either to Alcuin or to Theodulf of Orléans. There is a bibliography in my *Ecclésiologie du Haut Moyen Age* (Paris, 1968), p. 281, note 115. For the text, see *PL* 98; *MGH, Concilia* II, *Supplementum* (Hanover, 1924). For the debate about *ex* and *per*, see cols 1117f., p. 110. For the profession of the *Filioque* at the Council of Frankfurt, see Mansi 13, 905; *MGH, Concilia* II, *Concilia Aevi Karolini* (Hanover, 1896), p. 163. The history of this period has been retraced by H. B. Swete, *On the History of the Doctrine of the Procession of the Holy Spirit* (Cambridge, 1876), chapter IX, pp. 196–226, with the appendix, pp. 227–237, containing the text of the letter of the Jerusalem monks to Leo III, the Pope's letter to the emperor, the Pope's profession of faith, the emperor's letter to the Pope and the account of the dialogue between the Pope and the emperor's envoys. See also M. Jugie, *op. cit.* (note 5 below), pp. 261–277; B. Capelle, 'Le pape Léon III et le "Filioque" ', *1054–1954. L'Eglise et les Eglises (Mélanges L. Beauduin)* (Chevetogne, 1954), I, pp. 309–322, who shows that the text given as Pope Leo III's profession of faith is in fact Alcuin's; R. G. Heath, 'The Schism of the Franks and the Filioque', *Journal of Ecclesiastical History*, 23 (1976), 97–113.

3. *PL* 129, 1257f.; *MGH, Epistolae* V, pp. 64–66 (for the monks' letter); *PL* 129, 1259f.; *MGH, op. cit.*, pp. 66–67 (for the Pope's letter to Charlemagne).
4. Anastasius Bibliothecarius, *Hist. de vitis Pontif.* (*PL* 128, 1238). This fact was borne out by Peter Damian in the second half of the eleventh century: *De proc. Spir. sanct.* 2 (*PL* 145, 635); and in the twelfth century by Peter Abelard and Peter Lombard: see Swete, *op. cit.* (note 2), p. 224, note 1. The account of the conversations between Charlemagne's envoys and the Pope can be found in *PL* 102, 971ff.; *MGH, Concilia* II, *Concilia Aevi Karolini*, Pars I, pp. 240ff.
5. Cardinal Hergenröther's study is still of fundamental importance: *Photius Patriarch von Konstantinopel*, 3 vols. (Regensburg, 1867–1869); see also F. Dvornik, *The Photian Schism: History and Legend* (Cambridge, 1948). Photius' argument is outlined and then disputed and rejected in L. Lohn, *Doctrina Graecorum et Russorum de Processione Spiritus Sancti a solo Patre*, Pars I: *Photii temporibus* (Rome, 1934); M. Jugie, *De Processione Spiritus Sancti . . .* (Rome, 1936), pp. 282–386. See also J. Slipyi, *Die Trinitätslehre des byzantinischen Patriarchen Photios* (Innsbruck, 1921); E. Amann, 'Photius', *DTC*, XII, cols 1536ff.; R. Haugh, *Photius and the Carolingians* (Belmont, Mass., 1975).
6. See F. Dvornik, *op. cit.*, esp. App. I, pp. 435–447; J. Alberigo *et al.*, eds, *Conciliorum Œcumenicorum Decreta* (Bologna, 1973), pp. 157–158. For the Council of 869–870, see D. Stiernon, *Constantinople IV* (*Histoire des conciles œcuméniques*, 5) (Paris, 1967).
7. V. Grumel, 'Le "Filioque" au concile photien de 879–880 et le témoignage de Michel d'Anchialos', *Echos d'Orient*, 29 (1930), 257–264. Even more important is the article by M. Jugie, 'Origine de la controverse sur l'addition du Filioque au Symbole', *RSPT* 28 (1939), 369–385—but see also note 29, p. 56 above.
8. See F. Dvornik, 'Le patriarche Photius: père du schisme ou patron de la réunion?' *La Vie intellectuelle* (December 1945), 16–28.
9. Photius, encyclical letter to the Bishops of the Eastern Church, 867 (*PG* 102, 721–741); letter to Walpert, the Metropolitan of Aquileia, probably 882 (*PG* 102, 793–821); *Amphilochia*, q. 28, between 867 and 876 (*PG* 101, 205–209); *The Mystagogy of the Holy Spirit*, which was composed in exile after 886 and is the most important text (*PG* 102, 263–400).
10. *Mystagogy*, 20 (*PG* 102, 300A).
11. *ibid.*, 53.
12. M. Jugie, *op. cit.* (note 5), p. 297, quotes *Contra Man.* III, 17 (*PG* 102, 168B) and *Amph.* q. 188 (*PG* 101, 909B) here. The diagram is generally attributed to Photius.
13. The texts in question are either those which speak of *dia tou Huiou, per Filium*, or those which show the Spirit to be united to the Father through the Son—see Athanasius, *Contra Arian*. III, 24 (*PG* 26, 373)—or those which attribute to the Son everything that the Father is or has except for his fatherhood—see L. Lohn, *op. cit.* (note 5), no. 69, pp. 59–60—or those which contain a commentary on the *de meo accipiet*, 'he will receive from me' (Jn 16:14), inclining towards a dependence of being—see L. Lohn, *op. cit.*, no. 76, pp. 64–65. Photius understands this as 'de meo *Patre*'; letter to the Metropolitan of Aquileia, 15 (*PG* 102, 808–809); *Mystagogy*, 22, 23 and 29 (*PG* 102, 301, 304, 312).
14. Letter to the Bishops of the Eastern Church, 22 (*PG* 102, 732); M. Jugie, *op. cit.* (note 5), p. 290.
15. Letter to the Bishops of the Eastern Church, 12 (*PG* 102, 728); *Mystagogy, passim*; see M. Jugie, *op. cit.*, p. 291, note 1.
16. Several of the Fathers explained this 'greater than I' by the fact that the Father is the begetter and the principle: see T. de Régnon, *Etudes de théologie positive sur la Sainte Trinité*, III (Paris, 1898), pp. 166ff.; *Œuvres de S. Augustin*, 15: *La Trinité*, I (Paris, 1955), pp. 574–575; Hilary of Poitiers, *Tract. super Ps.* 138, 17 (*PL* 9, 801).
17. S. Bulgakov, *Le Paraclet* (Paris, 1946), p. 110.

5

A NOTE ON THE
THEOLOGY OF GREGORY PALAMAS

We must now turn to a very important subject which would call for a much more developed treatment if I were to deal with it as such. As regards the theme of this book, it is necessary to speak about Palamite theology, but it is sufficient to do so relatively succinctly. I have, in this, made considerable use of the many indispensable texts and excellent analyses available.[1]

Gregory Palamas (1296–1359) became a monk on Mount Athos about 1316 and there experienced Hesychastic spirituality, in which the body is very closely associated with the spirit in the search for recollection and concentration. In Hesychastic prayer, a breathing technique is used to enable the prayer to descend from the head and find its way to the heart. The particular prayer used is the 'Jesus Prayer': the words 'Lord Jesus Christ, Son of God, have mercy on me' are said again and again in time with the breathing until they become a continuous prayer of the heart. Hesychasm eventually fitted into the pattern of Church and social life of the empire and became a reforming movement, working for the humble and the poor and for the independence and transcendence of the Church.

In the meantime, a monk from Calabria, Barlaam, attacked the Hesychasts' claim that it was possible to know God, their practice of prayer, and their theology of the divine light of Mount Tabor. Palamas replied to these attacks, and his defence of the Hesychastic positions forms the basis of Palamite theology. Two synods took place in 1341. Barlaam's teachings were condemned by the first in June and those of Akindynos by the second, which met in August. Despite the approval of these synods, Palamas became involved in the vicissitudes of ecclesiastical politics which led at times to his being excommunicated and the triumph of his enemies and at other times to the confirmation of his teachings. In 1347 he was made Archbishop of Thessalonica, but did not take up his see until 1350. Years of struggle and frequently dramatic episodes followed. He died on 14 November 1359 and was canonized by the Church of Constantinople in 1368. His teaching had by this time already been approved, by a council that met in 1351.[2]

Palamas was almost completely forgotten for several centuries—so much so that T. de Régnon published his four great volumes in 1892–1898 without even referring to him, even in those passages where he was commenting on the term 'energy' (IV, pp. 425ff., 476ff.). In the nineteen-thirties and forties, however, there was a wonderful revival of interest in him and his theology. Broadly speaking, Eastern theologians have come to recognize in Palamism a clear expression of the genius and the tradition of their Church. It is therefore of great importance for the theme of this book.

It is also relatively simple. In the first place, there is the whole context of Eastern apophatism, according to which it is not possible either to know God or to express any positive idea of him, the deepest knowledge of him being purely experiential or mystical. At the same time, God calls us to become deified. This is such a fundamental datum in the teaching of the Greek Fathers that they constantly used it as proof of the divinity of the Son and the Spirit in their controversy with the Arians. It is within this context that should be placed the Hesychastic experience of communion with God and of a knowledge, through experience, of his light. According to the Greek tradition, then, there is, in God, a secret essence that cannot be known or shared and a radiation which, once it has been experienced and shared, ensures our deification. This accounts for the distinction that Palamas makes *in God*—without impairing the simplicity of God—not only between the essence and the hypostases, but also between the hypostases, the divine essence that cannot be known or shared, and the uncreated energies of God. These energies are God, not in his being in himself, which is not accessible to creatures, but in his being for us. The energies must be available for us to share in them, and they must be God as uncreated, or else we could never be deified. The Palamists are unable to accept that the created grace of the Scholastic theologians of the West and the intentional union of the Thomists, the depth and realism of which they do not fully understand, can bring about a true deification of man, and the direct vision of the divine essence without any created *species*, as affirmed by Thomas Aquinas, is, in their view, contrary to the unknowable character of that essence.

These uncreated energies are therefore what surround the essence of God that cannot be communicated to man—*ta peri auton* (or *autou*).[3] Scriptural terms for these are, for example, the glory, the face or the power of God. The light that transfigured Christ on Mount Tabor was the uncreated splendour that emanates from God. It was always with Christ because of his divinity, but it remained invisible to carnal eyes—the apostles were only able to perceive it miraculously because their bodily eyes were illuminated by grace. This perception of the divine light is, in the opinion of the Hesychasts and the Palamists, the peak of all spiritual experience, and this idea is very closely associated with the very fundamental decision not to separate the body from the highest spiritual life.

What, then, is the relationship between these energies and the hypostases or Persons of the Trinity? According to Sergey Bulgakov, 'Palamas hardly touches on the complex and important question of the relationship between the energies and the hypostases (except in a few isolated sentences that are lacking in precision)'.[4] The texts and the studies that have been published since Bulgakov said this enable us to make a better reply to our question. The divine energies are 'inhypostatized'.[5] The eternal and uncreated activity that flows from the divine essence is possessed, put to work and manifested by the divine Persons and communicated by them to our persons.[6] The energetic manifestations of God follow the order (*taxis*) of the Persons—from the Father, through the Son, in the Spirit.

In the particular case of the Holy Spirit, the part played by the latter in the economy of salvation was made manifest at Pentecost, when, however, no incarnation of the hypostasis of the Spirit or communication of the essence of God took place. But the manifestation of his Person by the energies confirms a dependence with regard to the Son. 'The grace is therefore uncreated and it is what the Son gives, sends and grants to his disciples; it is not the Spirit himself, but a deifying gift which is an energy that is not only uncreated, but also inseparable from the Holy Spirit' (*Triad*, III, 8).

At this point Palamas goes back to a statement by Gregory of Cyprus, the Patriarch of Constantinople (†1290),[7] and recognizes that the *Filioque* may possibly have a meaning in the order of energetic manifestation, that is, that the holy Spirit, not as hypostasis but as inhypostatizing the energy, is poured out from the Father, through the Son (*dia tou Huiou* or even *ek tou Huiou*). Vladimir Lossky discovered this openness as early as 1945, but he kept to the idea of an eternal manifestation of the Spirit through the Son.[8] His disciple O. Clément, however, went further than this and said:

If the 'monarchic' character of the Father as the unique principle of the Son and the Spirit is an absolutely incommunicable hypostatic character, is his character as the divine source (of the essence and energies)—to use a Latin theological term, his 'fontal' privilege—not communicated to the Son and then from the Father and the Son to the Spirit, the source of our deification? And would it not be this participation in the divine source, the rhythm that makes first the Son and then the Spirit the source with the Father, that is indicated by a certain Latin (and Alexandrian) *Filioque*?[9]

It may be because I am not sufficiently well informed, but I have to admit that I am not quite clear what Palamas thinks about his attribution to the energies or to the Person of the Holy Spirit. When he says, for example, ' "The new spirit and the new heart" of Ezek 36:26 are created things, . . . whereas the Spirit of God given to the new heart (Ezek 27:5) is the Holy Spirit',[10] is he speaking about the uncreated energies or the Person of the Holy Spirit? Again, when he says that the energies are nothing but the Holy Spirit, but that they are not the divine essence,[11] is he referring to the energies inhypostatized in the Holy Spirit or to the third Person of the Trinity? This may, of course, have to do with the fact that Palamas gives the name of Holy Spirit both to the uncreated energies and to the hypostasis. He says, for example: 'When you hear him (that is, Cyril of Alexandria) say that the Holy Spirit proceeds from the two, because he comes essentially from the Father through the Son, you should understand his teaching in this sense: it is the powers and essential energies of God which pour out, not the divine hypostasis of the Spirit'.[12] What the Fathers called *energeia* is the supernatural action of God, which is his Spirit—Father, Son and Spirit are the first subject, his power and his act.[13] Or else they spoke of the energies of the Spirit and meant by this his gifts, given to believers, but caused by him.[14]

This at once gives rise to the question—widely discussed by Palamas' opponents[15]—of the continuity between the statements made by the Fathers and Palamas' systematic treatment of the subject. This whole question would be well worth examining in depth and with scholarly objectivity.[16] It would, in my opinion, certainly be possible to dispute the meaning of the texts of the Cappadocian Fathers and John Damascene that have been quoted in favour of Palamas' thesis.[17] The ante-Nicene Fathers, and in particular Athanasius, always denied that there could have been any procession in God other than that of the Persons. According to them, apart from the hypostases, only creatures proceeded from God. In opposition to Eunomius, according to whom the term *agennētos* adequately expressed the essence of God, the Fathers stressed the unknowable aspect of that essence. God, they believed, could only be known by his properties and works, and Basil of Caesarea called these his 'energies', which, he claimed, 'descend towards us, while his substance remains inaccessible'.[18]

The Fathers frequently expressed this distinction by using the terms *kat' auton* (God in himself) and *ta peri auton* or *peri autou* ('about him', in other words, what can be known and said about him, that is, on the basis of his properties and his activity) or *peri tēn phusin*.[19] André de Halleux, who is a considerable expert in this field, has, however, defended the interpretation of *peri auton* which is favourable to Palamas.[20] From the philological point of view, he is clearly right, since *peri* followed by the accusative certainly means 'around' or 'in connection with'. The question as to what theological or metaphysical conclusion should be drawn from the term, however, still remains. Did the Fathers postulate a kind of corona of divine energies which were active *ad extra*, which could be shared and which were ontologically and really distinct from the divine essence and the hypostases? E. von Ivanka, who is also a considerable expert, disputes this (see note 16 below). The problem has, in my opinion, not yet been fully cleared up, and I am in no position to decide. I am, however, impressed by the formal decision reached by so many Greek and Slav Orthodox theologians, who are in the best position to judge and interpret the writings of those who have borne witness to their own tradition.

We must now consider the question whether Palamism can be accepted by Western Catholicism or whether it is irreconcilably contrary to our teaching—and to our faith? The negative and critical position has been held, with varying shades of emphasis, by M. Jugie, S. Guichardan (see note 1 below), E. Candal[21] and those who contributed to the 1974 number of *Istina* (see also note 1 below). On the other hand, there have been as many specialists in this sphere who have regarded it as possible to reconcile Palamism with the Catholic faith.[22] I say quite deliberately the 'Catholic faith', because, if we are thinking of the *theology* of Augustine or Thomas Aquinas, we are bound to admit that, after reading Palamas openly and sympathetically and after recognizing very wide possibilities of agreement, there are still many great divergences. This ground has been covered to a great extent by Cardinal Journet on the basis of Jean Meyendorff's excellent book.[23] The distinction between faith and theology is quite fundamental—so much so that T. de Régnon referred to it again and again throughout the four volumes of his work on the Trinity.

Cardinal Journet has pointed out first of all that there is no opposition between Palamism and the Catholic faith with regard to the following articles: the natural and the supernatural order, Christ and the Eucharist, the Church as a mystical reality, the Virgin Mary and the saints. There are divergencies in the case of that very ambiguous term 'original sin', the immaculate conception of Mary, and the procession of the Holy Spirit from the Father *and the Son* through the same spiration. The question of the real distinction between the essence and the divine energies, however, still remains, and this distinction is required by the affirmation of the full truth of our deification. The doctrine of the light of Mount Tabor is only an application of that distinction. I believe, together with Cardinal Journet, J.-M. Garrigues, G. Philips and, ultimately, also J. Kuhlmann (*op. cit.* (note 22 below), pp. 43–57), that this difference comes from the idea of participation. Let us look at this question more closely.

Kuhlmann and Journet have both compared the same Pseudo-Dionysian texts as interpreted by Thomas Aquinas (and Maximus the Confessor) on the one hand and by Palamas on the other. To 'participate' means to 'take part', *partem capere*. Palamas interprets this as taking part in God entitatively and ontologically, but this participation cannot be in his essence, which cannot be communicated—it must be in the energies which emanate from that essence and which surround it. This, however, makes it possible for us to be deified in a literal and absolute sense—we become God and therefore we become, by grace, uncreated.[24] From the philosophical point of view, this Palamite idea of participation is clearly elementary and material,[25] one might almost say Neo-Platonic. The interpretation provided by Thomas Aquinas (and Maximus the Confessor), on the other hand, is Aristotelian, although it has taken from Plato a note of exemplarism. Maximus and Thomas comment on Pseudo-Dionysius' *Divine Names* in the following way: God, as a sovereign artist, lets his creatures participate, not in his divinity as such, which would be as impossible for us as it was for Palamas, but in the likenesses of his perfections of being—this is the exemplarism of the divine ideas—and through the efficient causality which confers existence. Thomas comments on *The Divine Names* II, 4 as follows:

> God is manifested by the effects that come from him. It is the Deity itself which to some extent proceeds in these effects, when it pours a likeness of itself into things according to their capacity, in such a way, however, that its excellence and its singularity remain intact in itself; these are not communicated to us and they remain hidden from our sight.[26]

This expresses the same sense of God's transcendence as I welcome and admire in the teaching of Gregory Palamas, but the concepts used by Thomas are, of course, quite different. The participation of which Thomas speaks is in a likeness of God's perfections and is realized in existence by the efficient causality of the absolute Being. There is no distinction in God himself between the divine essence that cannot be shared and the energies that are communicated, not even when it is a question of our *supernatural* participation. To the extent to which that participation includes created realities such as grace, charisms and gifts of the Holy Spirit, those realities have a status that is similar to that of natural realities. Participation, then, is not in perfections which are God's common perfections. It is rather in the divine nature as a principle of activities with God himself in view (see 2 Pet 1:3–4). The divine causality of grace produces in us principles of existence and action which enable us to attain the reality of God himself, that is, the Tri-unity, as the object of the life of the spirit, of knowledge and of love. These principles of action are limited (because they are created) in their entitative being, but they are effectively open to the infinite aspect of God himself, which they can attain without exhausting (*totum, non totaliter*). This is the effect of grace, of the theologal virtues and of the light of glory. And just as grace is that supernatural gift with which God himself is given, the indwelling in us of the divine Persons follows the gift of grace, with the enjoyment of their presence (see Volume II of this work, pp. 83–84). This explanation, however, is as such not really dogmatic, but rather theological.

I do not dispute the underlying intention of Palamas' teaching, but find myself in disagreement with the concepts that he uses and his metaphysical mode of expression. Even if it is admitted that he is supported by several of the Fathers in his distinction *a parte rei* between the divine essence and the energies, he still only presents us with a theologoumenon in the precise sense in which this term has been defined by B. Bolotov: 'The opinions of the Fathers of the *one* and *undivided* Church are the opinions of those men among whom are found those who have rightly been called *hoi didaskaloi tēs oikoumenēs.* . . . But, however widely accepted it may be, a theologoumenon does not constitute a dogma.'[27]

Does Palamas' teaching constitute a dogma in the Orthodox Church? Certain Eastern Christians think so, including, for example, Professor Karminis and Archimandrite [now Bishop] Kallistos Ware (*op. cit.* (note 1 below), 58). Considerable importance has obviously also to be attached to the Council of Constantinople of 1351 and its decisions that were incorporated into the synodicon to be read on the First Sunday of Lent, the so-called Feast of Orthodoxy. (Are they still read then?) At the Council of Florence in 1439, the Greeks regarded the distinction between the divine energies and the uncreated character of the light of Mount Tabor as their teaching. Nowadays, Palamism is almost universally accepted by Orthodox theologians. But does all this evidence point to a dogma? There are strong reasons for doubting it.[28]

Did the Roman Catholic Church dogmatically condemn the Palamite theses at any time? J. Kuhlmann does not think so. He has examined the dogmatic statements concerning the vision of God.[29] Although the Latin participants at the Council of Florence regarded the Palamite thesis as heretical, no formal condemnation was pronounced by the Council itself. The Fathers of the Council spoke of 'intueri clare ipsum Deum trinum et unum sicuti est', but did not say 'per essentiam'. Palamas might have agreed with that formula by seeing it as pointing to a vision of energies *which are God*. The Constitution *Benedictus Deus* of 1336 speaks of seeing 'essentiam divinam visione intuitiva et etiam faciali', and Kuhlmann's comment on this is that all that was intended was to oppose a vision of something created. Palamas may, however, have disputed the vision of the divine essence, but he certainly admitted participation in the divine nature (2 Pet 1:4), not *kata phusin*, but *kata charin*, that is, through grace. Kuhlmann has therefore concluded that, as far as Palamism is concerned, there is no obstacle to re-establishing communion with the East. Is he being too optimistic here? Mgr Gérard Philips, who was the king-pin in the Theological Commission of Vatican II, has come to the same conclusion. This is, in my opinion, a firm guarantee.

NOTES

1. D. Stiernon has published a bulletin containing 303 items on Palamism in *Rev. Et. byz.* 30 (1972), 231–341. This alone shows that the subject is so full and technical that only specialists can deal adequately with it. For the works of Palamas, see J. Meyendorff, *Introduction à l'étude de Grégoire Palamas* (*Patristica Sorbonensia*, 3) (Paris, 1959), Appendix I, pp. 331–399 [the Eng. tr. (see below) lacks the Appendixes]. For our particular subject, only the following need to be consulted: *PG* 150, 809–828: *Chapters against Akindynos*; 909–960: dialogue *Theophanes*; 1121–1126: *Capita CL physica, theologica, moralia et practica*; 1225–1236: *Hagioritic Tome*; *PG* 151, 424–449: *Homilies* 34 and 35 on the Transfiguration and the Light of Tabor; see also J. Meyendorff, ed., *Pour la défense des saints hésychastes* (*Spicil. Sacr. Lov.*, 29) (Louvain, 1959: 2nd ed. 1973).

Studies and analyses of Palamas include: I. Hausherr, 'La méthode d'oraison hésychaste', *Or. Chr. Period*. 9 (1927), 97–210; M. Jugie, 'Palamas et Palamite (Controverse)', *DTC*, XI (1932), cols 1735–1776, 1777–1818; *idem*, *Theologia dogmatica Christianorum Orient. ab Ecclesia cath. diss.*, II (Paris, 1933), pp. 47–183; S. Guichardan, *Le problème de la simplicité divine en Orient et en Occident aux XIVᵉ et XVᵉ siècles. Grégoire Palamas, Duns Scot, Georges Scholarios* (Lyons, 1933); B. Krivocheine, 'The Ascetic and Theological Teaching of St Gregory Palamas', *ECQ*, 3 (1938–1939), 26–33, 71–84, 138–156, 193–215; V. Lossky, *The Mystical Theology of the Eastern Church* (Eng. tr.; London, 1957), especially pp. 67ff.: 'Uncreated Energies'; *idem*, 'The Procession of the Holy Spirit in the Orthodox Triadology' (Eng. tr.), *ECQ*, 7, Supplementary Issue (1948), 31–53, also tr. in *In the Image* . . . (see below), chapter 4, pp. 71–96: 'The Procession of the Holy Spirit in Orthodox Trinitarian Doctrine'; *idem*, *In the Image and Likeness of God* (Eng. tr.; London and Oxford, 1975), especially chapter 3: 'The Theology of Light in the Thought of St Gregory Palamas'; C. Lialine, 'The Theological Teaching of Gregory Palamas on Divine Simplicity', *ECQ*, 6 (1946), 266–287; C. Kern, 'Les éléments de la théologie de Grégoire Palamas', *Irénikon*, 20 (1947), 6–33, 164–193; J. Meyendorff, *A Study of Gregory Palamas* (Eng. tr. of *Introduction*, *op. cit.*; London, 1964): an original and fundamental work, and, at a less technical level, but more synthetic, *S. Grégoire Palamas et la mystique orthodoxe* (*Coll. Les Maîtres spirituels*) (Paris, 1959); *idem*, 'the Holy Trinity in Palamite Theology', *Trinitarian Theology: East and West* (Brookline, Mass., 1977), pp. 25–43; E. Boularand, 'Grégoire Palamas et "La Défense des saints hésychastes" ', *RAM*, 36 (1960), 227–240; O. Clément, *Byzance et le Christianisme* (Paris, 1964); R. Miguel, 'Grégoire Palamas, docteur de l'expérience', *Irénikon*, 37 (1966), 227–237; Amphilokios Radovic, ' "Le Filioque" et l'énergie incréée de la Sainte Trinité selon la doctrine de S. Grégoire Palamas', *Messager de l'Exarchat du Patriarche russe en Europe occidentale*, 89–90 (1975), 11–44; Kallistos Ware, 'Dieu caché et révélé. La voie apophatique et la distinction essence-énergie', *ibid.*, 45–59. A double number of the journal *Istina* on 'Orient et Occident. La Procession du Saint-Esprit' appeared in 1972 and a series of articles on Gregory Palamas in 1974, of which the editorial, 257–259, is especially valuable; see also in that number (19) J. P. Houdret, 'Palamas et les Cappadociens', 260–271; J.-M. Garrigues, 'L'énergie divine et la grâce chez Maxime le Confesseur', 272–296; J. S. Nadal, 'La critique par Akindynos de l'herméneutique patristique de Palamas', 297–328; M. J. Le Guillou, 'Lumière et charité dans la doctrine palamite de la divinisation', 329–338. The articles in this number of *Istina,* together with several other publications, give the impression of being a combined attack. For a Catholic reply, see A. de Halleux, 'Palamisme et tradition', *Irénikon*, 48 (1975), 479–493. Finally, for the epistemological debate, see G. Podskalsky, *Theologie und Philosophie in Byzanz. Der Streit um die theologische Methodik in der spätbyzantinischen Geistesgeschichte (14./15. Jahrhundert), seine systematischen Grundlagen und seine historische Entwicklung (Byzantinisches Archiv*, 15) (Munich, 1977), which contains an exhaustive documentation and a full bibliography. See also below, notes 15 to 20, for Palamas and the Fathers, and note 22 for the reception by Catholic theologians of Palamism.

2. J. Meyendorff, *A Study, op. cit.*, pp. 94–97; for the text see *PG* 151, 717–762.
3. See below, notes 19 and 20.
4. S. Bulgakov, *Le Paraclet* (Paris, 1946), p. 236.
5. See J. Meyendorff, ed., *Pour la défense des saints hésychastes, op. cit.* (note 1), III, 1, 18, pp. 591–593.
6. J. Meyendorff, *A Study, op. cit.* (note 1), pp. 216ff.; *idem*, 'The Holy Trinity in Palamite Theology', *op. cit.* (*ibid.*), 31–33, 38–39, in which the author quotes an article by Edmund Hussey, 'The Persons–Energy Structure in the Theology of St Gregory Palamas', *St Vladimir's Theological Quarterly*, 18 (1974), 22–43. In this context, it is also worth quoting from O. Clément, *Byzance et le Christianisme, op. cit.* (note 1), p. 46: 'This energy is not an impersonal radiation subsisting in itself. It is rather an expansion of the Trinity and

expresses *ad extra* the mysterious otherness of the Trinity in its unity. It is a "natural procession" from God himself, bursting or flashing out, like a flash of light, of the Father through the Son and in the Holy Spirit. It reveals the "interpenetration" or perichoresis of the divine Persons, who "interpenetrate each other in such a way that they possess only one energy" '. See also A. de Halleux, 'Palamisme et Scolastique', *op. cit.* below (note 22), 425, who refers to Palamas, *Capita CL physica, op. cit.* (note 1), 75 and 107 (*PG* 150, 1173B and 1193B).

7. Gregory's treatise on the *ekporeusis* of the Holy Spirit (*PG* 142, 269–300) has been analysed by O. Clément, 'Grégoire de Chypre "De l'ekporèse du Saint-Esprit" ', *Istina*, 17 (1972), 443–456.

8. V. Lossky, 'The Procession of the Holy Spirit', *ECQ, op. cit.* (note 1), 48–49; *In the Image and Likeness of God, op. cit.* (*ibid.*), pp. 90–93. In his article 'Vladimir Lossky, un théologien de la personne et du Saint-Esprit (Mémorial Vladimir Lossky)', *Messager de l'Exarchat du Patriarche russe en Europe occidentale*, 30–31 (April–September, 1959), 137–206, O. Clément referred to this openness on Lossky's part and, on pp. 192 and 178, points to expressions of it, taken from classes given on 10 November and 17 November 1955: 'The *Filioque* can be justified at the level of manifestation—the Holy Spirit manifests the common nature of the Trinity and proceeds from the Father and the Son not as a Person, but as a function. His function is essentially to make manifest. He manifests the nature of the Father and the Son (which is also his own)'; 'In this *taxis* (of manifestation), it is possible to say, if need be, that the Spirit proceeds from the Father and the Son. The Son shows in himself what the Father is; the Spirit shows what the Father is and what the Son is, insofar as they are the same principle, but a principle to which the Spirit himself belongs and which he manifests.'

9. O. Clément, *op. cit.* (note 7), p. 450. Amphilokios Radovic, *op. cit.* (note 1) shows that Palamas affirmed the procession of the Holy Spirit only from the Father, but that the Spirit also receives the divine essence from the Son (pp. 27ff.); he devotes pp. 42–43 to Gregory of Cyprus. In this context, it is also worth quoting Paul Evdokimov, *L'Esprit Saint dans la tradition orthodoxe* (Paris, 1969), p. 63: 'The distinction between essence and energy is the first of the possible solutions of the *Filioque* in the light of the Eastern tradition. It postulates the distinction and identity of the Spirit (*to Pneuma* with the article) as hypostasis and of Spirit (*Pneuma* without the article) as energy. At the level of the common essence, the Spirit as hypostasis proceeds from the Father alone, although conjointly with the Son on whom he rests. As divine energy, Palamas teaches, "the Spirit is poured out from the Father through the Son and, if one wants, from the Son" [quoted by J. Meyendorff, *Introduction, op. cit.*, p. 315 (= *A Study, op. cit.*, p. 230)]. The solution, then, is to be found in the distinction between the hypostasis of the Holy Spirit and the energy that it manifests *ex Patre Filioque*.'

10. Quoted by J. Meyendorff, *A Study, op. cit.*, (note 1), p. 164.

11. *Against Akindynos*, II, 17, quoted by J. Meyendorff, *A Study, op. cit.*, p. 225.

12. *Apodictic Treatises*, quoted by J. Meyendorff, *A Study, op. cit.*, p. 230.

13. See the many texts, together with full commentaries, in T. de Régnon, *Etudes de theólogie positive sur la Sainte Trinité*, IV (Paris, 1898), pp. 425–465. This is, in particular, what is found in Athanasius, *Ad Ser.* I, 19, 20 and 31; III, 5. See also G. L. Prestige, *God in Patristic Thought*, 2nd ed. (London, 1952), pp. 257ff.

14. This seems to me to be the case in the *Const. Apost.* V, 20, 4, with regard to Pentecost: 'We have been filled with his energy and have spoken in new tongues', and in Maximus the Confessor, *Q. ad Thal.* 63 (*PG* 90, 672); *Theol. Polem.* 1 (*PG* 91, 33). In his anti-Monothelite struggle, Maximum spoke of divine energy in the sense of the active faculty of a nature or essence. For him, however, it was the creative causality and not the energies in the sense in which Palamas distinguished them from the essence and the hypostases; that, at least, is how J.-M. Garrigues interprets it; *op. cit.* (note 1).

15. J. S. Nadal, *op cit.* (note 1).

16. All that we have at present is this partial study: E. von Ivanka, 'Palamismus und Vätertradi-
tion', *L'Eglise et les Eglises. Mélanges Lambert Beauduin* (Chevetogne, 1954), II,
pp. 29–46, who concluded that the texts in question do not speak of a real distinction in
God himself, but of a distinction made by our spirit, which can only think in distinctions;
see also J. P. Houdret, *op. cit.* (note 1). This conclusion is of crucial importance.

17. G. Florovsky, 'Grégoire Palamas et la patristique', *Istina*, 8 (1961–1962), 115–125,
especially 122 (only Basil of Caesarea, *Ep.* 234 *ad Amphilochium*, and John Damascene,
De fide orthod. I, 14); G. Philips, *op. cit.* below (note 22), 254.

18. Basil of Caesarea, *Contra Eunom.* I, 4 (*PG* 29, 544); *Ep.* 234 *ad Amphilochium* 1 (*PG* 32,
869 A–B).

19. See, for example, Gregory Nazianzen, *Orat.* 38, 7 (*PG* 36, 317B); 45, 3 (*PG* 36, 525C);
Maximus the Confessor, *Centuries on Charity*, IV, 7 (*PG* 90, 1049A); *First Century on
Theology and the Economy*, 48 (*PG* 90, 1100D); John Damascene, *De fide Orthod.* I, 4
and 10 (*PG* 94, 800C and 840).

20. A. de Halleux, *op. cit.* (note 1), 484: 'The contrast that the Cappadocian Fathers expressed
by the words *kat' auton* and *peri auton* cannot be translated as that between God as he is in
himself and what we are able to know about him. When it is followed by the accusative,
the preposition *peri* usually means "around" and not "about" in this sense. By *peri auton*,
the Fathers therefore meant what is "around" or what surrounds the essence of
God, the radiation of light coming from the dark nucleus of the essence. . . . This *peri auton*
is not what God reveals of his *kat' auton*, that is, the essence as we are able to know it, the
simple perceived as many. It is rather a flowing that is distinct in God himself from the
inaccessible source of his being.'

21. Many publications are listed in D. Stiernon's bulletin on Palamism, *op. cit.* (note 1).

22. I would mention here, in chronological order and for the most part in accordance with D.
Stiernon's very valuable bulletin, *op. cit.*, to which the page numbers in brackets refer: G.
Habra, 'The Source of the Doctrine of Gregory Palamas on the Divine Energies', *ECQ*, 12
(1957–1958), 244–252, 294–303, 338–347 (311); P. Bossuyt, 'Hesychasmus en
katholieke theologie', *Bijdragen* (1964), 229–238 (306); M. Strohm, 'Die Lehre von der
Einfachheit Gottes. Ein dogmatischer Streitpunkt zwischen Griechen und Lateiner',
Kyrios, New Series, 7 (1967), 215–228; *idem*, 'Die Lehre von der Energeia Gottes', *ibid.*, 8
(1968), 63–84; 9 (1969), 31–41 (309–311); J. Kuhlmann, *Die Taten des einfachen Gottes.
Eine römisch-katholische Stellungnahme zum Palamismus* (*Das östliche Christentum*, New
Series, 21) (Würzburg, 1968) (294–299), with reference to a criticism by B. Schultze, *Or.
Chr. period*, 36 (1970), 135–142; G. Philips, 'La grâce chez les Orientaux', *ETL*, 48
(1972), 37–50, reprinted in *L'union personnelle avec le Dieu vivant. Essai sur l'origine et le
sens de la grâce créée* (*Bibl. ETL*, XXXVI) (Gembloux, 1972), 241–260 (I shall be
returning to this article by G. Philips, because his position has not received the attention
that it deserves); A. de Halleux, 'Palamisme et Scolastique', *RTL*, 4 (1973), 409–422; *idem*,
'Orthodoxie et Catholicisme: du personnalisme en pneumatologie', *ibid.*, 6 (1975), 3–30;
idem, 'Palamisme et tradition', *op. cit.* (note 1). See also the following note.

23. C. Journet, 'Palamisme et thomisme. A propos d'un livre récent', *RThom*, 60 (1960),
429–452.

24. J. Meyendorff, *A Study, op. cit.* (note 1), pp. 176–177.

25. Thus, according to Palamas, if man were to participate in God's essence, he would himself
become omnipotent and there would consequently be an infinite number of divine hypostases: *Capita CL physica*, 108–109 (*PG* 150, 1193C–1196A). This accounts for G. Philips'
comment, *op. cit.* (note 22), p. 253: 'Palamas sees "participation" as a division into almost
materialized pieces, each participant possessing a fragment of the whole, which is clearly
absurd. In his view, everything that can be shared can also be divided (*Cap.* 110; *PG* 150,
1196C; *Theoph.* 944 A).'

26. Thomas Aquinas, *In lib. de Divinis Nominibus expositio*, Turin ed., p. 46, No. 136,
translated by Journet, *op. cit.* (note 23), p. 448. On p. 449, Journet has also translated

Thomas' commentary on XI, 6 (*PG* 3, 956) (Thomas, *op. cit.*, p. 346, no. 934), and that of Maximus, *Scholia in lib. de Div. Nom.* XI, 6 (*PG* 4, 401). J. Kuhlmann, *op. cit.* (note 22), pp. 43–57, has compared Thomas' and Palamas' commentaries on the *Divine Names*, XI, 6 (*PG* 3, 953ff.). For the idea of participation in the likeness, see also Thomas' fine passage *ST* IIIa, q. 23, a. 2 ad 3.

27. B. Bolotov, 'Thèses sur le "Filioque" ' (Fr. tr.), *Istina*, 17 (1972), 261–289, especially 262 and 263.

28. For the 'non-dogmatic' character in the strict sense of the distinction between essence and energies, despite the Council of 1351 and the Sunday anathemas of the Feast of Orthodoxy, see M. Jugie, *Theologia dogmatica*, *op. cit.* (note 1), pp. 132ff., who gives texts and summaries. What I. K. says, for example, in *Or. Chr. Period.*, 17 (1951), 488, is: 'Is it a true dogma? Is it now still held as such in all the Eastern Churches? As for the Russian Church, it is well known that that Church ceased to affirm this from the eighteenth century onwards. In 1767, that Church radically changed the office of the Sunday of Orthodoxy and removed every trace of Palamism from it.' See M. Jugie, *op. cit.*, pp. 176ff.

29. J. Kuhlmann, *op. cit.* (note 22), pp. 108–125, for the Council of Florence (*DS* 1305); pp. 126–135 for the Constitution *Benedictus Deus* of Benedict XII, 29 January 1336 (*DS* 1000–1001).

6

EASTERN PNEUMATOLOGY TODAY

Now that we have considered the patristic sources of the Eastern tradition, we are in a position to provide a conspectus of the present state of pneumatology in the Eastern Church. In this synthesis, I shall leave aside Sergey Bulgakov's *Le Paraclet* (1946), not because the book is not interesting—quite the reverse!—but rather because it is too personal a work to be really representative of the Orthodox tradition.[1] There are, however, many more classical studies available.[2]

They are all deeply indebted to Greek patristic literature, but they contain an element that is not present in the Fathers. Although their tone may be irenical, they incorporate the data of the anti-Latin polemics. The result is that these works are at the same time a very positive expression of deep insight into the Eastern theological tradition and a criticism of Latin theological or dogmatic constructions. They almost all go back to the difference that T. de Régnon observed, namely that the point of departure for the Latin Fathers was the divine nature, whereas for the Greeks it was the hypostases. De Régnon unfortunately extended this penetrating insight into a simplification that no longer expressed the full reality of the situation. I shall try, in what follows, to avoid this over-simplification and to keep to the fundamental truth of the insight.

The Orthodox first affirm the three Persons or hypostases. Their point of departure, it would seem, is a difference between the essence or substance and the hypostases of a kind that enables them to speak in two different ways about the divine Persons, according to whether they are regarded as hypostases or are seen in their relationship to the divine essence. In Latin dogmatic theology, on the other hand, the hypostases are really identical with the divine essence. This means that, as far as the Holy Spirit is concerned, dependence on the Son in respect of the divine essence also implies dependence on him with regard to the hypostasis. In Orthodox dogmatic theology, however, it is possible to claim a hypostatic dependence on the Father alone and at the same time a reception of the divine essence also from the Son. After the abortion—or rather the still-birth—of the union discussed at the Council of Lyons in 1274, the Patriarch of Constantinople, Gregory of Cyprus (†1290), wrote:

How could we affirm dogmatically that, because the Spirit is of the essence of the Son, he is from him, as from a cause? . . . We say in fact that the Holy Spirit has his essential *ekporeusis* from the Father and that he exists from his essence. Because, on the other hand, the Father and the Son do not have a different essence, but have a single and the same essence, we of necessity confess that the Spirit is also from that essence. That, because he is of the essence of the Son, he is also from his hypostasis, no reason could persuade us to confess it, insofar as it has not been established that the essence and the hypostasis are the same principle.[3]

The divine hypostases are affirmed as such without any apparent need for an explanation by means of an opposition in relationship, as is the case in Latin theology. In the latter, Son implies Father and Father implies Son. In the community and unity of substance, the hypostases are distinguished by the mutual relationship which opposes them by affirming them. That relationship is and can only be a relationship of origin, or of principle or beginning and end. On the one hand, spiration of the Spirit does not bring about any opposition in relationship between the Father and the Son and, on the other hand, the Spirit proceeding from the Father can be distinguished hypostatically from the Son only if he has a relationship of procession or origin with that Son. He is, in many scriptural texts, Spirit of the Father and Spirit of the Son and for this reason he must be confessed as proceeding from the two by a single common act of active spiration.

The Orthodox reject this theology for the following reasons:

1. The hypostases must be affirmed for themselves and as such because they are affirmed by revelation and in the formula of baptism. To distinguish the Spirit from the Son, it is sufficient to keep to biblical terms, according to which the Son comes from the Father by begetting. The Spirit, on the other hand, comes by 'procession' or *ekporeusis*. It is enough for there to be two different modes of coming from the Father. The relationships are not what define the persons—they follow and are constituted by the persons, like inseparable properties.[4] The Latins have developed reasons and make inferences from logical necessities, whereas it is sufficient—and indeed necessary—to revere the mystery, to accept it and to defend it as it is given to us, without attempting to rationalize it.[5]

2. Since the time of Photius, the Orthodox have continued to object to the procession of the Spirit 'from the Father and the Son as from the same principle and by a single act of spiration', claiming that the Father and the Son, who are distinguished in their hypostases, can only spirate the Spirit through a common nature. A hypostasis cannot, however, come from a common nature—a hypostasis can only come from a hypostasis. If the Spirit proceeded from a common nature, he must have proceeded from himself, because he also shares in that common nature, but that, the Orthodox theologians maintain, is absurd.

The Latins have, of course, been replying to this objection for centuries. The fact that it has been raised again and again shows how what is intellectually effective in one theological construction of faith can continue to be remote from another theological construction and even alien to it. The Orthodox are convinced that we have deduced the hypostases from the divine nature or essence; our idea of the hypostasis as a subsistent relationship does not appeal to them. We recognize for our part that the way in which the Scholasticism that has, as H. Clérissac put it, 'run to seed' has reasoned with an almost tactless lack of caution and beyond what the eye can see about the data of the mystery of the Trinity[6] may well have encouraged Eastern Christians to think that there has been excessive rationalization about the Trinity in the West. This, however, should not prevent us from trying to understand the great value of what saints and geniuses such as Thomas Aquinas have attempted to express in their use of such terms as 'subsistent relationships'.

It would be wrong to think that the Greek Fathers knew nothing about or simply neglected the question of consubstantiality through the divine essence. On the contrary, the Cappadocians affirmed the common essence before insisting on the specific aspect of the hypostases. Basil the Great (*Ep*. 38; *PG* 32, 325ff.), Gregory of Nyssa and Pseudo-Dionysius all did this. It is true that they insisted on the monarchy of the Father, claiming that only he was *archē*, the original and originating principle, but so did the Latin Fathers (see below, pp. 134–137). It is from the Father that the one substance of the deity is communicated, by begetting in the case of the Son and by procession in the case of the Spirit.[7] Gregory Nazianzen said: 'The divine nature is one in the three, but what makes their unity is the Father, on whom the others depend'.[8] Because it is a positive affirmation, I welcome what Paul Evdokimov said about this question, although I cannot welcome what he appears to exclude: 'For the Greeks, the principle of unity is not the divine nature, but the Father, who establishes relationships of origin with regard to himself as the one source of every relationship'.[9]

The unity of the three is also brought about by their being within each other, that is, by their *perichōrēsis* or circumincession. In their affirmation of the persons or hypostases without justifying the difference between them in terms of relationships of origin—although what I have said in the preceding section shows that this does not have to be so absolute—the Orthodox emphasize that, for the Greek Fathers, 'the relations only serve to *express* the hypostatic diversity of the Three; they are not the basis of it. It is the absolute diversity of the three hypostases which determines their differing relations to one another, not *vice versa*.'[10]

So far as these different relationships are concerned, there are not only different relationships of origin, but also different relationships of manifestation and reciprocity.[11] It is one of the most valuable aspects of the Orthodox view of the Tri-unity that the interaction of the Persons is so clearly envisaged, because they are affirmed together and the dependence of the Son and the Spirit with regard to the Father does not point to any immediate priority in the case of the latter. Each Person is always

Trinitarian. This is clearly expressed by Athanasius, for example, who said: 'As the Father has given all things to the Son, the Father again possesses all things in the Son and, as the Son possesses them, the Father again possesses them'.[12] With this datum, that the relationships are always Trinitarian, Paul Evdokimov was even able to say that 'In the act of begetting, the Son receives the Holy Spirit from the Father and therefore, in his being, he is eternally inseparable from the Holy Spirit, so that he is born *ex Patre Spirituque*. In the same way, the Holy Spirit proceeds from the Father and rests on the Son, and this corresponds to *per Filium* and *ex Patre Filioque*.'[13]

If it were simply a question of the birth of the Word made flesh in time, there would be no problem, but we have a discussion of eternal being. The formula can therefore be disputed, because it does not respect the order of the Persons in their eternal being and the fact that, as Basil the Great pointed out, the Spirit is numbered together with the others, but third. Athanasius can also be quoted in this context.[14] Nonetheless, we should welcome this idea of the in-existence of the hypostases one within the other, the idea, in other words, of exchange and reciprocity. It points to the fact that there is a Trinitarian life that does not simply consist of processions or relationships of origin. The Fathers and the Orthodox tell us again and again that the Spirit is received in the Son or that he takes from the Son and, in so doing, they are providing a foundation for relationships of reciprocity, the relationships, in other words, of the *perichōrēsis*. S. Verkhovsky had this to say about the *perichōrēsis*:

> I am sure that the doctrine of the *perichōrēsis* is the best commentary on *di' Huiou*. The Holy Spirit proceeds from the Father with the Son. . . . It is therefore possible to say, although in a hypostatic sense, that the Holy Spirit is for the Son because he is sent by the Father as his hypostatic Spirit, his Life or his Love in the Son. He is the living revelation of the Father to the Son. The Holy Spirit, who is sent by the Father, rests in the Son as an anointing. It is also possible to say that the Holy Spirit, who proceeds from the Father, leaps out towards the Son in order to find in him that Truth, that 'hypostatic Idea of God' that is, for the Holy Spirit, *quasi forma* of his existence as a Person. By receiving in him the hypostatic Wisdom, the Holy Spirit becomes the Spirit of Wisdom, his active Image. He therefore no longer remains in the Son, but comes from him by revealing him and in order to reveal him . . . that principle of the Orthodox triadology that all relationships in God are always Trinitarian. As a result of this, if the Holy Spirit is the revelation of the Father, he is also that revelation both for the Father and for himself and for the Son. If he is a manifestation of the Son, he is also that manifestation for the Son, for himself and for the Father. When the Holy Spirit reveals the Son, then, he reveals him to the Father, and that revelation is also a manifestation of the Son's infinite love for the Father. Thus it is possible to say that the Holy Spirit returns to the only one who has spirated him and he is the union not only of the Father with the Son, but also of the Son with the Father. The real meaning of *dia tou Huiou* is therefore not simply 'with'. It is also 'for' or 'after' (in the sense of the order of the hypostases) or 'from' the Son, but above all 'through' the Son, because the Holy

75

Spirit, in his inexpressible circumincession, proceeding from the Father, passes into the Son and through the Son while at the same time being reflected in him.[15]

This long text, which would be difficult to express in clear Latin theological concepts, indicates the main aspects of the in-existence/reciprocity of the Spirit in the divine Tri-unity. It also provides an interpretation of the 'through the Son' (*di' Huiou*), which the Council of Florence brought close to the meaning of the Latin *Filioque*. Most contemporary Orthodox Christians interpret it, not at the level of the origin of the third hypostasis, but at that of the eternal and immanent manifestation in the first place and then at that of the voluntary and economic manifestation. Gregory of Nyssa, for example, speaks of the Spirit shining eternally through the Son.[16] V. Lossky and other authors whom I have cited have interpreted this within the framework of the Palamite distinction between the essence of the hypostases and the energies.[17] As for the hypostatic procession, they believe that the Spirit comes from the Father alone. There is, however, *in God* and eternally, a procession of the common divinity which is brought about in the Holy Spirit 'through the Son'. In other words, 'in the order of natural manifestation (that is, the common manifestation outside the essence), the Holy Spirit proceeds from the Father through the Son, *dia Huiou*, after the Word, and this procession reveals to us the common glory of the three, the eternal splendour of the divine nature'.[18] 'From all eternity, the Father is "the Father of glory" (Eph 1:17), the Word is "the reflection of his glory" (Heb 1:3) and the Spirit is "the Spirit of glory" (1 Pet 4:14).'[19]

Do the patristic texts that I have cited not call for more than this? Are they not an undefined opening or a beginning, in the sense of pointing to the part played by the Son in the hypostatic existence of the Spirit? I am not alone to think that they are, although it is difficult to say exactly to what extent and in what sense. Probably not in the sense of *a Patre Filioque tanquam ab uno principio*, that is, 'from the Father and the Son *as from a single principle*'.

NOTES

1. S. Bulgakov provides first a number of interesting notes on the pneumatology of the Fathers, and then a personal reflection. He believed that it was necessary to go beyond the debate between the East and the West and, in order to do that, the problem of the origin of the hypostases had to be left aside. In his opinion, 'the divergence expressed by the two traditions—*Filioque* and *dia tou Huiou*—is neither a heresy nor a dogmatic error. It is a difference of theological opinion. There is no dogma about the relationship between the Holy Spirit and the Son': *Le Paraclet* (Paris, 1946), pp. 140–141. His aim was to work out a theology of the Trinity on new foundations and to analyse the inner dynamism of God who is Spirit and Love, and the correlation between the three hypostases who are situated within that absolute and living Subject. God is therefore 'one Person in three hypostases', who reveals himself in Wisdom identified with his *ousia* (this is sophiology, the object of discussion in its own right). An Orthodox theologian like V. Lossky could obviously only

reject this gnosis, since Lossky became the champion of Palamism and, as a member of the Confraternity of St Photius, regarded the *Filioque* as the radical cause of the differences between East and West—differences which he took so far that reconciliation is in danger of being made impossible (I have personally criticized him for this). On the other hand, another of my Orthodox friends, Paul Evdokimov, was more open and favourable to the insights of Bulgakov (whom I met on two occasions).

2. V. Lossky, *The Mystical Theology of the Eastern Church* (Eng. tr.; London, 1957); *idem, In the Image and Likeness of God* (Eng. tr.; London and Oxford, 1975), chapter 4; J. Meyendorff, 'La procession du Saint-Esprit chez les Pères orientaux', and S. Verkhovsky, 'La procession du Saint-Esprit d'après la triadologie orthodoxe', *Russie et Chrétienté* (1950), pp. 158–178 and 197–210 respectively, and the resulting discussions, pp. 193–196 and 219–224 respectively; P. Evdokimov, 'L'Esprit Saint et l'Eglise d'après la tradition liturgique', *L'Esprit Saint et L'Eglise. L'avenir de l'Eglise et de l'Œcuménisme. Symposium de l'Académie Internationale des Sciences religieuses* (Paris, 1960), pp. 85–111; *idem, L'Esprit Saint dans la tradition orthodoxe (Bibl. Œcum.,* 10) (Paris, 1969). See also numerous articles in *Le Messager de l'Exarchat du Patriarche russe en Europe occidentale.*

3. Gregory of Cyprus, 'On the *ekporeusis* of the Holy Spirit' (*PG* 142, 272); Fr. tr. O. Clément in *Istina* (1972), 446. Maximus the Confessor's letter to Marinus of Cyprus can also be mentioned in this context.

4. In this context, it is worth recording Karl Rahner's far-reaching comment: 'It has not been proved that a relationship that is peculiar to a person and a relationship that results in the constitution of a person are necessarily the same': *Mysterium Salutis*, I (Fr. tr.; Paris, 1971), p. 33 [the Eng. tr. (*The Trinity*, London, 1970, p. 26) is less clearly expressed].

5. 'The positive approach employed by Filioquist triadology brings about a certain rationalization of the dogma of the Trinity, insofar as it suppresses the fundamental antinomy between the essence and the hypostases. One has the impression that the heights of theology have been deserted in order to descend to the level of religious philosophy. On the other hand, the negative approach, which places us face to face with the primordial antinomy of absolute identity and no less absolute diversity in God, does not seek to conceal this antinomy but to express it fittingly, so that the mystery of the Trinity might make us transcend the philosophical mode of thinking. . . .' These words come from V. Lossky, *In the Image and Likeness of God, op. cit.*, p. 80; he also says, *ibid.*, p. 88: 'By the dogma of the *Filioque*, the God of the philosophers and savants is introduced into the heart of the Living God, taking the place of the *Deus absconditus, qui posuit tenebras latibulum suum*. The unknowable essence of the Father, Son and Holy Spirit receives positive qualifications. It becomes the object of natural theology: we get "God in General," who could be the god of Descartes, or the god of Leibnitz or even perhaps, to some extent, the god of Voltaire and the dechristianized Deists of the eighteenth century.' Surely this is going too far!

6. An attempt should be made—as I have done—to read M. Schmaus' monumental and massive work (over 1,000 pages), *Der Liber Propugnatorius des Thomas Anglicus und die Lehrunterschiede zwischen Thomas von Aquin und Duns Scotus*, II. Teil: *Die trinitarischen Lehrdifferenzen* (Münster, 1930). The effort merits admiration, and one is bound to appreciate the serious contribution made by the authors studied to the discussion of the arguments. It is certainly not to be despised, but the reasoning and the discussion of terms and concepts obscure the underlying theological insights almost completely.

7. See Athanasius, *Contra Arian.* I, 45; IV, 1 (*PG* 26, 105B, 468B–C); Basil the Great, *De spir. sanct.* XVIII, 47 (*PG* 32, 153B–C); Gregory Nazianzen, *Orat.* 2, 38, 40, 41 (*PG* 35, 445; 36, 417B); Gregory of Nyssa, *De comm. not.* (*PG* 45, 180C); John Damascene, *De fide orthod.* I, 8 (*PG* 94, 829A–C); . To these can be added the images expressing a dynamic linear diagram—the arm, hand and finger (Didymus); the root, branch and fruit (John Damascene); the source, river, sea or water that is drunk (Athanasius, John Damascene), and several others.

8. Gregory Nazianzen, *Orat.* 42, 15 (*PG* 36, 476B).

9. P. Evdokimov, *L'Esprit Saint dans la Tradition orthodoxe*, *op. cit.* (note 2), p. 46.

10. These words are by V. Lossky, *In the Image and Likeness of God*, *op. cit.* (note 2), p. 79. He continues: 'Here thought stands still, confronted by the impossibility of defining a personal existence in its absolute difference from any other, and must adopt a negative approach to proclaim that the Father—He who is without beginning (*anarchos*)—is not the Son or the Holy Spirit, that the begotten Son is neither the Holy Spirit nor the Father, that the Holy Spirit, "who proceeds from the Father," is neither the Father nor the Son. Here we cannot speak of relations of opposition but only of relations of diversity.'

11. P. Evdokimov, *L'Esprit Saint dans la tradition orthodoxe*, *op. cit.* (note 2), p. 41: 'According to Eastern Christians, the relationships between the Persons of the Trinity are not of opposition or separation, but of diversity, reciprocity, reciprocal revelation and communion in the Father'. This is a suitable point at which to point out a serious misunderstanding. Our Orthodox friends often speak of 'relationships of opposition' as a principle by which the Latins distinguish between the hypostases. Thus, in addition to Evdokimov, *op. cit.*, pp. 41, 42 and 65, and *L'Orthodoxie* (Paris 1959), pp. 137–138, Elie Melia, *Russie et Chrétienté* (1950), 223, and Vladimir Lossky, nine times in chapter 4 of *In the Image and Likeness of God*, *op. cit.* have also spoken of this. Is this due to a slip or an omission in reading? But such omissions often point to an unconscious inclination of the mind. To speak of 'a relationship of opposition' instead of 'opposition in relationship' (as in the case of Father–Son or Son–Father) could mean that, for the Latins, the persons are pure relations in essence, but this would point to a lack of understanding, both of the idea of subsistent relationships and of the way in which the Latins think of the diversity of the persons in the unity and simplicity of the divine Absolute.

12. Athanasius, *Contra Arian.* III, 36 (*PG* 26, 401C). For the permanently Trinitarian character of the relationships, see S. Bulgakov, *op. cit.*, (note 1), p. 70, note 67; P. Evdokimov, *L'Esprit Saint dans la tradition orthodoxe*, *op. cit.* (note 2), pp. 42, 70, etc.

13. P. Evdokimov, *ibid.*, pp. 71–72. The formula *Spirituque* can also be found on pp. 77 and 78 and in the last and unfinished work by the same author, 'Panagion et Panagia', *Bulletin de la Société française d'Etudes Mariales*, 27th year (1970), 59–71, especially 62–63. See also below, pp. 158, 164 note 25.

14. Athanasius, *Contra Arian.* III, 24; 'The Son does not participate in the Spirit in order to come about in the Father. He does not receive the Spirit, but rather distributes him to all. It is not the Spirit who unites the Son to the Father; the Spirit rather receives from the Logos' (*PG* 26, 373).

15. S. Verkhovsky, *Istina* (1950), 206–207.

16. Gregory of Nyssa, *Contra Eunom.* I (*PG* 45, 336D, 416C).

17. V. Lossky, *In the Image and Likeness of God*, *op. cit.*, pp. 90–95. Jean Meyendorff, *op. cit.* (note 2), pp. 169ff., keeps as a whole to the order of economic manifestation and communication, even in the texts of Cyril of Alexandria; cf. P. Evdokimov, 'L'Esprit Saint et l'Eglise', *op. cit.*, (note 2), p. 91.

18. Cf. V. Lossky, *In the Image and Likeness of God*, *op. cit.*, p. 93.

19. Cf. *ibid.*, p. 94.

(B) THE WEST AND THE REVELATION OF THE TRI-UNITY OF GOD[1]

It is not my intention to write a history of Christian doctrines, and this means that I do not have to attempt to be complete. I am simply looking for the theological view and possibly for the dogmatic construction that has been formed by Latin Catholicity. For this purpose, it should be sufficient (though still a monumental work) to present: (1) Augustine, who so determined the subsequent development in the West: (2) Anselm; (3) Richard of Saint-Victor and Bonaventure; and (4) Thomas Aquinas. It will then be possible for us to compare, with a full knowledge of the data, the theological approach of Greeks and Latins, that is, of Orthodox Catholics and of Roman Catholics. My ultimate aim, however, is to put forward a theology of the third hypostasis and I hope to do that under the sign of the freedom of grace and the Gift.

That is, of course, an enormous and perhaps excessive plan, but it is one that I regard as necessary in the name of theological honesty. I am all too aware of my own shortcomings. I have only been able to carry out this work in an environment of prayer and the celebration of the mysteries of faith—in other words, in a theological and doxological climate, and in the communion of saints.

NOTES

1. H. B. Swete, *The Holy Spirit in the Ancient Church. A Study of Christian Teaching in the Age of the Fathers* (London, 1912), pp. 295ff.; T. Camelot, 'La tradition latine sur la Procession du Saint-Esprit "a Filio" ou "ab Utroque" ', *Russie et Chrétienté* (1950), 179–192; P. Smulders, 'L'Esprit Saint chez les Pères', *Dictionnaire de Spiritualité*, IV, cols 1272–1283.

1
AUGUSTINE

Here we shall consider, although not exclusively, Augustine's *De Trinitate*, which he began in 399 and handed over to the public in 419.[1] He was not the first Christian in the West to write about the Trinity and the Holy Spirit. He knew the writings of Tertullian and had read the treatise on the Trinity by Hilary of Poitiers (†366),which he quotes. There can also be no doubt that he knew Marius Victorinus, who was greatly influenced by Plotinus (see Volume I, p. 77). He had heard Ambrose of Milan and had probably read his *De Spiritu Sancto* (*c*. 381), which was in many places inspired by Basil the Great and literally by Didymus the Blind and which transfers into Latin thought an exegesis of several passages in the Bible originally made by the Greek Fathers. As far as the latter are concerned, Augustine knew or may have known, in translation, Origen's *De principiis* and Didymus' *De Spiritu Sancto* and the references that he makes to their vocabulary show that he must have had access to the writings of Basil the Great and, at a relatively late period, to those of Gregory Nazianzen, although it is impossible to say exactly to what extent.[2]

Augustine's *De Trinitate* is less dominated than the writings of Athanasius and the Cappadocians by immediate polemics against the fourth-century heretics, although his adversaries were the same as theirs—the Arians and Eunomius. Arianism still had its followers and was at times favoured by those in authority. Augustine had it consciously in mind.[3] He also attacked Sabellius, who affirmed unity in the deity to such a degree that he went so far as to obscure the distinction between the hypostases, whereas the Arians made a distinction between the Word and the Spirit in such a way as to deny their consubstantiality with 'God'. The essential problem was to combine the identity with the distinction of the Persons. This is just how Augustine expressed it.[4] He declared his intention in these words: 'to undertake, with the help of the Lord and as far as we can ourselves, a justification (*reddere rationem*) of this affirmation: the Trinity is one true God and it is exactly true to say, believe and think that the Father, the Son and the Holy Spirit are of one single and the same substance or essence' (*De Trin*. I, 2, 4). A few lines later, he states more precisely the means that he intends to employ. These are firstly the authority of Scripture—he does this in Books I to IV of *De Trinitate*—and then a rational process of discussion—he does this in Books V to VII.

Augustine was sometimes very prolix, but the words that he uses in this context—*dicatur, credatur, intelligatur*—outline a programme. Like the Greek Fathers, he takes as his point of departure what Scripture says, that is, the texts and the terms employed. Later, Thomas Aquinas was to do the same. To a very great extent, the treatises on the Trinity consist of a search for a way of speaking. Is it possible to say this or that, is it wrong to utter a certain sentence? Then, after making sure of the truth by faith, reasoning continues on the basis of the terms chosen. What is sought is an understanding of what is believed.

The Theology of the Relationships

In his *De Trinitate*, then, Augustine takes biblical texts as his point of departure and shows that they disprove the Arian construction (Books I to IV). Then he goes on to consider the problem of an intellectually valid agreement between unity and diversity (Book V). It is necessary, but at the same time sufficient, to distinguish between absolute and relative terms. The terms 'Father', 'Son' and 'Holy Spirit' distinguish the Persons, and they are 'relative' terms, that is, terms of relationship, expressing an *ad aliquid*. *Relative dicuntur ad invicem*, they affirm the Persons by opposing one to the other. Augustine says what the Greek Fathers so often said—the Son is not the Father and the Father is not the Son, but the Father has never been without the Son; one term implies the other. But this 'relative' or 'relational' diversity can exist and does in fact exist within the same substance or, as Augustine preferred to say, 'essence'.

The absolute terms point, on the other hand, to the one substance that is common to all the Persons. 'Good' and 'all-powerful' are such absolute terms. They apply to each of the Persons without diversifying or multiplying the substance—the Father is God; he is also good and he is all-powerful; he is also Creator. The Son is also all this, and so is the Holy Spirit. This does not, however, make three gods or three creators. The Father, the Son and the Spirit are each one Person, and any person affirms himself for himself: *ad se dicitur (not ad aliud)* (*De Trin*. VII, 11). If, however, I search for how or of what it is made, I find inevitably that it consists of a relational opposition—*relative dicitur*, that is, the Son exists by his relationship with the Father and therefore by a relationship of origin or procession. The Persons of the Trinity are therefore, according to the aspect by which they are considered, both relational and absolute. As I. Chevalier pointed out, 'the substance of the Father comes from his being God, not from his being Father; his property as Father, on the other hand, comes from his being in relationship (*ad Filium*). Hence the identity of substance, despite the plurality of relationships; hence also the reality of the relationships which would not exist without that substance.'[5] Augustine did not know or use the term, but he had the fundamental idea of what Thomas Aquinas later called a 'subsistent relationship'.[6] In the same way, even before Thomas, he also expressed the fact that the Father, the Son and the Holy Spirit were one with regard to each other: *alius*, but *non aliud*; each was a different subject, but not of a different substance.[7] This had already been said by Gregory Nazianzen.[8]

It is worth noting in this context that the Greek Fathers recognized the distinction between the hypostases in terms of their relationships, or rather their characterization by correlative terms. In his treatise against Eunomius, for example, Basil accused the latter of translating the relative diversity between the Father and the Son into a diversity of substance.[9] Gregory of Nyssa followed his brother Basil in his defence of the unity of nature and repeated what Basil had said, namely that the words 'Father' and 'Son' are relative terms.[10] In the same way, Gregory Nazianzen stated that 'Father' and 'Son' were names not only of a relationship, but also of a relationship of origin.[11] Augustine only knew of this after 417. To the Cappadocian Fathers, we can also add Maximus the Confessor (†662): 'The name "Father" is neither a name of essence nor a name of energy. It is a name of a relationship and it tells us how the Father is with regard to the Son and how the Son is with regard to the Father.'[12]

In his study of the possible dependence of Augustine on the Greek Fathers, in which he stressed their real agreement in this whole question of relationships,[13] I. Chevalier also noticed certain important differences and commented on them:

> The two terms (*schēsis, oikeiōsis*) which Basil uses to characterize the divine begetting do not represent for him the same hierarchy of ideas that they do for Augustine and the Scholastic theologians. For the Greek doctor, what was in question was the community of nature which exists between a father and a son as a result of begetting. It is this relationship of origin as the only cause of difference between the Father and the Son which, far from destroying their identity, confirms it and explains it. But Basil does not mean to say that, because the unity and identity of the essence of God are presupposed, the immanent begetting can only result in a distinction of relationships. His point of departure is the relationship established by this begetting, and from this he ends up by way of the relationship with the community of nature, whereas Thomas Aquinas, for example, takes the simplicity of God as his point of departure and goes on from that to purely relative terms of procession. This last point of view is also that of Augustine. Although we must take care not to exaggerate it, and above all not to build it up into a system characteristic of 'the Latin mind', we cannot ignore this difference. The part played by the idea of relationship is somewhat changed in it. Basil notes these relationships, but, as it were, granted their divine subjects and above all their source, the begetting *ex ipsa natura* and the procession, he deduces from these the unity of the divine essence. Augustine notes the divine identity and then, since the processions have been revealed, deduces from these the relationships. What we have, then, are the same truths seen from different points of view. There is, surely, nothing surprising in this!

In the case of the Greeks, however, the result is that the idea of relationship is presented in a more realistic and, it could be said, more vital form. It is important to emphasize that the *schēsis* is not seen from a static point of view, that is, as a constitutive principle of the divine hypostasis. This idea is seen rather as a means of expressing the mystery of the divine life, those immanent processions from the one and the return to that one-principle from which those modes of subsistence which are the divine Persons, whose whole reason for existing is to be directed towards each other and who safeguard the unity of the divine essence, eternally come and circulate within each other. These two points of view still come to the same conclusion, namely that the three divine hypostases are distinguished by their properties and the latter are distinguished by differences in origin, which are oppositions of relationship within an essential identity. 'Between the three, everything is identical, apart from the relationship of origin.'[14]

Olivier du Roy has expressed the difference between Augustine and the Greeks in an even more radical way.[15] T. de Régnon tirelessly repeated his own argument, namely that, whereas the Greeks took the Persons as their first data and then showed that they were consubstantial in their unity of nature on the basis of the 'monarchy' of the Father, Augustine and the Latin Fathers took the unity and unicity of 'God' as their starting-point and from that unity of the sovereign divine Being went on to affirm the plurality of the Persons. It cannot be denied that there is an element of truth in what de Régnon maintained, but close examination reveals the emptiness of his formula that the Greeks saw the Persons *in recto* and the unity of the divine essence *in obliquo*, whereas the Latins considered the unity *in recto* and the Persons *in obliquo*. Du Roy does not deny the validity of de Régnon's insight, but points to another origin of difference in the case of Augustine, who undoubtedly had a powerful influence on later Latin theology. Augustine discovered the Trinity in the works of the Neo-Platonists before he discovered the incarnation in the letters of Paul. His approach was not purely theoretical. It was rather the beginning of a very deep existential conversion. As a priest and bishop, dedicated to meditating on the Scriptures and to studying and analysing them with the aim of defending the Christian faith, Augustine kept at heart to his original direction, which differed from that of the Greek Fathers, who spoke of a Tri-unity connected with its economic revelation.[16] Augustine, on the other hand, was fundamentally concerned with a *Deus-Trinitas* thought of in a static manner, independently of the incarnation and the economy of salvation. Du Roy therefore says: 'Augustine's special contribution to Western theology consists of this representation of God who is one in his essence and who deploys the Trinity of his inner relationships in the knowledge and love of himself. This was the logical conclusion of a Neo-Platonism applied to a deep reflection about faith before being converted.'[17]

It is quite certain that Arianism made Christian thinkers apply their minds to a different set of considerations. Before Arianism emerged, the Trinity was seen in its revelation and its economic commitment, at the risk of inclining towards subordinationism. Arianism and Nicaea turned their thoughts towards the unity and consubstantiality of the three Persons. In the case of Augustine, this tendency, which was justified by the persistent influence of Arianism, may have been inherited from and reinforced by his Neo-Platonic past and his own deeper existential approach. Even his reflection about the 'missions' of the Word and the Spirit did not improve the chances that he might consider the economy.[18] He was somewhat hampered by the question of theophanies, which the Arians used very effectively, and he therefore turned to the visible missions of the Word and the Spirit and then to the invisible missions, describing them theologically, on the one hand as a value of manifestation and knowledge and, on the other, by means of their connection with the processions. Even Hilary and Ambrose, whose works Augustine had read, went back from the temporal to the eternal procession. Augustine said: 'Sends, the One who begets; sent is the One who is begotten' (De Trin. IV, 20, 28). The missions reveal a divine Person in his eternal origin. According to Augustine, 'As for the Son to be born is to be from the Father, so for the Son to be sent is to be known in his origin from the Father. In the same way, as for the Holy Spirit to be the gift of God is to proceed from the Father, so to be sent is to be known in his procession from the Father. What is more, we cannot deny that the Spirit also proceeds from the Son. ... I cannot see what he could otherwise have meant when, breathing on the faces of the disciples, the Lord declared: "Receive the Holy Spirit" (Jn 20:20).'[19]

Augustine's thoughts about the theophanies in the first place and then about the divine missions were guided on the one hand by the affirmation of the unity and consubstantiality of God and, on the other, by his related desire to deepen and intensify the image of the Deus-Trinitas in the souls of believers. The soul is more God's image when, because of the knowledge that the Word communicates to it and the love that the Spirit places in it, it makes present the resemblance to the one of whom it is the image. The missions make possible an increase in faith and love.[20]

This theory of the relationships which make the Persons different within the substance or essence without dividing the latter is simple, grand and satisfactory. Nonetheless, it does involve a difficulty in characterizing the Holy Spirit. 'Father' and 'Son' are correlative, terms which comprise an opposition in a reciprocal relationship. If, however, the Spirit is the Spirit of the Father and the Son, as Scripture testifies, how does he affirm two Persons by a reciprocal relational opposition? What correlative term has the Spirit from which he proceeds and which points to a hypostasis? From Photius onwards, the Orthodox have continued to stress this difficulty in opposition to the Filioque. But on this view, which is based exclusively on the terms of

Jn 15:26, the theory of relationships does not fit easily, since, if the Spirit is in a relationship of procession only with the Father, he must be his Son. How, in that case, can he be distinguished from the monogenous one?[21]

Augustine was aware of this difficulty. In his reply to it, he made use of his theology of the Holy Spirit in which he attributed the personal title of Gift to the latter. I shall set out this theology briefly here, since it seems to me to be true and very profound. Augustine notes that 'Spirit' (holy Spirit) can be applied either to the Father or to the Son or can point to the third Person. He has this to say about the third Person:

> There is no need for anxiety (after this remark) about the absence, it would seem, of a term that corresponds to him and points to his correlative. We speak of the servant of the master or of the master of the servant, of the son of the father or of the father of the son, since these terms are correlative, but here we cannot speak in that way. We speak of the Holy Spirit of the Father, but we do not speak in the reverse sense of the Father of the Holy Spirit; if we did, the Holy Spirit would be taken to be his son. In the same way, we speak of the Holy Spirit of the Son, but not of the Son of the Holy Spirit, since, in that case, the Holy Spirit would be seen as his father.
>
> In many relatives, it is not possible to find a term that expresses the reciprocal connection between the relative realities. For example, is there a term that is more manifestly relative than 'pledge' (*pignus*)?[22] A pledge clearly refers to the thing of which it is the pledge[23] and a pledge is always a pledge of something. If we speak of the pledge or guarantee of the Father and the Son (2 Cor 5:5; Eph 1:14), can we speak in the reverse sense of the Father and the Son of the pledge? At least, when we speak of the gift of the Father and the Son, we obviously cannot speak of the Father and the Son of the gift. In order to have a reciprocal correspondence in this case, we must speak of the gift of the giver or the giver of the gift. In this latter case, then, it has proved possible to find a term that is in use, in the other case, not.[24]

It is true that the Father and the Son are not brought together in Scripture under the same title of 'giver', but Scripture does speak of the mission or sending of the Spirit by the Father and by the Son. It is on that basis that it is possible to call the Spirit 'Gift'—Augustine always quotes Acts 8:20, also Rom 5:5 and Jn 4:7—and both the Father and the Son 'givers'. It is therefore on the basis of the economy that Augustine constructs his theology of the eternal procession of the Spirit from the Father and the Son (see note 19), that is, not as 'Father' and as 'Son,' but as 'giver'. I have already said that I think that this theology is very profound. It is also Christian. But it does not, of course, satisfy the Orthodox, who have a different understanding of the Trinity and its homogeneity.

The Filioque

This teaching did not originate with Augustine. It had already been expounded in one form or another by Tertullian, Hilary, Marius Victorinus and Ambrose. Augustine deals with this question only in his *De Trinitate*.

We have to bear in mind that he borrowed a great deal from his commentary on St John and that it is difficult to date with certainty the composition of any particular book in his great work. To begin with, he does no more than simply affirm that the Spirit is the Spirit of the Father and the Son (*De Trin*. I, 4, 7; 5, 8; 8, 18). His point of departure is the fact that the Spirit is said to be both Spirit of the Father (Mt 10:28; Jn 15:26) and Spirit of the Son (Gal 4:6; Jn 14:26; 20:22; Lk 6:19; cf. Rom 8:15). The Spirit, then, is common to both. Thus, if the Spirit is said by Scripture to proceed from the Father (Jn 15:26), it cannot be denied that he also proceeds from the Son (*De Trin*. IV, 20, 29; V, 11, 12; 14, 15). The Son, however, has this faculty of being the co-principle of the Spirit entirely from the Father. Augustine stresses this fact very forcibly, either by using his term *principaliter*[25] or in formulae which could be taken to mean *a Patre solo*.[26] Whichever way he chooses, it is the equivalent of a *per Filium*.

The Spirit, then, is from the Father and the Son. Augustine reflects about this datum, often within the context of his ordinary preoccupations, such as the need to answer certain questions, to reply to the Donatists, or to throw light on the spiritual life of believers and their life in the Church. He says, for example: 'Scripture enables us to know in the Father the principle, *auctoritas*, in the Son being begotten and born, *nativitas*, and in the Spirit the union of the Father and the Son, *Patris Filiique communitas*. . . . The society of the unity of the Church of God, outside of which there is no remission of sins, is in a sense the work of the Holy Spirit, with, of course, the co-operation of the Father and the Son, because the Holy Spirit himself is in a sense the society of the Father and Son. The Father is not possessed in common as Father by the Son and the Holy Spirit, because he is not the Father of the two. The Son is not possessed in common as Son by the Father and the Holy Spirit, because he is not the Son of the two. But the Holy Spirit is possessed in common by the Father and the Son, because he is the one Spirit of the two.'[27]

Augustine was naturally loving and always gave priority to charity. As a pastor and teacher living in the midst of Donatists, he elaborated an ecclesiology at two levels, that of the *sacramentum* and that of *unitas-charitas-Columba*, in which the Spirit was the principle of life, unity and effectiveness to save. Even in his early writings, he called the Spirit *charitas*.[28] This idea emerges from the first evidence of his interest in a theology of the Holy Spirit. It can be found, for example, in his preaching and his commentaries on Scripture.[29] It is clearly present in *De Trin*. VI, 5, 7. Augustine concludes: 'They are three, the one loving the one who has his being from him, the other loving the one from whom he has his being, and that love itself'.

He also showed that, in God, that *charitas* is substantial, because 'God *is* charity' (1 Jn 4:16). This gives rise to a question: the Father is charity, the Son is also charity, and the *Deus-Trinitas* is also charity. Since it is substantial, then, how is it peculiar to the Spirit and characteristic of his Person? This question is not answered until the last book of the treatise (XV, 17, 27ff.). The answer is first of all related to the economy—it is the Spirit who gives us charity (XV, 17, 31 to 19, 35)—and then the answer is given at the intra-divine level (XV, 19, 36ff.), the Spirit being the substantial communion of the Father and the Son, *communio amborum*, because *communis ambobus*. Being common to the Father and the Son, he receives as his own the names that are common to both of them (XV, 19, 37).

Before concluding his treatise on the Trinity with a humble prayer, Augustine replies to the following difficulty: 'If the Holy Spirit proceeds from the Father and the Son, why does the Son say: the Spirit proceeds from the Father (Jn 15:26)?' In answering this question, he repeats the reply that he had already given a little earlier in his commentary *In Ioan. ev.* XCIX, 8–9, namely that the Father communicates to the Son all that he is, apart from his being Father. Thus, all that the Son has comes from the Father and is from the Father. This reminds us inevitably of the *principaliter* discussed above. Just as he said: 'My teaching is not mine, but his who sent me' (Jn 7:16), when he said 'the Spirit proceeds from the Father' the Son did not mean: 'He does not proceed from me'. There are therefore good reasons to believe that the Spirit also proceeds from the Son. It is clear, however, that the Orthodox could not declare themselves satisfied with this.

A Note on Augustine's Theology of the Trinity and the Eastern Tradition

In anticipation of a conclusion which I shall be in a better position to maintain at the end, when the situation has been fully examined, I can say now that what we have here are two theological constructions of the same mystery, each of which has an inner consistency, but a different point of departure.

Augustine's aim was to guarantee the perfect consubstantiality of the three Persons. He made sure of this by making the distinction between them consist in the relationship which opposes them correlatively to each other and which is a relationship of procession. The relationship between the Father and the Son does not give rise to any questions—it is clear, and our own experience provides a striking analogy. The Spirit is distinguished relationally from the two in the unity of the divine essence only by proceeding from the two as their common Spirit. If he did not proceed from the Son, he would not be distinguished from him by that relationship which safeguards the divine equality and consubstantiality. As H. B. Swete, who, as a historian, was not disposed to speculate, said: 'the Western *Filioque*, as Augustine states it, is almost a necessary inference from the Homoousion'.[30]

An initial difference, not to say difficulty, comes from the vocabulary. The same Latin verb, *procedere*—although Augustine also says *exire* (*De Trin.* V, 14, 15)—is used to translate the *proeimi* or the *erchomai* of Jn 8:42 and the *ekporeuomai* of Jn 15:26, although the Greeks make a distinction be-tween these terms in that the second, which is reserved for the 'procession' of the Holy Spirit, refers to the Father as the original source. From the time of Gregory Nazianzen—who did not give the matter any polemical emphasis—the Greeks have on many occasions remarked that the Latin lacks the subtlety of the Greek. In theological Latin, the word 'procession', means the fact of coming from another, in the more general sense. It therefore includes the sense of the Greek *ekporeusis*, but does not express the shade of meaning given to this word as a procession from an original and absolute principle.

The Greeks thought of and justified consubstantiality in terms of the monarchy of the Father,[31] the *perichōrēsis* and the Trinitarian character of all the relationships. In itself, the monarchy of the Father is not opposed to the Spirit's also deriving from the Son. This is clear from the various images that we have previously considered: the images of the arm, the hand and the finger (Didymus), the root, the branch and the fruit (John Damascene) and the source, the river and the water, as well as others. All these images illustrate a theology of the procession of the Spirit from the Father through the Son. It has to be recognized, however, that the Latin vocabulary fails to express the value that the Greeks rightly place on the *ekporeuetai* of Jn 15:26. Having said that, we can also say with Pusey in the nineteenth century that we in the West also condemn the heresy for which we have been criticized since the time of Photius, because the real meaning of the *Filioque* is quite different.

As we have already seen, the Greek Fathers were familiar with the category 'relationship'. This applies particularly to Gregory the Theologian. The concept, however, plays only an occasional part in their writings,[32] whereas, in the work of Augustine and Thomas Aquinas, it helps to justify the diversity of the hypostases in the unity of substance. The Greeks appeal to the particular character of each hypostasis as different from that of another.[33] They do this within a theological climate that is more apophatic than that of the Latins, although these too do not lack the apophatic sense.[34]

The idea of the Holy Spirit as communion between the Father and the Son is exceptional in the East. In the patristic period, it is only to be found in the writings of Epiphanius of Salamis.[35] Gregory Palamas was, however, also familiar with it and said, for example: 'The Spirit of the Word is like a love (*erōs*) of the Father for the mysteriously begotten Word, and it is the same love that the beloved Word and Son of the Father has for the one who begot him. That love comes from the Father at the same time as it is with the Son and it naturally rests on the Son.'[36] We should not therefore be surprised to find Sergey Bulgakov writing in this century: 'if God, in the Holy Trinity, is Love, then the Holy Spirit is Love of that love'.[37] No more surprising is the profound comment of Paul Evdokimov on the Person in the centre of the Andrei Rublev's wonderful icon; the Holy Spirit, he says, 'is in the middle of the Father and the Son. He is the one who brings about the communion between the two. He is the communion, the love between the Father and the Son. That is clearly shown by the remarkable fact that the movement comes from him. It is in his breath that the Father moves into the Son, that the Son receives his Father and that the word resounds.'[38]

These pieces of evidence are not sufficient, of course, to form a theological tradition, but they do create a link and point to an openness. 'The walls of separation do not reach as high as heaven!'

The Images of the Trinity[39]

Augustine continued, in Books VIII to XV of his *De Trinitate*, to look for an understanding of what Christians believed and he did this on the basis of the images of the Triad that could be found in the human spirit and its activity. It was, for him, certainly not a question of deducing a Trinity of Persons philosophically from the structure of man's spirit, as Hegel, Günther and perhaps also Gioberti have claimed to do. For Augustine, it was a search in faith, one which becomes deeper by an existential conversion to be conformed once again to the image of God by thinking of him and loving him. (The stages are: *credere Deo, credere Deum, credere in Deum, credendo in Deum ire*.) Augustine therefore analysed a series of triads, moving from more external ones to more intimate ones and from simple psychological analysis to an expression of supernatural experience. The following summary has been provided by Fulbert Cayré (*Bibl. August.* 16, p. 587):

1. *amans, amatus, amor* (*De Trin.* VIII, 10, 14; cf. IX, 2, 2);
2. *mens, notitia, amor* (IX, 3, 3);
3. *memoria, intelligentia, voluntas* (X, 11, 7);
4. *res (visa), visio (exterior), intentio* (XI, 2, 2);
5. *memoria (sensibilis), visio (interior), volitio* (XI, 3, 6–9);
6. *memoria (intellectus), scientia, voluntas* (XII, 15, 25);
7. *scientia (fidei), cogitatio, amor* (XIII, 20, 26);
8. *memoria Dei, intelligentia Dei, amor Dei* (XIV, 12, 15).

A little later, Cayré observes, Augustine wrote his *De Civitate Dei* and, in Book XI, 24–28 of this work there are six similar triads.[40] Each time and in related terms, Augustine finds in the structure of the soul (see A. Gardeil, note 39 below) and in the way in which it is supernaturally actualized an image of the Holy Triad: three in the unity of the same substance; one stable consciousness of self, one act of knowledge and one movement of love. To make God, the Christian God, present in these three aspects is to experience a conversion and restore the image.[41] It is also being able to perceive how the manifestations of the Persons in the economy and the three whom we confess in the baptismal formula are one inseparable Trinity.[42] In this way, the personalization and the consubstantial unity of the *Deus-Trinitas* are united.

In this case too, the way followed by Augustine has hardly any parallel in the East, apart from the theme of man's re-formation in the image and likeness of God.[43] In this case too, however, there is once again a parallel in the East in the work of Gregory Palamas, who drew attention to the analogy of the Holy Triad in the soul, with the *nous*, the *logos* and the *erōs*.[44] There can be little doubt that Gregory had read Maximus Planudes' translation of Augustine.

Augustine was very conscious of the distance separating the image from the model. Both his *Sermo* 52 and Book XV of his *De Trinitate* end with his expressing his feeling of inadequacy and with an appeal to prayer, thanks to which God may himself give man an experience and a knowledge of his mystery. Again and again Augustine expresses his awareness of the fact that the similitudes are dissimilar.[45]

In the same Book XV, Augustine looks back at what he has already written and expresses the feeling that he has spoken more about the Father and the Word than about the Holy Spirit. He therefore resolves to devote several chapters (17–20 and 26–27) to the latter. I too have the feeling that I have discussed Augustine's Trinitarian theology more than his pneumatology. One is, of course, contained within the other. As there are so many excellent texts, several of which I have quoted in Volume II of this work, I shall only consider two groups.

A.-M. La Bonnardière noted that 'from 387 to 429, Augustine quoted at least 201 times the verse of St Paul: "God's love has been poured into our hearts through the Holy Spirit which has been given to us" (Rom 5:5). His quotations of this verse were relatively rare until 411 (51 in all), but they became very frequent in the decade 411–421, which was the period in which he was engaged in controversy with the Pelagians over the question of grace, and they continued afterwards in his works of controversy with Julian of Eclanum.'[46] In fact the criticism which the Bishop of Hippo made of the Bishop of Eclanum was as follows: 'You would like to make the grace of Christ consist in his example and not in his life. You say that man is made righteous by imitating him, and not by the help of the Holy Spirit who leads him to imitate him, that Spirit whom he has poured out so abundantly on his own.'[47] The Spirit is the principle of all life according to the grace that Augustine continued throughout his Christian life to preach, discuss and further.

For the edification of his people and in his struggle against the Donatists, Augustine developed and defined more precisely the part played by the Spirit in the Church. There are dozens of texts to be found in his works, each one more magnificent than the last. There are, for example, those in which he shows how the Spirit brings about in the mystical Body of Christ what the soul brings about in our body. S. Tromp listed 83 of these texts, either as extracts or as references.[48] There is also the ecclesiology that Augustine developed in his controversy with the Donatists at two levels, that of the *sacramentum*, that is, the signs and institutions that the Donatists had in common with the Catholics, and that of the *res*, that is, the spiritual fruit that saves, which the Donatists did not have, the principle of which is the Holy Spirit.[49] The Spirit, for Augustine, was not only the principle of unity. He was also the principle of that catholicity which consists of the variety of gifts in the communion of the same Body.[50]

NOTES

1. See the *Œuvres de S. Augustin*, 15: *La Trinité*, Fr. tr. M. Mellet and T. Camelot, with an introduction by E. Hendrikx; 16, Fr. tr. P. Agaësse, with notes by J. Moingt (Paris, 1955); a full bibliography of works published up to that date will be found in these volumes, which give column references to *PL* 42. Apart from the works listed in note 29 on Volume I, p. 83, and articles mentioned below, see O. du Roy, *L'intelligence de la foi en la Trinité selon S. Augustin. Genèse de sa théologie trinitaire jusqu'en 391* (Paris, 1966); J. Verhees, 'Die Bedeutung des Geistes im Leben des Menschen nach Augustinus frühester Pneumatologie', *Zeitschrift für Kirchengeschichte*, 88 (1977), 161–189. I consider principally, but not exclusively, the *De Trinitate* in this section of my book. Arranged in terms and themes, a mass of other Augustinian texts dealing with the Holy Spirit will be found in the articles of F. Cavallera and these, however material they are, or rather, precisely because they are material, can be of great use in this respect: 'La doctrine de S. Augustin sur l'Esprit Saint à propos du "De Trinitate" ', *RTAM*, 2 (1930), 365–387; 3 (1931), 5–19.

2. I. Chevalier has concluded from a careful study: 'It is certain that Augustine read Athanasius', Basil's and Gregory Nazianzen's works on the Trinity as well as Epiphanius' *Recapitulation*, but it is probable, or simply possible, that he also knew the latter's *Panarion* and *Ancoratus* and the two works on the Trinity by Didymus the Blind': *S. Augustin et la pensée grecque. Les relations trinitaires* (Fribourg, 1940), p. 160.

3. *De Trin.* V, 3, 4; 6, 7; VI, 1, 1; see also *Contra sermonem arianorum* (418–419); *Collatio cum Maximino* and *Contra Maximinum*.

4. *In Ioan. ev.* 39; *De Civ. Dei* XI, 10; *De Trin.* I, 2, 4; 3, 5; 5, 8; VI, 6, 8; VIII, proem.; XV, 3, 5; *Enarr. in Ps.* 68; *Ep.* 170, 238.

5. I. Chevalier, *op. cit.* (note 2), p. 63, commenting on the following text, which resists translation: 'Quidquid est Pater quod Deus est, hoc Filius, hoc Spiritus Sanctus. Cum autem Pater est, non illud est quod est, Pater enim non ad se, sed ad Filium dicitur: ad se autem Deus dicitur. Itaque eo quod Deus est, hoc ipso substantia est . . . secundum substantiam tibi dixi hoc esse Filium quod Pater est, non secundum id quod ad aliud dicitur' (*Enarr. in Ps.* 68, 5; *PL* 36, 845): 'All that the Father is in that he is God, the Son is, the Holy Spirit is. But when one takes him as Father, he is not what he is thus, but he is taken in his relationship to the Son. It is in his being in itself that he is called God. Thus, from the fact that he is God, he is substance . . . and it is according to the substance that I have said that the Son is what the Father is, not according to what he is described in relationship to another (another thing).'

6. Thomas Aquinas, *De Pot.* q. 9, a. 1 and 2; *ST* Ia, q. 29, a. 4. It is clearly because of his Thomist training that I. Chevalier, *op. cit.*, p. 76, spoke of 'a double character of relationship—a character of inhering in, expressing the need of a subject in order to exist at all, and a character that is specific (*ad*), expressing an entering into a relationship with another'. But this is certainly Augustine's idea.

7. Augustine, *De anima et eius origine*, II, 5 (*PL* 44, 509); see the references in I. Chevalier, *op. cit.* (note 2), p. 62.

8. Gregory Nazianzen, *Orat.* 31 (*PG* 36, 141ff.); the Son is not the Father, but he is *what* the Father *is*. The Holy Spirit is not the Son, but he is *what* the Son *is*.

9. Basil, *PG* 29, 588C–589A; Fr. tr. in I. Chevalier, *op. cit.* (note 2), p. 131.

10. See Gregory of Nyssa, *Quod non sint tres dii* (*PG* 45, 133C) and other references in I. Chevalier, *op. cit.*, p. 103; see also T. de Régnon, *Etudes de théologie positive sur la Sainte Trinité*, I (Paris, 1892), pp. 77–78.

11. See Gregory Nazianzen, *Orat.* 29 (*PG* 36, 96); 31 (*PG* 36, 140C and 141C); I. Chevalier, *op. cit.*, pp. 146–147; de Régnon, *op. cit.*, I, pp. 76–77.

12. Maximus, *Ambigua* 26 (*PG* 91, 1265C-D).

13. Chevalier goes so far as to say, *op. cit.* (note 2), p. 174: 'The famous axiom "In God all is one, except where there is an opposition of relationship" is Greek as much as Latin in all its parts. Although it is not stated in exactly the same form and although it does not play precisely the same part as it does in Augustine, it is familiar to both. The Greek doctors always taught that the persons are distinguished by their properties, but that those properties should be seen as mutual relationships. They rejected as absurd the fact that they might be accidents. It is no more than a single step from this to the synthesis, subsistent relationship, but they did not make that step.'

14. Gregory Nazianzen, *Orat.* 34 (*PG* 36, 253A); 20 (*PG* 35, 1073A); 31 (*PG* 36, 165B); 41 (*PG* 36, 441C); quoted in I. Chevalier, *op. cit.*, pp. 168–169.

15. O. du Roy, in his difficult, but very suggestive thesis, *op. cit.* (note 1).

16. O. du Roy adopted an attitude that was opposite to that of A. Malet in *Personne et Amour dans la théologie trinitaire de S. Thomas d'Aquin* (Paris, 1956); Malet's claims are taken up by M.-J. Le Guillou in *Istina*, 17 (1972), 457–464, and *Le Mystère du Père* (Paris, 1973). The Cappadocians apparently abandoned the ante-Nicene view of the economy, according to Le Guillou, and taught a primacy of essence. G. Lafont, *Peut-on connaître Dieu en Jésus-Christ?* (Paris, 1969), pp. 67ff., and L. Scheffczyk, *Mysterium Salutis*, V (Fr. tr.; Paris, 1970), pp. 252, 261, have a similar attitude.

17. O. du Roy, *op. cit.* (note 1), p. 458.

18. Augustine discusses the 'missions' in *De Trin.* II, 5, 7–10; IV, 18, 24 to 20, 29; see also I, 22, 25; II, 7, 12–13; 12, 22; III, proem. 3 and 1, 4. See also J.-L. Maier's monograph, *Les Missions divines selon S. Augustin* (*Paradosis*, XVI) (Fribourg, 1960).

19. *De Trin.* IV, 20, 29. This link between the temporal mission and the eternal procession of the Spirit, with reference to the text of Jn 20:22, can also be found in *De Trin.* XV, 26, 45; *De Gen. ad litt.* 10, 5; *De Civ. Dei*, XIII, 24; *In Ioan. ev.* XCIX, 7 and CXXI, 4; *Contra Maxim.* II, 14, 1; see Cavallera, *op. cit.* (note 1) (1931), 17; Maier, *op. cit.* (note 18), p. 152. Only the Father is not sent 'quoniam solus non habet auctorem a quo genitus sit vel a quo procedat': *Contra serm. arian.* 4, 4 (*PL* 42, 686).

20. For faith, *De Trin.* IV, 20, 28; for charity, *In Ioan. ev.* LXXIV, 3.

21. In the colloquium that took place in 1950 between Orthodox and Catholic Christians, S. Verkhovsky reaffirmed that 'the Son and the Spirit as hypostases coming from the Father are sufficiently distinguished, so that there is no need to affirm an opposition of relationship between them'. H. Dondaine's response to this was: 'The Son is distinguished from the Father because he is a hypostasis coming from the Father. In the same way, the Holy Spirit is distinguished from the Father. How does that distinguish the Son from the Holy Spirit?': see *Russie et Chrétienté* (1950), 223.

22. 'Pledge' or 'guarantee' is one of the names for the Holy Spirit in the New Testament: 'You ... were sealed with the promised Holy Spirit, which is the guarantee (*arrabōn*) of our inheritance' (Eph 1:14). In 2 Cor 1:22 and 5:5, *arrabōn tou Pneumatos*, the genitive is a genitive of apposition: see H. Behm, '*arrabōn*', *TDNT*, I, p. 475; cf. Rom 8:23, *aparchē tou Pneumatos*. Augustine's texts on *pignus* have been gathered together by F. Cavallera, *op. cit.* (note 1) (1930), 370.

23. 'Ad id quippe refertur cuius est pignus'; is it not possible and even necessary to translate this as 'a pledge refers to that from which it comes as a pledge (to the being of which it is the pledge)'? Otherwise the sentence says the same thing twice.

24. *De Trin*. V, 12, 13. I. Chevalier said, for example (and I give in brackets what he placed in notes): 'By the character of his procession, which is holiness, love or gift, the Holy Spirit on the one hand ensures the unity of spirit of the Father and the Son and, on the other hand, the same Holy Spirit is distinguished from each of them (*De Trin*. VI, 5, 7; XV, 17–20). If there is a relative meaning, it is that he takes his origin from the Father and the Son. He proceeds as a Gift and the latter are a single Giver. The Giver and the Gift are, then, essentially relative (V, 14, 15; 15, 16; 16, 17). That Gift and that giving are, like the Giver, eternal (V, 15, 16; 16, 17). The relationships that result from the second procession are therefore no more accidents than the relationships of the Son and the Father': *op. cit.* (note 2), pp. 79 and 81.

25. *De Trin*. XV, 17, 29 and 26, 47; *Sermo* 71, 26 (*PL* 38, 459); see the crit. ed. in *RBén*, 75 (1965), 94. The term *principaliter* can be found in Tertullian, *Adv. Prax*. 3. The following is the first of these texts: 'God the Father, the only one from whom the Word is begotten and from whom the Holy Spirit proceeds as from his original principle (*principaliter*). I say "as from his original principle", because it is proven that the Holy Spirit also proceeds from the Son. But it is also the Father who gives him'; cf. *De Trin*. IV, 20, 29: 'totius divinitatis, vel, si melius dicitur, deitatis, principium est Pater'; *De vera rel*. 31, 58: '(Filius) non de seipso est, sed primo summoque principio, qui Pater dicitur: ex quo omnis paternitas' (*PL* 34, 148).

26. Apart from the text quoted in the preceding note, it is also possible to cite from *De fid. et symb*. IX, 19 (in 393): 'nulli debere sed Patri ex quo omnia, ne duo constituamus principia sine principio'; *Contra Maxim*. II, 14 (428): 'cum de illo (Spiritus) Filius loqueretur ait "de Patre procedit", quoniam Pater processionis eius est auctor qui talem Filium genuit et gignendo ei dedit ut etiam de ipso procederet Spiritus Sanctus'.

27. *Sermo* 71, 18 and 33 (*PL* 38, 454 and 463–464); crit. ed. P. Verbraken, *RBén*, 75 (1965), 82 and 102. Augustine worked at this text intensely, because he was treating in it the *difficillima quaestio* of blasphemy against the Holy Spirit; it was written about 417.

28. *De quant. anim*. 34, 77 (388 A.D.): 'in quo omnia, id est incommutabile principium, incommutabilem sapientiam, incommutabilem charitatem, unum Deum verum' (*PL* 32, 1077); *De mus*. VI, 17, 56 (389); 'qua inter se unum et de uno unum charissima, ut ita dicam, charitate junguntur' (*PL* 32, 1191); *De fid. et symb*. IX, 19–20 (393), where Augustine reported the opinion of those (Marius Victorinus) for whom the Spirit was the Deity, or the charity that was common to the Father and the Son. Valuable in this context is the rather complicated, but very rich study written by J.-B (= O.) du Roy, 'L'expérience de l'amour et l'intelligence de la foi trinitaire selon S. Augustin', *Recherches Augustiniennes* II: *Hommage au R.P. Fulbert Cayré* (Paris, 1962), pp. 415–445.

29. See the reference and texts quoted in F. Cavallera, *op. cit.* (note 1) (1930), 382 ff.

30. H. B. Swete, *The Holy Spirit in the Ancient Church* (London, 1912), p. 353.

31. See Gregory Nazianzen, *Orat*. 42, 15 (*PG* 36, 476).

32. This was observed by W. Ullmann in 'Das Filioque als Problem ökumenischer Theologie', *Kerygma und Dogma*, 16 (1970), 58–76, especially 64; the article as a whole is disappointing in view of what the title suggests.

33. See Gregory Nazianzen, *Orat*. 25 (*PG* 35, 1221): what is peculiar to the Father is that he cannot be born, to the Son his being begotten, and to the Spirit his procession (*ekporeusis*); Gregory of Nyssa, *Contra Eunom*. I, 22 (*PG* 45, 355ff.): 'In his uncreated nature, the Holy Spirit is united with the Father and the Son and is, on the other hand, distinguished from them by the marks that are peculiar to him (*tois idiois gnōrismasin*). His most characteristic mark is that he is nothing of what is rightly thought peculiar to the Father and the Son—he is neither unbegotten nor monogenous, but he is simply what he is. One with the Father in that he is uncreated, he is distinguished from him in that he is not Father. One with the Son, since both are uncreated and derive their substance from the God of all things, he differs

from the Son in that he is not monogenous and has been manifested by the Son'; Leontius of Byzantium (†c. 543), *De sectis*, 1 (*PG* 86, 1196): 'These three Persons differ from one another in no way, except for their properties. . . . The Son and the Spirit differ only in this, that the Son is begotten of the Father and the Spirit proceeds from him. We do not have to look for how the one is begotten and the other proceeds'; Anastasius of Sinai, *Hodēgos* (*PG* 89, 60).

34. V. Lossky has himself pointed to this in the case of Augustine: 'Les éléments de "Théologie négative" dans la pensée de S. Augustin', *Augustinus Magister*, I (Paris, 1945), pp. 575ff.

35. The Holy Spirit is *sundesmos tēs Triados*: see Epiphanius' *Anc.* 7 (*PG* 43, 28B).

36. Gregory Palamas, *Cap*. 36 (*PG* 150, 1144D–1145A).

37. S. Bulgakov, *Le Paraclet* (Paris, 1946), p. 74. Augustine is quoted. The theme is connected with Bulgakov's personal construction.

38. P. Evdokimov, 'L'icône', *VS*, 82 (1956), 24–27, especially 36.

39. M. Schmaus, *Die psychologische Trinitätslehre des heiligen Augustinus* (Münster, 1927); A. Gardeil, *La structure de l'âme et l'expérience mystique* (Paris, 1927); F. Cayré, 'Le mysticisme de la sagesse dans les Confessions et le De Trinitate de S. Augustin', *Année théolog. august.*, 13 (1953), 347–370; G. B. Ladner, 'St. Augustine's Conception of the Reformation of Man in the Image of God', *Augustinus Magister*, II (Paris, 1954), pp. 867–878; P. Verbraken, 'Le sermon LII de S. Augustin sur la Trinité et l'analogie des facultés de l'âme', *RBén*, 74 (1964), 9–35.

40. The last three triads are: 4. *sumus, novimus, diligimus* (*De Civ. Dei* XI, 26 and 27); 5. *essentia, notitia, amor* (XI, 28); 6. *aeternitas, veritas, caritas* (XI, 28). Complete tables either of the most diverse triads or of the Trinitarian images and comparisons in the works of Augustine will be found in the French translation, *Bibl. August.* 15, p. 571 and in O. du Roy, *op. cit.* (note 1), pp. 537–540.

41. G. B. Ladner, *The Idea of Reform. Its Impact on Christian Thought and Action in the Age of the Fathers* (Cambridge, Mass., 1959), pp. 185–203.

42. In *De Trin*. XV, 7, 12; 17, 28; 20, 37, Augustine insists on the fact that each of the three Persons is memory, understanding and love, because they are only one substance. In his *Sermo* 52 (*PL* 38, 354–364; see also P. Verbraken, *op. cit.* (note 39)), Augustine shows that the three Persons reveal themselves *separabiliter* in the economy, while acting *inseparabiliter*. Then, treading on very delicate ground as a teacher, he explains this by the analogy of our soul, our activity and our experience. At the level of the economic revelation, he seems to go beyond simple appropriation (*De Trin*. XV, 21).

43. This is found above all in Gregory of Nyssa; see G. B. Ladner, *op. cit.* (note 41), pp. 96ff.; H. Merki, *Homoiōsis Theō* (Fribourg, 1952).

44. Gregory Palamas, *Cap*. 35–39 (*PG* 150, 1144–1147). See also the *Confession* of Gennadius Scholarios (*c*. 1450): spirit, reason and will. Other approaches to this theme can also be found—in Gregory of Nyssa, for example, who said: 'The one therefore who sees himself sees in himself the object of his desires . . . looking at his own purity, he sees the archetype in the image': *Beatitudes*, 6 (*PG* 44, 1272); Photius: 'God, in his pre-eternal counsel, decreed to place the logos in man so that man would approach in his own structure the enigma of Theology': *Amph.* CCLII.

45. For *similitudo dissimilis*, see *Ep*. 169, 6; *De Trin*. I, 1; V, 8; VIII, 5 and 6; XV, 5; 16; 20; 23 and throughout.

46. A.-M. La Bonnardière, 'Le verset paulinien Rom. V, 5, dans l'œuvre de S. Augustin', *Augustinus Magister*, I (Paris, 1945), pp. 657–665, especially pp. 657 and 658.

47. *Opus imperfect. Contra Julianum* II, 146 (*PL* 45, 1209). In what follows, Rom 5:5 is quoted. The Spirit gives charity: *De Trin*. XV, 18, 32.

48. S. Tromp, *De Spiritu Sancto anima Corporis mystici*. II: *Testimonia selecta e Patribus latinis* (Rome, 1952). See also F. Hofmann, *Der Kirchenbegriff des heiligen Augustinus* (Munich, 1933), pp. 148–173. It is also possible to quote passages from Augustine's *Sermo* 71, for example, 71, 33 (*PL* 38, 463–464); see above, note 27.

49. See my general introduction to Augustine's anti-Donatist treatises, *Bibl. August.*, 28 (Paris, 1963), pp. 109–115. The following text is relevant here: 'Isti autem (donatistae) . . . non sunt desperandi: adhuc enim sunt in corpore. Sed non quaerant Spiritum Sanctum nisi in Christi corpore, cuius habent foris sacramentum, sed rem ipsam non tenent intus, cuius illud est sacramentum. . . . Extra hoc corpus, neminem vivificat Spiritus Sanctus': *Ep.* 185, 50 (*PL* 33, 815).
50. For example, *Sermo* 267, 4 (*PL* 38, 1231); 268, 2 (*PL* 38, 1232–1233); *De Trin.* XV, 19, 34.

Augustine's profound thought and valuable work provided material for the reflection of Christian teachers in the Middle Ages. In the theology of the Trinity, he opened two great ways, each of which was followed further in mediaeval thinking. The first of these took up the analysis of the activities of the spirit, understanding and love, and was followed above all by Anselm and Thomas Aquinas. The second way followed the theme of God-charity and the Spirit as the mutual love between the Father and the Son. This was the way which attracted, with individual differences, Achard and Richard of Saint-Victor, Bonaventure and the Franciscan school.

2

ANSELM (1033 – 1109)

Anselm wrote his *Monologion c.* 1070 as Abbot of Bec. During one of his exiles, he took part in a council held at Bari in 1098 with the bishops of the Greek rite of Apulia, Calabria and Sicily. In 1100, when he was at Canterbury, where he died as Archbishop on 21 April 1109, he finished a treatise *De Processione Spiritus Sancti*. His theology of the third Person of the Trinity, which had an undoubted influence on early and high Scholastic thought, is to be found in these two treatises.[1]

Anselm's point of departure is Augustine's psychological analogies, since it is clear that Augustine was his master,[2] but he dealt with them as a born metaphysician and used arguments which strictly inter-linked and were expressed in precise and sober language, the only beauty of which is its exactness. In the *Monologion*, he declares his intention: to understand, by the use of reason, what he believes. He does this in accordance with a statement made elsewhere: 'I thank you, because what I already believed by your grace I now understand by your illumination, to the point that, if I refused to believe it, my understanding would force me to recognize it'.[3]

Anselm believed that the fact that the spirit, and therefore the *summus spiritus* as well, could produce an act of intellectual understanding and therefore a word—he did not make a distinction between the act and its term[4]—and that, in knowing itself, it could love itself, could be traced back to a nature and a necessity of what the spirit was. It was, in his view, a simple and absolute perfection, like goodness or wisdom. As a result, it was necessary to affirm it in God. In us it was, of course, no more than a likeness of what was perfect in God.[5] This was enough for Anselm to state, as a necessary reason, the existence in the *summus spiritus* or *summa natura* of a memory, an understanding and a love of itself, in which he saw the Father, the Son and the Holy Spirit.

This intellectual understanding or Word is the Son because he comes from the supreme spirit as his image and likeness and therefore *nascendo*, *sicut proles parentis*.[6] This is the beginning of a plurality within the unity of God. The *parens* and his *proles* are a single supreme spirit, *unus spiritus*, distinguished from each other and made two by the relationship which makes one Father and the other Son: 'Sic sunt oppositi relationibus, ut alter numquam suscipiat proprium alterius; sic sunt concordes natura, ut alter semper teneat essentiam alterius'.[7] Their essence is identical, but they are distinguished in that one essence by the pure relationship of the one who begets and the one who is begotten.

As early as the *Monologion* (chapter 49 onwards), Anselm states that the supreme spirit loves himself because he is memory and understanding of himself; that the Father loves himself, the Son loves himself, and that they love each other (*Mon.* 51). That love is simply what the Father and the Son are, that is, the *summa essentia* (*Mon.* 53). It is a single, unique love (*Mon.* 54). It is not 'son' and it does not verify the quality of likeness that is brought about by the Word (*Mon.* 55). Only the Father is *genitor* and *ingenitus*. The Son is *genitus*, and the Spirit, who is the love of the two, is neither *genitus* nor *ingenitus* (*Mon.* 56). Thus Memory, Understanding and Love are identical *essentialiter*, that is, through and in the divine essence (*Mon.* 60), and they are one in each other (*Mon.* 59—although Anselm does not use the term, he is clearly speaking of circumincession). They are identical in *summa essentia* and yet they are not confused because, in that identity of essence and activities, there is a *genitor*, a *genitus* and a *procedens* (*Mon.* 61).

When he speaks of the Spirit, Anselm always uses this term, which is biblical and which comes close to the practice of the Greek Fathers. The *quomodo sit*, that is, the manner of that procession, the intimate being of the three whose existence can be deduced by reason, goes beyond our understanding, however, and cannot be expressed (*Mon.* 64–65). Anselm therefore concludes that there is 'a unity because of the unity of essence; a trinity because of the three I know not what (*trinitatem propter tres nescio quid*)' (*Mon.* 79; see Schmitt, *op. cit.* (note 1 below), I, p. 85). It is therefore hardly possible to say 'three Persons' because persons exist separately from each other—they are, in other words, individual substances. It is only because it is necessary to speak and because usage authorizes one to speak that, having expressed oneself clearly about the unity of the absolute essence, one can speak at all about an essence and about three Persons or substances.[8]

Dealing with the procession of the Holy Spirit, Anselm speaks at some depth in the treatise that resulted from his participation in the Council of Bari. In *De processione Spiritus Sancti*, he no longer tries, as he did in the earlier treatise, to understand what he believes by drawing attention to the inner consistency and logical necessity of the affirmations of faith. He takes as his point of departure what the Western Church has in common with the Greeks in faith in God and his Tri-unity in order to lead them to agreement with the West in the article on the procession of the Holy Spirit 'a Patre *et Filio*'. There are two possible ways which can be followed in this, and Anselm in fact follows each in turn. The first is the way of logical argument (the two very long and difficult chapters which open *De Processione Spiritu Sancto*). The second way is that of the implications of the scriptural texts. Anselm does not appeal to the Fathers, because the Greeks were ignorant of the writings of the Latin Fathers and he himself apparently did not know the Greeks.

The logical argument, which is extremely complicated and abstract, can, I think, be summarized as follows. The Father, the Son and the Spirit are equally God. Hence, there is a rigorous logic of identity. There can only be a difference by opposition of relationship of origin or of procession. That and that alone is what limits the identity. The latter, left to itself, would require the Father to be the Son and the Spirit, because they are also the one God, but to this is opposed the fact that it is not possible to be the one from whom one has one's being. The Son is from the Father by mode of begetting, *nascendo*, and the Spirit is from him by mode of procession, *procedendo*. That is the opposition of relationship which establishes the differences within the unity of God. Anselm did not create the definition of the Persons by relationships—we have already found that in Augustine and the Greeks. He is the origin of the axiomatic formula which, although it is not strictly speaking a dogma, is nonetheless more than a theologoumenon: 'in Deo omnia sunt unum, ubi non obviat relationis oppositio'.[9]

In this one divinity, the Spirit is not from nobody, *a nullo*, he is from God, *a Deo*. He is *God from God*, from that God who is Father, Son and Spirit. He cannot be 'a se ipso, quoniam nulla persona a se ipsa potest existere'.[10] He is therefore from the Father and the Son, not as Father and Son, but as God, the divine essence—'secundum eandem deitatis unitatem'—and therefore, in this respect, not distinct from each other.[11] The Spirit, then, proceeds from the Son at the same time as he does from the Father, as from the same principle.

Anselm also insists that he proceeds *equally* from the two as from the one principle. This is necessary, because he proceeds from the two according to the essence that is common to both. Here, Anselm meets Augustine's *principaliter a Patre*. He does not deny this, but explains it within the framework of his own teaching, in which the begetting of the Son and the procession of the Spirit are seen within the context of an identity of essence and an equality of divinity:

Ex eo enim quod pater et filius unum sunt, id est ex deo, est spiritus sanctus, non ex eo unde alii sunt ab invicem. . . . Et quoniam pater non est prior aut posterior filio, aut maior aut minor, nec alter magis aut minus est deus quam alter, non est spiritus sanctus prius de patre quam de filio.[12]

The Holy Spirit comes from that in which the Father and the Son are one, that is, from God, not from that in which they differ from each other. . . . And because the Father is neither before nor after the son, neither greater nor lesser, and because the one is neither more nor less God than the other, the Holy Spirit is not from the Father before [being from] the Son.

Si ergo dicitur quod spiritus sanctus principaliter sit a patre, non aliud significatur, quam quia ipse filius de quo est spiritus sanctus, habet hoc ipsum ut spiritus sanctus sit de illo, a patre (Schmitt, II, p. 213).

If, then, it is said that the Holy Spirit comes from the Father as the principle, nothing more than this is meant: the Son himself, from whom the Spirit comes, has it from the Father that the Spirit comes from him.

It is important not to transfer to God what *principaliter* implies for God's creatures. In God, Anselm teaches, everything is not so much 'aequale vel simile sibi et coaeternum quam idem sibi ipsi' (Schmitt, II, p. 214). There is nothing wrong with this teaching, but it does not really contain the traditional idea of the monarchy of the Father and it is a long way from the Greek understanding of the mystery.

This same distance is also reflected in Anselm's treatment of the *a Patre per Filium*. The bishops who took part in the Council of Bari must have spoken to him about this question, but he was clearly unaware of the important place that this formula had in Greek patristic literature. He himself says that he could not see what the formula could mean (Schmitt, II, pp. 201ff.). He says: 'As the Father and the Son do not differ in the unity of the deity and as the Holy Spirit only proceeds from the Father as the deity, if that deity is similarly in the Son, it is not possible to see how the Spirit would proceed from the deity of the Father through the deity of the Son and not (immediately) from that same deity of the Father, but from his fatherhood, and that he proceeds through the sonship of the Son and not through his deity—but that idea is clearly stupid' (Schmitt, II, p. 202).

After this, Anselm, probably not knowing that the comparison can be found in the Greek Fathers, whose linear plan it expresses, critically examines the image of the source which, through the river, produces a lake.

The lake, he comments, certainly comes from the river and in the same way the Spirit comes from the Son. If, however, it is insisted that the lake strictly speaking comes only from the source and not from the channel between the source and itself, Anselm's reply is: that is true in the material order, but in the case of God it is not possible to speak of the Son differently from the way in which we speak of the Father, because he is *in* the Father and is in no way different from him in essence. And if the source, the channel and the lake are three, the same water is in all three, that is to say, the divine essence or the deity itself.[13] Gregory Nazianzen's comments about this comparison are very similar to Anselm's. All this is quite true, but nonetheless, Anselm's approach to the mystery of the Trinity is different from that of the Eastern tradition.

Anselm's aim, in taking as his point of departure in his theology of the Trinity what the Orthodox have in common with the Western tradition, was to take the Greeks to the point where they might confess what they had hitherto rejected, namely the procession of the Spirit *a Patre Filioque tanquam ab uno principio*. In chapters 4 to 7 of *De Processione*, he pursues his intention and his argument no longer by reasoning, but by interpreting a number of New Testament texts. These are Jn 20:22 and 16:13, reinforced by Mt 11:27 and Jn 10:30. In chapter 11, he shows that the Son is also affirmed in Jn 15:26: 'Who proceeds from the Father'. I shall not discuss this exegesis in detail, but go on to chapter 13, in which Anselm deals with the question of the addition of the *Filioque* clause to the creed. He deals with it very quickly and without realizing how important it is—as has frequently been the case in Western Catholic circles until our own time!

I would like on the other hand, to draw attention to a more favourable element in Anselm's treatise. He does not use the word *procedere* as a generic term, but as an expression of the coming to be of the Spirit or of Love, whereas he uses *gigni* or *nasci* for the Son.[14] These are two different ways of being 'God from God'. He does not, however, regard the difference between these two modes of origin as sufficient to form a basis for distinguishing between the Son and the Spirit. In his view, it is necessary to go back to the opposition of relationship of origin; the Spirit is distinct from the Son because he proceeds from him. This was also Thomas Aquinas' view, whereas Duns Scotus held a position that was close to that of the Greeks. This is, however, not a strictly dogmatic question.

Anselm was above all a speculative theologian. He did not develop his pneumatology within the framework of the history of salvation; indeed, he did not refer to the latter at all. He moves immediately from the activity of God in the economy to the eternal procession, for example, in the case of Jn 16:13, 'he will not speak of himself'. Even his prayers and meditations are not pneumatological. They do not even mention the Holy Spirit. He has, however, great dynamism, although he has certain limitations. Like Augustine (see Volume I, p. 78), he tends to block together the essential and the notional. He is interested in the divine essence and does not take the hypostases as his point of departure. The notion of 'person' seems to have perplexed him. He does not, therefore, make a very clear distinction between their principle *quo*, their nature, and their principle *quod*, the person, in the processions. However much we have to admire him, there is always a feeling that there is a need to go beyond his thinking. He would himself have agreed with that sentiment.

*   *   *

It is not because they have the same name that I add a note at this point on Anselm of Havelberg (†1158). It is rather because of the content of his dialogue with Nicetas of Nicomedia. The whole of Book II of his *Dialogi* deals with the Holy Spirit, and in it he discusses the theology of the Latins with its supporting scriptural texts and arguments. Nicetas complies a little too easily and is above all anxious to affirm the monarchy of the Father. He finds the term 'proceed' an obstacle, while Anselm stumbles over *ekporeusis*. Each refers to the Fathers of his own tradition, although Anselm declares that he reveres the Greeks as he does the Latins and respects every orthodox Christian who has received the gift of the Spirit (*Dial*. 24; *PL* 186, 1204).

NOTES

1. I follow in this section the critical edition of S. Schmitt: for the *Monologion*, I (Seckau, 1938), pp. 5–87; for the *De Processione Spiritus Sancti*, II (Rome, 1940), pp. 177–279. The following studies of Anselm's work are worth consulting: B. Bouché, *Le doctrine du 'Filioque' d'après S. Anselme de Cantorbéry. Son influence sur S. Albert le Grand et S. Thomas d'Aquin* (this is a duplicated thesis I have not been able to read) (Rome, 1938); R. Perino, *La dottrina trinitaria di S. Anselmo nel quadro del suo metodo teologico e del suo concetto di Dio* (*Studia Anselmiana*, 29) (Rome, 1952); C. Vagaggini, 'La hantise des *rationes necessariae* de S. Anselme dans la théologie des processions trinitaires de S. Thomas', *Spicilegium Beccense*, I (*Congrès internationale du IXᵉ centenaire de l'arrivée d'Anselme au Bec*) (Le Bec-Hellouin and Paris, 1959), pp. 103–139; P. del Prete, *Il concilio di Bari nel 1098* (Bari, 1959).
2. *Mon*. Prol. (Schmitt, I, p. 8, 1. 8f.). The editor gives, at the foot of his pages, Augustine's similar texts.
3. *Prosl*. 4 (Schmitt, I, p. 104); cf. *Ep. de Inc. Verbi*, VI (Schmitt, II, p. 20).
4. 'Cum idem sit illi sic dicere aliquid quod est intelligere': *Mon*. 32 (Schmitt, I, p. 51). Thomas Aquinas makes a distinction here: see *De ver*. q. 4, a. 2 c and ad 7.
5. *Mon*. 65.
6. *Mon*. 39–41. In *Mon*. 42, Anselm asks why Christians speak of the Father and the Son and not of the Mother and the Daughter; this is, he says, because the father comes before the mother in the causality of begetting.
7. *Mon*. 43 (Schmitt, I, p. 60).
8. 'Potest ergo hac necessitatis ratione irreprehensibiliter illa summa et una trinitas sive trina unitas dici una essentia et tres personae sive tres substantiae': *Mon*. 79 (Schmitt, I, p. 85). This equivalence between 'Person' and 'substance' came to Anselm from what he knew of

the Greeks: 'Quod enim dixi summam trinitatem posse dici tres substantias, Graecos secutus sum, qui confitentur tres substantias in una persona eadem fide, qua nos tres personas in una substantia. Nam hoc significant in deo per substantiam, quod nos per personam': *Mon.*, Prol. (Schmitt, I, p. 8). See also *Ep. de Inc. Verbi*, XVI (Schmitt, II, p. 35); *Ep.* 83 *ad Rainaldum* (Schmitt, III, p. 208), in which the following interesting text can be found: his *Monologion* had been criticized by those who 'nesciebant enim sic non dici proprie de deo tres personas quomodo tres substantias, quadam tamen ratione ob indigentiam nominis proprie significantis illam pluralitatem quae in summa trinitate intelligitur, Latinos dicere tres personas credendas in una substantia, Graecos vero non minus fideliter tres substantias in una persona confiteri'.

9. This axiom is not to be found as such in Anselm's work, but its meaning and use can be found: see *De proc. spir. sanct.* 1 (Schmitt, II, p. 180, 1. 27; 181, 1. 2–4; 183, 1. 3). It can only be found, in connection with the Council of Florence, in the decree of 4 February 1442 for union with the Copts: see J. Alberigo *et al.*, *Conciliorum Œcumenicorum Decreta*, 3rd ed. (Bologna, 1973), p. 571; *DS* 1330. According to Heribert Mühlen, the axiom was applied in that case to a tritheism which the Monophysites who were opposed to the definition of Chalcedon had adopted in the sixth century from John Philoponus. Its dogmatic implication would therefore be limited: see H. Mühlen, *Der Heilige Geist als Person in der Trinität, bei der Inkarnation und im Gnadenbund; Ich-Du-Wir*, 3rd ed. (Münster, 1966), p. 314. 'It is not of faith', H. Dondaine told the Orthodox: *Russie et Chrétienté* (1950), 223. It is, however, a commonly accepted principle in Catholic theology. Is it not possible to find the equivalent in Greek patristic thought in the following text from Athanasius, *Contra Arian.* I, 22: 'Because they are one and the divinity is itself one, the same things can be said of the Son that are said of the Father, although it cannot be said that he is Father'; see also *De decr.* 23.

10. *De proc. spir. sanct.* 2 (Schmitt, II, p. 188). It is astonishing that Anselm does not explain how this statement applies or does not apply to the Father. He does not, however, have the monarchy of the Father in mind, but only the divinity. In the case of the latter, the Father is only Father when the Son is affirmed, and that through his relationship as *genitor* to the *genitus*.

11. *Mon.* 54 (Schmitt, I, p. 66): 'non ex eo procedit in quo plures sunt pater et filius, sed ex eo in quo unum sunt. Nam non ex relationibus suis quae plures sunt . . . sed ex ipsa sua essentia quae pluralitatem non admittit, emittunt pater et filius pariter tantum bonum'; *De proc. spir. sanct.* 1 (Schmitt, II, p. 183): 'non est filius aut spiritus sanctus de patre nisi de patris essentia'. See also below, pp. 109, 114 note 7, and p. 120.

12. *De proc. spir. sanct.* 14 (Schmitt, II, p. 212); cf. *ibid.* 9 (Schmitt, II, p. 204).

13. *De proc. spir. sanct.* 9 (Schmitt, II, pp. 203–205). The comparison can also be found, for example, in John Damascene (*PG* 94, 780). For Gregory Nazianzen, see *Orat.* 31 (= *Orat. theol.* V), 31 (*PG* 36, 169). Anselm's explanation was explicitly rejected by Abelard, but not for a good reason—it would not be *simul* and would presuppose a *successio temporis*: *Intro. ad Theol.* II, 13 and *Theol. Christ.* IV (*PL* 178, 1071 and 1287).

14. See, for example, *De proc. spir. sanct.* 1 (Schmitt, II, p. 178, 1. 3ff.; p. 179, 15ff.; p. 180, 15ff.; etc.). Again and again *nascens* and *nascendo* are found for the Word, the Son, and *procedens* and *procedendo* for the Spirit: see Schmitt, II, p. 179, 12ff.; p. 185, 3ff.: 'habent utique a patre esse filius et spiritus sanctus, sed diverso modo: quia alter nascendo, alter procedendo'.

3

SPECULATIVE TRIADOLOGY
CONSTRUCTED IN FAITH AND UNDER
THE SIGN OF LOVE

[*Note*: the numbered notes are collected at the end of each of the two sections in this chapter.]

A. RICHARD OF SAINT-VICTOR

For half a century, the abbey of Saint-Victor in Paris was a centre of intense theological speculation in a climate that was marked by an astonishing trust in the power of reason, an acute intellectual curiosity, an intense religious and doxological life and a deep interest in love or charity. G. Dumeige has considered a large number of texts relating to this interest on the part of the Victorines.[1] The leading members of Saint-Victor were Hugh (†1141), Achard (†1171), Richard, Walter, Adam, Godfrey and Andrew.

Richard, who died in 1172, wrote a remarkable treatise *De Trinitate* late in life.[2] It has been demonstrated that he was directly indebted to his abbot, Achard,[3] for it, and more distantly to Augustine and Anselm. Like the latter, he believed that it was possible to find the 'necessary reasons' to support the affirmations of faith in a reflection made in faith. He was conscious of the inadequacy of our concepts and of all that we can say with regard to the transcendent mystery of God, and we today are less convinced of the effectiveness of his reasons, but he developed and repeated them with what was intended to be vigorous consistency.

Whereas Anselm took as his point of departure *id quo nihil maius cogitari potest*, 'that than which it is not possible to conceive anything greater', Achard said: *Deo nihil pulcrius et melius esse vel cogitari potest*—'nothing better or more beautiful than God can exist or be conceived of'. Richard's point of departure was: *id quo nihil est maius, quo nihil est melius*, that is, 'a being, greater or better than whom there is nothing'.[4] Unlike Achard, he did not appeal to the *summum* of beauty, although he often made use of the aesthetic argument. To Anselm's teaching, he added the *summum* of goodness, that is to say, the *summum* of a value, not of a purely ontological reality.

In Book III of his treatise on the Trinity, Richard deduces the plurality, or more precisely the Trinity of the Persons in the unity of the divine substance. It is valuable to quote his own summary of his argument. He begins by showing that it is necessary for there to be a plurality in God, through the existence of a second Person who, in order to be the term of a perfect love, will be the *condignus* or equal of that love:

103

In God, the supreme and absolutely perfect good, there is total goodness in its fullness and perfection. Where there is a fullness of total goodness, however, there is necessarily true and supreme charity. . . . It is never said of anyone that he possesses charity because of the exclusively personal love that he has for himself—for there to be charity, there must be a love that is directed towards another. Consequently, where there is an absence of a plurality of persons, there cannot be charity.

You may say: 'Assuming that, in this true divinity, there is only one Person, that Person might be able to have and in fact would have charity with regard to his creatures'. Yes, but with regard to a created person, it would be impossible for him to have a sovereign charity, because it would be a disorder in that charity to love sovereignly what is not sovereignly lovable.[5]

Richard gave a character that was personal, and not purely essential to charity by conceiving it in the form of friendship, which in itself presupposes an interpersonal relationship. The perfect one, the deity, has everything, Richard taught, from himself.[6] He is *innascibilis*.[7] Richard showed that what perfect love implies is that there is one who is personally over and against that perfect presence and who is the Son.[8] He also deduces, in the name of the same perfect love, a third, who is *condilectus*:

Sovereign charity must be perfect in every respect. To be sovereignly perfect, it must be of such an intensity that there can be nothing more intense and of such a quality that there can be nothing better. . . . In true charity, the supreme excellence is to want another to be loved as one is loved oneself. . . . The proof of consummate charity is the desire for the love with which one is loved to be communicated.[9]

The procession of the second and the third Person can therefore be understood thanks to the concept of perfect love or charity, and by making a distinction in that love. There is, for example, the love that is simply given. This gratuitous love is the Father.[10] There is the love which is received (*debitus* or due to another) and which gives (*gratuitus*). That love is the Son.[11] The love that is purely received (*debitus*) is the Spirit.[12] He enjoys the privilege of a love that is exclusively due and he loves those who give everything to him perfectly. Each divine Person is therefore equally love that is sovereign but possessed in a distinct way which corresponds to his mode of existence.[13] In this context, Richard uses a precise vocabulary and works out a distinctive concept of 'Person'. He is critical of the definition given to the term by Boethius—'an individual substance of reasonable nature'[14]—and replaces it by a different definition: 'one who exists in himself alone, according to a certain mode of reasonable existence'[15] and who is distinguished from everyone else by a property that cannot be communicated.[16] Richard therefore defines the person in terms of being, but does so within a personalistic and not within a purely ontic perspective. The person is not a *quid*, but a *quis* (see *De Trin*. IV, 7). He also uses the term *existentia* for the person; this word expresses both the nature or essence (*sistere*) and the origin (*ex*) of the person. It can, Richard insists, be applied suitably to the divine Persons each of whom has, within the community of substance, his own mode of subsistence.[17] In this way, then, Richard affirms the unity of the divine essence and the plurality of the divine Persons. It would be futile to ask whether he affirms the one or the other first, whether he is more Greek than Latin, according to the difference between the two traditions emphasized in such an over-simplified way by T. de Régnon. The fact that he begins by outlining the essential attributes of God does not make him into an 'essentialist' any more than it does John Damascene. What is certain, however, is that his idea of the person is very close to that of the Greeks.[18]

Although he does not engage in polemics or even in debate with the Greeks, he parts company from them on the question of the procession of the Holy Spirit from the Father and the Son. He says, for instance: 'If the two (the Father and the Son) possess the same power in common, it must be concluded that it is from both that the third Person of the Trinity received his being and has his existence'.[19] In the Trinity, he claims, the third Person proceeds both from the one who was born and from the one who cannot be born (*innascibilis*).[20] This does not mean that the Spirit is, according to Richard, what he was for Augustine—the love of the Father and the Son for each other.[21] The Spirit is, according to Richard, the particular and incommunicable mode of existence of the divine substance, which is Love. This special way of existing which characterizes the divine Persons consists in a manner of living and realizing Love. That Love is either pure grace, or it is received and giving, or it is purely received and due. This can then be expressed equally well in terms of procession and therefore also in terms of origin. Beginning with the one who is *innascibilis*, there is an immediate procession, that of the Love-Son, and one that is simultaneously immediate (from the Father) and mediate (from the Son), that of the *Condilectus* or the Spirit.[22]

No other Person proceeds from the Spirit, but it is through the latter that God as Love is given to the believer and takes root in him. The Spirit therefore merits the name of 'Gift':

> The Holy Spirit is given by God to man at the moment when the due (*debitus*) love that is found in the divinity is breathed into the human soul. . . . Insofar as we enable the love that is due (*debitum*) to our creator to go back to him, we are quite certainly configured into the property of the Holy Spirit. It is precisely for this end that he is given, that he is breathed into man, so that the latter may be, to the full extent of what is possible, configured into him. For the rest, this gift is sent to us, this mission is given to us at the same time and in the same way by the Father and by the Son. It is, after all, from the one and from the other that the Spirit has everything that he possesses. And because it is from the one and from the other that he has his being, power and will, it is right to say that it is they who send and give him, who has received from them the power and the will to come from them into us and to dwell in us.[23]

Richard does not make use of the principle formulated by Anselm: 'in Deo omnia sunt unum ubi non obviat relationis oppositio'.[24] He does not make an inference from the relationship between the Father and the Son, the Giver and the Gift, in order to distinguish between the Persons. He too distinguishes between them by means of the principle of origin, but in so doing he only uses an analysis of love in its absolute perfection and the distinctions that are contained within that love.

Despite appearances, Richard does not base his ideas on a pure deduction from sacred metaphysics. They presuppose not only revelation—taking expressions of faith as a point of departure—but also spiritual experience, and indeed Richard refers explicitly to this.[25] He justifies the fact that he bases his teaching on the human experiences of love in its most intense state by quoting at least ten times a Pauline text: 'The invisible nature of God . . . can be clearly perceived in the things that have been made' (Rom 1:10). This frequent quotation is all the more remarkable because of the paucity of quotations in the treatise as a whole. This appeal to human experience does not, however, mean that Richard also looked for the life of the Spirit in history or in the economy of salvation. He gives us a theology of the third Person of the Trinity, but not a full 'pneumatology'.

NOTES

1. After I had written this chapter, I read Jean Leclercq's *Monks and Love in Twelfth-Century France* (Oxford, 1979). The author is principally concerned in this remarkable and suggestive study with Bernard, and this is right, but he also cites the Victorines. The new religious orders in the twelfth century found recruits among adults who were acquainted with the expressions of human love. These men developed a spirituality in which love played a new part and was studied with a new richness and delicacy. It became a special theme in spiritual reflection.

   In Volume I, pp. 86–87, I quoted the fine prayer of William of Saint-Thierry (†1148), who said that God loves himself in and through us with the same love with which he loves himself. For his theology of the Trinity, see M.-J. Le Guillou, 'Guillaume de Saint-Thierry: l'équilibre catholique de la triadologie médiévale', *Istina*, 17 (1972), 367–374.

   Bernard can also be placed within this context. He spoke of 'caritas, quae Trinitatem in unitate quodammodo cohibet et colligat in vinculo pacis': *De diligendo Deo* XII, 35 (*PL* 182, 996). In his commentary on the verse of the Song of Songs, 'May he kiss me with a kiss of his mouth', he suggests that this kiss is the Holy Spirit and adds: 'It is enough for the spouse to be kissed by a kiss of the bridegroom, even if she is not kissed by his mouth. It is not a trivial matter or an everyday thing to be kissed by a kiss. It is simply being penetrated by the Holy Spirit. If it is the Father who kisses, the Son is the one who is kissed and it is not out of place to see in that kiss the Holy Spirit, who is the unchangeable peace of the Father and the Son, their firm bond, their unique love and the inseparable unity': *Sermo 8 in Cant.* 2 (*PL* 183, 811).

2. See *PL* 196, 887–902 (which is not complete or perfect); J. Ribaillier, *Richard de Saint-Victor, De Trinitate. Texte critique* (Paris, 1958); *idem*, crit. ed., in *Richard de Saint-Victor, Opuscules théologiques* (Paris, 1967), of the brief text *Quomodo Spiritus Sanctus est amor Patris et Filii* and another text, *De tribus Personis appropriatis in Trinitate*, which is partly

reproduced in *De Trin*. VI, 15; G. Salet, *Richard de Saint-Victor, La Trinité* (Latin text, Fr. tr. and notes; *SC* 63) (Paris, 1959). There are several studies, including T. de Régnon, *Etudes de théologie positive sur la Sainte Trinité*, II (Paris, 1892), pp. 233–335; A.-M. Ethier, *Le 'De Trinitate' de Richard de Saint-Victor* (*Publ. de l'Inst. d'Etudes méd. d'Ottawa*, IX) (Paris and Ottawa, 1939); F. Guimet, 'Notes en marge d'un texte de Richard de Saint-Victor', *Arch. hist. doctr. litt. M. A.,* 14 (1943–1945), pp. 361–394; *idem*, ' "Caritas ordinata" et "amor discretus" dans la théologie trinitaire de Richard de Saint-Victor', *Rev. M. A. latin*, 4 (1948), 225–236; G. Dumeige, *Richard de Saint-Victor et l'idée chrétienne de l'amour*) (*Bibl. de philos. contemp*.) (Paris, 1952), which contains a bibliography with 101 items.

3. M. T. d'Alverny, 'Achard de Saint-Victor, *De Trinitate, de unitate et pluralitate creaturarum*', *RTAM*, 21 (1954), 299–306; J. Ribaillier, *De Trinitate, op. cit.* (note 2), pp. 27–33; J. Chatillon, *Théologie et spiritualité dans l'œuvre oratoire d'Achard de Saint-Victor* (Paris, 1969).

4. *De Trin*. I, 11 and 20; V, 3.

5. *De Trin*. III, 2; G. Salet, *op. cit.* (note 2), p. 169. There is an implicit quotation of Gregory the Great here: 'Minus quam inter duos caritas haberi non potest. Nemo enim proprie ad semetipsum habere caritatem dicitur, sed dilectio in alterum tendit ut caritas esse possit': *Hom. in Ev.* I, *Hom*. 17 (*PL* 76, 1139). Quoting the same passage, Abelard saw it as realized by the extension of God's love to creatures; *Theol. Summi Boni* III, 3; ed. H. Ostlender (Münster, 1939), p. 103. Richard is replying to his statement here.

6. *De Trin*. V, 7 and 8.

7. *Innascibilis* is a commonly used word: see *De Trin*. V, 7, 8 and 19; VI, 2, 3, 5, 6 and 8.

8. *De Trin*. V, 7; VI, 5; begotten, VI, 16; the image of the Father, which the Spirit is not, *because*, like the Father, he produces a different Person, he is charity that gives: VI, 11, 18 and 20. Thinking of the first procession within the framework of love and not as a procession of intellectual understanding, Richard did not connect 'image' with 'Word'. He shows, however, that the second Person is 'Word' (VI, 12) within a personalistic perspective of communication.

9. *De Trin*. III, 11: G. Salet, *op. cit.* (note 2), p. 191; cf. III, 19; V, 20.

10. *De Trin*. V, 16 and 17.

11. *De Trin*. V, 16 and 19.

12. *De Trin*. V, 16 and 18. The distinction between the three conditions of love is expressed in III, 3 and V, 16.

13. *De Trin*. V, 20 and 23.

14. *De Trin*. IV, 21; Boethius, *Liber de persona et duabus naturis*, 3 (*PL* 64, 1343). Thomas Aquinas accepted Boethius' definition after correcting it and explicitly quoted Richard: *ST* Ia, q. 29, a. 3, ad 4.

15. *De Trin*. IV, 24; G. Salet, *op. cit.* (note 2), p. 285.

16. *De Trin*. IV, 17 and 20; in this final chapter of his treatise, Richard affirms the identity of meaning in the difference between the terms used by the Greeks and the Latins: see below, p. 175.

17. *De Trin*. IV, 12 and 19, where this formula can be found concerning two distinct Persons in God: 'Quamvis enim utrisque sit unus modus essendi, non tamen utrisque est unus modus existendi'. There is another excellent statement in IV, 20: 'nihil aliud est persona ista quam dilectio summa alia proprietate distincta'.

18. G. Salet quoted John Damascene in this context, *op. cit.* (note 2), p. 254, note 1: 'The word hypostasis has two meanings. It can mean simply existence, in which case it has exactly the same value as ousia. . . . On the other hand, it can also mean that existence which is in itself and subsists in its individuality, in which case it points to the numerically distinct individual—Peter, Paul or a certain horse': *Dial*. 42 (*PG* 94, 612).

19. *De Trin*. V, 8; G. Salet, *op. cit*., p. 321.

20. *De Trin*. V, 13; G. Salet, *op. cit.,* p. 377; see also *De Trin*. VI, 13, end.

107

21. In his brief treatise or letter *Quomodo Spiritus Sanctus est amor Patris et Filii* (*PL* 196, 1011–1012); see J. Ribaillier, *Opuscules*, *op. cit.* (note 2), pp. 164–166. Richard takes as his point of departure the Augustinian view which had been brought to his attention by the question asked by his correspondent and which was not exactly his own. Ribaillier, *op. cit.*, pp. 159–160, has shown that, although the two views are different, they do not contradict each other. *De Trin*. III, 19 indicates an openness on Richard's part to the idea of mutual love. The latter is explictly discussed in *De tribus appropriatis*: ed. Ribaillier, *op. cit.*, p. 184.

22. *De Trin*. V, 6–10.

23. *De Trin*. VI, 14; G. Salet, *op. cit.* (note 2), pp. 413 and 417.

24. The only place where a 'relationship of opposition' is possibly called to mind—and then only remotely—is *De Trin*. V, 14, but even here it is only between receiving and giving, or giving and receiving.

25. *De Trin*. III, 3; G. Salet, *op. cit.*, pp. 171ff., translates this text as: 'Let everyone reflect about this and, without the slightest doubt, he will indisputably recognize that there is nothing better or more agreeable than charity'. What he says in *De Trin*. III, 16 about the sweetness of friendship presupposes personal experience.

B. ALEXANDER OF HALES AND BONAVENTURE

Both these theologians continued in the tradition of Richard of Saint-Victor and their triadology is deeply indebted to his teaching. As members of the high Scholasticism of the thirteenth century, they continued to develop, within faith itself, a rational and consistent discourse about faith. Bonaventure taught that 'fullness' was the source and that 'first' meant the 'principle' and therefore the beginning of a communication, and this teaching was based not on the rational content of the concepts, but on faith itself. Those concepts, however, seen in the light of his affirmations about faith, gave his theological vision grandeur and coherence. I have already spoken in Volume I of this work (pp. 87–88 with the bibliography p. 91 note 7) about the theme of the Spirit as the link of mutual love between the Father and the Son,[1] and I shall later on discuss the theology of the *innascibilis*, that is, of the Father as the source of the divinity (see below, pp. 135–136).

Alexander of Hales (†1245) dealt briefly with the Trinity in his *Glossa* on the Sentences, but nonetheless outlined quite clearly the course that he was to follow and that his disciples were to follow after him. This amounted to an accord between John Damascene on the one hand and Augustine on the other, John representing the Greek and Augustine representing the Latin tradition, John speaking of God's relationship with his creatures and Augustine of the inner life of God.[2]

This is, however, clearly unsatisfactory. The questions *Antequam esset frater* reveal a truly irenical intention in their treatment of the 'controversy between the Greeks and the Latins about the procession *ab utroque*'.[3] It is possible that they contain an echo of dialogues that really took place ('concedebant . . .'). The Greeks maintain, Alexander's argument runs, that the Spirit is the Spirit of the Son, but that he does not proceed from him. As the *responsio pro illis*, in accordance with the teaching of John Damascene, whom Alexander quotes frequently, the Spirit is the Father's love for the Son and proceeds from the Father to the Son, but he is the Son's love for the Father without proceeding from the Son to the Father. That is why the Greeks call him, Alexander says, the Spirit of the Son and do not say that he proceeds from the Son to the creature. They do not say that he proceeds *simpliciter* from the Son, because he does not proceed from the Son to the Father.[4] Alexander is therefore conscious of *utriusque positionis concordia*.[5] It was sufficient in his opinion to affirm with Augustine the inner procession of the Spirit *a Filio*, but not *in Patrem*, and with John Damascene the procession *ad creaturas*. But is this question really so simple? Has Alexander reached the real facts in the debate?

There is a change of style in his *Summa Theologica*, in which his pneumatology is presented in a more systematic way, and which was continued by his disciple John de la Rochelle. The divine life is seen as a good that is communicated, since good is naturally and essentially something that is diffusive of itself.[6] This takes place, according to Alexander, in two ways—by mode of nature, which is the begetting of the Son, and by mode of love or gift, which is the procession of the Spirit. Alexander quotes Richard of Saint-Victor frequently here (c. 1). He also makes use of Richard's idea of the *condilectus* in his reply[7] to the Greek objection, namely that, if the Spirit proceeds from the Father and the Son, this procession takes place either from the common essence—but he shares in that common essence—or in accordance with the difference between the Father and the Son—but then *non conveniunt in aliquo*: they have no common fund. Alexander's reply to this objection is that the Spirit does not proceed from the Father and the Son either in accordance with their unity (in essence) or in accordance with their difference, but rather in accordance with the fact that, although they are different, they are still one, that is to say, insofar as they are, as Father and Son, God. Their unity is one of essence as hypostatized in the Father and in the Son in a personal way.

*   *   *

Bonaventure's triadology is constructed on a very conceptual basis, but always in faith.[8] He attempted to decipher the mystery of God in three books. In the first he dealt with nature, in the second with the soul and in the third with revelation. The third book throws light on the other two, since it is itself read under an inner light or illumination that enables us to sense God *altissime* and *piissime*, in other words, in accordance with the most sublime, the most religiously profound and fervent way one can think.[9] The work is certainly constructed on the basis of intellectual concepts, but the criteria of the most sublime, the most profound and the most fervently religious things one can think are always followed. This can be detected in the following summary from Bonaventure's *Itinerarium mentis ad Deum*, which he wrote in 1259:

See and note well—the best is simply the best that can be conceived. It is such that it cannot validly be conceived as not existing, because it is better to be than not to be and it is also such that it cannot validly be conceived other than threefold and one. 'Whoever says "good" says "diffusive of itself" ', so that the sovereign good is sovereignly diffusive of itself. A sovereign diffusion can only be present and intrinsic, substantial and hypostatic, natural and voluntary, full of grace and necessary, without restriction and perfect. If, then, there were not eternally in the sovereign good a present and consubstantial fertility and a hypostasis of equal dignity, as the fertility by mode of begetting and spiration is, so that it is from an eternal principle that is in eternity doubly principle, with the result that there is a Beloved and a loved Companion [*dilectus* and *condilectus*], begotten and an outcome of spiration, in other words, Father, Son and Holy Spirit, there would never have been a sovereign good, because that good would not have diffused itself sovereignly. Diffusion of a temporal kind in the creature is no more than a point in the centre of a sphere in comparison with the immensity of eternal goodness. It is therefore possible to conceive of a greater diffusion, namely that in which the principle of diffusion communicates the whole of its substance and nature to another. There would therefore not be a sovereign good if this did not exist in the idea that is conceived of it and in reality.

If you can, then, with the eye of your spirit, seize hold of (*contueri*) the purity of the goodness which is the pure act of the principle of charity that loves with a gratuitous love and a due (love) and (a love) that is a mixture of the two, which constitutes the fullest diffusion by mode of nature and (by mode) of will—it is a diffusion by mode of the Word, in whom (God) says all things, and by mode of Gift, in whom the other gifts are given—then you will see through the sovereign communicability of the good that it is necessary for the Trinity of the Father, the Son and the Holy Spirit to exist. In them, by reason of the supreme goodness, there must be supreme communicability and, by reason of that supreme communicability, there must also be a sovereign consubstantiality and, by virtue of that sovereign consubstantiality, there must also be a sovereign configurability and, because of (all) that, a sovereign co-equality and, for that reason, a sovereign co-eternity and, as a result of all that, a sovereign co-intimacy, by virtue of which the one is necessarily in the other through a sovereign circumincession, the one functions with the other through the totally undivided substance, virtue and functioning of the blessed Trinity itself.[10]

This synthesis is dominated and inspired by two great values. In the first place, the idea that the supreme good is diffusive of itself comes from Pseudo-Dionysius[11] and expresses the primacy that is recognized in Neo-Platonism to value and the supreme good over being. It is simply a question of seizing hold of this property of the good in its supreme degree, in other words, in supreme or sovereign love. In the second place, there is also Richard of Saint-Victor's application of the idea of love to the intra-divine life, for which he may or may not have been indebted to Pseudo-Dionysius, in its supreme form of altruism or friendship. Bonaventure took from Richard the ideas of *dilectus condignus* and *condilectus*, the distinction between gratuitous love, due or received love, and the mixture of the two.

To this he added the theme of communication or emanation by mode of nature and by mode of will and liberality. It was this theme, together with that of the *condilectus*, which enabled Bonaventure to justify the existence of the third Person of the Trinity as 'necessary'.[12] The Spirit is therefore, for Bonaventure, Love and Gift. He also defines this Love more precisely. In what sense, he asks, is this title 'Love' personal to the Holy Spirit, since love must, after all, be attributed to all three Persons?[13] Love exists in God in the essential and in the notional sense, that is, as the personal name of the Spirit, It is, he claims, in this second sense that the Spirit is the mutual love of the Father and the Son.[14] For that is what he is. Bonaventure comes back again and again to this point, which is fundamental for him:

> Love has the perfection of its delectable value and of its value of union and uprightness from its character of reciprocity. As a consequence of this, we have either not to speak of a person in God who proceeds by mode of love or, if there is such a procession, it must be by mode of reciprocal charity.[15]

> The love that the Holy Spirit is does not proceed from the Father insofar as he loves himself, nor does he proceed from the Son insofar as he loves himself, but he proceeds insofar as the one loves the other, because he is a *nexus* (a bond or link).[16]

If there is a first procession by mode of nature and a second procession by mode of will and liberality, Bonaventure taught, it is that the principle of both is essentially the Source of being. The idea of hierarchy and that of communication predominated in Bonaventure's thinking; in every sphere, there is a first who is for that reason the principle of communication or emanation, in his own words, 'primum, ergo principium':[17]

Ratione primitatis persona nata est ex se aliam producere; et voco hic primitatem innascibilitatem ratione cuius, ut dicit antiqua opinio, est fontalis plenitudo in Patre ad omnem emanationem, ut infra patebit.	By reason of his quality of first, one person is, by nature, inclined to produce another. I call here a 'quality of first' the *innascibilitas*, the fact that he cannot be born, by virtue of which, as an early view states, there is in the Father the fullness of a source from which everything emanates, as we shall see later.[18]

These words go back to a passage in Bonaventure's distinction 27, in which he discusses and justifies his decision about the question whether God begets because he is Father—this was to be Thomas Aquinas' position—or whether he is Father because he begets. But in that case, what is the reason for his begetting? Bonaventure claims that it is because he is first and distinguished by the fact that he cannot be born (*innascibilitas*). For Thomas, this *innascibilitas* is a negative quality that cannot positively describe anyone. Bonaventure, however, says:

111

It is, on the contrary, important to stress that this *innascibilitas*, under a negative form, is a perfect and positive reality. The Father cannot be born because he does not proceed from another. Not to proceed from another is to be the first, and primacy is a noble affirmation. In fact, 'first', seen in the formal sense of 'first', is such a positive affirmation that, as we shall see, the position of second follows the position of first. He is first and therefore he is the principle; he is the principle and therefore there is, in act or in potency, a term that proceeds from that principle (*Quia primum, ideo principium; quia principium, ideo vel actu vel habitu est principiatum*). Once it is admitted that the sense of primacy is always the sense of principle for things of the same order, we must conclude that, if the Father begets and produces by 'spiration', this is because he is the first with regard to every emanation, either by begetting or by spiration. And because being first in the order of begetting, that is to say, being *innascibilis*, at the same time includes being first in the order of spiration, that is to say, *improcessibilis*, we must say that he begets because he is the God who cannot be born. There is no value in asking why he is *innascibilis*, because this *innascibilitas* implies primacy and we have to stop at the first. . . . This is what will be said below, at the beginning of my twenty-ninth distinction, in the sentence: *Pater est principium totius divinitatis quia a nullo*. I have already touched on this truth in several other passages.

Quod movet ad hoc dicendum—what prompts me to maintain this doctrine is the early statement made by the great teachers who said that the Father's *innascibilitas* pointed to a flowing fullness (*fontalem plenitudinem*). A flowing fullness is, after all, a productive fullness. It is clear, however, that this flowing fullness is not attributed to the Father because he produces the creatures, since that is an act which is common to all three Persons. Nor is it attributed to him because he produces the Holy Spirit, because that act is common both to him and to the Son. This flowing fullness in the Father, then, affirms the active begetting in the same Person. If his *innascibilitas*, then, is his flowing fullness, it is clear that. . . .

Movet etiam communis opinio—what also prompts me is the common opinion, according to which this *innascibilitas* is peculiar to the Father. What is peculiar to the Father, however, characterizing him in the most excellent way, cannot be a notion that is purely negative. In this respect, the idea of *innascibilitas* is more suitable for the essence and the Holy Spirit. This notion nonetheless points to something—but neither to an absolute reality, since nothing that is absolute is a personal priority, nor to anything relatively positive which refers to the producer. This *innascibilitas* therefore has a positive relationship with a term that is produced. In accordance with our way of understanding, however, the first mode of production is by begetting. The position of *innascibilitas* therefore leads to the position of begetting. . . .

Movet etiam verbum Hilarii—what also prompts me is the statement mady by Hilary in the twelfth book of the Trinity, in which he says that the Father is the 'author' of the Son. It is clear that by 'author' here he does not mean the creator, but the one who begets. He is the author, then, by what constitutes authority in the Father. But the supreme authority in the Father has *innascibilitas* as its reason. Thus, it is by reason of innascibility that the hypostasis of the Father begets. This is what Hilary seems to be saying in the twelfth book of the Trinity, if his words are interpreted in depth, and the same applies to the fourth book.

Movet etiam verbum Philosophi—what also prompts me are the words of the philosopher, who speaks of principles that are all the more powerful the more they are first, who says that the first cause has more influence than the others and who claims that the cause which is absolutely and simply the first has a sovereign influence. If, then, we see, in the order of those causes between which there is an essential connection, that primacy confers a sovereign influence on the first cause and an influence that is in proportion to their essential rank on the second causes, the same reasoning must be applied when there is an order of persons and we must affirm that primacy in the first person is the reason for producing the others. And because *innascibilitas* connotes primacy, it also connotes the flowing fullness with regard to all personal production. A sign of this can be found in the hierarchy of kinds. The first kinds are the principles of the lower kinds. Those that are so much the first that it is necessary to stop there have an infinite power, like the point with regard to the line or the unit with regard to the numbers; the same applies to the divine essence insofar as it is the first with regard to the creatures. It is possibly because the divine essence is the first that it is omnipotent. And because all essence is posterior to the essence of the three Persons, it is impossible for one Person to produce something without the others. Therefore, although the ability to produce persons should not be extended to an infinite number, as I have shown above, if the impossible supposition is made that a thousand persons were produced, it would be necessary for all of them to proceed immediately from the Person of the Father. The first cause functions not only immediately in all mediate production, but also in the processions of the Persons.[19]

Bonaventure provides four more reasons in the text that follows. If I were asked what Bonaventure's position was in his teaching about the Trinity, I would say that he is certainly in the Augustinian tradition, not only in his idea of the Spirit as the bond of love between the Father and the Son, but also in his psychological analysis of the image of God in the *mens*. But Bonaventure, who outlined this in his *In I Sent*. d. 3, did not make it the principle of organization of his synthesis, which is indebted to Richard of Saint-Victor, Alexander of Hales and John Damascene and is ultimately closer to Greek thought, not so much in its style, which is clearly Scholastic, but rather in its great and decisive values.

Examples of this are his description of the monarchy of the Father, expressed in such concepts as *primitas*, *innascibilitas*, fertility and 'ideo principium quia primum'[20] and his definition of the Person as the 'supposit of a reasonable nature that is distinguished by a property'.[21] This property is, of course, the relationship, but Bonaventure does not, as Thomas Aquinas was to do, make use of the principle singled out and expressed by Anselm, namely that in God everything is one, except where there is an opposition of relationship. The Persons are distinguished by their different properties, each of which is identical with their origin and therefore with the relationship. They cannot be distinguished by anything absolute. It is, however, indisputable that, in his affirmation of the unity of the divine substance, Bonaventure keeps close to the idea of the communication of life from one Person to another. This sense of mystery is also clear from the fact that he may have been the first in the West to give a place to the circumincession (which he spelt in this way). We have already seen this in the passage that is quoted above from his *Itinerarium* (p. 110, and below, note 10), but he speaks of it elsewhere as well.[22] It points to a mysterious but admirable aspect of the life of the Trinity as a life of *Persons* in unity of nature.

NOTES

1. Alexander of Hales, *ST* I, pars 2, inq. V, tract. II, sect. II, q. 3, memb. 3 (Quaracchi ed. (1924), pp. 460ff.). Alexander says in this context: 'Magistri concedunt hanc "Pater et Filius diligunt se Spiritu Sancto", sed dissentiunt in determinatione ablativi'. Bonaventure also asks how this ablative should be interpreted and replies: 'quasi effectus formalis' and 'aliquo modo in ratione formae': *In I Sent.* d. 32, a. 1, q. 1 (Quaracchi ed. (1924), p. 560). Odo Rigaldus also spoke in the same way: see Volume I, p. 91 note 7.
2. Alexander of Hales, *Glossa in quatuor libros Sententiarum. In librum primum (Bibl. Franciscana Scholastica Medii Aevi*, XII) (Quaracchi, 1951), dist. XI; pp. 135ff.
3. Alexander of Hales, *Quaestiones disputatae 'Antequam esset frater' (Bibl. Franciscana Scholastica Medii Aevi,* XIX) (Quaracchi, 1960), q. 8, memb. 1, 2 and 3; pp. 67ff.
4. *Ibid.*, memb. 1, nos 16 and 18; pp. 71 and 72.
5. *Ibid.*, memb. 3, nos 29–35; p. 75.
6. *ST* I, pars I, inq. II, tract. I, q. 1 (Quaracchi ed., pp. 436ff.). T. de Régnon discussed Alexander's triadology exclusively on the basis of the *Summa Theologica*, insofar as the text was known at the time: *Etudes de théologie positive sur la Sainte Trinité*, II (Paris, 1892), pp. 338–431.
7. *ST* I, c. 5; pp. 452–453. He returns to it again in Pars II, inq. II, tract. III, sect. II, q. 1, tit. II, a. 3; pp. 602ff.: 'sunt unum in spirando'; see also a. 6; pp. 696–697: 'spiratio convenit Patri et Filio secundum hoc commune quod est unitas naturae sive rationis naturae, quae non est unitas naturae absolute vel essentialiter dictae, sed relative dicitur'. He also quotes a text of Isidore of Seville, *In Sent. V*, 15, 2 (*PL* 83, 569), who himself quotes Jn 17:22: 'ut sint unum sicut et nos unum sumus'. I do not know how the Greek Fathers commented on this text.
8. Bonaventure stresses this from the very beginning: see *In I Sent.* d. 2 (Quaracchi ed., I, p. 24): 'sicut fides dicit'; see also d. 3; p. 93.
9. *De myst. Trin.* q. 1, a. 2 (Quaracchi ed., V, pp. 51ff.).
10. *Itin.* VI, 2 (Quaracchi ed., V, pp. 310–311).
11. Pseudo-Dionysius, *De coel. hier.* c. 4, 1 (*PG* 3, 177); *De div. nom.* c. 4 § 5 and c. 5 § 20 (*PG* 3, 593, 720); see Bonaventure, *In I Sent.* d. 2, q. 2 (Quaracchi ed., I, p. 53).
12. *In I Sent.* d. 2, q. 4 (Quaracchi ed., V, p. 57); d. 10, a. 1, q. 1 (Quaracchi ed., V, p. 195); and q. 2 (Quaracchi ed., V, p. 197). See also J.-F. Bonnefoy, *Le Saint-Esprit et ses dons selon S. Bonaventure* (Paris, 1929), pp. 26–28.
13. *In I Sent.* d. 10, a. 2, q. 1 (Quaracchi ed., V, p. 201). T. de Régnon provided the following translation of this text, *op. cit.* (note 6), p. 549: 'The word "dilection" can be understood in the context of God as referring to the divine essence, the notional act or the Person. It can be used with reference to the essence, since each Person loves himself. It can be applied to the notional act, since the Father and the Son agree with each other to produce the Holy Spirit, "concordant in spirando spiritum sanctum", and that agreement is a love or "dilection". Finally, it can be employed in the personal sense, because the one who is produced by way of perfect liberality can only be love or "dilection". An example of this can be found in the affection of creatures, through which a bridegroom and his bride love

each other. They love one another with a "social" love so that they can live together. What is more, they love one another with a "conjugal" love so that they can procreate a child. If that child were produced by the agreement of wills alone, it would be "love". In fact, the child is only the "loved one", although it may be called "love" by virtue of a kind of emphasis. In God, however, it is truly "love", because it has the characteristics of love and hypostasis. It has the character of love because of the immediate procession from a very liberal will by means of perfect liberality. It has the character of hypostasis because, being distinguished from its productive principle and not being able to distinguish itself from it essentially, it is distinguished from it personally.'

14. *In I Sent.* d. 32, a. 1, q. 1 and a. 2, q. 1 (Quaracchi ed., pp. 552 and 562).

15. *In I Sent.* d. 10, a. 1, q. 3 (Quaracchi ed., p. 199).

16. *In I Sent.* d. 13, a. unic., q. 1, No. 4 (Quaracchi ed., p. 231); d. 10, a. 2, q. 2 (Quaracchi ed., p. 202).

17. 'Ideo principium quia primum': *In I Sent.* d. 7, a. un. q. 2 (Quaracchi ed., p. 139). For this *primitas* as a very important category in Bonaventure's thought, see *De myst. Trin.* q. 8 (Quaracchi ed., V, p. 114); and the *Lexique S. Bonaventure* (Paris, 1969), under the entry 'Primitas'. Another idea that is much favoured by Bonaventure is that of *reductio ad unum primum*. He also makes use of this idea in his ecclesiology. See, for example, *De myst. Trin.* q. 2, a. 1 (Quaracchi ed., V, p. 61); *In II Sent.* d. 37, a. 1, q. 3, fund. 3 (Quaracchi ed., II, p. 867).

18. *In I Sent.* d. 2, q. 2 (Quaracchi ed., p. 54). This is an opening statement, made on the threshold of the *De myst. Trin.*

19. *In I Sent.* d. 27, q. 1, a. 1, q. 1 ad 3; tr. T. de Régnon, *op. cit.* (note 6), pp. 484ff. Further relevant quotations are: 'innascibilitas quae idem est in Patre quod primitas, cum primum et principium sint idem': d. 11, a. un. q. 2 (Quaracchi ed., p. 215); 'auctor dicit in Patre fontalem plenitudinem, quia ipse non est ab alio sed alii ab ipso, et inde dicit, ut credo, eandem notionem quem dicit innascibilis, sed differenti modo': d. 13, dub. IV (Quaracchi ed., p. 240). See also below, pp. 135–136. Bonaventure believed that this *innascibilitas* implied fertility, that there was no antecedent or father and that it could give being to another: see, for example, the long *retractatio* in the prologue to *In II Sent.*, reproduced in the scholion of the editors; *In I Sent.* d. 27, p. 1 to 2 (Quaracchi ed., pp. 472ff.).

20. See the previous note. The Holy Spirit proceeds *prius a Patre origine* and *auctoritate*: *In I Sent.* d. 12, a. un. q. 1 and 2.

21. *In I Sent.* d. 23, a. 1, q. 1 (Quaracchi ed., p. 409); d. 25, a. 1, q. 1 (Quaracchi ed., p. 436); in q. 2, Bonaventure accepted Boethius' definition; d. 34, a. un. q. 1 (Quaracchi ed., p. 587), where he also says *hypostasis*.

22. *In I Sent.* d. 19, q. 1, a. un. q. 4 (Quaracchi ed., p. 349); *Coll. in Hexameron* XXI, 19 (Quaracchi ed., V, p. 434). Peter Lombard wrote an excellent chapter on this question, but did not use the word. It is also worth noting, in this context, the comment made by William of Saint-Thierry, that we cannot name one of the Persons of the Trinity without implying another—the Son calls for the Father, and the Spirit as Gift calls for a Giver. This, William thought, was evidence that the Persons were related to each other and that they existed within each other.

4

THOMAS AQUINAS[1]

According to Thomas Aquinas, it is impossible to prove or understand by human reason the mystery of the Tri-unity of God. All that can be grasped by reason alone is the existence and the attributes of God the creator. God acts as creator through his nature, which is common to the three Persons, while revealing the latter only in traces, like the traces of a man whose face and voice remain unknown.

Thomas' theology is thus based on faith and his thinking is done in faith.[2] He did so with an exceptional use and mastery of the resources of reason, which was formed in the Aristotelian school and Scholastic disputation. He was firmly convinced of the value and the consistency of the truth that human reason was able to deduce from the reality of creation. He applied the rules of that reason and observed the demands made by it in elaborating his theological arguments, within the framework of affirmations of faith and on the basis of certain scriptural statements. This gives his work an impression of overriding rationality. This impression is particularly powerful, for example, in a text such as question 10 of *De Potentia*. It is, however, at the same time impossible to avoid being struck by his masterly knowledge and use of Scripture, and of the writings of the Fathers, although it has to be admitted that his knowledge of the Greek patristic texts was incomplete.[3]

A whole book could be written on his pneumatology. Such a book would contain at least four chapters: (1) the great principles of the theology of faith in the Trinity; (2) the procession of the Holy Spirit *a Patre et Filio tanquam ab uno principio*; (3) the theme of the Spirit as the mutual love of the Father and the Son (see Volume I of this work, pp. 88–90); (4) the part played by the Holy Spirit in the life of the Christian and of the Church. The last chapter has not been greatly studied, except for the question of the indwelling of the Holy Spirit and that of the gifts of the Spirit. I have already dealt with these questions in Volumes I and II.[4] Later in this volume, I shall look at the part played by the Spirit in the sacraments. Thomas Aquinas' consideration of the rôle of the Holy Spirit in the whole economy of grace and in his view of the Church has, however, still to be discussed with the full and precise attention that it deserves.[5]

Any attempt to present him as an 'essentialist', that is, as being conscious of and as affirming first of all the common divine essence, and only secondarily the Persons in that essence, would be to betray the balance of his theology. Such an interpretation should no longer be possible since the

116

appearance of the studies by A. Malet, H. F. Dondaine, E. Bailleux, M.-J. Le Guillou and others.[6] This interpretation has all too frequently been based on the fact that Thomas' study of the Trinity of Persons in the *Summa* is preceded by a study of the divine essence. Surely, however, it is hardly possible not to proceed in this way from the point of view of teaching? Is this procedure not justified by the economy of revelation itself? Did John Damascene not begin with the unity of 'God'? Thomas had a very lively sense of the absolute character of God, his transcendence, his independence and his sufficiency.[7] In his mystery, which is both necessary and absolute, God knows and loves himself. He communicates his goodness with sovereign freedom in the free mystery of creation and of the 'divine missions' through which creatures, who are made 'in his image', are included in that life of knowledge and love and are in this way 'deified'.

Through the Word of God and in faith, we know that there are three Persons in the unity of the divine substance. Thomas accepts this article of faith from no other source than the faith, but, as a theologian, he attempts to understand it: 'utcumque mente capere' (*Contra Gent.* IV, 1). God descended to us in the forms and words of our world, and we have to use the same instruments in order to re-ascend to him.

In a very resolute way, Thomas follows the path traced first by Augustine and especially by Anselm. He is aware of the path followed by Richard of Saint-Victor and Bonaventure, and he criticizes it cautiously.[8] He retains the idea of the Holy Spirit as Love and Gift and affirms that these titles are correctly bestowed on the Spirit (*ST* Ia, q. 37 and 38). He also preserves the idea that the Spirit is the mutual love of the Father and the Son. He does not, however, make these ideas the principle by which the mystery of the holy Triad should be understood *theologically* or that on which a *theological* construction should be erected. The principle that he prefers is the structure of the spirit itself, which includes knowledge and love of itself.[9] He does not, however, deduce these faculties or these acts from the essence of God, nor does he see in this structure the equivalent of Anselm's *rationes necessariae*. He is familiar with the work of Anselm and follows him, but rejects the idea of 'necessary reason'.[10] For him, what affirms the Triad of Father, Word-Son and Spirit is faith. The best way of approaching this mystery of faith intellectually, he claims, is through our knowledge of the structure of a spiritual being. This being exists in three ways—in its being as reality, in its thought as a known 'object' and in its will as a loved 'object'. Thinking and will are immanent functions which remain in the subject as its life. The term of these functions, the intellectual expression or the mental word, and the impression made in the one who loves by the act of loving are also immanent.

There are two 'processions' in God, but the term 'procession' is used in a very general sense by Thomas and, in his teaching, points simply to the fact that one reality comes from another.[11] From the theological point of view, these processions can be understood on the model of the functioning of the spirit—as emanations or communications of the nature of that spirit by mode of intellectual understanding and by mode of will.[12] The mode of will clearly produces dynamic movement, and Thomas stresses the fact that the very name 'spirit' indicates a movement or an impulse.[13] He makes a similar commènt with regard to the gifts of the Holy Spirit and the text of Isaiah in which they are listed.[14]

These emanations of the divine nature do not, Thomas believes, take place in the same way as the human faculties emanate from man's essence, from which the faculties are really quite different. The divine processions in fact constitute Persons who are both really identical with the essence of God and at the same time different from each other. This is the whole problem of the Trinity—it is one in the absolute sense and at the same time several. These several Persons are identical with the absolute one and yet really different from each other, to the point of being Persons, that is, a spiritual reality existing in itself in a way that cannot be communicated. The solution to these aporias can be found in the ideas of *relationship, relationship of origin*, with the *opposition* between the two terms that this idea implies, and *subsistent relationship*.

The Son is not the Father and the Father is not the Son. But the Father is God and the Son is God. Each is everything that the other is, apart from that character which describes it by reference to another and which in this way also distinguishes it within the unity of both.[15] What defines the Person, then, is the relationship which both unites and opposes that Person to the other. This opposition is an opposition of the relationship itself—to say Father is to say Son and vice versa. The unity is in the communication of the entire good of the nature (or the essence or substance) of God. This communication takes place by means of the fact that one Person is the origin of the other—the Father is the origin of the Son as the spirit is similarly the origin of the word in which it is expressed. What constitutes the Person, then, according to Thomas, is his relationship of origin.[16] Through that relationship, the Person is *really* distinguished from the Person who is correlative to him. But in God, these relationships are *really* identical with the sovereignly simple essence and this means that they have that quality of 'subsistent relationships' that Thomas defines and employs in his triadology.[17] As H. F. Dondaine pointed out,[18] 'the divine Person is the divine and subsistent relationship regarded as distinctly subsistent. In other words, it is the relationship of origin insofar as that relationship enjoys in God the prerogatives of substance and insofar as it is absolute, while at the same time being intra-divinely incommunicable.'

Thomas' theology of the Person and the relationship of origin is also applied to the second procession, the one that takes place in God by mode of will or love. The procession of the Holy Spirit is not only *ex Patre*, from the Father, but also *ex Filio*, from the Son. Thomas deals with this question in his *Summa* in a dialectic and highly rationalized way. In other writings, he provides proofs derived from Scripture and the Fathers.[19] The scriptural texts that he uses are those that had been employed for centuries by the Latins, but their value as proofs is heightened by rational explanations. The Spirit is, for example, the Spirit of the Son (or of Christ) (Rom 8:9; Gal 4:6). The Spirit is sent by the Son (Jn 15:26), but the 'mission' of a Person is linked to his procession. 'He will take what is mine' (Jn 16:14)—this declaration that the Spirit will receive from Jesus is followed by the decisive reason: 'All that the Father has is mine; therefore I said that he will take what is mine'. The Greeks, as we have seen, thought that these texts referred to the economy and not to the eternal relationships, but Thomas shows that they cannot be applied to the humanity of Christ, but only to his divinity. He is above all concerned to provide reasons for this.

His main reason is derived from the essence of the Trinitarian theology elaborated by Anselm. The divine Persons are distinguished not by an absolute perfection, but only by a mutual opposition in their relationships. If these relationships are not opposed, there is no question of different Persons. The Father produces the Son by begetting and the Spirit by spiration, but, as begetting and spiration are not opposed, this duality of relationships does not bring about a duality of Persons in the Father. In the same way, these two processions or modes or proceeding are not opposed, so that they are not in themselves sufficient to distinguish the Son from the Spirit as two different Persons. In God, the only relationships that are really opposed are those of origin, which are opposed as the beginning or principle and the term. Consequently, if the Holy Spirit is to be personally distinguished from the Son, there must be a relationship of origin between them, in other words, the Spirit must proceed from the Son at the same time as he proceeds from the Father. Thomas is categorical and even almost rough in his affirmation of this, saying: If the Spirit did not proceed from the Son, he would not be distinguished from him![20] He thus decisively rejects Photius' triadology.

Thomas was, however, more positive in his acceptance of the theme of *per Filium* than Anselm had been before him.[21] The Father is the *auctor*, the absolute principle, from whom the Son is able to perform the 'spiration' of the Spirit.[22] The Word begotten by God the Father is not an ordinary conception. In his very reality as Word, he is a Word from whom Love proceeds—as Thomas himself said, he is 'Verbum non qualecumque, sed spirans amorem'.[23] Thomas is, however, more anxious to affirm the unity of the hypostases than to stress their order. He does not fully recognize the implication of the *dia tou Huiou* on which the Greeks insisted so much, but he does sense the complementarity of the two formulae.[24] Although he accepts the *per Filium*, he, like Anselm, is anxious to exclude any inequality. The Father, as *auctor*, communicates the faculty of spiration to the Word, but he does so by making him a single and identical principle, along with himself.

The Greeks, however, have been raising objections to the Western teaching and asking critical questions since the time of Photius. Nilus Cabasilas[25] asked such questions in the fourteenth century and they were asked a century later at Florence by Mark Eugenikos. The identical objections are raised by my Greek friends and contemporaries, and it is at this point that we must consider them. They can be summarized as follows: If the Spirit also proceeds from the Son, then either he proceeds from two principles or else he proceeds from the essence that is common to the Father and the Son, but in that case he would also proceed from himself, because that essence is also common to him. This situation is clearly absurd, the Greeks claim, unless the divine essence is not shared by all three Persons and the two first Persons have a reality that the third lacks.

These objections are, of course, justified within the perspective of Eastern triadology and within the context of the Greek vocabulary applied to the Trinity. The hypostases and the monarchy of the Father are aspects of great importance in the Orthodox triadology. One hypostasis proceeds only from another hypostasis, who communicates the fullness of the divine nature or essence to him. The terms *ekporeusis*, *aitia* and *archē* are only applied in the East to the Father and they express above all the *first* origin. The Latins were wrong to translate them as *processio*, *causa* and *principium* respectively, in the belief that these words had the same meaning as the Greek words, when in fact they can be applied more widely to include the Son with the Father.[26]

The Latin theologians, especially Thomas Aquinas, but before him Alexander of Hales (see above), have provided reasons for their belief. It is not enough to say that 'the spiration comes from the divine nature insofar as it is common to the Father and the Son',[27] because it does not come from that nature, but from supposits or Persons who have in common a nature that exists only in a hypostatized form. Thomas follows the logic of the principle according to which the divine Persons are distinguished from each other only by a relationship of opposition and goes on to distinguish, in the properties, those which are identical with the Persons because they are constitutive of those Persons—fatherhood and sonship—and those which, not being constitutive (because they do not include a relationship of opposition), can be common to several Persons. This is so in the case of active spiration, in which the Father and the Son are not, as such, opposed. Thomas' insistence on these relationships and their opposition leads him to make a further subtle, but very important definition, namely that the Father is not, *as Father*, the principle of the Spirit, because he is only the Father of the Son. He is, the Greeks claimed, the principle of the Spirit as *archē* and has the title of *proboleus*.[28] The Latins, on the other hand, maintained that the Spirit proceeds not from God his Father, but from God who is Father,[29] or else that he proceeds from the Father as *auctor* or absolute Principle. They also claim that, in the equal status of the *virtus spirativa*, there is also an order—just as the Persons in the Trinity are equal, yet proceed from each other, the Father being the Principle without principle and the Son receiving from him his faculty which enables him to produce the Spirit in a simple and unique act of spiration that is common to both.

The Latin theologians, including Thomas, based their reasoning on the principle that the Father gives the Son all that he has apart from his quality of being Father. He therefore also gives him the faculty of spiration. The Father does not, however, give the Son the faculty to beget, nor does he give the Spirit the faculty of spiration. Even if the Father gives the Son the faculty of spiration with him, he does not communicate to him the nature to be *principaliter* at the origin of the Spirit. As Thomas pointed out, 'the essence and the dignity of the Father and the Son are identical, but in the Father they exist according to the relationship of the one who gives, whereas in the Son they exist according to the relationship of the one who receives'.[30] The Latins were therefore careful to preserve the full truth of the monarchy of the Father, although they did not make it the axis of their theological construction, as the Greeks did in their triadology.

The Holy Spirit proceeds by mode of will or love. The personal names that he receives are Love and Gift (see *ST* Ia, q. 37 and 38). Thomas also pursued the theme of the Spirit as the mutual love of the Father and the Son at every stage of his life and in all his writings (see Volume I, pp. 88–90).

There is, then, a procession in God in accordance with will and love. This procession enables the Holy Spirit to exist eternally. The latter is therefore hypostatically Love. The word 'love', however, at once evokes the idea of an impulse or a movement towards a good. In man, it is because of a lack and the need to acquire what we do not have, except in friendship, which is a communication with the other, whereas in God that love is a superabundance and a great generosity. God is Love, *agapē*. He is the source of Love, a Love that gives itself in grace. His love does not try to satisfy a hunger, but to arouse and communicate being.[31] If the Spirit, then, is hypostatic Love in God—and his name 'Spirit', Thomas believed, points to an impulse (see note 13 below)—everything that is gift, grace and the communication of being and good must be traced back to him as manifesting his property as a Person.

It is in this line of love of self (and of all things in himself) by God that Thomas looks for a theological understanding of what he believes through faith regarding the third Person. Secondly, he considers essential love of the kind that is common to the three Persons. This accompanies the first procession. The Father experiences it with regard to the Son and the Son experiences it with regard to the Father. In this question, Thomas goes back to the theme of mutual love and sees the Holy Spirit as the link between the two Persons—the *nexus amborum* or *amor unitivus duorum*.[32] All those who have considered pneumatology in the context of the mutual love of the Father and the Son have always quoted scriptural texts in which Jesus speaks

121

of the love of the Father for him and of his love for the Father.[33] These texts have the incarnate Word in mind. The 'I' of these texts is certainly that of the eternal Son, but one in whom human consciousness and freedom must be acknowledged. It is therefore a metaphysical 'I', but an 'I' who is also psychologically human.

The theme of the Spirit as the mutual love of the Father and the Son has been widely discussed in recent works on triadology and in spiritual books. It is not difficult to explain and it can easily be applied to other forms of expression. It is in accordance with human experience and it has strong echoes in the psychological study of interpersonal relationships. It also quickly arouses a warm response. On the other hand, however, it presents certain difficulties to the theologian. Above all, it takes anthropomorphic expressions to the limit of doctrinal precision. Also, it goes back to a different way of thinking from that of the Eastern Orthodox. But we should have no illusion about this—Thomas' way of thinking may be more accessible than that of the Eastern Christians because it is more dogmatic, but it is not the same as theirs either.

According to Thomas, then, the Spirit proceeds by mode of will and love. He is uncreated, hypostatic Love and he deserves to be called Love and Gift. In that case, he clearly is, by appropriation, the principle of what God freely produces outside himself as a participation of his goodness. Thomas develops this idea in three very dense and rewarding chapters in his *Contra Gentiles*—I shall come back to these below—and in a short chapter in his *Compendium theologiae* which is a gloss on the third article of the creed. The text of the latter is as follows:

> The second effect caused by God is the government of the world and in particular of those creatures who are gifted with reason and to whom he has given grace and whose sins he has remitted. All this is called to mind in the creed, on the one hand when we confess the Holy Spirit as God—this means that all things are ordered to the end of divine goodness, since it is God's function to order his subjects to their end (the Spirit is called 'Lord')—and, on the other hand, it is clear that he gives movement to all things—he is called the 'giver of life'. In the same way, just as the movement that passes from the soul to the body is the life of the body, so too is the movement with which God animates the world a kind of life of the universe. It was suitable that the effects of divine Providence should be situated close to the Holy Spirit, since the whole of divine government is dependent on divine goodness, which is appropriated to the Holy Spirit, who proceeds as love. For what is of the effect of supernatural knowledge, which God brings about in men through faith, we say 'the holy Catholic Church', since the Church is the assembly of the faithful; for what is of the grace that he communicates to men, we say 'the communion of saints'; for what is of the remission of faults, we say 'the remission of sins'.[34]

What is stated in the rational and rather barren style of this *Compendium* is set out more explicitly in:

(1) The very rich biblical chapters of *Contra Gentiles* IV. These are chapter 20: 'the effects attributed to the Holy Spirit with regard to the whole of creation', that is, everything that exists of goodness, movement towards the end, and life; chapter 21: 'the effects attributed to the Holy Spirit with regard to the creature gifted with reason, as regards what God grants to us or lavishes on us', that is, everything that is given through love to a friend; chapter 22: 'the effects of the Holy Spirit through whom God enables his creature to return to himself', that is, according to what a life of friendship, a filial life, a life in freedom includes. I dream of an eloquent translation of these three chapters with a commentary and notes, pointing out especially the use that Thomas has made of so many magnificent biblical texts elsewhere in his writings. . . .

(2) Part IIa of the *Summa*. Thomas describes the general structures of Christian action in Part Ia IIae and studies the composite parts of that action in IIa IIae. He shows that it is a supernatural form of human activity sustained by the law of God and the grace of the Holy Spirit and that the principal aspect of this Christian law is grace itself, which operates in such a way that the law is a law of freedom (see Volume II, pp. 124–126). It is a life as children of God.[35] Grace places charity in us and Thomas defines this as friendship.[36] This friendship means that the Trinity dwells in us (see Volume II, pp. 79–90). Thomas' sense of the theologal character of faith, hope and charity was exceptionally acute, with the result that he believed that these virtues, which make us children of God, could only be practised according to their divine demands if there were impulses from the Holy Spirit. This constitutes his theology of the gifts, to which the fruits of the Spirit and the beatitudes, which are the supreme acts of forms of Christian life, correspond. I have spoken about these in Volume I, pp. 117–121, and Volume II, pp. 134–139. Finally, there is the question of merit, the principal agent of which is the Holy Spirit (see Volume II, p. 108).

(3) All this actively concerns the life of the Christian, which is personal, but not simply individual. Thomas is conscious of the believer as a member of the Church and sees charity as a virtue of the common good of the City of God.[37] That City is also the Church, which Thomas sees as unified, sanctified and animated by the Holy Spirit.[38] Unfortunately it is not possible for me to discuss in detail here the many scattered, but quite consistent indications in his writings that form part of his pneumatology. This is all the more regrettable, since this question has not yet been studied as exhaustively as it should have been.

*   *   *

Many of the later, less successful imitators of the great thirteenth-century theologians of the Western Church, some of whom were very active and vigorous workers, elaborated and discussed the great questions of Trinitarian theology with an excessive reliance on philosophical concepts and arguments. M. Schmaus[39] analysed and partly edited this copious body of writing in which these sublime questions were discussed with great confidence in the unlimited scope of theological reasoning: Does the Father beget because he is Father or is he Father because he begets? Are the two processions, begetting and spiration, to be distinguished by their term or by their principle or beginning? If the Father and the Son love each other through the Spirit, can this 'through the Spirit' be regarded as a 'formal effect'? What is the principle by which (*quo*) of spiration? What is the difference between begetting (generation) and spiration? Would the Spirit be different from the Son because of an absolute quality if he did not proceed from him? In the thirteenth and fourteenth centuries, there were two traditions or schools. One was in the path followed by Thomas Aquinas. The other was the tradition of Henry of Ghent and Duns Scotus, and before that of Bonaventure and, before him again, up stream, Richard of Saint-Victor.

NOTES

1. The most important texts are: *In I Sent*. d. 3 to 31; *Contra Gent*. IV, 1 to 28; *Contra Err. Graec*. (1264); *De Pot*. q. 8 to 10; *ST* Ia, q. 27 to 43; see H. F. Dondaine's translation, with commentary, 2 vols (Paris, 1943). Apart from T. de Régnon, *Etudes de théologie positive sur la Sainte Trinité*, II (Paris, 1892), the following studies are valuable: H. F. Dondaine, 'La théologie latine de la procession du Saint-Esprit', *Russie et Chrétienté* (1950), 211–218; M. T. L. Penido, ' "Cur non Spiritus Sanctus a Patre Deo genitus". S. Augustin et S. Thomas', *RThom* (1930), 508–527; *idem*, 'Gloses sur la procession d'amour dans la Trinité', *ETL*, 14 (1937), 33–68; for the discussion that followed this article, see *BullThom* (1937–1939), 135–139 and 547–549; A. Malet, *Personne et amour dans la théologie trinitaire de S. Thomas* (*Bibl. thomiste*, XXXII) (Paris, 1956); J. Pelikan, 'The Doctrine of the Filioque in Thomas Aquinas and its Patristic Antecedents. An Analysis of Summa Theologica Part I, q. 36', *S. Thomas Aquinas. Commemorative Studies*, I (Toronto, 1974), pp. 315–336. See also Volume I, pp. 88–90, 91–92 notes 9 to 14, and 118–121, 124 notes 17 to 26.
2. Thomas frequently stated and justified this, for example, in *In I Sent*. d. 3, q. 1, a. 4; *Contra Gent*. I, 3 and 9; IV, 1; *De Pot*. q. 9, a. 5 and 9; q. 10, a. 1; *ST* Ia, q. 1, a. 8, ad 2; q. 32, a. 1; q. 45, a. 6. See also *Quodl*. IV, 18: 'quomodo sit verum'.
3. In his Trinitarian theology, he only really cites Pseudo-Dionysius and John Damascene. There is a vague and general reference to the 'doctores Graecorum' in *ST* Ia, q. 35, a. 2 c. and ad 4. His references to the Greek Fathers in *ST* Ia are concerned with anthropology and the work of the six days of creation: see G. Bardy, 'Sur les sources patristiques grecques de S. Thomas dans la 1re partie de la Somme théologique', *RSPT*, 12 (1923), 493–502. Thomas thought very highly of Gregory Nazianzen: q. 61, a. 3 c. end. There is also a general comment in *Contra Err. Graec*. I, 10.
4. For the indwelling of the Spirit, see Volume II, pp. 82–90; for the gifts, see Volume I, pp. 117–121, and Volume II, pp. 134–139.
5. M. Grabmann, *Die Lehre des heiligen Thomas von der Kirche als Gotteswerk* (Regensburg, 1903), has some interesting observations; references in my article, 'Vision de l'Eglise chez S. Thomas d'Aquin', *RSPT*, 62 (1978), 523–542, especially 532–536.
6. A. Malet, *op. cit.* (note 1), and 'La synthèse de la personne et de la nature dans la théologie trinitaire de S. Thomas,' *RThom*, 54 (1954), 483–522, and 55 (1955), 43–84; E. Bailleux,

'Le personnalisme de S. Thomas en théologie trinitaire', *ibid.*, 61 (1961), 25–42; *idem*, 'La création, œuvre de la Trinité selon S. Thomas', *ibid.*, 62 (1962), 27–60; M.-J. Le Guillou, *Le Christ et l'Eglise. Théologie du mystère* (Paris, 1963); *idem*, *Le Mystère du Père* (Paris, 1973). *Contra Err. Graec.* I, 4 criticizes all the formulae in which the procession of the Persons is linked with the divine essence.

7. May I record the evidence of my personal experience here? We had to begin our theological studies with *De Deo uno* because of the way in which Thomas' treatises to be studied were distributed at the time. This coincided with our reception of minor orders. The benefit that we derived from this was a very lively sense of the absolute nature of God.

8. Thomas criticizes Richard's argument with regard to the communication of good, which is necessary to God's perfect state of blessedness. See *De Pot.* q. 9, a. 5, videtur quod non 24; *ST* Ia, q. 32, a. 1, ad 2. For a criticism of Bonaventure's construction on the basis of God's *innascibilitas*, see *ST* Ia, q. 33, a. 4, ad 1.

9. See *Contra Gent.* IV, 19, 23, end, 26; *De Pot.* q. 10, a. 1 and 2; *ST* Ia, q. 27, a. 1, 3 to 5; q. 37, a. 1. In the enigmatic *Comp.* I, 50, we read: 'Deus in esse suo naturali existens, et Deus existens in intellectu, et Deus existens in amore suo unum sunt'.

10. See C. Vagaggini, 'La hantise des *rationes necessariae* de S. Anselme dans la théologie des processions trinitaires de S. Thomas', *Spicilegium Beccense*, I (*Congrès internationale du IXᵉ centenaire de l'arrivée d'Anselme au Bec*) (Le Bec-Hellouin and Paris, 1959), pp. 103–139. I do not believe that an 'obsession [*hantise*] with the *rationes necessariae*' is a good category, since it is a question of rationality of faith and in faith. The fact that the sending out of a word by intelligence is treated as a simple perfection shows us, subject to the presupposition of faith, that there is a procession in God of a Word, the Son, but it does not enable us to infer the fact, since we do not know the positive mode by which this perfection is realized in God or the way in which God is this perfection in the absolute unity of his substance. Is it a simple attribute? Is it a hypostasis? Or is it a subsistent relationship? It is, however, true to say that, when grounds of fittingness (*convenientia*) are taken from the formal structure of realities, they come close to the proof of existence.

11. See *De Pot.* q. 10, a. 1; a. 4 ad 13: *procedere* has the advantage of being the 'verbum communissimum eorum quae ad originem spectant', although this excludes an understanding of the meaning and the importance that *ekporeuesthai* had for the Greeks, despite the fact that Thomas was very near to an understanding of this in his *In I Sent.* d. 12, q. 1, a. 2, ad 3. See also *Contra Err. Graec.* II, 16; *ST* Ia, q. 36, a. 2, c. end.

12. In *De Pot.* q. 10, a. 2, Thomas uses this formula in place of the one that appears in the *Sentences*: 'per modum naturae, per modum voluntatis'. Logically enough, the theme of 'Son' was given priority over that of 'Word' in the *Sentences*. The Greek Fathers had also tended to follow the theme of 'Son', although they had also stressed the theme of 'image'. Thomas shows very rigorously that the Word proceeds in God in accordance with a process of begetting—the second Person is the Son because he is the Word and he is the Word because he is the Son; see *Contra Gent.* IV, 11; *ST* Ia, q. 27, a. 2; q. 34, a. 1 and 2. See also Gregory Nazianzen, *Orat.* 30 (= *Orat. theol.* IV), 20 (*PG* 36, 129A).

13. See *Contra Gent.* IV, 19, in which Thomas uses the word *inclinatio* again and again; see also IV, 20: 'amor vim quandam impulsivam et motivam habet'; *ST* Ia, q. 27, a. 4, c. end and q. 36, a. 1: 'nomen spiritus impulsionem quamdam et motionem significare videtur'.

14. *ST* Ia IIae, q. 68, a. 1: Isaiah speaks not of 'gifts', but of 'spirits', which means that they are *ab inspiratione divina*.

15. As Maximus the Confessor said, *Amb.* 26 (*PG* 91, 1265C-D), 'the name of Father is neither a name of essence nor a name of energy, but rather a name of *schēsis*, that is, of relationship, and it says how the Father is towards the Son and how the Son is towards the Father'.

16. *De Pot.* q. 8, a. 1. Thomas believed that the relationship logically preceded the origin and that it was what defined the Person. Consequently, in a discussion in which Bonaventure, taking as his point of departure the ideas that we have outlined above, held a different view,

Thomas said: 'quia Pater est, generat', in other words, he is not the Father because he begets, but he begets because he is the Father. This is, of course, a very subtle distinction. It is a question which preoccupied the Scholastic theologians, not because of the words themselves, but because of the need to establish order in our human ways of thinking and speaking. It is the famous *modus significandi*. It means that the subsistent Person, with all that constitutes it (the relationship), is absolutely first. It is logically first and precedes its act: see *ST* Ia, q. 40 and the explanations provided by H. F. Dondaine. In the relationship itself, if what it is in God is considered, the *esse in*, which makes it subsistent, logically precedes the *esse ad*, which distinguishes it from another Person by opposing it relationally.

17. *De Pot.* q. 8, a. 1, ad 4; a. 2; a. 3, ad 7 and 9; a. 4; q. 9, a. 4; a. 5 ad 13; q. 10, a. 1 ad 12; a. 2, ad 1; *ST* Ia, q. 28, a. 2; q. 29, a. 3 and 4; q. 40, a. 1; q. 42, a. 5. This real identity between relationship and substance, two terms which seem to be situated at the extreme end of reality, is possible because 'substance' in God is not in a genus: see *De Pot.* q. 8, a. 2, ad 1.

18. Fr. tr. H. F. Dondaine, *op. cit.* (note 1), I, p. 245; *In I Sent.* d. 23, a. 3, c. See also A. Malet, *op. cit.* (note 1).

19. Thomas did this before his rational argument in *Contra Gent.* IV, 24, but after that provided in *De Pot.* q. 10, a. 4. See also the second part of the *Contra Err. Graec.*, where several of the patristic texts quoted are known to be, at least in part, unauthentic. Thomas refrained from using them in his *Summa*.

20. *In I Sent.* d. 13, q. 1, a. 2; *De Pot.* q. 10, a. 5, a very well developed article; *ST* Ia, q. 36, a. 2; *Comm. in ev. Ioan.* c. 15, lect. 5, No. 7. See also *Contra Gent.* IV, 25, where Thomas deals with the Greek rejection of the *Filioque* with a vivacity which shows that he had not really grasped their reasons.

21. *De Pot.* q. 10, a. 5; the *a Filio* is established in the body of the article; cf. *ST* Ia, q. 36, where the *a Filio* is established in art. 3.

22. See below, p. 136, for Thomas Aquinas' acceptance of Augustine's *principaliter* and of the theme of *auctor*.

23. *In I Sent.* d. 27, q. 2, a. 1; *ST* Ia, q. 43, a. 5, ad 2; *Comm. in ev. Ioan.* c. 6, lect. 5, No. 5.

24. In his *De Processione Spiritus Sancti* (*PG* 161, 397C-400A), John Bessarion observes that *ex Filio* means equality and not order, whereas *per Filium* points to order rather than to equality and sees in these two different and yet complementary aspects the anxiety of the Latins and the Greeks respectively.

25. Cabasilas rejected the possibility of proving the procession from the Son by means of syllogisms and studied and criticized fifteen such syllogisms. These have been examined by E. Candal, *Nilus Cabasilas et theologia S. Thomae de Processione Spiritus Sancti* (*Studi e Testi*, 116) (Vatican, 1945): Cabasilas' treatise is edited on pp. 188–385. See also the criticism of Thomas Aquinas' syllogisms in *Contra Gent.* IV, 24, by Cabasilas and the reply made by the translator, Demetrios Kydones, in M. Rackl, 'Der heilige Thomas von Aquin und das trinitarische Grundgesetz in byzantinischer Beleuchtung', S. Szabó, ed., *Xenia Thomistica* (Rome, 1925), III, pp. 363–389.

26. V. Grumel pointed this out in his article 'S. Thomas et la doctrine des Grecs sur la procession du Saint-Esprit', *Echos d'Orient*, 25 (1926), 257–280. This is an excellent article, which has lost nothing of its value with the passage of the years.

27. This is T. de Régnon's formula, *Etudes de théologie positive sur la Sainte Trinité*, I (Paris, 1892), pp. 308–309.

28. *Proboleus*—see above, pp. 38, 47 note 69; John Damascene, *PG* 94, 849A. This question has been discussed by A. de Halleux, 'La procession de l'Esprit Saint dans le symbole de Constantinople', *RTL*, 10 (1979), 34. According to this author, in Gregory Nazianzen, *Orat.* 31, 6, 'the Father is understood as divine nature and as the source of divinity before being seen as a pole of personal opposition', and with the creed of 381, 'the title of God, which is necessary because of the Johannine text (15:26), does not point here to the first

Person in his personal uniqueness, but only to him as the source of divinity': *op. cit.*, pp. 33–34.

29. T. de Régnon, *op. cit.* (note 27), IV (Paris, 1898), p. 275.

30. *ST* Ia, q. 42, a. 4, ad 2.

31. See Thomas' frequently repeated axiom: 'amor Dei creans et infundens bonitatem in rebus', *ST* Ia, q. 20, a. 2, 3 and 4; q. 23, a. 4; Ia IIae, q. 26, a. 3, ad 4, *Tabula aurea*, 'amor', No. 21.

32. *ST* Ia, q. 36, a. 4, ad 1; q. 37, a. 1, ad 3; q. 39, a. 8.

33. The Father loves the Son: see Jn 3:35; 5:20; 10:17; 17:23, where the evangelist is clearly speaking of the incarnate Christ; 17:24, where he presupposes the pre-existence of Christ (see Volume II, pp. 229, 230 note 1); 17:26. The Son loves the Father: see Jn 14:30; 15:10, where the evangelist is speaking of the incarnate Son.

34. *Comp.* I, 147.

35. See E. Bailleux, 'Le Christ et son Esprit', *RThom*, 73 (1973), 373–400. For our life as sons, see Volume II, pp. 90–92 and 104–106.

36. *ST* IIa IIae, q. 23. It is surprising that Thomas does not name the Spirit in this text as the mutual love of the Father and the Son; but see *Contra Gent.* IV, 21 and 22. For his moral teaching in the perspective of charity, see H. D. Noble, *L'amitié avec Dieu. Essai sur la vie spirituelle d'après S. Thomas d'Aquin* (Tournai, 1929).

37. See *Quaest. disp. de virtutibus in communi*, a. 9; *de caritate*, a. 2; *Comm. in I Cor.* c. 13, lect. 4; *Comm. in Eph.* c. 2, lect. 6.

38. See above, note 5; see also below, Part Two, and Volume II, Part One.

39. M. Schmaus, *Der Liber Propugnatorius des Thomas Anglicus und die Lehrunterschiede zwischen Thomas von Aquin und Duns Scotus*, II: *Die trinitarischen Lehrdifferenzen (Beitr. zur Gesch. der Phil. und Theol.*, 29) (Münster, 1930), xxvii–666 and iv–334 pages!

5

DOGMATIC DEFINITIONS IN PNEUMATOLOGY
A NEED FOR HERMENEUTICS

There are different norms of faith and it is important to weigh them. They include canonical Scriptures, conciliar definitions, professions of faith, liturgy, the teachings of the ordinary magisterium and those of the 'authentic' doctors of the Church, and finally the experience of Christians themselves and the witness borne by spiritual men.

The professions of faith, which can be found, for example, in the collection of A. and G. L. Hahn and at the beginning of Denzinger and Schönmetzer, are sober expressions of the 'economic' activity of the third Person—the remission of sins, the resurrection of the body and eternal life. The Spirit has spoken through the prophets. He is the giver of life and he dwells in the saints.

It is, of course, not possible for me to study the ancient liturgies here, but it is possible to state that they express doxologically the faith of baptized Christians. In the ante-Nicene Church, these liturgical expressions of faith preceded theological expressions.[1] In the anaphora of the liturgy of St Basil, for example, the reference to the Spirit is linked to the mention of the Word by the words: 'by means of whom (the Word) the Holy Spirit manifests himself'.[2] Finally, we have already seen how rich is the pneumatology contained in the Syrian liturgy [above, pp. 41–43].

I have already spoken about the First Council of Constantinople, held in 381 (see Volume I, pp. 74–75, and above, p. 34). It was at Constantinople that the article on the Holy Spirit was completed in opposition to the Pneumatomachi and Macedonius:[3] we believe 'in the Holy Spirit, the Lord and giver of life, coming from the Father, co-adored and conglorified (with the Father and the Son), having spoken through the prophets'. The Council wanted to affirm the consubstantiality and therefore the divinity of the Spirit without in fact using these words and therefore retained the economic context of the text of Jn 15:26, to which it refers.[4] Its intention was not to define precisely the mode of procession followed by the Spirit, the mystery of which it revered. Both 'filioquism' and 'monopatrism' were alien to the spirit of Constantinople. No Latin bishop had been called to the Council, nor was any Latin bishop present at it; it was convoked by the emperor

Theodosius I. It described itself as 'ecumenical' because it was of the empire, but, if it was 'received' by the West, it was not described as such before the end of the fifth century by the Western Church.[5] This text is, in any case, absolutely normative. It expresses our faith.

A decree which begins with a profession of faith insisting on the relationship between the Spirit and Christ and which appeared at about the same time is attributed to Pope Damasus. According to the *Decretum Damasi*, the Spirit is not simply the Spirit of the Father, but also the Spirit of the Son. Christ himself said: 'he proceeds from the Father' (Jn 15:26) and 'he will receive from me and declare it to you' (16:14).[6] This was the Roman faith, as expressed later by Pope Pelagius I when he addressed King Childebert in 557.[7] Rome did not in fact adopt the *Filioque* until the eleventh century.[8]

It was introduced into the profession of faith in the seventh century, however, by the national Councils of Toledo. Such national councils, however, assume an importance which goes far beyond their local character when, on the one hand, they deal with faith, as is the case here, in order to combat dogmatic errors and, on the other, the teaching that they promulgate has already been widely 'received' by other Churches.

It is generally agreed that the Roman councils over which the Pope presided have increased authority by virtue of the fact that the Roman Church and its pontiff are a kind of mirror or epitome of Catholicity. Louis Bouyer, for instance, said: 'The Church has always recognized that partial councils could, in certain cases, express the *mens ecclesiae* in a definitive manner. This must, to some extent, be the case with all the councils convoked by the Pope and confirmed by him after a considerable episcopal representation has met.'[9]

This comment can certainly be applied to the Fourth Lateran Council, which was of great importance for the whole Latin Church in the thirteenth century. Its chapter on the 'Catholic faith', *Firmiter credimus*, was received as a fourth creed.[10] According to this conciliar statement, the Spirit is *ab utroque*.

It is customary to include the five Lateran Councils and the two Councils of Lyons among the so-called 'ecumenical' councils. I have mentioned elsewhere, as the decisive studies of the question by V. Peri have shown, that there is no official list with overriding authority of the 'ecumenical councils' of the Church, apart from the first seven which were common to both the Eastern and the Western Churches.[11] The application of the description 'ecumenical' not only to Lateran IV, but also to Lyons II of 1274 can therefore be called seriously into question. In any case, this qualification of 'ecumenical' is very difficult to define adequately. Paul VI published an important *actum* of the Apostolic See in 1974 which authorized this questioning of the term. In his letter written on 5 October of that year to Cardinal Jan Willebrands, *Lugduni, in urbe Galliae nobilissima*,[12] he described the Second Council of Lyons as the 'sixth of the general councils held in the

West'. The other five are, of course, the four Lateran Councils and the First Council of Lyons, held in 1245. The Pope also took note of the fact that the 'reception' of the union of Lyons was absent in the East.

In Lyons, on 6 June 1274, the logothete read, in the name of Emperor Michael VIII, a profession of faith that had been sent by the Pope. This profession stated that the Holy Spirit proceeded *ex Patre Filioque*.[13] In the sixth session of the same Second Council of Lyons, on 17 July, the Catholic teaching was proclaimed: 'The Holy Spirit proceeds eternally from the Father and the Son, not as from two principles, but as from a single principle, not by two spirations, but by a single spiration'.[14]

There was no debate at Lyons. The Byzantine emperor was represented, but it is not possible to say that the Greek Church was really represented. The situation was quite different at the Council of Florence, as we shall see. This council really deserves to be given the title of 'ecumenical council' and in fact it is often included in the list as the eighth (see note 11 below). The union that was reached there—I give the text of this below [p. 186], recognizing at the same time both its serious implications and its limitations—was denounced in the East.[15] The text of the Council of Florence is therefore not a link between the two parts of the Church. It has, however, served as a basis for a later union, such as that of Brest, which was prepared by a profession of faith compiled in 1575.[16]

Louis Bouyer went on to say this, not directly about Florence, but about councils held and accepted since the eleventh century in the West:

> It is no less true to say that, even when they can be regarded as infallible and, for that reason, unchangeable, their decisions, because they were taken in the absence of a considerable part of the episcopate, that part which would have represented a very venerable theological tradition, may still call for later additions and augmentations which would not have been necessary in the case of an ecumenical council in the earliest and fullest sense of the word.
>
> . . . The whole of the West may and indeed should ask the East to accept these councils at least provisionally and in a favourable sense, as a positive element that is essential if the questions involved are to be reconsidered together more broadly and more profoundly. At the same time, the West should offer the East the same promise—that the councils and decisions which the Eastern Church unanimously regards as equally important will be seriously considered in the West.

There is no doubt at all that the procession of the Holy Spirit from or through the Son as well forms part of the Roman Catholic expression of faith in the Trinity. It is taught by the ordinary universal magisterium of the Church and professed in the creed. But it is the *Latin* expression of that faith. It is more or less formally supported by a few Greek Fathers such as Cyril of Alexandria. It is not the Greek expression of Trinitarian faith. Bonaventure said of John Damascene, *graecus erat*—he spoke in Greek! An Eastern Christian could say of Augustine, Anselm, Thomas Aquinas and Bonaventure himself—they thought and spoke as Latins. The same applies to the

Second Council of Lyons and, at Florence, a Greek point of view was reduced to a Latin point of view, without the other Greek points of view having been really effectively taken into consideration. At least, as we have already seen, a door is left relatively open for Palamism.

An Anglican author once said: 'Rome cannot change, but she can explain'. The Roman Catholic Church cannot be asked to deny its teaching about the part played by the Son in the eternal procession of the Spirit. It can, however, reasonably be expected to recognize that the Western formulae do not express everything that the Catholic Church believes,[17] that certain points of doctrine are a matter, not absolutely of faith as such, but of theological explanation,[18] and that it is possible for other expressions of the same faith to exist, taking different insights as their point of departure and using other instruments of thought. There is a need to invite Orthodox theologians to engage in an analogous critical hermeneutical examination of their own doctrines. In other words, we must re-create the situation of the Church Fathers, who were in communion with each other while following different ways, and admit the possibility of two constructions of dogmatic theology, side by side, of the same mystery, the object of the same faith.

NOTES

1. H. B. Swete, *The Holy Spirit in the Ancient Church* (London, 1912), pp. 151–159. A. de Halleux, *op. cit.* (note 3 below), 9, says, with reference to G. Kretschmar's studies: 'There was a clear break in the fourth century between spontaneous, charismatic or sacramental experience of the Holy Spirit as a Person and as a divine and Christological gift, and a reflected form of pneumatology'.
2. B. Capelle has the translation 'proceeds' here: 'La procession du Saint-Esprit d'après la liturgie grecque de S. Basile', *L'Orient syrien*, 7 (1962), 69–76. I have criticized him about this. According to him, the text is by Basil himself.
3. *DS* 150; G. L. Dossetti, *Il simbolo di Nicea e di Constantinopoli. Edizione critica* (Rome, 1967); A.-M. Ritter, *Das Konzil von Konstantinopel und sein Symbol* (Göttingen, 1965); J. Ortiz de Urbina, *Nicée et Constantinople (Histoire des Conciles œcuméniques,* 1) (Paris, 1963); A. de Halleux, 'La procession de l'Esprit Saint dans le symbole de Constantinople', *RTL*, 10 (1979), 5–39.
4. An indication of this is to be found in the preservation in the text of the mode of the present particle, *ekporeuomenon*, instead of the aorist, as in the case of *gennēthenta* with regard to the Son; this would have stressed the eternity of the *ekporeusis*: see A. de Halleux, *op. cit.*, 34–45.
5. J. Ortiz de Urbina, *op. cit.*, pp. 223–240.
6. *DS* 178. The date of this decree is perhaps 382.
7. *DS* 441.
8. See above, p. 54. The profession of faith which Leo IX sent to the Patriarch Peter of Antioch on 13 April 1053 contains the *Filioque* (see *DS* 682), but the Roman Council of 680 said only: 'ex Patre procedentem' (see *DS* 546).
9. See L. Bouyer, *L'Eglise de Dieu, Corps du Christ et Temple de l'Esprit* (Paris, 1970), Excursus II, pp. 678–679.

10. *DS* 800; see also Y. Congar, 'S. Thomas et les archidiacres', *RThom*, 57 (1957), 657–671; R. Foreville, *Latran I-III. Latran IV* (*Histoire des conciles œcuméniques*, 6) (Paris, 1968).

11. Documentation and a bibliography will be found in my article, '1274–1974. Structures ecclésiales et conciles dans les relations entre Orient et Occident', *RSPT*, 58 (1974), 355–390.

12. *AAS* 66 (1974), 620–625.

13. *DS* 853.

14. *DS* 850.

15. See below, pp. 185–188. The text will be found in *DS* 1300. To this should be added the decree of 4 February 1442, *Decretum pro Iacobitis* (*DS* 1330–1331), in which the principle of Anselm and Thomas Aquinas figures, namely: 'in Deo omnia sunt unum ubi non obviat relationis oppositio'. This decree is a statement of classical Scholastic theology.

16. *DS* 1968.

17. This is, the *principaliter a Patre*. The Orthodox Christians, on the other hand, could perhaps recognize that the creed does not express the relationship between the Spirit and the Son.

18. This can be seen in the principle of Anselm, included only in the *Decretum pro Iacobitis* (see above, note 15).

THEOLOGICAL REFLECTIONS

1

THE FATHER,
THE ABSOLUTE SOURCE OF DIVINITY

> *Mian gar isasin Huiou kai*
> *Pneumatos ton Patera aitian*
> Maximus the Confessor, letter to
> Marinus of Cyprus, 655 (*PG* 91, 136)

THE GREEK FATHERS

The first insight into the mystery of the Trinity is that concerning its origin in the monarchy of the Father. That is the import of the well-known text of Dionysius of Alexandria (*c*. 230): 'We extend the monad without dividing it in the Triad and at the same time we recapitulate the Triad without diminishing it in the monad'.[1] This insight continued to play a decisive part in the theology of the Greek Fathers even after the time when, in opposition to Arianism, they insisted on the consubstantiality of the three Persons on the basis of identity of *ousia* or *phusis*. There is evidence of this in these texts of Gregory Nazianzen and John Damascene:

> The Father is the principle of the goodness and the divinity that we contemplate in the Son and the Spirit.[2]

> There is one single nature in the three and that is God. The union is the Father, from whom proceed and to whom return those who follow (that which follows).[3]

> The Father is the source by begetting and procession of all the good hidden in that source itself.[4]

The description of the Father as 'source of divinity', *pēgē tēs theotētos*, can be found in Origen,[5] and Pseudo-Dionysius speaks of *pēgaia theotēs*, 'divinity-source', or in Latin *fontana deitas*,[6] which will recur later. Tertullian included 'source' among a list of images[7] and Athanasius, Basil, Cyril of Alexandria and John Damascene called the Father the 'source' of what proceeded from him.[8]

Pēgē, source, is not the only image of the Father. There is also *archē*,

133

principle or beginning: *tēs theotētos archē*, 'Principle of divinity'.[9] The Father is the Principle without any other principle or beginning apart from itself; he is, in other words, *anarchos*. It was necessary to explain this term because the Arians both used and misused it, saying that the Father was the only *anarchos*, the only one without a beginning, whereas the Son had a beginning—there was a time when he was not. There was a need to overcome the ambiguity of the term—the Son was without any beginning, because he was consubstantial with the Father, but he was not without a principle, since he proceeded from the Father, who was the only *anarchos* in this sense.[10]

The Arians also seem to have misused another term taken from Neo-Platonism—*agennētos*, the one who cannot be born, *innascibilis*. Only the Father was, in their opinion, *agennētos*, just as only he was *anarchos*. The begotten Son had a beginning; he had been created before the centuries.[11] Eunomius believed that *agennētos* was a definition of God, since a knowledge of God's name meant a knowledge of his nature.[12] This is why the Fathers at first rejected the term *innascibilis* (Athanasius) or at least avoided it and disputed its application to God (Basil). After Basil had shown, however, that it could not be applied to the *ousia*—which included the Son—but could only be applied to the *hypostasis*, the Fathers used it and made this *innascibilitas* a characteristic of the Father. Those who employed it include, among the Greeks, Basil himself,[13] Gregory Nazianzen,[14] Gregory of Nyssa,[15] Epiphanius of Salamis[16] and John Damascene[17] and, among the Western Fathers, Hilary of Poitiers, writing in his difficult Latin and preceding the Greeks (†366).[18]

THE LATIN WEST

Clearly Augustine must be mentioned first, because he had such a deep influence on Western thinking and, although he did not initiate the idea, continued to be the major source in the question of the *Filioque*. He said, for example: 'The Father is the principle of all divinity or, to be more precise, of the deity, because he does not take his origin from anything else. He has no one from whom he has his being or from whom he proceeds, but it is by him that the Son is begotten and from him that the Holy Spirit proceeds.'[19] Later in the same treatise, he reaffirms this conviction: 'The Son has all that he has from the Father; he therefore has from the Father that the Holy Spirit (also) proceeds from him'.[20] This 'also' is my insertion, not Augustine's. Augustine, on the contrary, expresses the monarchy of the father in the following words: 'It is not in vain that God the Father is called the one by whom the Word is begotten and from whom the Holy Spirit principally proceeds. I have added *principaliter*, "principally", because the Holy Spirit also proceeds from the Son. But it is the Father who gave it to him.'[21] This *principali-*

134

ter has a very strong import—it expresses the idea of the first and absolute source. In his translation in the *Bibliothèque augustinienne*, Fr Agaësse renders this as 'proceeds as from his first principle' (*De Trin*. XV, 17, 29) or as 'proceeds originally [*originairement*]' (XV, 26, 47). As I have already said and as I shall say again later, this *principaliter* should lead to a difference in the way of stating the affirmation of the procession of the Spirit 'from the Father and the Son as from one principle'. Despite my respect for and devotion to Anselm, I regret that he had so little regard for this *principaliter*.

If the Councils of Toledo received the *Filioque* from Augustine, then they also took from him the statements 'Fons ergo ipse (Pater) et origo totius divinitatis' and 'Patrem, qui est totius fons et origo divinitatis'.[22]

These formulae were not very much in favour in the Carolingian period, which was preoccupied with the affirmation of the *Filioque*. It is interesting to note, however, that Ratramnus of Corbie takes up the *principaliter* again and refers to Augustine's *De Trin*. XV, 17.[23]

Bernard, on the other hand, makes an almost Eastern statement: 'Fontem assigna Patri, ex qua nascitur Filius et procedit Spiritus Sanctus'—'Attribute the source to the Father; from it the Son is born and from it the Spirit proceeds'.[24] Bernard's friend William of Saint-Thierry returned insistently to the *principaliter*: 'The Father, who takes his origin from no one else, is the origin of the divinity'.[25] Richard of Saint-Victor was responsible for this excellent statement: 'In Patre origo unitatis, in Filio inchoatio pluritatis, in Spiritu Sancto completio Trinitatis'.[26]

Both Albert the Great (†1280) and Bonaventure (†1274) were influenced by Pseudo-Dionysius, who used the expressions *pēgaia theotēs ho Patēr*, translated into Latin as *fontana deitas*, and *theogonos theotēs*, translated as *deitas deigena*.[27] Albert commented favourably on these formulae and presented the Son and the Spirit as a 'pullulatio deigenae deitatis'. These are Dionysian terms.[28]

Of all the great thirteenth-century teachers. Bonaventure worked out a theology that was most clearly inspired by the idea of the Father as the absolute source.[29] That theology is a reflection of his own warm nature and his use of striking images. It is influenced by Richard of Saint-Victor and at the same time by the Greek Fathers.[30] He takes as his point of departure the fact that the Father is *innascibilis* (the *agennētos* of the teaching of the Greek Fathers).[31] This fact results in a fullness of the source: 'Innascibilitas dicit in Patre plenitudinem fontalitatis sive fontalem plenitudinem'—it 'places in the Father a fullness that is characteristic of a source'.[32] This *plenitudo fontalis* is equivalent to *primitas*, and *primus* means *principium*: 'quia primum, ideo principium'.[33] The fact that the Father is first means that he has a propensity to communicate himself: 'ratione primitatis persona nata est aliam producere'.[34]

There are two modes of communication in God according to Bonaventure—communication by nature and communication by generous free will. As such, the fullness of the source cannot be communicated, because it is peculiar to the Father. The Father, however, communicates to the Son the capacity to communicate the divine nature, by means of generosity. Being the *auctor* is connected with being the *plenitudo fontalis*. The Father is the only *auctor*. The Son is not the *auctor* of the Holy Spirit, because he receives his fertility from another, that is, the Father. Bonaventure's *auctor* is here the equivalent of Augustine's *principaliter*, and it may even be more expressive. Alan of Lille (†1203) had written: 'Pater auctor Filii; Spiritus auctoritate Patris procedit a Filio'.[35] Albert the Great is very insistent on the *principaliter*, which he identifies with the *auctoritas processionis*. He attributes this—and justifies and defines more precisely this attribution—to the Father.[36]

Turning now to Thomas Aquinas, we find that he too, in his *Sentences*, calls the Father the only *auctor*, whereas he called the Son the *principium* of the Holy Spirit.[37] In his *Summa*, he explains how a statement of Hilary of Poitiers saying that the Spirit 'a Patre et Filio auctoribus confitendus est' should be interpreted.[38] He traces Augustine's *principaliter* back to this datum of *auctoritas* on the only occasion when he quotes it, that is, in his first book of *Sentences*, the quotation having been taken from the work of Peter Lombard (see *In I Sent.* d. 12, q. 1, a. 2, ad 3). He does not use this term in the *Summa*. According to *ST* Ia, q. 36, a. 3, ad 2, he does not do so because he is afraid of suggesting that the Spirit proceeds more from the Father than from the Son or proceeds from the Father before he proceeds from the Son.

In a number of texts which reveal an insight into the divine reality rather than a concern for conceptual precision, Bonaventure shows that the *auctor* is equivalent to the *fontalis plenitudo* or the *innascibilitas* of the Father.[39] The Father's supreme authority comes from his *innascibilitas*, which in itself means *primitas* and therefore firstly *esse principium* and secondly being *principians*.[40] In this context, Bonaventure quotes Hilary of Poitiers. The Son is not the *auctor* because he receives his fertility from another. The Father, on the other hand, as the original or flowing fullness, practises to perfection the two modes of communication, that is, by nature and by generosity. Because he is not the original source, the Son cannot practise communication by nature—he does not, for example, beget—but he can and does receive from the Father the ability to practise communication by generosity.

Thomas does not follow Bonaventure here. Without in fact naming him, he even criticizes him. He was, of course, familiar with the *fontana deitas* of Pseudo-Dionysius.[41] He accepts this idea in the sense in which Augustine spoke about the Father as the 'principium totius divinitatis'.[42] It is therefore not correct to say, as Nilus Cabasilas did, that the Latins unite or merge together the Father and the Son in the state of the source (*fontalitas*).[43] Pseudo-Dionysius' text, especially when it goes on to speak of 'pullulationes, sicut flores, sicut divina lumina', undoubtedly provides a number of excellent images, but it is not possible to base a rational argument on it. As Pseudo-Dionysius himself admits: 'locutiones illae sunt symbolicae; et ideo ex eis non procedit argumentatio'.[44]

Thomas, then, believed that *innascibilitas* was a property of the Father, but not a personal notion enabling us to know the Person positively as such.[45] He reacted, however, against an interpretation of the character 'unbegotten' that would identify it with this *innascibilitas* in such a way that would give this property not a simply negative value, but a positive value, characterizing the quality of the Father as 'a nullo esse, esse principium aliorum, esse fontalis plenitudo'. For Bonaventure, *innascibilis* did not characterize the Father simply in the negative sense, that is, it did not simply describe him as having his being from no one else—it also characterized him positively, as having the ability to give being to another. The term, in other words, is negative only in appearance. Thomas was open to the reality of the mystery of the Father expressed in this way, but he preferred to speak of that mystery by respecting the vigour of our concepts, since they are inadequate but valuable means of our talk about God. Even Cyril of Alexandria and Augustine had perceived that 'unbegotten' and 'Father' were not synonymous.[46]

Here I conclude my investigation; for the rest, I would simply quote L. Cognet on the subject of Cardinal Bérulle (†1629): 'Bérulle believed that the Father was essentially the principle in the life of the Trinity. This is an idea to which he returned again and again, even outside the *Grandeurs de Jésus*. He saw in the Father the "source of divinity" (68). This idea occurs frequently in patristic writings and especially in the Greek Fathers. Bérulle was able to remember the teaching of his master at the Sorbonne, Philippe de Gamaches, who had called the Father *fons et origo divinitatis* (69). Bérulle also characterized this function of the Father by calling it the "fontal deity" (70). He atributed this expression to Pseudo-Dionysius; it is true that Dom Goulu, in his seventeenth-century translation of the *Corpus dionysiacum*, spoke of the "fontal and originating deity" (71) and these terms may have inspired Bérulle. Elwhere, using a rather strange pleonasm, he spoke of the "fontal source of the divinity" (72).'[47]

*   *   *

I agree with Thomas Aquinas in his assessment of the *innascibilis*, but I have to admit that Bonaventure's insights continue to attract me. Beyond the concepts, with which he deals in a masterly way, there is the reality of the living God as perceived by the religious soul in the prayer that accompanies his *lectio divina*, that is, his meditation on the Scriptures and the liturgy in which the mysteries are celebrated and experienced.

What is particularly striking is that God is presented in the biblical revelation both as transcendent and as immanent, both as beyond and above everything and as with and for us, in other words, as given and handed over to us.

God appeared to Jacob in the place that was to be called Bethel. He appeared to him in a prophetic dream (see Gen 28). Waking, Jacob 'was afraid and said: "How awesome is this place!" ' (28:17). This is the *terribilis est locus iste*, 'This is a place of awe', of our Masses for the dedication of a Church, a heartfelt cry expressing our consciousness of the transcendence of the most high God. But, in the Old Testament story, a ladder is placed on the earth with its top reaching up to heaven, and angels go up and down it. An interchange is established between the most high God and here below. God has come down to us and will come to us in Jesus Christ, God-with-us (Jn 1:51).

A second example is Moses on Horeb (Sinai). God manifests himself there to Moses as a flame in the heart of the bush which is burnt without being consumed (see Ex 3). God calls to Moses, but, when he comes, tells him: 'Do not come near; put off your shoes from your feet, for the place on which you are standing is holy ground' (Ex 3:5). So we have 'come' and 'do not come near'—Moses may come because God has come near, but he may not come near because God continues to be sublime, the most high, beyond and above everything and all men. But Moses asks God: 'What is your name? Who are you?' and God calls himself both absolutely transcendent and at the same time the companion of our destiny in human history on this earth. Immediately after calling himself 'I am' or 'I will be (who I will be)', he adds: 'Yahweh, the God of Abraham, the God of Isaac and the God of Jacob has sent me to you' (Ex 3:15). Augustine pointed to the unity that exists between these two names.[48] Confronted with the sublimity of the 'I am who I am', man can only be conscious of the distance caused by his smallness and ignorance. But that is what God is in and for himself. From that distance, however, he has come to us and made himself near to us—he is the God of Abraham, Isaac and Jacob: '*Ego sum qui sum* ad Me pertinet. *Deus Abraham* . . . ad te pertinet'. The absolute Being, the eternal, transcendent one, has entered with us into our history: 'I will be with you', in other words, 'I will be Jesus Christ'.[49]

This revelation on Mount Sinai is renewed in the same place, after the making of the golden calf. Yahweh refuses to accompany the rebellious people of Israel, lest he should have to exterminate them on the way (Ex 33:3). This is a sign of his transcendence. Moses, who has beseeched him to make himself known to him, sees only his back, because, as he says, 'you cannot see my face . . . my face shall not be seen' (Ex 33:20, 23)—another sign of his transcendence. Yet, when he comes down and makes himself known as he passes by, he is 'Yahweh, a God merciful and gracious, slow to anger and abounding in steadfast love and faithfulness'.[50] Because he is such a God, he will go with his people. He is able to go with them without exterminating them, because he is merciful and therefore close to them, as he is still close to us in our misery.

The God who revealed himself twice on Mount Sinai is the same God

138

whom we invoke in the psalms—the God who is so sublime, yet so pre-occupied with me that he is 'my God'. The God who is 'enthroned upon the cherubim' manifests himself to those who believe in him and 'comes to save them' (Ps 80:2). It is true to say that 'the exaltation of God was not his exile. He who dwells in the high and holy place, dwells no less with him that is of a contrite and humble spirit . . . he is lofty enough to think nothing beneath him, great enough to count nothing too small to be his concern.'[51]

There is the case of the prophet Isaiah, who, in 740 B.C., the year when King Uzziah died, had a vision of the Lord Yahweh 'sitting upon a throne, high and lifted up. . . . Above him stood the seraphim. . . . And one called to the other and said: "Holy, holy, holy is Yahweh Sabaoth" ' (Is 6:1ff.). The prophet was aware that he was confronted with the transcendent God, for he said: 'Woe is me, for I am lost; I am a man of unclean lips and I dwell in the midst of a people of unclean lips; for my eyes have seen the King, Yahweh Sabaoth!' (6:5). This is, of course, very similar to Jacob's 'How awesome is this place', but at once one of the seraphim purifies Isaiah's unclean lips with an ember taken from the altar. Isaiah becomes God's messenger among his people and for that people, in him, Yahweh Sabaoth becomes the 'holy one of Israel', which is a very frequent expression in the book of Isaiah.

We too sing every day that 'holy, holy, holy', but, even though we are conscious that we are 'mystically representing the cherubim', as the Eastern liturgy expresses it, we add: 'blessed is he who comes in the name of the Lord', since, in Jesus Christ, Yahweh made himself Emmanuel, God-with-us, for ever.

The Wisdom writings also provide examples of God's transcendence and immanence. The fact that statements from these writings have often been applied to the Holy Spirit and that some of them speak explicitly of the Spirit (see Volume I, pp. 9–12) makes this even more interesting. These texts, which express a much more elaborate theoretical thought than those considered so far, say that it is because God is transcendent and immense that he can, through his Wisdom and his Spirit, be with and in all things. In this context, the following texts are particularly relevant: Job 37 to 39; Sir (Ecclus) 1:3; 24:5–6; Wis 1:7 (the Introit for the Mass of Pentecost); 7:22–26; 8:1. Precisely because he is transcendent, God can be given to us and become close and intimate.

Finally, there is God the Father—but when we invoke him by this tender and close name, we add 'who art in heaven'—who has sent us his Son, his Word, his image, and his Holy Spirit, who is the Gift above all. 'No one has ever seen God' (Jn 1:18; 6:46)—a source is not seen; all that is seen is the river that flows from it. 'God', the unbegotten fountain of divinity, is invisible.[52] He made himself visible in his Son who became man, the *Unigenitus* who became *Primogenitus in multis fratribus*. He comes to dwell in our hearts through his Holy Spirit. These are the 'divine missions' which are, in the creature, the outcome of the intra-divine 'processions', a communication of the very mystery of God.[53] The one who exists before everything—everything that has a beginning—entered time. The Absolute entered what is relative and exposed to risk.

Why did this happen? Because that Absolute *is* Love. 'God is Love' (1 Jn 4:8 and 16). We know that, in the New Testament, 'God', with only two or three exceptions, means the Father. *Agapē*—love flowing like a source, love initiating being and life—is attributed to God as a hypostatic mark, that is, as a personal characteristic (see 2 Cor 13:13; 1 Cor 13:11). The Father is the subject of this *agapē* (see 1 Jn 2:15; Jn 3:14; Eph 2:4). He is often the subject of the verb *agapan*, which means 'to love with *agapē*'.[54] This is intimately concerned with his plan of love and with his gift of mercy for the world, but its truth is to be found first of all in the mystery of the intra-divine life. Maximus the Confessor (†662), who forms a link between the East and the West, said: 'God the Father, moved by an eternal love, proceeded to the distinction between the hypostases'.[55] His Son is therefore called his beloved Son—*agapētos*.[56] This love is obviously the essential love that is hypostatized in the Father, the first Person, the Principle without a principle and the source of divinity.

NOTES

1. See Athanasius, *De sent. Dion.* 17.
2. Gregory Nazianzen, *Orat.* 2, 38 (*PG* 35, 445) and 20, 6 (*PG* 35, 1072C).
3. *Idem*, farewell discourse at the Council, 15 (*PG* 36, 476B).
4. John Damascene, *De fide orthod.* I, 12 (*PG* 94, 848).
5. Origen, *Comm. in Ioan.* II, II, 20 (*SC* 120, p. 121).
6. Pseudo-Dionysius, *De div. nom.* II, 7 (*PG* 3, 645B): 'The divinity-source is the Father. Jesus and the Holy Spirit are so to speak the divine buds and like the flowers of that divinely fertile divinity'.
7. Tertullian, *Adv. Prax.* 8 (*PL* 2, 163; *CSEL* 47, 238).
8. Athanasius, *Contra Arian.* I, 19 (*PG* 25, 52); Basil the Great, *Hom. contra Sab.* 4 (*PG* 31, 609); Cyril of Alexandria, *Comm. in Ioan.* I, 1 (*PG* 73, 25); John Damascene, *op. cit.* (note 4). See also T. de Régnon, *Etudes de théologie positive sur la Sainte Trinité*, III (Paris, 1898), pp. 164–165.
9. Gregory Nazianzen, *op. cit.* (note 2). The Son is 'ek tēs archēs tou Patros': see Basil the Great, *Hom.* 24, 4 (*PG* 31, 605).
10. Gregory Nazianzen, *Orat.* 25, *In laudem Heronis Philos.* 15 (*PG* 35, 1220; Fr. tr. in T. de Régnon, *op. cit.*, IV (Paris, 1898), p. 257); see also *Orat.* 20, 6 (*PG* 35, 1072C); 30, 19 (*PG* 36, 128); 39, 12 (*PG* 36, 348).
11. Arius, *Thalia*, quoted by Athanasius, *De syn.* 15 and 16 (*PG* 26, 705 and 708); see T. de Régnon, *op. cit.*, III, p. 202, who devotes pp. 185–259 to this idea of *innascibilis*.
12. Gregory of Nyssa, *Contra Eunom.* (*PG* 45, 929).
13. Basil, *Ep.* 125, 3 (*PG* 32, 549); *Adv. Eunom.* II, 28 (*PG* 29, 637).
14. Gregory Nazianzen, *Orat.* 25, 16 (*PG* 35, 1221); 31 (= *Orat. theol.* V), 8 (*PG* 36, 141).
15. Gregory of Nyssa, *Contra Eunom.* I, 1 (*PG* 45, 369).
16. Epiphanius, *Anc.* 7 (*PG* 43, 28).
17. John Damascene, *De fide orthod.* I, 8 (*PG* 94, 828D); 10 (*PG* 94, 837); 13 (*PG* 94, 856).

18. Hilary, *De Trin*. IV, 6, 15; 33 (*PL* 10, 90; 108; 120); *De syn*. 60 (*PL* 10, 521). See also P. Smulders, *La doctrine trinitaire de S. Hilaire de Poitiers* (Rome, 1944).

19. Augustine, *De Trin*. IV, 20, 29 (*PL* 42, 908); this is a text frequently quoted, for example, by Peter Lombard, *I Sent*. 29, Bonaventure, Thomas Aquinas and even by Leo XIII, in his encyclical *Divinum illud munus* of 9 May 1897 (*DS* 3326).

20. *De Trin*. XV, 26, 47 (*PL* 42, 1094).

21. *De Trin*. XV, 17, 29 (*PL* 42, 1081); 26, 47 (*PL* 42, 1095; *principaliter*); *Contra Maxim*. II, 14 (*PL* 42, 770). The word also occurred in Tertullian; see *Adv. Prax*. III, 3. Tertullian used it to affirm the monarchy of the Father in begetting the Son.

22. The Eleventh and the Sixteenth Councils of Toledo respectively (675 and 693); see Mansi XI, 132 and XII, 640; J. Vivès, ed., *Concilios Visigóticos e Hispano-Romanos* (Barcelona and Madrid, 1963), pp. 346 and 489; *DS* 525 and 568.

23. Ratramnus, *Contra Graec. opp*. III, 3 (*PL* 121, 282). See. W. Schulz, *Der Einfluss Augustins in der Theologie und Christologie des VIII. und IX. Jahrhunderts* (Halle, 1913), p. 56.

24. Bernard, *In vig. nat., Sermo* 4, 9 (*PL*, 183, 104D).

25. William of Saint-Thierry, *Enigma fid*. (*PL* 180, 430D–431A, 435D, 439B). See also J. M. Déchanet, *Guillaume de Saint-Thierry. L'homme et son œuvre* (Bruges and Paris, 1942), pp. 99–110.

26. Richard of Saint-Victor, *De trib. approp*. (*PL* 196, 992); see J. Ribaillier, *Richard de Saint-Victor. Opuscules théologiques* (Paris, 1967), p. 184.

27. Pseudo-Dionysius, *De div. nom*. II, 7 (*PG* 3, 645B); cf. II, 5 (*PG* 3, 641D): 'monē de pēgē tēs huperousiou theotētos ho Patēr'.

28. See F. Ruello, 'Le commentaire inédit de S. Albert le Grand sur les Noms divins. Présentation et aperçus de théologie trinitaires', *Traditio*, 12 (1956), 231–314. This commentary has been edited since the time of F. Ruello's article by P. Simon, *S. Alberti Magni Operum omnium*, XXXVII, *Pars I* (Münster, 1972). The commentary on the text quoted above (see note 27) will be found on pp. 82ff.; it is emphatically 'Scholastic'.

29. See O. González, *Misterio trinitario y existencia humana. Estudio histórico teológico en torno a San Buenaventura* (Madrid, 1966); A. de Villalmonte, 'El Padre plenitud fontal de la deidad', *S. Bonaventura 1274–1974* (Grottaferrata, Rome, 1974), IV, pp. 221–242; see also T. de Régnon, *op. cit*. (note 8), II (Paris, 1892), pp. 435–568.

30. A. de Villamonte, 'Influjo de los Padres Griegos en la doctrina trinitaria de S. Buenaventura', *XIII Semana Española de Teología* (Madrid, 1954), pp. 554–577.

31. See *In I Sent*. d. 27, q. 2, ad 3 (Quaracchi ed., I, pp. 470–472); d. 28 (Quaracchi ed., pp. 495–505); *In II Sent*. proem. (Quaracchi ed., II, pp. 2–3); *Breviloquium*, p. 1, c. 3 (Quaracchi ed., V, p. 212).

32. *In I Sent*. d. 29, dub. 1 (Quaracchi ed., I, p. 517); *Breviloquium*, *op. cit*.: 'Cum enim proprium sit Patris esse innascibilem sive ingenitum . . . innascibilitas in Patre ponit fontalem plenitudinem'. Bonaventure refers to Hilary of Poitiers and the Greek Fathers.

33. References in A. de Villalmonte, *op. cit*. (note 29), 236, note 26. The formula is taken from Aristotle, *Post. Anal*. I, c. 2,

34. *In I Sent*. d. 2, q. 2, concl. (Quaracchi ed., I, p. 54). See also A. de Villalmonte, *op. cit*., 231, note 21.

35. Alan of Lille, *Reg. theol*. 3 (*PL* 210, 625) and 53–54 (*PL* 210, 647).

36. Albert, *In I Sent*. d. 12, a. 5 (ed. A. Borgnet, XXV, p. 359); see also a. 6 (Borgnet, p. 361). For the application of this *principaliter* to the procession of the Holy Spirit *a Filio*, see d. 13, a. 6 (Borgnet, p. 379).

37. Thomas Aquinas, *In I Sent*. d. 29, q. 1, a. 1 sol. end: 'Nomen auctoris addit super rationem principii hoc quod non est esse ab aliquo; et ideo solus Pater auctor dicitur, quamvis etiam Filius principium dicatur notionaliter'. See also d. 12, q. 1, a. 2, ad 3; a. 3, ad 1; *ST* IIIa, q. 21, a. 3: 'ut ostenderet Patrem suum esse auctorem a quo et aeternaliter processit'; see also *De Pot*. q. 10, a. 1, ad 9 and ad 17.

38. *ST* Ia, q. 36, a. 4, ad 7. See also Hilary of Poitiers. *De Trin*. II (*PL* 10, 69). In this text, however, Hilary deals with the witness to the Father and the Son which is expressed in the baptismal confession of faith and not with the intra-divine procession.

39. Bonaventure, *In I Sent*. d. 13, dub. 4 (Quaracchi ed., I, p. 240).

40. *In I Sent*. d. 27, p. 1, q. 2, ad 3 (Quaracchi ed., pp. 470–471). This important text is translated in T. de Régnon, *op. cit*. (note 8), II, pp. 484ff. See also *In II Sent*. prol.

41. Not only in Thomas' commentary on Pseudo-Dionysius' *De div. nom*., but also in *In I Sent*. d. 11, q. 1, a. 1, obj. 1; d. 28, q. 1, a. 1.

42. *In I Sent*. d. 28, 1. 1, a. 1; *In III Sent*. d. 25, q. 1, a. 2; ed. Moos, no. 36: 'fons totius deitatis'; *Comm. in Eph*. c. 4, lect. 2: (super omnes) 'appropriatur Patri, qui est fontale principium divinitatis'; *ST* Ia, q. 39, a. 5, obj. 6 and ad 6; see also *In I Sent*. d. 29, expos. textus.

43. Folio 72ᵛ of the Greek manuscript in the Vatican Library: see E. Candal, *Nilus Cabasilas et theologia S. Thomae de Processione Spiritus Sancti* (*Studi e Testi*, 116), (Vatican, 1945), p. 86.

44. *In I Sent*. d. 11, q. 1, a. 1, ad 1. The saying 'symbolica theologica non est argumentativa' can be found no less than six times in Thomas' writings.

45. *In I Sent*. d. 26, q. 2, a. 3; d. 28, q. 1, a. 2; *ST* Ia, q. 32, a. 3; q. 33, a. 4, the ad 1 of which refers to Bonaventure word for word. See also q. 40, a. 3, ad 3; Basil the Great, *Adv. Eunom*. I, 15 (*PG* 29, 545).

46. Cyril of Alexandria, *De sanct. Trin. Dial*. II (*PG* 75, 720); Augustine, *De Trin*. V, 6 (*PL* 42, 914), quoted by Peter Lombard, *I Sent*. d. 28. Gregory Nazianzen, on the other hand, said: 'the quality of the Father is non-begotten': *Orat*. 25, 16 (*PG* 75, 1221B), but this was in comparison with the Son, who is begotten. See also Hilary of Poitiers, *De Trin*. IV, 6 (*PL* 10, 90).

47. L. Cognet, *La spiritualité moderne*, I: *L'essor, 1500–1650* (Paris, 1966), p. 332. The notes given in brackets in the text refer to: (68) Bérulle, *Œuvres*, CLXXXII, §7, col. 1242 in Migne's edition; probably c. 1624; (69) *Philippi Gamachi, Summa theologica* (Paris, 1634), I, p. 270; (70) Bérulle, *Grandeurs*, V, §3 and VI, §2, cols 230 and 246 respectively; J. Dagens made a slight mistake when he said that Bérulle applied these words to the divine essence: see *Bérulle et les origines de la restauration catholique* (Paris, 1952), pp. 307 and 353; (71) *Les œuvres du divin S. Denys Aréopagite* (Paris, 1629), folio 146ᵛ; (72) *Grandeurs*, VII, §3, col. 267.

48. Augustine, *Enarr. in Ps*. 101, *Sermo* 2, 10 (*PL* 37, 1311); *Enarr. in Ps*. 134, 4 and 6 (*PL* 37, 1341–1343); *Sermo* 6, 4 and 5 (*PL* 38, 61); *Sermo* 7, 7 (*PL* 38, 66).

49. An article which I wrote a long time ago may be useful here: 'Dum visibiliter Deum cognoscimus', *M-D*, 59 (1959/3), 132–161; Eng. tr. in *The Revelation of God* (London and New York, 1968), pp. 67–96.

50. Ex 34:6; cf. Ps 86:15; 103:8; 145:8; Joel 2:13; Neh 9:17; Jon 4:2.

51. G. F. Moore, *Judaism*, I (Cambridge, Mass., 1972), p. 442. Compare also the statement by Gregory the Great in connection with the Scriptures, taken up in the Middle Ages and frequently quoted by Luther: 'est fluvius, ut ita dixerim, in quo et agnus ambulet et elephas natet': *Moralia* (*PL* 75, 515); even more pertinent is his other pronouncement: 'Omnipotens Deus, qui nec in magnis tenditur nec in minimis angustatur': *Comm. in Ezech*. (*PL* 76, 957B); see also this statement from the *Imago Primi Saeculi (Societatis Jesu)* of 1640: 'Non coerceri a maximo, contineri tamen a minimo, divinum est'.

52. Col 1:15; 1 Tim 1:17; 6:16; Rom 1:20.

53. See Volume II, pp. 79–90. See also the Decree *Ad Gentes divinitus*, on the Church's Missionary Activity, 2, which claims that the latter flows from the 'fountain of love within God the Father', *ex fontali amore Dei Patris*. See also below, note 56.

54. See Jn 3:35; 15:9; 17:23–26; 8:12; 14:21 and 23; Rom 5:8; 8:39; Eph 2:4; Jude 1. A. Nygren showed the nature of *agapē* to be love as the source, without antecedent; I assume that his ideas on this subject are known and accepted. He was rightly criticized for

unilateralism and excessive systematization, but these faults have since been corrected. His insight is still illuminating. See also 1 Jn 4:10; Rom 5:8; 8:32.

55. See Pseudo-Dionysius, *Scholia on the Divine Names*, 2 (*PG* 4, 221). See also Origen, *Comm. in Rom.* IV, 9 (*PG* 14, 997B–C): 'Paul speaks of the Spirit of charity (Rom 4:30) and God is called Charity (1 Jn 4:8) and Christ is called the Son of Love (Col 1:13). If there is a Spirit of charity and a Son of love and if God is Charity (Love) it is certain that the Son and the Spirit come from the source of the paternal deity'; Gregory of Nyssa, *De anim. et res.* (*PG* 46, 96C): 'Love is the very life of the divine nature', *hē te gar zōē tēs anō phuseōs agapē estin*. This can be compared with the Decree of Vatican II, *Ad Gentes divinitus*, cited above (note 53): 'Hoc autem propositum (Patris mittentis Filium et Spiritum Sanctum) ex "fontali amore" seu caritate Dei Patris profluit, qui, cum sit Principium sine Principio, ex quo Filius gignitur et Spiritus Sanctus per Filium procedit'—'this decree (of the Father sending the Son and the Holy Spirit) flows from that "fountain of love" or charity within God the Father. From him, who is the Origin without Origin, the Son is begotten and the Holy Spirit proceeds through the Son.'

56. Mk 1:11 and par.; Mt 12:18; 17:5; 2 Pet 1:17; Col 1:13.

2

A THEOLOGICAL MEDITATION
ON THE THIRD PERSON

The Spirit is without a face and almost without a name. He is the wind who is not seen, but who makes things move. He is known by his effects. He is the one who produces everything that I have discussed in Volume II. He is the one who *is given* in order to produce everything that can be summarized as the community of the sons of God, the universal body of the only Son made man. He is, above all, the Gift. The Word or the Son of God has also, of course, been given to us (see Jn 3:16; Rom 8:32), but it is only the Spirit who is called 'Gift'. There is abundant evidence of this in Scripture and the writings of the Fathers in the East and the West.

The Spirit is presented by Jesus, and then by Peter and Paul, as what the Father had promised.[1] He is not the only object or content of God's promise, since Jesus, as the Saviour and as the risen Lord, was also promised,[2] but it was the Spirit who raised him (Rom 1:4, 8:11). Eternal life[3] is also our inheritance, and with regard to this the Spirit who is given here and now has the function of *arrha* or earnest-money (see Eph 1:14). The eschatological era has already commenced since Jesus' exaltation (Acts 2:33) resulted in the gift of the Spirit, and that era leads to total salvation, the kingdom of God.

The Spirit is the one who completes all things and who brings a perfection in which we can rest in peace. This creation calls for a renewal which will pass from persons to nature itself and from man to the cosmos (see Rom 8:1–25). The Spirit will be and is already given to us as *arrha* or as a pledge. He is the agent of that fulfilment of creation in God by a new creation, the first-fruits of which he has affirmed in the resurrection and glorification of Jesus Christ, the *eschatos Adam* (see 1 Cor 15:20–28 and 42–50). The Spirit, then, is the Gift par excellence. He is often called in Greek *dōrea*, which contains the meaning 'formal donation' as opposed to *dōron*, which means either a 'present' in the wider sense or a cultic 'offering'.[4] Let me give some examples of the use of this word in the New Testament:

Simon is condemned because he thought he could buy the 'gift of God' with silver, whereas that gift, the Spirit, is 'given by the laying on of hands by the apostles' (Acts 8:20).

Jesus says to the Samaritan woman: 'If you knew the gift of God' (Jn 4:10). That

Gift is salvation by faith, the living water of the Spirit, 'welling up to eternal life' (4:14).[5]

Peter proclaims on the day of Pentecost: 'Repent and be baptized every one of you in the name of Jesus Christ for the forgiveness of your sins and you shall receive the gift of the Holy Spirit' (Acts 2:38). The words 'Holy Spirit' are, in Greek, in the 'epexegetical' genitive—the gift is the Holy Spirit himself.

At Caesarea, in the house of Cornelius, who had just been converted, 'the gift of the Holy Spirit was poured out even on the gentiles' (Act 10:45). In this case too, the gift is the Spirit accompanied by the signs that point to his coming. The disciples had received the same gift on the day of Pentecost (11:17).

'It is impossible to restore again to repentance those . . . who have tasted the heavenly gift and have become partakers of the Holy Spirit . . . if they then commit apostasy' (Heb 6:4–6).

There are many other New Testament texts containing the verbs *didōmi*, to give, or *lambanō*, to receive, which have the Spirit as their complement and which could be added to the above list. (I include them in a note below, so as not to overburden the text.[6]) All these cases where 'gift' or 'to give' is used with reference to the Spirit give an impressive density to the theme of the Spirit as the eschatological Gift and the agent of the fulfilment of God's plan and work.

The Fathers reflected this revelation in their writings. Dionysius Petavius observed that the description 'Gift (of God)' was less often used by the Greek than by the Latin Fathers.[7] The theme is, however, undoubtedly present in their work, although they use different terminology. It can be found especially in the dynamic diagram Father→Son→Spirit, which is developed above all by Athanasius and Basil the Great in their affirmation of the monarchy of the Father and, against the Arians, the consubstantiality of the three Persons. 'The Father, through the Son and the Holy Spirit, gives all good things'—*ta panta charizetai*.[8] 'It is the Father himself who does everything and gives everything through the Word in the Spirit'—*energei kai didōsi ta panta*.[9] It was only occasionally that the Greek Fathers attributed the title of Gift to the Spirit. Pseudo-Justin, for example, spoke of *tou Theou dōrean*—'the Gift of God (the Father)'[10]—and Irenaeus spoke of 'that drink that the Lord received as a "gift" from the Father and also gave to those who participate in him, by "sending the Holy Spirit over the whole world" '.[11] Athanasius used the word *dōrea* in the following text:

Just as the Son is the only begotten one, so too is the Spirit, who was given and sent by the Son, equally one and not many . . . for, just as the Son, the living Word, is unique, so too must his living sanctifying and illuminating effectiveness be unique, perfect and full, as well as his donation (*kai dōrean*), who is said to have proceeded from the Father, because, through the Son, who is confessed (as proceeding) from the Father, he shines and is sent and is given (*kai didotai*).[12]

145

Cyril of Alexandria also pointed out that 'the good donation (*dosis*) and the perfect gift (*dōrēma teleion*) are nothing other than obtaining a participation in the Holy Spirit'—*metalachein hagiou Pneumatos*.[13] Basil the Great used the word 'Gift' for the Spirit, although the Pneumatomachi concluded from this use that the giver was honoured, but not the gift.[14] The Spirit is called *dōrea* at the beginning of the anaphora in the Greek text of the liturgy of St James.[15]

In the West, it was above all Augustine who developed the theme of the Spirit as Gift, although he claimed that he owed this to Hilary of Poitiers, who in turn owed a great deal to the East in his teaching about the Trinity. It is interesting to quote the main text on the Spirit as Gift in Hilary's *De Trinitate*:

> He (the Christ) commanded (his disciples) to baptize in the name of the Father and the Son and the Holy Spirit, that is, by confessing the Author, the only Son and the Gift (*Doni*). There is only one author of all things, since there is only one God, the Father, from whom all things come, and only one Son, our Lord Jesus Christ, through whom all things are, and only one Spirit, the Gift, in all things. All are therefore ordered according to their virtues and their merits—only one power, from which all things come, only one Son, through whom all things come, only one Gift (*munus*) of perfect hope. Nothing is absent from such a consummate perfection, within which there are, in the Father and the Son and the Holy Spirit, infinity in the Eternal, beauty in the Image and activity and enjoyment in the Gift (*usus in munere*).[16]

Augustine quotes these last lines of Hilary's text in *De Trin*. VI, 10, 11, and interprets the terms used. In his text, he makes these terms express not the logic of the divine economy, but an intra-Trinitarian process: 'The inexpressible embrace (*complexus*) of the Father and the Image does not take place without enjoyment (*perfruitione*), without charity and without joy. This dilection, this pleasure, this felicity, this happiness—if any human word can suitably express it—was called in a very concise way "enjoyment" (*usus*) by Hilary and, in the Trinity, this is the Holy Spirit. He is not begotten, but is the sweetness of the begetter and the one who is begotten. He overwhelms with his generosity and his abundance all creatures according to their capacity, so that they retain their respective ranks and rest in their places.'

As early as his treatise *De vera religione*, Augustine called the Holy Spirit by the personal name of *Donum* or *Munus*.[17] This name 'Gift' is personal because it is relative and it relates not only to the creatures who benefit from the Gift, which is something that could not be verified freely and in the course of time, but also to the Giver.[18] The Giver is the one who sends the Holy Spirit, mission and gift being identical: it is the Father and the Son. They are eternally Giver. The Spirit is sent by both in time, but proceeds eternally from both as the Spirit who is common to both, as their Love and as their substantial Communion.

What is given to us, then, according to Augustine, in the Holy Spirit is God himself, hypostatized as Gift: 'ipse (Spiritus) proprie sic est Deus ut dicatur etiam Dei donum'.[19] God gives nothing less than himself.[20] On this basis, Augustine develops a very great and profound teaching about the Spirit. We love God, he teaches, but we also love each other. The Church, as the Body of Christ, is one because of what—and here we should say because of the one who—in God is Love and Communion.[21] We have been made fully happy and we reach the fullness of our being as men because we enjoy God—*frui Deo*—by the same reality of which Augustine, speaking here of the intra-divine life in the text of *De Trin*. VI, 11, 12, which I have already quoted above, said: 'this dilection, this pleasure, this felicity, this happiness'. At present, of course, we have the Spirit only as *arrha* or earnest-money. The Gift is communicated to us as a *pignus* or 'pledge'.[22]

Peter Lombard (*I Sent.*, d. 18), and the classical theologians of the Western Church re-used the biblical and Augustinian theme of the Holy Spirit as Gift, and Thomas Aquinas gave special emphasis in his teaching to two personal names of the third Person: Love (*ST* Ia, q. 37) and Gift (q. 38.)[23]

*   *   *

I shall now try to contemplate and, as far as possible, to express the mystery of the Spirit as the absolute Gift. May he be gracious enough to illuminate, support and guide me in this attempt, since 'no one comprehends the thoughts of God except the Spirit of God' (1 Cor 2:11)!

(1) The Greek Fathers continually repeated the formula: 'from the Father, through the Son, in the Spirit'—*ek Patros, di' Huiou, en Pneumati*. This is a statement of the dynamism in which the Spirit is that in which—or the one in whom—the process is completed. To this statement can be added their numerous quotations, in a Trinitarian sense, of a doxology taken from certain New Testament texts: Rom 11:36, which is given in the Vulgate as 'Quoniam ex ipso et per ipsum et in ipso sunt omnia: ipsi gloria in saecula',[24] 1 Cor 8:6, which speaks of the Father and the Son,[25] and Eph 4:6, applied to the Father who is above all, the Son through whom everything is and the Spirit who is in all.[26] These texts are often merged together in the writings of the Greek Fathers and used in a doxological form that is of a liturgical type. The same is found, for example, in Augustine and in a canon of the Second Council of Constantinople (the Fifth Ecumenical Council: 553): 'God the Father, from whom all things are, is one; the Lord Jesus Christ, through whom all things are, is one; and the Holy Spirit, in whom all things are, is one'.[27]

Here we have an economic order, but one expressing the order of the immanent Trinity. According to that order, the Spirit is the one through whom God's communication of himself is completed. His economic attributes are sanctification or the ability to make perfect.[28] He is the completion, the *telos* or *teleiōsis*, in the Tri-unity of God.[29] I have quoted the Greek

147

Fathers here, because this attribute is in accordance with their linear pattern, but, as I have indicated above, the same can be found in Augustine's theme of the Spirit as the link of love between the Father and the Son. The Father and the Son remain in the Spirit and set the seal on their communication of life in him, Richard of Saint-Victor, an original disciple of Augustine in the twelfth century, said, for example: 'In Patre origo unitatis, in Filio inchoatio pluritatis, in Spiritu Sancto completio Trinitatis'—unity has its origin in the Father, plurality begins in the Son, the Trinity is completed in the Holy Spirit.[30]

(2) God is a Triad. His unity is not limited to only one mode of subsistence or to only one 'figure'. As Karl Barth has said, 'in equal Godhead the one God is, in fact, the One and also Another, . . . He is indeed a First and a Second . . . because in the same perfect unity and equality He is also a Third . . . the One who makes possible and maintains his fellowship with himself as the one and the other'.[31] An Other who is the perfect Image of the Father comes (or proceeds) by begetting from the Father. The Father and the Son are for each other, they are relative to each other. The Spirit is the one in whom they are united, in whom they receive each other, in whom they communicate with one another, and in whom they rest. Does God, then, remain tied to what psychologists have called a narcissistic structure, which they have further described as the essential foundation for love of self? Taking human experience as his point of departure, Christian Duquoc has pointed to a very deep aspect of *theo*-logy which calls on us to go beyond a static attitude that is not suited to the concept of the *living* God:

> The 'Trinitarian symbolism' not only sets aside the image of narcissistic self-contemplation as an ideal of perfection—it also equally strongly rejects the idea of a 'face to face' which is sufficient in itself, and points to a life or a communion that is both differentiated and open. The Spirit makes it impossible for such a self-sufficient 'face to face' between the two first figures to take place. The Christian tradition has accorded to the Spirit a creative and dynamic rôle and, in this sense, he is the one who gives rise to other differences. He makes the divine communion open to what is not divine. He is the indwelling of God where God is, in a sense, 'outside himself'. He is therefore called 'love'. He is God's 'ecstasy' directed towards his 'other', the creature.[32]

This text makes the transition to the economy, but it does so as the continuation of a *theo*-logy in which the Spirit is shown to be an opening to communion between God and man. He is the communion between the Father and the Son, but he is first of all the Breath of God. The Son is the Image, but he is first of all the Word coming from the mouth of the Father and accompanied by the Breath, and therefore accompanied by a power that sets things in motion. The life of God is, according to Duquoc, 'ecstasy, because each divine "figure" only exists in his relationship with the other "figures" and those figures are different because of that relationship'.[33] If

148

this is so, then the Holy Spirit is, as his name indicates, a going out, an impulse, an 'ecstasy'. That is why, if the Spirit is, in God, the term of the substantial communication that goes out from the Father, it is suitable, though not necessary, that this movement should continue, no longer by mode of substantial transference, but by mode of free and creative will. The *Spiritus creator* is the one who creates the *communicatio Spiritus Sancti*. As Walter Kasper has said, 'There is in God something that is most intimate, the unity of a freedom which transcends itself, and, at the same time, something that is most external, the freedom and the possibility of self-communication in God in a new way, that is to say, outside himself. The Spirit is therefore the bond of unity not only in God, but also between God and creation, a unity of love.'[34] God, in other words, can exist, as it were, outside himself.[35] Not only the possibility of this is there—there is also the inclination. God is Love and he is Grace. Love and Grace are hypostatized in the Spirit.

Grace is a synthesis of generosity, freedom and power. For the most high God, it is also the possibility of being not only with the lowliest, but also with the most wretched of creatures. Grace even makes God prefer what is wretched to what is sublime.

This is the fact of 'God'. Revealing himself, as we have seen, as the One who is, he also adds that he is the God of Abraham, Isaac and Jacob.[36] 'Who is like Yahweh our God, who is seated on high, who looks far down upon the heavens and the earth?' (Ps 113:5–6). Hannah's canticle (1 Sam 2:1–10) and the Magnificat (Lk 1:46–55) also point to this. It was the Spirit who came down on Mary and inspired her thanksgiving: the one who is mighty has looked down on me, his humble servant; he has 'filled the hungry with good things' and so on. In other words, the almighty God comes above all to the weak, lowly and poor.

What is the situation with regard to Jesus, the Son of God? Although his condition was divine, he came in the form of a servant. Nothing is more eloquent than the words which John uses to describe the washing of the disciples' feet: 'Jesus, knowing that the Father had given all things into his hands and that he had come from God and was going to God, rose from supper, laid aside his garments . . .' (Jn 13:3–4).

The Spirit is the water which flows towards the lowest, because he is grace, and can spring up into eternal life because he is grace from on high. He is implored as riches and as Gift, in the name of what is wretched and lacking. We ask him to come to us in the sequence *Veni, Sancte Spiritus*:

> Come, father of the poor. . . .
> Rest in hardship,
> moderation in the heat. . . .
> Water what is arid,
> heal what is wounded.
> Bend what is stiff,
> warm what is cold. . . .

In this context, I would also like to quote a prayer by Søren Kierkegaard (†1855), despite its rather excessive paradoxes and its Lutheran pessimism about man's fate:

> It is in a fragile vase of clay that we men carry the holy one, but you, O Holy Spirit, when you dwell in a man, you dwell in what is infinitely inferior—you, spirit of holiness, dwell in impurity and dirt, you, spirit of wisdom, dwell in foolishness, you, spirit of truth, dwell in deceit!
>
> Oh dwell in me for ever!
>
> O you, who do not look for the comfort of a desirable residence, something that you would certainly look for in vain, you who create and regenerate and make your dwelling-place for yourself—dwell in me for ever! Dwell in me for ever, so that you will, one day, end by being pleased with that dwelling-place that you have prepared for yourself in the impurity, wickedness and deceitfulness of my heart![37]

Grace is, by definition, free. Jesus compared the Spirit with the wind that 'blows where it wills': 'you hear the sound of it, but you do not know whence it comes or whither it goes'.[38] We have evidence every day of the freedom of God's grace in the inspirations, the charisms and the movements that appear again and again in our history. We also experience ourselves the paradox of the gratuity of God's gift on the one hand, as the prophet Isaiah said: 'Every one who thirsts, come to the waters, and he who has no money—come, buy and eat! Come, buy wine and milk without money and without price!' (Is 55:1)—and on the other hand, of what Dietrich Bonhoeffer called the 'price of grace'.

(3) God, as it were, outside himself is God in us—God in his creatures. He is in us in his activity and the movement by which he directs and inspires history.[39] He is there, in us, above all by the gift that he makes of himself. As Augustine said, God gives us nothing less than himself.[40] This gift is in accordance with a deep desire that is present in our nature, if it is true that we are made in God's image. We are therefore destined to become children of God by receiving the Spirit of his Son.[41]

Do we grasp the realism of such a statement? We receive the reality of the Spirit who has made Jesus' humanity a humanity of the Son of God: on this earth, in obedience and in the prayer 'Abba, Father!' and then, through the resurrection, in glory. The image of God comes more intimately alive in the leading of our filial life which the Spirit brings about in us and through which we return to the Father.

It is important to give its fullest realistic sense to the theologal character of this life. It is our life and it is firmly rooted in us because of the gifts that are really ours, but its principle and its term are, in a very real sense, God. We are sons of God (1 Jn 3:1–2). We are really deified! God is God not only in himself, but also in us! He is God not only in heaven, but also on earth! The Holy Spirit, who is the term of the communication of the divine life *intra Deum*, is the principle of this communication of God outside himself and beyond himself.[42]

According to Orthodox theology, which was systematically formulated in Palamism, this is the work of the uncreated energies which are God insofar as he is open to participation. This would then be the sense in which to interpret the texts of the Fathers which speak of a participation *in the Holy Spirit* by attributing directly to that Spirit the process of our deifying sanctification. We have, of course, encountered many such texts in the course of our reading. This does not, however, presuppose a personal presence that is distinctively and especially that of the Holy Spirit. Dionysius Petavius' thesis about this question has been criticized very effectively by Paul Galtier, but, in spite of this criticism, it continues to reappear, because it has to be admitted that the feeling expressed by the texts is stronger than the explanations that have been given of them.

According to our classical theology, God is present through his creative power in the things that he sets in being and moves. This creative power is that of the three consubstantial hypostases, according to the order in which they process from the Father. In the communication of covenant and grace, God gives himself in a new way to the creatures made in his image, through the gifts that enable them to reach him in a very real way as the reality towards which their knowledge and love are directed. The divine Persons are made present by means of the gifts of grace, the effect of the invisible movements of the Word and the Spirit, as partners in a spiritual communion. Sometimes—witness the experience of the great mystics—their presence is felt in a life of knowledge and love of great intensity. Christ and the Holy Spirit in fact become the life of these mystics.

Is this a deification'? It will be, in the perfect possession of heaven. In it, God will become 'everything to everyone' (1 Cor 15:28). He himself will become our peace, our joy and our 'everything'. Peace and joy will become ours, but they will also be his. We shall in the fullest sense be children of God. Here on earth we only taste the first-fruits, but does our theological talk about the divine missions and created grace suffice to do justice to the terms in which the mystics and the spiritual writers have spoken about the transforming union—iron which becomes fire in contact with a source of intense heat, air which glows when the sun penetrates it, and so on?[43] The Orthodox think that Latin theology does not express a true *deification*. All the same, based as it is on the very profound teaching about the divine missions, Western theology sees the communication of grace as a prolongation, in the created world, of the eternal processions. This doctrine thus takes its place, as H. F. Dondaine has suggested, 'among the most spacious ideas of mediation between the finite and the Infinite'. Through the missions of the Word and the Spirit and with their effects of grace, God, as the Trinity, is really able to exist outside himself.

NOTES

1. Lk 24:49; Acts 1:4; 2:33 and 38; Gal 3:14; Eph 1:13.
2. Acts 13:23 and 32; 26:6.
3. 1 Jn 2:25; Heb 4:1; 9:15; 10:36; 2 Tim 1:1.
4. *Dōron* is used in a way which most closely approaches the cases in which *dōrea* is applied to the Spirit in Eph 2:8, which refers to salvation as a gift from God; cf. *dōrea* in Rom 5:15 and 17; 2 Cor 9:15.
5. The well of Jacob, beside which the conversation wih the Samaritan woman took place, was sometimes called 'gift': see A. Jaubert, *Approaches de l'évangile de Jean* (Paris, 1976), p. 59, who says that the water of the well represents the Holy Spirit in certain rabbinical texts: p. 60, note 13, and p. 144. On the other hand, there is also a connection between 'our father Jacob gave us the well and drank from it himself and his sons' (4:12) and 'whoever drinks of the water that I shall give him' (4:14): see C.-J. Pinto de Oliveira, *RSPT*, 49 (1965), 82–83.
6. *Didōmi*: Acts 5:32: 'We and the Holy Spirit whom God has given'; 8:18; 15:8: 'God . . . gave them the Holy Spirit just as he did to us'; Lk 11:13; Rom 5:5: 'through the Holy Spirit which has been given to us'; 2 Cor 1:22: 'he has given us his Spirit in our hearts as a guarantee' (= as *arrha* or earnest-money); similarly 5:5; Eph 1:17; 1 Thess 4:8: 'God, who gives his Holy Spirit to you'; 2 Tim 1:7; Jn 3:34: 'It is not by measure that he (God) gives the Spirit'; 4:14, which can be compared with Rev 21:6; 14:16: 'I will pray the Father and he will give you another Paraclete'; 1 Jn 3:24 and 4:13: 'By this we know that we abide in him and he in us, because he has given us of his own Spirit'.

    Lambanō: Acts 1:8: 'But you shall receive'; 2:33; 2:38; 8:15: Peter and John 'prayed for them that they might receive the Holy Spirit', which can be compared with 8:17 and 19; 10:47; 19:2; 1 Cor 2:12: 'We have received . . . the Spirit which is from God'; 2 Cor 11:4; Gal 3:2 and 14: 'that we might receive the promise of the Spirit through faith'; Jn 7:39: 'he said this about the Spirit, which those who believed in him were to receive'; 14:17: the world cannot receive him; 20:22: 'he breathed on them and said to them: "Receive the Holy Spirit" '.
7. Dionysius Petavius, *Dogmata Theologica. De Trinitate*, VIII, c. 3, §3; see also T. de Régnon, *Etudes de théologie positive sur la Sainte Trinité*, IV (Paris, 1898), p. 475 and pp. 466–498, where the author deals with the Holy Spirit as a Donation.
8. Cyril of Jerusalem, *Cat.* XVI, 24 (*PG* 33, 953).
9. Athanasius, *Ad Ser.* III, 5 (*PG* 26, 633; *SC* 15, p. 171); see also Basil the Great (*PG* 32, 133C).
10. Pseudo-Justin, *Coh. ad Graec.* 32 (*PG* 6, 300).
11. Irenaeus, *Adv. haer.* III, 17, 2 (*PG* 7, 930; ed. W. W. Harvey, II, 93; Sagnard, pp. 306 and 307).
12. Athanasius, *Ad Ser.* I, 20 (*PG* 26, 580; *SC* 15, pp. 119–120, Fr. tr. J. Lebon).
13. Cyril of Alexandria, *De sanct. Trin. Dial.* III (*PG* 75, 844; *SC* 250, p. 237).
14. Basil, *De spir. sanct.* XXV, 58 (*PG* 32, 173A–B; *SC* 17, p. 218).
15. Liturgy of St James, ed. B. C. Mercier, *Patr. Or.* XXVI/2 (Paris, 1946), pp. 198–199.
16. *De Trin.* II, 1 (*PL* 10, 50); cf. II, 29 (*PL* 10, 70A). It is very difficult to translate this word *usus*. In other passages, it is clear that Hilary employs it in the sense of the welcome that we give to the Gift or the usefulness that God is or could be for us as given in the Holy Spirit: see *De Trin.* II, 33–35 (*PL* 10, 73–75). For this meaning of Hilary's text, see P. Smulders, *La doctrine trinitaire de S. Hilaire de Poitiers* (*Anal. Greg.*, 32) (Rome, 1944), pp. 270–278. For the way in which Augustine employed the word *usus*, see O. du Roy, *L'intelligence de la foi en la Trinité selon S. Augustin* (Paris, 1966), pp. 320–322. Du Roy quotes Ambrose, p. 320, note 3: 'Sanctificatio autem Spiritus donum munusque divinum sit': *De spir. sanct.* I, 7, 83, but he observes that Ambrose did not make it a title or a name of the Spirit.

17. See the texts in F. Cavallera, 'La doctrine de S. Augustin sur l'Esprit Saint', *RTAM*, 2 (1930), 368–370. With the passage of time, the word *donum* was used by Augustine rather than *munus*. When he wanted to speak of the mission of the Holy Spirit, however, he tended to use *datio*. See J. L. Maier, *Les missions divines selon S. Augustin* (*Paradosis*, XVI) (Fribourg, 1960), p. 168.

18. Augustine, *De Trin.* V, 11, 12 and 15; see also Volume I, pp. 79–80, 84 notes 39 to 42. For this theology taken over word for word by the Sixteenth Council of Toledo in May 693, see *DS* 570.

19. *Ench.* 40 (*PL* 40, 252)

20. *De fid. et symb.* 9, 19 (*PL* 40, 191); *Bibl. Augustin.*, 9, pp. 56ff.: 'ut Deum credamus non seipso inferius donum dare'; cf. *Sermo* 128, 4 (*PL* 38, 715): 'donum dat aequale sibi, quia donum eius Spiritus Sanctus est'; *Enarr. in Ps.* 141, 12 (*PL* 37, 1840): 'quid dabit amanti se, nisi se?'.

21. *De Trin.* XV, 19, 35: 'The Spirit is the gift of God as given to the one who, through him, loves God'; cf. *Sermo* 71, 12, 18 and Fénelon: 'It is the love that God has for us which gives us everything, but the greatest gift that he can give us is to give the Love that we should have for him'; quoted by F. Varillon, *Fénelon et le pur amour* (1957), p. 101. See also Volume I, pp. 86–87: the prayer of William of Saint-Thierry.

22. See above, p. 92, note 22. All the theology summarized here will be found in Augustine's *De fid. et symb.* 9, 19.

23. Thomas speaks of the created gift and the uncreated Gift and makes use in this context of the categories *uti* and *frui*, which come from Augustine.

24. O. du Roy, *op. cit.* (note 16), pp. 479–485 has an appendix on the quotations from Rom 11:36 in Augustine's work. He finds that there are 46 of these and that the text is often combined with that of 1 Cor 8:6 and also frequently applied formally to the three Persons, sometimes with a doxological emphasis.

25. This text is often compared with Rom 11:36 (see Augustine, *De Trin.* I, 6, 12) or merged with it in patristic writings. For Origen, see Cécile Blanc's Fr. tr. of his *Commentary on St John, SC* 120 (1966), p. 252, note 1. For Cyril of Alexandria, see the Introduction to G. M. de Durand's *Dialogues sur la Trinité*, I, *SC* 250 (1976), pp. 74ff.

26. See Irenaeus, *Adv. haer.* V, 18, 1 (*PG* 7, 1173; *SC* 153, p. 374); *Dem.* 5; Hilary of Poitiers, *De Trin.* II, 1 (*PL* 10, 51): 'unus est enim Deus Pater, ex quo omnia; et unus unigenitus Dominus noster Jesus Christus, per quem omnia; et unus Spiritus, donum in omnibus'. See also Athanasius (note 28 below).

27. *DS* 421; O. du Roy, *op. cit.* (note 16), p. 484, compared this with Justinian's confession of faith in 551–553: see Mansi, 9, 540.

28. Athanasius, *Ad Ser.* I, 14 (*PG* 26, 565B; *SC* 15, pp. 107–108): 'The grace which (coming) from the Father through the Son is completed in the Holy Spirit (*en Pneumati hagiō plēroumenē*) is one; the divinity is one and there is only one God who is over all and through all and in all'; Basil the Great, *De spir. sanct.* XVI, 38 (*PG* 32, 136B; *SC* 17, p. 175); Gregory Nazianzen, *Orat.* 34, 8 (*PG* 36, 249A): the Father is *aitios*, the Son is *dēmiourgos* and the Spirit is *telepoios*; we have already seen that both Basil and Gregory made the ability to 'sanctify' the characteristic property (*gnōristikē idiotēs*) of the third Person; Gregory of Nyssa, *Quod non sint tres dii* (*PG* 45, 129): 'every action comes from the Father, progresses through the Son and is completed in the Holy Spirit (*en tō Pneumati tō hagiō teleioutai*)'; Didymus the Blind, under the name of Basil, *Contra Eunom.* V (*PG* 29, 728): *teleiourgon*; John Damascene, *De fide orthod.* I, 12 (*PG* 94, 136): the *telesiourgikē dunamis* is given to the Holy Spirit.

29. T. de Régnon, *op. cit.* (note 7), IV, p. 120, provides an excellent documentation: Basil the Great, *De spir. sanct.* XVIII, 45 (*PG* 32, 152A; *SC* 17, p. 194): 'the Holy Spirit is connected by the one Son and by the one Father and by himself he completes the blessed Trinity' (*di' heautou sumplēroun tēn poluhumnēton kai makarian Triada*); Gregory Nazianzen, *Orat.* 31 (= *Orat. theol.* V), 4 (*PG* 36, 137A; *SC* 250, p. 283): 'What kind of

divinity is it if it is not complete? . . . Something would be absent from it if it was without holiness. And how would it have it if it did not have the Holy Spirit?'; Cyril of Alexandria, *Thes.* (*PG* 75, 608): 'The Holy Spirit is the completion of the Trinity (*sumplērōma*), . . . completing the Holy Trinity (*sumplērōtikon tēs hagias Triados*). Finally, see Thomas Aquinas, *Contra Err. Graec.* II, 30.

30. Richard of Saint-Victor, *De trib. approp.* (*PL* 196, 992).
31. K. Barth, *Church Dogmatics*, IV. 1 (Eng. tr.; Edinburgh and New York, 1956), pp. 202–203.
32. C. Duquoc, *Dieu différent* (Paris, 1977), pp. 121–122. See also O. Clément, 'A propos de l'Esprit Saint', *Contacts*, 85 (1974), 87; and the mystic Adrienne von Speyr: H. Urs von Balthasar, *Adrienne von Speyr et sa mission théologique. Anthologie* (Paris, 1978), p. 108.
33. C. Duquoc, *op. cit.*, p. 120.
34. W. Kasper, *Kirche, Ort des Geistes* (Freiburg, 1976), p. 34.
35. H. Mühlen, *Morgen wird Einheit sein* (Paderborn, 1974), p. 128: 'the Pneuma is God's being outside himself'; *idem*, *Die Erneuerung des christlichen Glaubens. Charisma-Geist-Befreiung* (Munich, 1974), p. 186.
36. See above, p. 142, note 48.
37. Based on Fr. tr. of Kierkegaard quoted in Sr Geneviève, *Le trésor de la prière à travers le temps* (Paris, 1976), p. 119.
38. Jn 3:8. See also the parallels: Eccles 11:5; Prov 30:4; Sir (Ecclus) 16:21.
39. The Pastoral Constitution *Gaudium et spes*, on the Church in the Modern World, 11, 1; 38, 1; 26, 4, pointed to this fact.
40. See Augustine's *De fid. et symb.* 9, 19 (*PL* 40, 191; *CSEL*, 41, 22): we have scarcely learnt only one thing about the Holy Spirit, 'nisi quod cum Donum Dei esse praedicant, ut Deum credamus non seipso inferius Donum dare'.
41. Rom 8:14ff.; Gal 4:5–6; Athanasius, *Contra Arian.* III, 24 (*PG* 26, 373).
42. This idea was shared by Bérulle, Louis-Marie Grignion de Montfort and others: see Volume II, pp. 67, 72 note 2. See also A. Stolz, *De SS. Trinitate* (Freiburg, 1941), pp. 88ff.; *Anthropologia*, p. 71.
43. For a purely literary and historical study of these formulae and their prehistory in Aristotle, the Stoics and Alexander of Aphrodisias, see J. Pépin, ' "Stilla aquae modica multo infuso vino, ferrum ignitum, luce perfusa aer". L'origine des trois comparaisons familières à la théologie mystique médiévale', *Miscellanea André Combes*, I (Rome and Paris, 1967), pp. 331–375.

3

THE MOTHERHOOD IN GOD AND THE FEMININITY OF THE HOLY SPIRIT

The question of the femininity present in God, or even of the femininity of God, is raised insistently nowadays, in reaction to an overwhelming, centuries-long, male dominance. In every language, the word for 'God' is masculine. In triadology we always speak of his 'Son'. The Word was made flesh—in the masculine form.

These are, of course, indisputable facts, but one will not insist on them too much if it is remembered how careful the canonical Scriptures are to avoid attributing sex to God. Israel was surrounded by religions with female deities,[1] but there was no goddess alongside the one living God in its own belief and practice. In obedience to his word and to the revelation of Jesus Christ, we call God 'Father', but this does not mean that he has a female partner, a bride or mother, alongside him. If we were not afraid of anthropomorphism, we would say, together with Bérulle, that, in the begetting of the Word, God 'performed the functions of father and mother, begetting him in himself and bearing him in his womb'.[2] Thomas Aquinas observed that Scripture attributed to the Father, in begetting the Word, what, in the material world, belonged separately to a father and a mother, but that there was no reason in this case to speak of a mother in God because he was pure Act, whereas in the process of begetting, the mother represents what receives passively[3]—this is, of course, an idea no longer acceptable to modern physiology. The Word of God remains.

On the other hand, however, 'God created man in his own image, in the image of God he created him, male and female he created them' (Gen 1:27). If this is true, then there must be in God, in a transcendent form, something that corresponds to masculinity and something that corresponds to femininity.

In fact, there is no lack of feminine characteristics in the God of the biblical revelation, and these are emphasized by the vocabulary of Scripture itself. In the first place, there is the theme of tenderness. This is, of course, not a uniquely feminine attribute: there is a paternal tenderness, and, in Scripture, God, as father, is tender (see Ps 103:13; Is 63:16). Sometimes tenderness is attributed simply to Yahweh (see Ps 25:6; 116:5; Ex 34:6). It is, however, indisputably feminine in many of the texts of the prophets and especially in the very concrete image incorporated into the term itself:

When Israel was a child, I loved him and out of Egypt I called my son. . . . Yet it was I who taught Ephraim to walk, I took them in my arms, but they did not know that I healed them. I led them with cords of compassion, with the bands of love. . . . How can I give you up, O Ephraim! How can I hand you over, O Israel! . . . My heart recoils within me, my compassion grows warm and tender (Hos 11:1–4, 8).

. Is Ephraim my dear son? Is he my darling child? For as often as I speak against him, I remember him still. Therefore my heart yearns for him; I will surely have mercy on (tenderness for—*raḥam*) him (Jer 31:20).

But Zion said: 'Yahweh has abandoned me, the Lord has forgotten me'. Can a woman forget her sucking child, that she should have no compassion on the son of her womb (*mereḥem*)? (Is 49:14–15).

As one whom his mother comforts, I will comfort you (Is 66:13).

The word used in Hebrew for 'tenderness' is *raḥamîm*, 'bowels', 'entrails', which is the plural of *reḥem* (*raḥam*), 'womb', matrix.[4] Tenderness, then, is feminine. God has the disposition and the love of a mother. Jesus had the same disposition—he is often shown in the gospels as [literally translated] 'moved in his bowels'.[5] Feminine qualities, activities and attitudes, such as feeding with milk, gentleness, love and so on, are celebrated in Christ, giving rise to the devotion to 'Christ our Mother'.[6] This was especially an ideal for the superior of a monastic community—the abbot, the father, should be maternal. This ideal was followed in detail by the great abbots and Cistercian monks of the twelfth century—Bernard, Aelred of Rievaulx, Guerric of Igny, Isaac of Stella, Adam of Perseigne, Hélinand of Froidmont and William of Saint-Thierry.[7] These are, however, psychological attitudes rather than *theo*-logy. The Holy Spirit is not mentioned at all in the monastic texts in this context. The idea of maternity in God does recur in a somewhat curious form in the writings of the English mystic Julian of Norwich, at the beginning of the fifteenth century. She saw three attributes in the Trinity: fatherhood, motherhood and lordship. It is, however, rather the theme of wisdom that she relies on in attributing motherhood to the second Person.[8]

Wisdom is, as the *šekinah*, Presence or Indwelling of God, a mode of being or action on the part of God and especially with reference to the world, to men, and to Israel. It is a feminine attribute and it is loved and sought like a woman (Sir 14:22ff.). Wisdom is a bride and a mother (Sir 14:26ff.; 15:2ff.). She is the source of fertility, intimacy and joy. In the New Testament and theological tradition, Wisdom is appropriated to the Word, Christ.[9] In the Old Testament, on the other hand, Wisdom is often identified with the Spirit (Wis 9:17) and many of the ante-Nicene Fathers thought of it as representing the Holy Spirit.[10]

G. Quispel recently suggested a new interpretation of the well-known text about the woman in Rev 12. She is, he thinks, the Holy Spirit accompanying the Christian community in its flight from persecution and seeking refuge at Pella, as the *šekinah* accompanied the people of God into exile. The birth of the male child would correspond to the baptism of Jesus, at which the Spirit is presented as *genetrix* in the *Gospel of the Nazarenes*.[11]

In Christian reflection, the feminine character of God is ultimately attributed to the Holy Spirit. The fact that the words *rûah* or *ruho* are feminine in Hebrew and Syriac respectively has often been used as evidence of this. We shall see later that this may play a part, but, apart from the fact that the Syriac *meltha*, 'word', is also feminine, the word *rûah* is often masculine in both languages; in Syriac, it is always masculine when it refers to the third Person.[12] Furthermore, Jerome noted that 'Spirit' is feminine in Hebrew, neuter in Greek and masculine in Latin, and interpreted this as a sign of God's non-sexuality.[13]

Nonetheless, it is in the linguistic and cultural domains of Judaism and the Syriac world that the Holy Spirit is most frequently called 'mother'.[14] In the climate of Judaeo-Christianity, this occurred especially in the *Gospel of the Hebrews* or the *Gospel of the Nazarenes*, which are mentioned by Clement of Alexandria, Origen and Jerome.[15] In Jerome's quotations, we read of the coming of the Spirit on Jesus at the time of his baptism, with the words: 'You are my beloved Son'. In the *Odes of Solomon*, which originated in Syria, the Dove-Spirit is compared to the mother of Christ who gives milk, like the breasts of God. Finally, within the framework of Judaeo-Christian Ebionism, Elkesai saw in a vision an immense angel, who gave him a book: 'This angel was immense, ninety-six miles high, and "was accompanied by a feminine being whose dimensions were of the same scale. The masculine being was the Son of God, the feminine was called the Holy Spirit." '[16] In the Syrian liturgy, the Spirit is compared to a merciful mother, and Aphraates, a Syrian writing in Persia about 336–345, said that 'the man who does not marry respects God his father and the Holy Spirit his mother, and he has no other love'.[17] R. Murray quotes these words from the *Homilies* of Macarius: after the fall, men 'did not look on the true, heavenly Father, or the good, gentle kind Mother, the grace of the Spirit, nor the sweet and longed-for Brother, the Lord'.[18]

Methodius of Olympus (†c. 312) evinces, if not speculation, at any rate an insight the depth of which we should not ignore on account of certain surprising statements.[19] As A. Orbe has shown, these insights did not come from the Gnostics, but from a very early common tradition, according to which the making of Eve was interpreted in the light of Christ and the Church.[20] God took Eve from Adam's side and gave her to him as his spouse. The Spirit of truth similarly came from the breast or the side of the Logos on the cross (Jn 16:13). The septiform Spirit (Is 11:2) came in this way to form the Church, his bride. That Church is the life and unity of the Spirit, especially in the pure souls of virgins, who are brides *par excellence*. Christ, the new Adam, and the Church-Spirit are the spiritual Adam and Eve. There is therefore, in this view, a real typological continuity or even identity. The Church-Spirit is Eve and it is the bride or spouse.

157

This idea was taken up again in the nineteenth century by M. J. Scheeben (†1888), who explicitly quoted Methodius as well as a rather different text by Gregory Nazianzen, in this way merging together two different themes, thereby not making his own thought any clearer.[21] In order to find some clarity and respect the course of history, I shall return to Scheeben later and say something now about the third- and fourth-century Fathers.

They had to reply to the difficulty raised since the third century, and again later by the Arians and Macedonius, namely: how could the Spirit proceed from the Father and not be the Son, that is, not proceed by begetting? If he does not proceed by generation, how can he be of the same essence? A. Orbe has brought together a great deal of evidence (see note 19 below). There are differences between individual authors, but the general consensus appears to be that Eve had a different origin and a different mode of coming into existence from Adam. She did not come by begetting. She is therefore not a daughter, although she is of the same nature as Adam. The same applies to the Spirit after the Son.[22] There was a certain amount of assimilation of the Spirit to Eve, but only in order to justify his consubstantiality in that his mode of coming into existence is not that of begetting, but there is no insistence on his feminine character, except in Methodius.

Gregory Nazianzen (†389–390) was similarly preoccupied with this question, but he introduced a third term into the discussion. Eve, he maintained, was taken from Adam by means of a coming out or immediate procession. It was in this way that the Spirit also proceeded. Seth, however, came out of Adam (and Eve!) by begetting, as a son.[23] John Damascene's teaching was very similar to Gregory's, although he replaced Seth with Abel: 'There was in Adam the one who was not born, in Abel the one who was begotten, in Eve the one who proceeded'.[24] It is clear that Gregory was only interested in showing that there could be an identity of nature despite different modes of coming into existence or of proceeding. He was not interested in the femininity of the Spirit, whom he compared to Eve only in their similar modes of procession. If his teaching in this case were to be taken to its ultimate conclusion, it would be necessary to say that the Son, who comes about by begetting, proceeds *a Patre Spirituque*. This teaching has, in our own time, been upheld by Paul Evdokimov, within the framework of a subtle and very profound triadology.[25] This is, however, not what Gregory wanted to say; his comparison was taken up again by several Greek writers, some of whom replaced Seth with Abel.[26]

The Greeks, then, were not concerned with a comparison between the Trinity and a family consisting of father, mother and child, save in the purely material sense. That idea was, however, current—Augustine came across it and rejected the image of the father, mother and child as false and unworthy of God, although he believed that the creation of Eve pointed to a mode of procession that ensured the consubstantiality of a son or a daughter, without the need for begetting.[27] He did not, however, concern himself in any way with the femininity of the Spirit. For him, woman, in the image of God that is realized in the individual person, represented the *ratio inferior*!

It is clear that Thomas Aquinas also came across the analogy of the family. He opted for Abel rather than Seth and obviously believed that this could illustrate the procession *a Patre et Filio*. The Son here is prefigured by Eve. Thomas does not refer at all the Holy Spirit's possible femininity:

> The Holy Spirit proceeds from the Father immediately insofar as he has his being from the Father, and mediately insofar as he has it from the Son. It is in this sense that we say that he proceeds from the Father and through the Son. It is in this way that Abel proceeded from Adam immediately, because Adam was his father, and mediately, because Eve was his mother and proceeded from Adam. To tell the truth, this example, taken from a material source, is badly chosen to represent the immaterial procession of the divine Persons.[28]

Thomas' criticism has not deterred a considerable number of contemporaries, attracted by the analogy based on interpersonal relationships, from gladly using the image of the family in connection with the Trinity.[29] In this comparison, the Holy Spirit is seen as the child. This has nothing to do with the theme of his femininity. Let us return at this point of Scheeben.

In *The Mysteries of Christianity* (see also below, note 21), Scheeben tried to establish a link between the Spirit and woman. He was familiar with the teaching of the Greek Fathers and noted first that, in man, the child (the son) came third, as the fruit of the union between the father and the mother, whereas, in God, the Son proceeded as the second Person, as the immediate and exclusive fruit of the Father. This is because, whereas there is a duality in the creature, a distance between the act and power, the active and the passive principles, God is pure act as the fertile Father. But Scheeben re-introduced the Holy Spirit between the Father and the Son as the bond of love between the two and as the expression of the unity of nature between them (Paul Evdokimov's 'manifestations' or, better still, the idea suggested by Gregory of Cyprus and Gregory Palamas), since he is the fruit of their love. Scheeben thus re-found a relationship here between the procession of the third Person and the creation of the first woman, Eve. It is at this point that he quotes Methodius of Olympus and suggests the following relationship:

$$\frac{Adam}{Eve} = \frac{Christ}{Church\text{-}Spirit}$$

Scheeben likewise brought together, in his *Dogmatik* (see also note 21 below), the Christological reality of the Church and the account of the origin of man, which is a very early tradition (see below, note 20) and in accordance with Jerome's quotations from the *Gospel of the Hebrews* (see below, note 15). He compared the procession of the Word, the Son, with the production of Adam and the procession of the Holy Spirit with the production of Eve. In the case of man, he insisted, man, who is *virtus et sapientia*, and woman, who is *suavitas et caritas*, are thus like Christ and the Holy Spirit. In the economy, the relationship between Christ and the Church corresponds to the relationship between Adam and Eve, and the Holy Spirit—the Church-Spirit—is the substantial unity of believers.

In an original, but ponderous attempt to base the difference and the relationship between the sexes on the intra-divine mystery of the Trinity, H. Doms relied a great deal on Scheeben's study.[30] The duality and complementary unity of action that we have noted and stressed between Christ and the Holy Spirit are reflected in the duality and the dynamic and symphonic unity of man and woman in society and the Church.[31] In the Church especially, but also in society as a whole, a pre-Trinitarian monotheism or a 'Christomonism'—in other words, a neglect of the Holy Spirit and of pneumatology—has led to the predominance of a patriarchal type and of an emphasis on masculinity.[32] The Church is consequently now confronted with a twofold task—on the one hand, it has to become more fully both masculine and feminine and, on the other, it has to preserve feminine values without keeping women in the 'harem' of passive and charming qualities from which they wish to emerge to be treated simply and authentically as persons.

There is an obstacle here that attempts to develop a 'theology of woman' have encountered. I would mention two of these, both by German-speaking Christians which, with varying degrees of basis, develop such a theology, in the light of the Holy Spirit. The first is by Mother Maura Böckeler and the second by Willi Moll.

(1) Maura Böckeler expounds a vision of the whole economy of grace, illustrating her reflections with numerous quotations from the Fathers, the liturgy and Hildegard of Bingen.[33] The intra-divine mystery of the three Persons has a parallel in the signs culminating in that of Rev 12. First there is Wisdom, in which the Breath accompanies the Word as Eve is given to help Adam. According to the author, then, as in the Fathers (see below, note 20) and in Methodius of Olympus, several passages of whom the author cites under the name of Pseudo-Gregory (of Nyssa), the origins are the sign of the Trinitarian mystery and Eve is the image of the Spirit. The Word calls for a response, the *Wort* for an *Antwort*. That response is love: the Spirit returns to the Father and completes the Triad, and consecrated virginity returns the praise of the cosmos to God. Eve fell, but the response of the virgin was taken up by Mary and then in the new Eve, the Church, which gives a body to love and to the Holy Spirit. Methodius is quoted again here, this time under his own name (*The Banquet*, III, c. 8): the Logos who became man received, by the thrust of the lance when he was on the cross and at Pentecost (*op. cit.* below (note 33), p. 400), when the Church was born, his opposite, the new Eve, the Church, that is, the Spirit in a human existence. Woman, then, is the great symbol of the response of love given to God. In God, that response is the Holy Spirit.

(2) Willi Moll tried to establish the specific character of the masculine person in the fatherhood of the first divine Person. The specific character of woman was based, according to Moll, on the Holy Spirit, in his property of Love in the three tasks or situations that are peculiar to woman as a *virgin*, that of welcoming or receiving, as a *spouse* or bride, that of union—the Spirit is the great 'and' of God, the copula that unites—and as a *mother*, that of communicating life.[34] Do these three characteristics, exemplified in the highest and most perfect way in Mary, really throw light on a theology of the Holy Spirit and of the femininity in God which would belong to him? Certainly, tradition recognizes in the Spirit a certain maternal function.

In Gen 1:2, the Spirit is shown, in a sense, as God's *rûah* hatching the egg of the world.[35] He is likewise at the principle of the second creation, as if realizing the Father's plan in a maternal manner—the Word, the Son, is begotten in our humanity (Lk 1:35), in his messianic function, the dove descending on Jesus when the Father's voice declares: 'You are my beloved Son',[36] and in his new creation, when he was raised and glorified in the condition of a humanity of the Son of God (Rom 1:4, together with Acts 13:33; Phil 2:6–11; Heb 5:5).

The Spirit, however, exercised and continues to exercise this motherhood with regard to Christ, our Head, in the first place and then with regard to the Church as Christ's body and members. For the Church, Pentecost was what the Annunciation was for Christ. The Spirit has never ceased to form Christians. In an article written in 1921, but frequently quoted ever since. A. Lemonnyer described 'the maternal part played by the Holy Spirit in our supernatural life'.[37] Firstly, he said:

> Of all the divine Persons, he is the one who is, in a more special way, 'given' to us. He is *par excellence* the Gift of God and he has that name. In the Trinity, he is Love, and that is also one of his names. These titles, however, are more suitably applied to the mother than to any other person. To some extent, they define what a mother is. No one on earth is 'given' to us in exactly the same way as our mother is and she personifies love in its most disinterested, most generous and most devoted form.

What Lemonnyer showed, however, above all in his article was that, in the imperfect state of the divine life in ourselves in our condition of faith, we are still living in the supernatural order as children and, what is more, as children picked up out of the gutter and called to live as children of the king. The part played in our upbringing by the Holy Spirit is that of mother—a mother who enables us to know our Father, God, and our brother, Jesus. The Spirit also enables us to invoke God as our Father and he reveals to us Jesus our Lord, introducing us gradually to his inheritance of grace and truth. Finally, he teaches us how to practise the virtues and how to use the gifts of a son of God by grace. All this is part of a mother's function. The mother fashions her child's mind by her daily presence and a communication more of feeling than of the intellect. That is, as I have shown elsewhere, the part played by Tradition in the Church.[38] The Spirit, who is the transcendent subject of that Tradition, completes the contribution made by the Word by making it interior and present here and now in the course of time. He does this by an intimate educative activity and a kind of impregnation and, so that the seal may be set on this work, his maternal and feminine part is combined with the function of the Father and that of the Son.

As I observed in Volume I of this work (pp. 163–164) the maternal function of the Holy Spirit has often been replaced in recent Catholic devotion by the Virgin Mary. The value of this may perhaps be ambiguous, but it forms part of the deep Christian mystery.[39]

NOTES

1. Inanna of Sumer, Ishtar of Akkad (see Jer 44:19), Astarte of the Phoenicians (see Judges 2:13), Cybele of the Phrygians, Isis of the Egyptians, Anath of the Canaanites, who is associated with Yahweh in the Elephantine papyri, as well as Gaia and Demeter of the Greeks. I pass over here the invocations and forms of worship of God as mother in non-Christian religions, such as Ramakrishna Paramahamsa celebrating the divine mother, Kali.
2. Bérulle, *Les Grandeurs de Jésus*, X, §2, ed. J. P. Migne (Paris, 1856), col. 355.
3. Thomas Aquinas, last chapter of *Contra Gent*. IV, 9; *Comp*. I, 39. The idea that fatherhood precedes motherhood in causality is the reason that Anselm gives us a justification for speaking of Father and Son and not of Mother and Daughter, although there is no sex in God. It is interesting to note in this context that Bonaventure rejected the Aristotelian idea that the woman was a passive principle, and the male was the only active principle: *In III Sent*. d. 4, a. 3, q. 1. Modern physiology and recent developments in the rôle of woman in society have led theologians nowadays to reconsider the question of God's maternity and femininity. In Anita Röper, *Ist Gott ein Mann? Ein Gespräch mit Karl Rahner* (Düsseldorf, 1979), Rahner accepts the attribution, in a transcendent and analogical way (*simpliciter diversum!*), of the function of motherhood, together with that of fatherhood, to God, but does not accept that we should call him man and woman. He also observes that, in a patriarchal society such as our own, the mother's status is secondary and subordinate. There is constantly a risk that controversial characteristics may be introduced into our speaking about God. Anita Röper, on the other hand, wishes in fact to transcend the representations of a patriarchal society and the results that these involve for the situation of woman in the Church.
4. The *Vocabulaire biblique* refers to Gen 43:30—Joseph is moved in the presence of his brethren—and 1 Kings 3:26—the real mother of the child is moved with tenderness after Solomon's judgement. To these can be added Prov 12:10.
5. The verb used is *splagchnizomai*: see Mt 9:36; 20:34; Mk 1:41; 6:34; Lk 7:13.
6. A. Cassabut, 'Une dévotion médiévale peu connue, la dévotion à "Jésus notre Mère" ', *RAM*, 25 (1949; *Mélanges Marcel Viller*), 234–245.
7. Caroline Walker Bynum, 'Jesus as Mother and Abbot as Mother: Some Themes in Twelfth-Century Cistercian Writings', *Harvard Theological Review*, 70 (1977), 257–284; this article has a very full bibliography and promises a second article on this subject by the same author.

8. 'The great power of the Trinity is our Father, the deep wisdom our Mother and the great love our Lord': Julian of Norwich, *Revelations of Divine Love*, tr. Clifton Wolters (Harmondsworth, 1966), p. 165.

9. Wisdom is the Son who reveals the Father: see E. Wurz, 'Das Mütterliche in Gott', *Una Sancta*, 32 (1977), 261–272. *Ibid.*, 273–279, G. K. Kaltenbrunner, 'Ist der Heilige Geist weiblich?', applies these texts to the Spirit together with other common themes and several quotations from modern poets.

10. Especially Theophilus of Antioch, Irenaeus and the Clementine *Homilies*. For the theme of Wisdom and the Holy Spirit, see Volume I, pp. 9–12. The *šekinah* is also identified with the Holy Spirit: see Volume II, p. 79. In the Zohar, I, 91–93, it has a feminine aspect— God will be united to this *šekinah* as man and woman are united. The motherhood of the *šekinah* is developed in Shmuel Trigano's very complex book, *Récit de la disparue* (Paris, 1978). Finally, it is also present in the Cabbala.

11. Professor Quispel made this suggestion at the Patrological Congress at Oxford in 1979, in a paper entitled 'The Holy Spirit as Woman in Apocalypse 12'. He kindly let me have the text of this paper before its publication.

12. K. Albrecht provided a list of texts in which *rûaḥ* is masculine: *ZAW*, 16 (1896), 42ff. For the Syriac, see E.-P. Siman, *L'expérience de l'Esprit par l'Eglise d'après la tradition syrienne d'Antioche* (*Théol. hist.*, 15) (Paris, 1971), p. 212, note 89.

13. *Comm. in Isaiam* XI, in which Jerome comments on Is 49:9–11 (*PL* 24, 419B). According to Gregory Nazianzen, God is neither masculine nor feminine: *Orat.* 31 (= *Orat. theol.* V), 7 (*PG* 36, 140–146; *SC* 250, pp. 288–289).

14. I only know the title of P. A. H. de Boer's brief account, *Fatherhood and Motherhood in Israelite and Judean Piety* (Leiden, 1974). I have, on the other hand, read R. Murray's *Symbols of Church and Kingdom. A Study in Early Syriac Tradition* (Cambridge, 1975), pp. 312–320, 'The Holy Spirit as Mother'.

15. J. Daniélou, *The Theology of Jewish Christianity* (London, 1964), pp. 22–23. The quotations from Jerome, *Comm. in Is.* IV and *Comm. in Mich.* II (*PL* 24, 145 and 25, 1221) are especially interesting, since they have to do with the coming of the Spirit on Jesus at the time of his baptism and the proclamation 'You are my beloved Son'.

16. *Elench*. IX, 13; see Daniélou, *op. cit.*, p. 65.

17. References will be found in E.-P. Siman, *op. cit.* (note 12), p. 155. See also Aphraates, *Dem.* XVII, *De virginitate et sanctitate* (*Patr. Syr.* I, p. 839).

18. R. Murray, *op. cit.* (note 14), p. 318.

19. Methodius of Olympus, *The Banquet (Symposium)* III, c. 8, §69–75 (*SC* 95, pp. 106–110 (Greek), pp. 107–111 (Fr. tr)). See also A. Orbe, 'La procesión del Espíritu Santo y el origen de Eva', *Greg*, 45 (1964), 103–118, especially 110ff. I hesitate to suggest it here, because the meaning is obscure, but the verse of Synesius of Cyrene († after 412), in which the Spirit, in the feminine (*Pnoia*), is presented as mother, sister and daughter (!), 'so that there was a pouring out from the Father to the Son', would seem to have to do with the part played by the Spirit in the incarnation: 'She has her place in the middle, God from God through the Son who is God, and it is also by this sublime pouring out of the immortal Father that the Son also came to be': *Hymn* II (at one time IV), ed. and Fr. tr. C. Lacombrade in the Budé collection (1978), p. 63.

20. For evidence of this tradition, see Anastasius of Sinai, *Hexaemeron*, I and VII (*PG* 89, 860B-C and 961D).

21. M. J. Scheeben, *The Mysteries of Christianity* (Eng. tr.; St Louis and London, 1946), pp. 181ff.: Appendix I, following §31; *Dogmatique*, Fr. tr. P. Bélet, II (Paris, 1880), nos 1019ff. (pp. 685ff.) and III (Paris, 1881), nos 375 (pp. 241ff.) and 445ff. (pp. 296ff.).

22. In chronological order, these authors are Methodius of Olympus, who situated the Son between Adam and Eve (*PG* 44, 1329C–D); Ephraem Syrus (†373), *Diat*. XIX, 15 (*Patr. Syr.* 145, p. 199); Gregory Nazianzen (see below, note 23); Procopius of Gaza († *c.* 529), *Comm. in Gen*. 1, 26 (*PG* 87, 125); Anastasius of Antioch (mid-sixth century), *Orat*. I, 13

(*PG* 89, 1318B–D); Anastasius of Sinai (mid-seventh century), *Hexaem.* X (*PG* 89, 1059A–B).

23. Gregory Nazianzen, *Orat.* 31 (= *Orat. theol.* V), 11 (*PG* 36, 144ff.).

24. John Damascene, *De duabus Christi vol.* 18, 30 (*PG* 95, 167).

25. In *La femme et le salut du monde. Etude et Anthropologie chrétienne sur les charismes de la femme* (Paris, 1958), p. 216, P. Evdokimov spoke of *a Patre Spirituque* exclusively with regard to the manifestation. In *L'Esprit Saint dans la Tradition orthodoxe* (Paris, 1969), pp. 71–72, 77, 78, and in his last work, 'Panagion et Panagia', *Bulletin de la Société française d'Etudes Mariales*, 27 (1970), 59–71, especially 62–63 (this text repr. in *La nouveauté de l'Esprit* (Bellefontaine, 1977), pp. 259–262), however, he spoke of the eternal procession of the Son, in which the Holy Spirit, he believed, had a 'begetting function' which could also be found in the conception of Christ by Mary. He situated this function within the context of a very profound understanding of the relationships, always Trinitarian, never dyadic, between the divine Persons, both *ad intra* and *ad extra*.

26. See above, p.45, note 38.

27. Augustine, *De Trin.* XII, 5 and 6 (*PL* 42, 1000ff.); F. K. Mayr, 'Trinität und Familie in Augustinus, De Trinitate XII', *Revue des Etudes Augustiniennes*, 18 (1972), 51–86.

28. Thomas Aquinas, *ST* Ia, q. 36, a. 3, ad 1; q. 93, a. 6, ad 2.

29. See, for example, Taymans d'Epernon, *Le mystère primordial* (Tournai, 1950), p. 57; S. Giuliani, 'La famiglia a l'immagine della Trinità', *Angelicum*, 38 (1961), 257–310; H. Cafferel, 'Notre Dieu, la Sainte Trinité', *L'Anneau d'Or*, 138 (1967), 440, 443–444; B. de Margerie, *La Trinité dans l'histoire* (*Théol. hist.*, 31) (Paris, 1975), pp. 370ff.

30. H. Doms, *Du sens et de la fin du mariage* (Tournai, 1937), pp. 29ff.

31. This is clearly why P. Evdokimov, *La femme et le salut du monde, op. cit.* (note 25), p. 16, said: 'If woman is ontically connected with the Holy Spirit, that bond only has universal validity and special application if man, for his part, is also ontically connected with Christ. The two together, in a mutual relationship, fulfil the requisite task. . . . The creation, together with man, of the whole new reality of masculine and feminine forms the body of the royal priesthood.'

32. See F. K. Mayr, 'Patriarchalisches Gottesverständnis? Historische Erwägungen zur Trinitätslehre', *TQ*, 152 (1972), 224–255; *idem*, 'Die Einseitigkeit der traditionellen Gotteslehre. Zum Verhältnis von Anthropologie und Pneumatologie', *Erfahrung und Theologie des Heiligen Geistes*, ed. C. Heitmann and H. Mühlen (Munich, 1974), pp. 239–252. There are suggestions as to how this can be applied to temporal society in my articles 'La Tri-unité de Dieu et l'Eglise', *VS*, 128 (August–September 1974), 687–703; 'La supériorité des pays protestants', *VS* (Suppl), 123 (November 1977), 427–442.

33. M. Böckeler, *Das grosse Zeichen. Apok. 12, 1. Die Frau als Symbol göttlicher Wirklichkeit* (Salzburg, 1941, but published after the war).

34. W. Moll, *Die Antwort der Liebe. Gedanken zum christlichen Bild der Frau* (Graz, 1964); *idem*, *Vater und Väterlichkeit* (Graz, 1962).

35. L. Bouyer, *Woman and Man with God* (Eng. tr.; London and New York, 1960), p. 189, gives references to a Jewish exegesis of this text.

36. Mk 1:10–11; Lk 3:22. See also notes 15 and 19 above.

37. A. Lemonnyer, *VS*, 3 (1921), 241–251, repr. in *Notre Vie divine* (Paris, 1936), pp. 66–83, and also pub. separately in the collection *Lectures chrétiennes*, 3rd series (Paris, 1941).

38. Y. Congar, *Tradition and Traditions* (Eng. tr.; London, 1966), Part Two, pp. 348–375, esp. p. 373, which deals with a formal expression of the feminine aspect; for the Holy Spirit as the transcendent subject of Tradition, see pp. 338ff.

39. See A. M. Greeley, *The Mary Myth. On the Femininity of God* (New York, 1977).

4

TOWARDS A
PNEUMATOLOGICAL CHRISTOLOGY

In recent years, many Christological studies have been written. At the same time there has also been reflection and books and articles about the Holy Spirit and pneumatology.[1] There are even signs that a beginning has been made in formulating a Christology based on the intervention of the Holy Spirit in the mystery of Christ. The first move in this direction should perhaps be attributed to Heribert Mühlen, who has worked assiduously to establish a firm connection between the mystery of the Church and, not the incarnation as such, but the baptism of Jesus, as anointed by the Holy Spirit in order to carry out his messianic ministry.

This type of Christology in no sense contradicts the classical Christology that has been developed since Chalcedon. What it in fact does is to develop certain important aspects to which both the New Testament and Church Fathers such as Irenaeus have borne witness, but which have not been sufficiently developed in the classical Christology based on the incarnate Word. It has two important preconditions:

(1) Christology should not be separated from soteriology: 'qui propter nos homines et propter nostram salutem'. The incarnation has an aim and that aim is Easter, the resurrection and eschatological fulfilment. The *katabasis* is there with an *analēpsis* or *anabasis* in view. In Pars IIIa of his *Summa*, Thomas Aquinas shows Christ as 'the way by which we can, by rising again, achieve the blessed state of eternal life' (Prol.) and considers the *acta et passa* of Christ, that is, the facts of his life which are the data of the history of salvation.

It is in fact almost true to say that Christology must be situated *within* soteriology, which embraces it. P. Smulders has shown how the need to define the formal constitution of Christ in precise terms as the Word made flesh has in the past led to a neglect of Christ's saving and messianic work in the history of man's salvation. This happened, according to Smulders, even at the Council of Chalcedon. It was only the crisis caused by Monothelitism and the solution provided by the Councils held in the Lateran in 649 and at Constantinople in 680–681 that threw a clearer light on the fact that, in the truth of his human nature, Christ had been called to realize himself and his mission as Messiah and Saviour by acting consciously and in freedom.[2] In

165

view of the important issue at stake, I do not regret my criticism of Luther's Christology, written for the fifteenth centenary of Chalcedon, even if I am now inclined to supplement and correct it in certain respects.

(2) God's work takes place in human history. It is achieved in a series of events situated in time, which, once they have happened, contribute something new and bring about changes. There are *kairoi*, times that are auspicious and favourable for a given event (see, for example, Mk 1:15; Gal 4:4; Eph 1:10). On the other hand, according to non-historical theology and even for Thomas Aquinas, Christ possessed everything from the time of this conception and, in what are reported in Scripture as institutive events, there is simply a manifestation *for others* of a reality that is already there. The theophany at the baptism of Jesus is an example of this.[3] We hold that the historical stages punctuated by events pointing to God's work are true qualitative moments in his communication of himself to and in Jesus Christ. There were successive events in which the Spirit descended on Jesus as Christ the Saviour. This is clear from the New Testament texts, as we read and interpret their teaching.

The hypostatic union is a metaphysical fact by means of which a human nature subsists through the Person of the Son of God. It clearly requires the man who is thus called into existence to be holy. In Scholastic theology, this is the work of the Holy Spirit, who follows the presence of the Word, and of sanctifying grace, which follows the grace of the union as its consequence (see *ST* IIIa, q. 7, a. 13). That grace, which is given in its absolute fullness to Christ, is both his personal grace and his grace as the Head (*gratia capitis*).[4] In the New Testament, the coming and the action of the Spirit made the fruit conceived by Mary 'holy', that is, realizing the will of 'God' (= the Father) perfectly (see Lk 1:35).

This will of God, which Irenaeus called the 'Father's good pleasure', was that the man Jesus should live perfectly in obedience as the Son (Heb 10:5–9). The way that the Father wanted him to follow was the way that led, through the cross, to glory. It was, in other words, not the way of (beatific) vision, but the way of obedience. That obedience consisted in going where God wanted him to go without knowing where it led (see Heb 11:8). It was the way of prayer—for how is it possible not to see Jesus' own life of prayer and the prayer that he himself taught us (see Mt 6:9–11) within the context of his whole 'mission' and the history of salvation? It was also the way of *kenōsis* and of the suffering Servant (Phil 2:6–8). It was, then, in this way that Jesus acted as a son.

What consciousness did he have, in his human soul, of his quality of Son of God? This is something that is hidden from us. The hypostatic union left his human soul, which was consubstantial with ours, in his human condition of *kenōsis*, obedience and prayer.[5] The Spirit, who sanctified him in that condition (see Lk 2:40 and 52), however, enabled him to understand more and also more deeply than the teachers of the law (2:47) and even than his mother, to whom he replied: 'Did you not know that I must be in my Father's house?' (2:49). What consciousness of himself and of the fatherhood of God is concealed within this reply?[6] The 'I' is that of the eternal Son, but it is at the level of the 'me', the objectively conscious content (or the content that is qualified to be conscious) of his experience, which may be called 'personality'. Jesus only realized his relationship with the Father in and through the acts of his spiritual life as a son, the Spirit being the source of these in him. These acts include his prayer, his clinging in love to the Father's plan for him, and the 'works' that the Father gave him to fulfil.[7]

The decisive event was the one that accompanied Jesus' baptism by John the Baptist. This event was a theophany of the Trinity. The Spirit descended and remained on Jesus as he came out of the water of the Jordan. According to the three synoptic gospels, a voice was heard—that of the Father—quoting the messianic psalm (2:7): 'You are my son, today I have begotten you'. Luke cites this psalm as it is (3:22), but Matthew (3:17) and Mark (1:11) combine it with a few words from the first song of the suffering Servant (Is 42:1). According to Mark (1:11), the words are addressed to Jesus: 'Thou art my beloved Son; with thee I am well pleased'. In all three synoptics, the same words occur in the theophany of the transfiguration, although in the latter there is no manifestation of the Spirit.[8]

The event in the Jordan marks the beginning of the messianic era. The period of John the Baptist is over and that of Jesus begins.[9] The fact that Luke has John the Baptist put in prison before Jesus' baptism and the theophany is no doubt intentional—it points to this end and beginning. The Spirit who descends on Jesus anoints him as Messiah or the 'Christ' (see Acts 10:38). He then leads him out into the desert and makes him begin his messianic activity: 'The time is fulfilled and the kingdom of God is at hand' (Mk 1:15; cf. Acts 1:22). That time was to be a time of a new humanity, in the image and in the wake of Jesus, the son and servant, through the Spirit.[10] Jesus is proclaimed the Son of the Father. He had always been that Son since the time of his conception—Luke, who has the words 'today I have begotten thee' in his account of the theophany, knew very well that Jesus had been Son and Lord since his conception (see Lk 1:35, 43, 76; 2:11, 26, 49). This is what Jesus was in himself, as the *Unigenitus a Patre*. He was to become this and be proclaimed this for us, as the *Primogenitus in multus fratribus*. This event brought about no change in Jesus himself, but it denoted a new *kairos* in the history of salvation. Jesus himself entered a new era, that of which Peter speaks in Acts 10:38. It was disclosed to Jesus by the voice 'from heaven'. At the same time, he also entered in a new way into his consciousness of being the Son, the Messiah and the Servant (see Lk 4:18). This is also borne out by his temptation in the desert and his first proclamation at Nazareth, to which he was led by the Spirit who had come down on him (Lk 4:1).

Jesus' temptation has a precise bearing on what he was told at the time of his baptism in the Jordan—it was a test of his quality of Son and Servant. The tempter says to him: 'If you are the Son of God'. The tempter knows only one temptation—the desire to be god (see Gen 3:5)—and therefore suggests to Jesus: If you are the Son of God, work miracles, use your power. Jesus, however, knows that he is the Servant and that he has come to do the Father's will (Heb 10:5–9). Through the Spirit, he follows the way of the Servant and Son (Lk 4:18ff.), choosing the apostles (Acts 1:2), driving out demons (Mt 12:28; Lk 11:20) and bringing the kingdom of God close and present as a kingdom of mercy and salvation (see Lk 10:9–11, 21ff.). Finally, he offers himself as Servant (Mk 10:45) and does so through the Spirit (Heb 9:14; cf. 9:8).[11]

The second decisive event leading to a new acquisition of Jesus' quality of son by virtue of an act of 'God' through his Spirit is, of course, Jesus' resurrection and glorification. Let us consider the essential New Testament texts:

> The gospel concerning his Son, who was descended from David according to the flesh and designated Son of God in power according to the Spirit of holiness by his resurrection from the dead, Jesus Christ our Lord (Rom 1:3–4).[12]

For to what angel did God ever say:

> 'Thou art my Son,
> today I have begotten thee' (Ps 2:7)?

Or again:

> 'I will be to him a father,
> and he shall be to me a son' (2 Sam 7:14)?

And again, when he brings the first-born into the world, he says:

> 'Let all God's angels worship him' (Deut 32:43 Gk) (Heb 1:5–6).[13]

> This Jesus God raised up. . . . Being therefore exalted at the right hand of God, and having received from the Father the promise of the Holy Spirit, he has poured out this which you see and hear. For David did not ascend into the heavens, but he himself says:
> 'The Lord said to my Lord, Sit at my right hand. . . .' (Ps 101:1)
> (Acts 2:32–35; Peter's address on the day of Pentecost).[14]

> And we bring you the good news that what God promised to the fathers, this he has fulfilled to us their children by raising Jesus; as also is written in the second psalm:

168

'Thou art my Son,
today I have begotten thee' (Ps 2:7)

(Acts 13:32–33; Paul's address at Antioch in Pisidia).

What is sown is perishable, what is raised is imperishable. It (the body) is sown in dishonour, it is raised in glory. It is sown in weakness, it is raised in power. It is sown a physical body, it is raised a spiritual body. . . . Thus it is written, 'the first man Adam became a living being'; the last Adam became a life-giving spirit (1 Cor 15:42–45).

The above texts have been called the texts of 'Christology of exaltation'.[15] This is a historical Christology, according to which there are two states in the destiny of Jesus-Christ. The first is the state of *kenōsis*, that of the Servant, and this culminated in the cross and the 'descent into hell'. The second is the glorious state, that of the resurrection and 'sitting on the right hand of God'. In the first of these two states, Christ received the Spirit and was sanctified by him. He also acted through the Spirit. In the second state, he is 'seated at the right hand of God; he is assimilated to God and can therefore, even as a man, give the Spirit'.[16] He is penetrated by the Spirit to such an extent that Paul could even say that 'the Lord is the Spirit' (2 Cor 3:17). The communication of divinity took his humanity, united without separation to the Person of the Word, to the condition of a *humanity of the Son of God*. This divinity communicated to him bestowed on him not only glory, but also the power to make sons by giving the Spirit, since it is the Spirit who places the life of Christ in us, who makes us sons in the divine Son and who dedicates us to resurrection after him (see Rom 8:9–11 and 14–17; Gal 4:6; 1 Cor 12:13).

Both the Church Fathers and the Scholastic theologians insisted that Christ gave the Spirit as God, but that as man he received it.[17] I would agree that this is correct from the ontological point of view. If, however, we are to think historically and in the concrete, with the New Testament, we are bound to say, together with Basil the Great, that 'the Spirit was first of all present to the Lord's flesh when he made himself the "anointing" of that flesh and the inseparable companion of the Word, as is written: "He on whom you see the Spirit descend and remain is my beloved Son" and "Jesus of Nazareth, whom God has anointed with the Holy Spirit". Then all the activity of Christ took place in the presence of the Spirit. He was with him. . . . He did not leave him even after his resurrection from the dead. When the Lord, to renew man and to give him what he had lost, namely the grace received from the breath of God, breathed on the faces of the disciples, what did he say? "Receive the Holy Spirit".'[18] Thomas Aquinas, whose understanding of the organic union between the soul and the body was different from that of Augustine, believed that Christ's humanity was an 'organ' of his divinity for the purpose of giving the Holy Spirit.[19]

Both the Fathers and the Scholastic theologians also used various images to express that communication of the Spirit by Christ, who was inseparably both God and man and who was, by virtue of his two natures, the Head of his Body, the Church. The image of anointing in Ps 133:2—'like the precious oil upon the head, running down upon the beard of Aaron, running down on the collar of his robes'—was tirelessly evoked and applied to the Holy Spirit.[20] From the Head, the oil of the Holy Spirit was communicated to the Body. The Scholastic treatise *De gratia Capitis* was not confined to a theology of created grace—it was open to an intervention by the Spirit.[21] The same Spirit who was given to Christ and who dwelt in him and moved him also dwelt in and moved his followers, the members of his Body.[22] What took place 'mystically', that is, through the Spirit, was the formation of a single filial being which prayed 'Our Father'.

This is the prayer that Jesus taught us. In a sense, its meaning is contained in the word 'our': Jesus and we are one being in this prayer. We are not, of course, 'sons' at the same level as Jesus, nor is God his Father and ours in the same way. The risen Christ, after all, said to Mary Magdalen: 'I am ascending to my Father and your Father, to my God and your God' (Jn 20:17). Jesus clearly expresses both the community and the difference between himself and us.[23]

Jesus is Son on several accounts. He is Son by eternal generation: 'begotten, not made'. He is therefore the *monogenitus* or *monogenēs*.[24] In a theology of the economy of salvation, however, we must take very seriously the texts in which Ps 2:7—'You are my son, today I have begotten you'—is applied to history. It is so applied, in the first place, as we have already seen, to the annunciation by the angel: 'he will be called the Son of God' (Lk 1:35). Later, it is applied to the theophany at Jesus' baptism (Mt 3:17; Mk 1:10; Lk 3:22) and to the resurrection and exaltation of Christ (Acts 13:33; Heb 1:5; 5:5). These are all moments when Jesus became—and was not simply proclaimed as—the 'Son of God' in a new way, that is, not from the point of view of his hypostatic quality or his ontology as the incarnate Word, but from the point of view of the plan of God's grace and the successive moments in the history of salvation. That point of view, then, is the one according to which Jesus was destined to be *for us*. He was to be the Messiah and Saviour as the Servant, and Lord as raised to God's 'right hand'. As Peter said on the day of Pentecost: 'God has made him (*epoiēsen*) both Lord and Christ, this Jesus whom you crucified' (Acts 2:36). This means that, from then onwards, Jesus was seen no longer as the *monogenēs*, but rather as the *prōtotokos*, that is, the first-born to divine and glorious life, with regard to the multitude of brothers who are called and predestined by God to be conformed to his model. There is one begetting—and even two—of Jesus as the first-born Son, that is to say, with us in mind and including us in the divine sonship. Like him in his humanity, we too shall only be fully sons through the glorious transfiguration of the resurrection, but, again like him, we are already sons according to the first-fruits of this life, 'amid sighings'.[25]

For us as for Jesus himself, the quality of sonship is, in both its stages, the work of the Spirit. The Spirit is not only the third in the intra-divine life, although he is equal in consubstantiality—he is also, in the economy of salvation, the agent of sonship as the effect of the grace and reality of holy living. The whole of our filial life is animated by the Spirit (see Rom 8:14–17; Gal 4:6).

In the case of Jesus, it is important to avoid Adoptianism. He is ontologically the Son of God because of the hypostatic union from the moment of his conception. Because of that too, he is the Temple of the Holy Spirit and is made holy by that Spirit in his humanity. We have, however, as believers, to respect the successive moments or stages in the history of salvation and to accord the New Testament texts their full realism. Because of this, I would suggest that there were two moments when the *virtus* or effectiveness of the Spirit in Jesus was actuated in a new way. The first was at his baptism, when he was constituted (and not simply proclaimed as) Messiah and Servant by God. The second moment was at the time of his resurrection and exaltation, when he was made Lord.

The Son is conceived eternally (= here and now) as due to become incarnate and due to be the first-born of many brothers whom he is to conform to his own image through the Spirit. That takes place in our history as the times (*kairoi*) come to fulfilment (see Gal 4:4; Eph 1:10). Parallel to this truth concerning the Son is one concerning the Father—he is eternally the 'Father of our Lord Jesus Christ'.[26] There is, of course, a distinction between the essential mystery of God in his Trinitarian life and the free mystery of his plan of grace. In God, however, his freedom and his essence are really identical. We affirm that identity in our own inability to represent it and to understand it. We can only revere that mystery and make it the object of our praise.[27]

NOTES

1. The most important recent studies concerned with this subject are: H. Mühlen, *Una mystica Persona. Eine Person in vielen Personen* (Paderborn, 1964); J. D. G. Dunn, 'Rediscovering the Spirit', *Expository Times*, 84 (1972–1973), 9–12; W. Kasper, *Jesus der Christus* (Mainz, 1974); Eng. tr., *Jesus the Christ* (London and New York, 1976); *idem*, 'Esprit-Christ-Eglise', *L'expérience de l'Esprit. Mélanges E. Schillebeeckx* (Paris, 1976), pp. 47–69; *idem*, 'Die Kirche als Sakrament des Geistes', *Kirche, Ort des Geistes* (Freiburg, 1975), pp. 14–55; P. J. Rosato, 'Spirit Christology. Ambiguity and Promise', *ThSt*, 38 (1977), 423–449; P. J. A. M. Schoonenberg, 'Spirit Christology and Logos Christology', *Bijdragen*, 38 (1977), 350–375.
2. P. Smulders, 'Développement de la christologie dans le dogme et le magistère', *Mysterium Salutis*, 10 (Fr. tr.; Paris, 1974), pp. 235–350; cf. K. Adam, 'Jesu menschliches Wesen im Licht der urchristlichen Verkündigung', *Wissenschaft und Weisheit*, 6 (1939), 111–120, especially 116ff.
3. If Jesus possessed the sovereign attribute of kingship from the beginning, however, he only

received its *executio* eschatologically: see the sermon edited by J. Leclercq in *RThom*, 46 (1946), 152–160 and 572.

4. Thomas Aquinas, *ST* IIIa, q. 7 and 8; see also C.-V. Héris, *Le mystère du Christ* (Paris, 1928).

5. C.-V. Héris, 'Problème de christologie. La conscience de Jésus', *Esprit et Vie*, 81 (1971), 672–679; H.-M. Féret, 'Christologie médiévale de S. Thomas et christologie concrète et historique pour aujourd'hui', *Memorie Domenicane* (1975), 107–141, especially 128ff. and 135ff.; see also my *Christ, Our Lady and the Church: A Study in Eirenic Theology* (Eng. tr.; London, New York and Toronto, 1957), esp. pp. 51ff., 96 note 11.

6. The first two chapters of Luke's gospel reflect the situation and the categories of the Old Testament—messianic times began with the arrest of John the Baptist and the baptism of Jesus (Lk 3:19ff.): see J. D. G. Dunn, *Baptism in the Holy Spirit*, 4th ed. (London, 1977), pp. 31ff.

7. B. Sesboüé, *RSR*, 56 (1968), 635–666, quotes J. Maritain, *De la grâce et de l'humanité de Jésus* (Bruges, 1967), pp. 97 and 107; C. Duquoc, *Christologie*, I (Paris, 1968), pp. 327–328.

8. Mt 17:5; Mk 9:7; Lk 9:35. There is a parallel between the scene of Jesus' baptism and that of his transfiguration: see J. Legrand, 'L'arrière-plan néotestamentaire de Lc 1, 35', *RB*, 70 (1963), 162–192.

9. J. D. G. Dunn, *op. cit.* (note 6), pp. 25ff.

10. What the event in the Jordan was for Jesus, the event at Pentecost was for his disciples: see J. D. G. Dunn, *op. cit.*, pp. 40–42; in Jn 1:33, the descent of the Spirit on Jesus denotes him as the one who was to baptize in the Spirit; see also Mk 1:8. For Jesus as the new Adam, see J. D. G. Dunn, *op. cit.*, p. 29.

11. According to C. Spicq, *Epître aux Hébreux* (Paris, 1952–1953), pp. 258–259, and the majority of exegetes, verse 14 does not deal with the Holy Spirit, but with the nature of Christ, who is divine. See, however, *DTC*, V, col. 222, and A. Vanhoye, *De epistola ad Hebreos, Sectio Centralis* (c. 8–9) (Rome, 1966), p. 158.

12. M. E. Boismard,' "Constitué" Fils de Dieu (Rom 1, 4)', *RB*, 60 (1953), 5–17, showed that this 'constitution' of Jesus as 'Son of God' was the same as his enthronement as the Messiah and the ruler of the nations. This can be compared with Rom 1:4; 1 Tim 3:16: 'he was manifested in the flesh, justified in the Spirit'; 1 Pet 3:18: 'put to death in the flesh, but made alive in the Spirit'.

13. This text, which can be applied to the incarnation (see W. Michaelis, '*prōtotokos*', *TDNT*, VI, p. 880), can be better understood if it is seen as referring to the enthronement of the First-born: see Ps 89:28; Col 1:15ff. The invocation of the angels and their bowing down, which recurs in Heb 2:5, suggests the situation of Lord; cf. Eph 1:18–22; Phil 2:9–11; Heb 5:5.

14. See Acts 5:30–31, in which Peter replies to the Sanhedrin: 'The God of our fathers raised Jesus whom you killed by hanging him on a tree. God exalted him at his right hand as Ruler and Saviour.'

15. See R. Schnackenburg, 'La christologie du Nouveau Testament', *Mysterium Salutis*, 10 (Fr. tr.; Paris, 1974), pp. 55–64.

16. See M. Gourges, *A la droite de Dieu. Résurection de Jésus et actualisation du Ps 110:1 dans le Nouveau Testament (Etudes bibliques)* (Paris, 1978), pp. 163ff., 209ff.

17. Augustine, *De Trin.* XV, 46 (*PL* 42, 1093); Cyril of Alexandria, *Comm. in Nahum* 2:27, II, 35 (*PG* 71, 777–780); *Comm. in Luc.* 4, 1 and 18 (*PG* 72, 525 and 537); *Comm. in Ioan.* 17, 18–19 (*PG* 74, 548B); *De recta fide, Or. alt.* 34, 35, 50 (*PG* 76, 1381 and 1405).

18. Basil the Great, *De spir. sanct*, XVI, 39 (*PG* 32, 140; *SC* 17, pp. 180–181); see also Irenaeus, *Adv. haer.* III, 9, 3 (*PG* 7, 872A).

19. *ST* Ia IIae, q. 112, a. 1, ad 1 and 2; IIIa, q. 8, a. 1, ad 1, in which Thomas replies to Augustine's text quoted above. For Thomas, it was a question of giving the Spirit insofar as he was the principle of grace and gifts: see *ST* Ia, q. 43, a. 8. In his commentary on

1 Cor 15, lect. 7 (see R. Cai, no. 993), Thomas says: 'sicut Adam consecutus est perfectionem sui esse per animam' (and therefore he was only a living soul), 'ita et Christus perfectionem sui esse inquantum homo per spiritum Sanctum' (and therefore he can be the Spirit who gives life).

20. See, for example, Origen, *Contra Cels*. VI, 79 (*PG* 11, 1417D); Athanasius, *Exp. in Ps.132* (*PG* 27, 524B-C); *Orat. III contra Arian*. 22 (*PG* 26, 369); Jerome, *Tract. in Ps. 132* (ed. G. Morin, CCL, 58, 277; Augustine, *Enarr. in Ps. 132*, 7–12 (*PL* 37, 1753ff.); Prosper of Aquitaine, *Expos. in Ps. 132* (*PL* 51, 381–382); frequent examples in mediaeval theology.

21. If Christ is the Head, then the Holy Spirit is the Heart, from which the Head receives the impulse and the warmth of life; see Thomas Aquinas, *De ver*. q. 29, a. 4, ad 7; *ST* IIIa, q. 8, a. 1, ad 3. For Thomas' teaching about this datum, see M. Grabmann, *Die Lehre des heiligen Thomas von Aquin von der Kirche als Gotteswerk* (Regensburg, 1903), pp. 184–193.

22. Thomas Aquinas, *In III Sent*. d. 13, q. 2, a. 1, ad 2; *Comm. in ev. Ioan*. c. 1, lect. 10, no. 1.

23. Jesus 'always says "my Father" or "your Father", but never "our Father". The prayer which according to Matthew begins with the last phrase is not spoken by Jesus with the disciples, but is part of the prayer he taught them to pray': O. Cullmann, *The Christology of the New Testament* (Eng. tr.; London, 1959), p. 289. John reserves the title of *huios* for Jesus, when it is a question of his relationship with the Father, and calls Christians *tekna*.

24. This term is peculiar to the Johannine writings: see Jn 1:14, 18; 3:16, 18; 1 Jn 4:9.

25. Rom 8:29–30. See also W. Michaelis, '*prōtotokos*', *TDNT*, VI, p. 877.

26. See Rom 8:11 and 16–25. For the meaning, see Col 3:3–4; 2 Cor 3:18; 1 Jn 3:1–2; Eph 1:5 and 13–14.

27. See Paul's formula in Rom 15:5; 2 Cor 1:3; Eph 1:3. It is worth quoting Louis Bouyer here: 'it is in time that he makes himself man, i.e. it is in a definite moment of time that our humanity is assumed. But as far as he is concerned he assumes it eternally. Thus the Father eternally generates his Son, not only as before his incarnation but also as the Word made flesh': *The Eternal Son* (Eng. tr.; Huntington, Ind., 1978), p. 401.

IV

CONTRIBUTIONS TO AN AGREEMENT

1

UNITY OF FAITH BUT A DIFFERENCE OF THEOLOGICAL EXPRESSION GREEKS AND LATINS IN THE UNDERSTANDING OF WESTERN THEOLOGIANS

Difficulties were encountered from the fourth century onwards in the translation of Greek terms into Latin. *Hypostasis* was rendered as *substantia*, but whereas the Latins believed in one *substantia*, the Greeks spoke of three *hypostases*. A synod held at Alexandria at the beginning of 362, after Athanasius had returned from exile, declared that the Latins meant *ousia* when they spoke of *substantia* and that there was no question of tritheism in the Greeks' speaking about three hypostases.[1] Jerome went no further than an acceptance of the fact that *substantia* and *ousia* were equivalent to each other and he was consequently scandalized when he was asked to declare that there were *tres hypostases*. Did this mean, he asked, that he was to accept *tres substantiae*?[2] His mistrust of the term 'hypostasis' continued into the Middle Ages in the West, when his hypochondriacal statement about this question: 'nescio quid veneni in syllabis latet' was frequently cited.

Thus orthodox thinking was dogged by a problem of terminology. Augustine bore witness to this in his treatise on the Trinity: 'Essentiam dico, quae *ousia* graece dicitur, quem usitatius substantiam vocamus. Dicunt quidem et illi *hypostasim*; sed nescio quid volunt interesse inter *ousiam* et *hypostasim*: ita est plerique nostri qui haec graecio tractant eloquio, dicere consueverint *mian ousian, treis hypostaseis*, quod est latine unam essentiam, tres substantias.'[3] Augustine preferred 'essence' to 'substance' in order to express the unity of the divine nature[4] and ended by speaking of 'one essence and three substances'.[5]

Anselm, who supported the *Filioque* in opposition to the Greeks living in southern Italy at the Council of Bari of 1098, made the following declaration at least four times: 'Latinos dicere tres personas credendas in una substantia. Graecos vero non minus fideliter tres substantias in una persona confiteri.'[6]

174

The formula used by the Apulian Greeks expressed the Trinitarian faith no less than that used by the Latins.

Abelard was familiar with the passage in *De Trinitate* in which Augustine discussed the difference in vocabulary between the Greeks and the Latins, the first speaking of 'one essence, three substances' and the second of 'one essence or substance, three persons'. Augustine had recognized the identity of meaning despite the difference between the terms, and Abelard added this gloss: 'We do not intend to speak against the Greeks here and there is no doubt that they do not differ from us with regard to the meaning, but only in their use of words; they unfortunately employ the term "substance" instead of "person", yet they do not refuse to speak of *ousia*, that is, of the substance in the sense of essence and not of what is peculiar to the person'.[7] In illustration of this, Abelard used the term *homoousion* and cited the well-known passage of Jerome on the dangers of the word 'hypostasis'.

This important question of terminology also concerned Richard of Saint-Victor, whose *De Trinitate* dates from a little before 1172. Here is his text.

> Perhaps my readers would like me to explain how the different formulae should be understood and how it is possible to make them agree with each other. Some speak of 'three substances and one essence', while others speak of 'three subsistences and one substance' and others again of 'three persons and one substance or essence'. There seems to be a clear opposition and an absolute contradiction between the Latins, who speak of one substance in God, and the Greeks, who speak of three. I am, however, far from thinking that their beliefs are disparate and one or the other party is erring in faith! We need to grasp the one truth in the diversity of formulae (*in hac ergo verborum varietate intelligenda est veritas una*): the words used by one party and the other are understood in different senses.[8]

It was relatively easy to reach agreement when it was only a question of vocabulary, since it was always possible to find equivalents, although the words themselves involved the use of categories of thought and therefore theological constructions. Thomas Aquinas explicitly formulated this rule governing equivalents and applied it himself to various statements about the theology of the Trinity.[9] This question became much more difficult when dogmatic judgements and statements became involved, as, for example, in the case of the article on the procession of the Holy Spirit. Even in that particular case, however, some remarkable declarations were made by Latin theologians in the Middle Ages. Hugh of Saint-Cher, whose commentary on the *Sentences* appeared at the same time as the texts of Alexander of Hales, *antequam esset frater*, said, for example:

> Is the controversy between ourselves and the Greeks real, or is it simply about words? It would seem that it is real, since they deny the procession of the Holy Spirit, which we affirm. There could in fact be no greater controversy that one concerned with an opposition in affirmations. It can, however, be seen to be only about words from the fact that they agree that the Holy Spirit is the Spirit *of the*

175

Son, that is, *a Filio*, which is the same thing as proceeding from the Son. The contradiction, then, is purely about words. We may conclude by saying that they contradict themselves when they say that the Spirit does not proceed from the Son, yet at the same time that he is *a Filio* or of the Son, and they are mistaken in their belief that proceeding from the Son and being *a Filio* is something different, when it is in fact the same thing. We are therefore not really opposed to them. The opposition is simply one of words. They do, however, really contradict themselves.[10]

Hugh clearly loaded the dice in his own favour when he affirmed that for the Greeks to speak of the Spirit *of the Son* was to say that the Spirit was *a Filio*. What is interesting for us, however, in his text is his attempt to bring about an agreement between the Greeks and the Latins. There is also an echo of Hugh's attempt in this direction—a very prudent echo—in Thomas Aquinas' statement: 'et quidam eorum (the Greeks) *dicuntur* concedere quod sit a Filio vel profluat ab eo, non tamen quod procedat'.[11]

From the time of Anselm onwards, the Latins were convinced that what the Greeks believed in agreement with the Latins in the case of the Holy Spirit logically implied that the Spirit also proceeded from the Son, despite the fact that this was denied by the Greeks themselves. Thomas also thought that 'if the expressions that are used by the Greeks are carefully examined, it will be seen that they differ from us more in words than in meaning'— *inveniet quod a nobis magis differunt in verbis quam in sensu.*[12] He adds that they in fact profess either that the Spirit is the Spirit *of the Son*, or that he proceeds from the Father *through the Son.*[13] This argument by implication from what is professed as belief, would appear to be also that of Thomas of Sutton at the beginning of the fourteenth century: 'Although the Greeks explicitly deny the procession of the Holy Spirit *a Filio*, they concede it implicitly in its antecedent'. There cannot, in other words, be a difference in origin without the principle being different.[14]

The Franciscans in particular felt that the Greeks and the Latins both had fundamentally the same faith in the Trinity and that they differed only in their theological constructions and modes of expression. Was this perhaps because of Robert Grosseteste, who taught at the Franciscan house in Oxford from 1224 onwards and who wrote a commentary on the works of the Pseudo-Areopagite?[15] His text can be read in Duns Scotus. Although it is less probable, it may be because many Franciscans were sent to Constantinople and Nicaea from 1231 onwards, particularly Haymo of Faversham in 1234.[16]

Alexander of Hales wrote a commentary on the *Sentences* of Peter Lombard *c.* 1225. He dealt in it with the question of the differing opinion between the Greeks and the Latins concerning the procession of the Holy Spirit. He believed that the Latins, as represented by Augustine, and the Greeks, as represented above all by John Damascene, both of whom he quotes a great deal, had different points of departure, consisting of two different levels or aspects in the created analogies of the sending out of the Word and the Spirit.[17] Augustine, he thought, considered the *inner* structure of the spirit and therefore maintained that it was from the *mens* that the *cogitatio* or word proceeded and the latter was followed by the spiration of the *affectus*. The Damascene, on the other hand, according to Alexander considered the *external* word, so that the point of departure was the intellect, followed by the word, which emerged as a word with a breath, which was connected in an immediate way to the intellect. The Spirit, then, was *Spiritus Verbi, non a Verbo*. These were, then, two different ways of representing the *proportio* or relationship between the Spirit and the Word.

This attempt to harmonize two different theologies met with some success. M. Roncaglia quotes, on p. 194 of his work (*op. cit.*, note 16 below), a text from the University Library of Münster (cod. 257), in particular a treatise *De fide* by an unknown author, which is worth translating:

It has been said that the Greeks are mistaken in claiming that the Spirit proceeds only from the Father. . . . If they are mistaken in this, then it is an error in an matter of faith. Others have expressed themselves differently. The Latin doctors, they say, have come to know the Trinity differently from the Greeks. The first have come to understand it from considering the image and the trace of the Trinity in the creature. Augustine therefore came to know the Father, the Son and the Spirit through this triad: the spirit, knowledge and love. The first is like the father, the second his child, and the third the Spirit that proceeds from both. The Latins, observing that love, which they call inner spirit, proceeds from understanding as from the Father and from knowledge or the inner word, therefore say that the same applies to the uncreated Trinity and that the Spirit consequently proceeds from both.

The Greeks, on the other hand, came to a knowledge of the Trinity through the external intellect and word and the external spirit and here I call 'spirit' the breathing in and out of air. There is first the intellect, then the word, and the word expressed in the breath is like the vehicle of the word. The intellect forms the word by breathing and is itself manifested in the breathed word. This is the position adopted by John Damascene. . . . He says that our word is not without the spirit-breath, although the latter does not come from the substance of the word. That is why the Greeks have insisted that, just as our external spirit-breath depends only on the intellect which forms it, in the uncreated Trinity, the Holy Spirit similarly comes from the Father alone as from the one who breathes (out) and the Word also comes from the same Father as from the one who pronounces, that is, begets him. There is therefore no contradiction between the Greeks and the Latins, each of whom express themselves quite consistently (*proportionaliter*). This is the solution provided by Alexander and Pagus.[18]

When John de la Rochelle edited the first part of the *Summa Alexandri* from 1256 onwards, basing his edition on Alexander's teaching and as far as possible on his text, he made use of the same ideas, although he did so with a precision that can later be found in other theological works. 'Proceed' can be understood in two different ways—either as a purely local proceeding, that is, as a movement *ab aliquo in aliquid*, or in a simply causal way, that is, *in exitu causati a causa*. Two terms have to be postulated in the case of the first—an *a quo* and an *ad quem*. This was the way in which the Greeks understood *procedere* and it presupposed that the Spirit proceeded from one Person into another. If he had proceeded from the Son, he would have had to proceed from him to the Father, and this was clearly untenable. He therefore did not proceed from the Son. The Latins, on the other hand, thought of 'proceed' in the causal sense: *ab aliquo exire, quamvis non in aliquam*. They were therefore able to maintain that the Spirit proceeded from the Father and from the Son, 'velut amor a notitia et mente'.[19]

This idea that there were two ways of understanding the procession of the Holy Spirit can also be found in the work of Bonaventure[20] and Odo Rigaldus[21] although it must be admitted that the value of this idea is not increased by its frequent occurrence. Thomas Aquinas appears not to have made use of it. It would also be difficult to find really significant Greek references to illustrate it. It is fundamentally a reconstruction. This also applies to the way in which Odo Rigaldus presented the course of the controversy, which is of value as pointing to the opinions of a magister of Paris, rather than as a historical summary:

> We agree that the Holy Spirit proceeds from the Son. And I believe that those among the Greeks who were really learned and understood the question have never denied it. This is clear from the texts quoted by the Master (*I Sent.* d. 11). Those who, on the other hand, were outraged, at the period when the addition was made to the creed, because they had not been summoned, refused to accept it, although we do not believe that even they denied that it was true. Less cultured men (*simpliciores*) who came later, having heard that their élite refused to concede it, simply denied it. In this way, the situation went from bad to worse. Their main reason for maintaining their position was that they saw the procession as going from one person to another (*esse ab aliquo in aliquem*). . . .
>
> It is, however, important to note that the Latins made a distinction in the statement *Spiritus Sanctus procedit a Filio*. If the preposition *a* means that the Son has the *auctoritas* of the procession of the Spirit, then the Latins accept it no more than the Greeks. If, on the other hand, it does not point to that *auctoritas*, then the Latins accept it and this may be what the Greeks meant to say.

In his commentary on the same distinction (11) in 1250–1251, Bonaventure is more interesting and more profound[22]. He distinguished between three levels or aspects. The first was the aspect of faith in divine revelation as contained in Scripture, about which Greeks and Latins were agreed. The second aspect was that of explicitation, that is, of the knowledge and use of categories and terminology, and it was this aspect that had given rise to the difference between the Greeks and the Latins. The third was that of the profession of the teaching in a formula and that was the controversy.

What is common to both Greeks and Latins is the scriptural basis of the procession, according to which the Spirit is the Spirit of the Son and is sent by the Son. There is, however, also the *ratio intelligendi*. The Greeks understood the procession as a local movement *ab uno in alium*, whereas the Latins saw it simply as a causal process, *unius ex alio*. What is more, the Greeks understood spiration as a *flatus exterioris*, while the Latins regarded it as the spiration of an inner love. Where Scripture says that the Spirit proceeds as a bond and as fellowship, the Greeks interpreted 'bond' as a mean between the two, whereas the Latins understood it as the term in which the two were united. In these various exercises in theological reasoning, the Latins made use of more spiritual and therefore more true ideas.[23] They were therefore able to understand Scripture better. The Greeks, on the other hand, were less open, since they had closed their own approach to a full development of its meaning and had limited that meaning to the purely temporal procession of mission of the Holy Spirit.

The controversy came fully into the open when the Latins introduced this article into the profession of faith. They did it with good reasons and legitimately—the teaching was correct and it was necessary to oppose error with the authority that the Roman Church had at its disposal. The Greeks were opposed to this addition because of ignorance, pride and obstinacy. Their ignorance had been revealed at three levels—they lacked an understanding of Scripture, they did not use the correct concepts, and they were not open to the illumination that was required for a true profession of faith. They were proud men who thought that they were well informed, but were offended because they had not been summoned and had therefore rejected what had been discovered by others. Finally, their obstinacy made them invent reasons to justify their own position. They consequently accused the Latins of having themselves incurred the excommunication that applies to those who tried to change the creed. The Latins had, however, not changed the creed. They had simply made more explicit and perfect what it had already contained.

There was a question about the text of John Damascene, *De fide orthod*. I, 8 (*PG* 94, 832): 'We do not say that the Spirit comes from the Son, although we call him the Spirit of the Son'. John was very highly regarded by the Scholastics of the West. Alexander of Hales explained a similar text by saying that John Damascene wanted to avoid saying that the Spirit proceeded from the Son *in Patrem*.[24] Alexander was deeply irenical and attempted to reconcile Augustine and John by saying that the first had dealt with the inner life of God, whereas the second was speaking of God's relationship with his creatures.[25]

Bonaventure was less accommodating. Like Thomas Aquinas, he said of John Damascene *non est in ista parte ei assentiendum*, adding 'I understand that he was writing at the time when the controversy first emerged. There is no need to support him in this because he was simply Greek. Nonetheless, he expressed himself subtly. He did not say that the Spirit did not have his being from the Son. What he said was: we do not say that he had it from him.

179

The Greeks did not in fact confess this truth, but nor did they deny it.'[26]

Duns Scotus was more favourable not only to John Damascene, but also to the Greeks as a whole. In his *Lectura* on the *Sentences*, a work that he wrote as a young man at Oxford in the last years of the thirteenth century, he refers to Robert Grosseteste's note on John Damascene but comments: 'In hac quaestione (that of the procession of the Spirit from the Son, *a Filio*) discordant graeci vario modo a latinis'.[27] Later on, however, in his *Ordinatio Oxoniensis* or *Opus Oxoniense*, he was more cautious: 'In ista quaestione *dicuntur* graeci discordare a latinis, sicut *videntur* auctoritates Damasceni sonare' and quoted the whole of Grosseteste's note. Because it is of such great interest, I translate it here:

> If two learned scholars, one Greek and the other Latin, both really loving the truth and not their own way of expressing it from their individual point of view, were to discuss this opposition, they would end by finding that it is not a real one, but one based on words. Otherwise, either the Greeks or ourselves, the Latins, are really heretical. But who would dare to accuse of heresy such an author as John Damascene and such saints as Basil, Gregory the Theologian, Cyril and other Greek Fathers? In the same way, who would impute heresy to blessed Jerome, Augustine and Ambrose, Hilary and the skilled Latins? It is therefore probable that, despite these different modes of expression, there is no real disagreement between the thought of these Fathers who are opposed to each other. There is more than one way of expressing oneself. One man expresses himself in one way and another way is derived or comes from another man. If we were to understand and distinguish the great number of modes of expression, it would appear that there is no disagreement in meaning or intention between these opposing terms. However, since the Catholic Church has declared it as having to be held as faith, it is necessary to maintain that the Holy Spirit proceeds *ab utroque*.[28]

Duns Scotus was very open to the Greek way of expressing the mystery and therefore defended pluralism in this question. The following important statement is very interesting in this respect:

> It should be understood in this debate that there are two articles which are of the substance of faith and these are discussed in the first book of *Sentences*. The first article is that there are only three Persons and one God. The second is that these Persons do not exist of themselves alone, but one Person produces another and those two produce a third. We are not permitted to think differently about these two articles. It is, however, possible to think differently about whether the Persons are constituted by relationships or by their mode of being, so long as we respect the articles mentioned above. It is permitted to discuss and to seek (*exerceri*), because I am not bound by faith to any particular true assertion.[29]

In fact, Duns Scotus kept close to the teaching of Bonaventure and several other theologians, according to whom the Person in God is constituted, not by relationships, but by something absolute, namely the (first) substance or supposit that is distinguished by a certain property. That property is identical with the relationship in question. But 'person' connotes in the first place a substance or supposit.[30] The Greek way of distinguishing the Holy Spirit from the Word—not by their relationship, but by the different mode of processing—was therefore seen by Duns Scotus to be acceptable. Thomas Aquinas did not accept this judgement.

Thomas regarded it as impossible to distinguish the Spirit from the Son if he did not proceed from him and if they did not both proceed from the Father.[31] This was the position that was in general held by the Dominican school. The question continued, however, to be disputed.[32] From the time of Robert Grosseteste onwards—he was not a Franciscan, although he taught them—the Franciscan school continued generally to maintain a different position from that held by Thomas and, before him, by Anselm. Those who opposed Thomas in this included William of Ware,[33] John Peckham,[34] Matthew of Aquasparta,[35] Petrus Johannis Olivi and, of course, John Duns Scotus. Outside the Order of Friars Minor, there were Praepositinus, William of Auvergne, Henry of Ghent[36] and James of Viterbo.

All these theologians regarded the procession of the Holy Spirit from the Father *and the Son* as a dogma of the Church. Many of them did not hesitate to describe the Greeks not simply as teaching error, but as heretics. In using this word, however, we should remember that the idea of heresy was wider in its meaning at that time than it is today.

NOTES

1. Athanasius, *Tomos ad Antiochenos*; see also H. B. Swete, *The Holy Spirit in the Ancient Church* (London, 1912), p. 173.
2. Jerome, *Ep.* 15, 3–4, written to Pope Damasus in September 374 (*PL* 22, 356–357).
3. Augustine, *De Trin.* V, 8, 9–10 (*PL* 42, 917).
4. *De Trin*, VII, 5, 10 (*PL* 42, 942).
5. *De Trin*. VII, 4 and VIII, proem. (*PL* 42, 939ff., 947).
6. See the critical edition of Anselm by S. Schmitt: *Mon.*, prol. (Schmitt, I, p. 8) and 79 (p. 86); *Ep.* 83 (III, p. 208) and 204 (IV, pp. 96–97); *Ep. de Inc. Verbi*, XVI (II, p. 35). Anselm's position was very similar in the case of the celebration of the Eucharist—whether it was unleavened or leavened, it was still bread!
7. See Abelard, *Theol. Christ.* IV (*PL* 178, 1268). The first sentence of this text is found, after an appeal to Augustine, *De Trin*. VII, 4, in the *Theol. Summi Boni* III, 1, No. 7: see H. Ostlender, *Peter Abaelards Theologia Summi Boni* (*Beiträge zur Geschichte der Philosophie und Theologie des Mittelalters*, XXXV, 2–3) (Münster, 1939), p. 77.
8. Richard, *De Trin.* IV, 20 (*PL* 198, 943); see the crit. ed. of J. Ribaillier (Paris, 1958), p. 184; Fr. tr. G. Salet, *SC* 63 (1959), pp. 273 and 275.
9. Examples are: *hypostasis–substantia*: *Contra Err. Graec.* I, prol.; *ST* Ia, q. 30, a. 1, ad 1 and q. 39, a. 3, ad 2; *causa–principium*: *ST* Ia, q. 33, a. 1, ad 1 and 2; *De Pot.* q. 10, a. 1, ad 8, in which Thomas generalizes: 'aliquid enim inconvenienter in lingua latina dicitur quod propter proprietatem idiomatis convenienter in lingua graeca dici potest'. See also my article 'Valeur et portée œcuméniques de quelques principes herméneutiques de S. Thomas d'Aquin',*RSPT*, 57 (1973), 611–626. For Thomas' respect for the Greek Fathers: 'quia praesumptuosum est tantorum doctorum expressis auctoritatibus contraire'; *ST* Ia, q. 61, a. 3: 'quamvis contrarium non sit reputandum erroneum propter sententiam

Gregorii Nazianzeni, cuius tanta est in doctrina christiana auctoritas ut nullus unquam eius dictis calumniam inferre praesumpserit, sicut nec Athanasii documentis, ut Hieronymus dixit'.

10. Text edited by M. Schmaus in *Der Liber Propugnatorius des Thomas Anglicus und die Lehrunterschiede zwischen Thomas von Aquin und Duns Scotus*, II. Teil: *Die trinitarischen Lehrdifferenz (Beiträge zur Geschichte der Philosophie und Theologie des Mittelalters*, XXIX) (Münster, 1930), p. 314.

11. *ST* Ia, q. 36, a. 2; cf. *Contra Err. Graec.* II, c. 9.

12. *De Pot.* q. 10, a. 5 c.—a very important article.

13. The Spirit of the Son: *De Pot.* q. 10, a. 5, ad 14; *ST* Ia, q. 36, a. 2; cf. *Contra Err. Graec.* II, 1. The Spirit proceeding through the Son: *De Pot.* q. 10, a. 4, c. end; *ST* Ia, q. 36, a. 3; *Contra Err. Graec.* II, 8.

14. Thomas of Sutton, *Quaest. disp.* 9; M. Schmaus, *op. cit.* (note 10), p. 95.

15. The Franciscans would seem to have owed their fundamental arguments in the debate with the Greeks, the principal concern being that they should believe that the Spirit was the Spirit of the Son, to Robert Grosseteste, in his note added to the *Ep. ad Trisagion* of John Damascene; see the evidence of Duns Scotus, *Oxon*. I, d. 11, p. 1 (ed. L. Vivès, *Opera*, IX, p. 325); Robert Grosseteste, MS. British Museum Royal 6, E. V, fol. 109 and 7 F. 2, fol. 72ᵛ–73ʳ; M. Roncaglia, *op. cit.* (note 16 below), p. 239; Oxford, Magd. cod. 192, fol. 215, quoted in the edition of the *Lectura* of Duns Scotus.

16. See M. Roncaglia, *Les Frères Mineurs et l'Eglise grecque orthodoxe au XIIIᵉ siècle (1271–1274)* (Cairo, 1954). The report by Haymo of Faversham (in 1234) was edited by G. Golubovich in *Arch. Franc. Hist.*, 12 (1919), 418–470.

17. Alexander of Hales, *Glossa in quatuor Libros Sententiarum*, lib. I, d. XI (Quaracchi ed. (1951), pp. 135ff.).

18. Münster, Universitätsbibliothek Cod. 257, fol. 72d–73c, quoted by Roncaglia, *op. cit.*, p. 195. For John Pagus, see the brief reference by P. Glorieux in *Répertoire des Maîtres en Théologie de Paris au XIIIᵉ siècle*, I (Paris, 1933), pp. 328–329.

19. Alexander of Hales, *ST* I, pars I, inq. II, tract. unicus, q.1, tit. II, c. IV (Quaracchi ed., p. 450). In his reply to the sixteenth objection, Alexander uses the idea expressed above to make a distinction between the inner word (and spirit) favoured by Augustine and the Latins and the external word of John Damascene and the Greeks.

20. Bonaventure, *In I Sent.* d. 11, art. un., q. 1, reply to the first objection.

21. Odo Rigaldus, *Utrum Spiritus Sanctus sit Patris et Filii ita quod ab utroque, vel sit Filii non tamen procedens a Filio, sicut volunt Graeci. Solutio*. This text was edited by Roncaglia, *op. cit.* (note 16), p. 215 in accordance with the Paris MS. BN lat. 14.910, but an integral edition of the whole question was prepared by M. Schmaus, *op. cit.* (note 10), pp. 281–286, especially p. 284, where our text appears.

22. Bonaventure, *In I Sent.* d. XI, art. un., q. 1 (Quaracchi ed., I, pp. 211ff.). J. Ratzinger commented on this article in 'Offenbarung, Schrift und Überlieferung. Ein Text des heiligen Bonaventura und seine Bedeutung für die gegenwärtige Theologie', *Trierer Theologische Zeitschrift*, 67 (1958), 13–27.

23. It is interesting to record a more favourable statement. In the question as to whether the personal name may be applied to God, Bonaventure raised this objection: 'vocabula nostra debent respondere Graecis, ut unitas fidei ostendatur; sed Graeci non utuntur vocabulo *prosopon* in divinis, quod est idem quod *persona*; ergo cum ipsi proprius habeant vocabula quam nos, nec nos debemus uti': *In I Sent.* d. 23, a. 1, q. 1, arg. 4 (Quaracchi ed., I, p. 405). In his reply to this objection, Bonaventure says that the word 'person' is used because of the lack of other terms; the Greeks have their own word, 'hypostasis', but we cannot say 'substance', because it is synonymous with 'essence'.

24. Alexander of Hales, *Quaestiones disputatae 'Antequam esset frater'*, q. 8, membr. 1, Nos. 16 and 18 (*Bibl. Franciscana Scholastica Medii Aevi*, XIX; Quaracchi ed. (1960), pp. 71 and 72).

182

25. *Glossa in quatuor Libros Sententiarum*, Lib. I, d. XI (*Bibl. Franciscana Scholastica Medii Aevi*, XII; Quaracchi ed. (1951), pp. 135ff.).

26. Bonaventure, *op. cit.* (note 22 above); cf. d. XXXI, a. 1, q. 2 ad 1, (Quaracchi ed., I, p. 542), in which the same explanation can be found: *fuit Graecus*. The finer interpretation is that he simply thought in Greek, with all its limitations. For Thomas Aquinas, see *ST* Ia, q. 36, a. 2, ad 3; *De Pot*. q. 10, a. 4, ad 24. For the introduction of John Damascene's texts to the Scholastics, see J. de Ghellinck, 'L'entrée de Jean de Damas dans le monde littéraire occidental', *Byzantinische Zeitschrift*, 21 (1912), 448–457; P. Minges, 'Zum Gebrauch der Schrift "De fide orthodoxa" des Johannes Damaszenus in der Scholastik', *TQ* (1914), 225–247. In the *Summa* alone, Thomas quotes him more than 200 times. For the Scholastic theologians, he was a very valuable authority. Peter Lombard said, for example: 'Ioannes Damascenus inter doctores Graecorum maximus, in libro quem de Trinitate scripsit, quem et papa Eugenius transferri fecit': *I Sent.*, d. 19. Albert the Great was anxious to show that he agreed with Augustine: see *In I Sent*. d. 27, a. 7 (ed. A. Borgnet, XXVI, pp. 46–47). Duns Scotus insisted that John Damascene was not heretical in his article on the procession of the Holy Spirit: 'Damascenus reputatur doctor authenticus et catholicus adeo ut liber suus translatus fuerit mandato papae de graeco in latinum, propter quod non videtur quod liber suus contineat aliqua opposita traditioni ecclesiae Romanae, et tamen ipse posuit ibidem non quod Spiritus Sanctus sit a Filio, sed quod est Filii': quoted by M. Schmaus, *op. cit.* (note 10), p. 374, note 199.

27. Duns Scotus, *Lectura in librum primum Sententiarum* (D. VIII–XLV), *Opera omnia*, XVII (Vatican, 1966), p. 128 = d. 11, q. 1.

28. *In I Sent*. d. XI, q. 1; *Opera omnia* (Paris, 1893), IX, p. 325. I have not been able to consult the most recent edition, the *Opera omnia*, V, pp. 2–3.

29. *Lectura*, d. II, No. 164 in the Vatican edition of the *Opera omnia*, XVI, pp. 166–167.

30. Duns Scotus, *Lectura*, d. XXVI; Vatican ed., *op. cit.*, pp. 328ff., in which William of Auvergne and Robert Grosseteste are given, in a note, as antecedents. Bonaventure, *In I Sent*. d. XXV, a. 1, q. 1 and q. 2, ad 3 (Quaracchi ed., pp. 436–437 and 441).

31. Thomas Aquinas, *In I Sent*. d. 13, q. 1, a. 2; *De Pot*. q. 10, a. 5; *ST* Ia, q. 36, a. 2; *Comm. in ev. Ioan*. c. 15, lect. 5.

32. See pp. 253ff. of M. Schmaus' enormous study, *op. cit.* (note 10 above). According to the list given in a Munich manuscript, it was the thirteenth of the articles on which the *magistri* disagreed: see A. Dondaine, 'Un catalogue des dissensions doctrinales entre les Maîtres parisiens à la fin du XIIIe siècle', *RTAM*, 10 (1938), 374–394.

33. See the texts of William of Ware in J. Slipyj, *De principio spirationis in SS. Trinitate. Disquisitio historico-dogmatica* (Lwow, 1926).

34. The text of John Peckham will be found in M. Schmaus, *op. cit.* (note 10), pp. 295–296.

35. Matthew of Aquasparta, *Quodl*. II, q. 3; see M. Schmaus, *op. cit.*, pp. 291–292.

36. Henry of Ghent, *Quodl*. V, q. 9 (Paris, 1518), fol. 167.

2

ATTEMPTS AT AND SUGGESTIONS
FOR AN AGREEMENT

The procession of the Holy Spirit from the Father *and the Son* was, for the Latins, an article of faith or a dogma. It had been professed by the Church's councils at least since the beginning of the seventh century, and before that by the Fathers of the Church, the Popes and the creed *Quicumque*. What is more, this had taken place during a period when the East and the West had—sometimes only with great difficulty—been in communion. After this communion had been broken, this same article of faith was proclaimed in the West by successive councils. These included Bari of 1098,[1] the Fourth Lateran Council of 1215,[2] the Second Council of Lyons in 1274, when the delegates of the Greek basileus chanted this passage in the creed twice, once in Greek and once in Latin,[3] and finally the Council of Ferrara-Florence in 1438–1439. We shall be returning to this last council later in this chapter.

The centuries in which East and West have been divided, but never totally separated, have been marked by efforts to re-establish communion and attempts at elucidation and agreement.[4] Unfortunately, however, on both sides, the main consideration has almost always been to reduce the other side to one's own level.[5] The Greeks put forward their own formula and the Latins proposed theirs—each formula was given as an absolute which excluded the other.[6] In particular, the numerous conferences held in the East by the Dominicans and the Franciscans, while providing an opportunity for the formulation of precise statements which are of interest to theologians, resulted in a hardening of the situation rather than a reduction of the difficulties between East and West. An abortive attempt to reach agreement has always involved the risk of creating a greater distance between the two sides. Was this the case with Ferrara-Florence? That is a possible view, especially considering the aversion that the Greeks still feel, even nowadays, for it. I have studied this council very carefully and asked searching questions about it. It seems to me that, as far as the article of faith that interests us here is concerned, Ferrara-Florence was at once a very serious confrontation between East and West, and (too brief) an attempt to look for a possibility of communion in diversity.

The Council of Florence

The debate began at Ferrara in 1438 on whether the addition of the *Filioque* clause to the creed was justified. I shall consider this extremely important point after I have summarized the whole debate and evaluated the agreement reached on the doctrinal question.[7]

The doctrinal discussion proper began on 2 March 1439 at Florence. It was at first concerned mainly with terminology: the meaning of the word 'procession'. Mark Eugenikos' definition was *huparktikē proodos*—a 'substantial going out or emanation'. A little later, it became necessary to clarify—once again—the relationship between 'substance' and 'hypostasis'. Then there was a long discussion about the real meaning of the texts of Basil the Great and Athanasius (see above, pp. 30, 44 note 9).[8]

The Greeks were anxious to safeguard the unity of the source of divinity, the Father from whom everything proceeded. The Latins replied to this by claiming firstly that the Son's spiration of the Spirit was derived entirely from the Father and secondly that the Holy Spirit proceeded from the two (*duo spirantes*) as from a single principle (*unus Spirator*). They did not want to say that the Son had a different function from that of the Father with regard to the Spirit proceeding *a Patre per Filium*. To claim this would have been to compromise on the one hand the real identity of the hypostases and the divine substance and, on the other, the community of essence of the Father and the Son. For this reason, then, it seemed important to them to interpret the *a Patre per Filium* in the sense of 'a Patre et Filio tanquam ab uno principio'.[9] They believed that an affirmation of the procession of the Spirit *a Patre solo* did violence to the divine unity by destroying the real identity of the hypostases and the divine substance because it attributed to the Father something, apart from fatherhood, that the Son did not have.

Obviously, this Latin theological construction of the mystery of the Trinity was alien to the Greek mind. They thought that it introduced a non-personal principle into the reality of the Triad. Instead of a Triad, the Latins, they believed, were postulating two dyads: Father→Son and Father-Son→Holy Spirit. The Greeks wished to recognize only relationships between the Persons, within which the Father was the Principle or beginning, the Cause, the Author and the Source. In fact, the Latins also recognized that, as Mgr Sergey, who was the Bishop of Yamburg and Rector of the Ecclesiastical Academy at St Petersburg at the beginning of the present century and became the second head of the restored Patriarchate of Moscow in 1925, pointed out in 1903 [see Appendix to this chapter, pp. 190–191].

A door was opened to possible agreement at Florence on 19 March when the Greeks presented the text of the letter written by Maximus the Confessor to Marinus, a priest in Cyprus, declaring that the Latins acknowledged that the Father was the only Cause of the Son and the Spirit.[10] Since John of Montenero had also produced texts by the Latin Fathers showing that the *Filioque* had the same meaning as *per Filium* as well as texts by Basil, Epiphanius, Didymus the Blind and Cyril of Alexandria saying much the same as the Latin texts, Isidore of Kiev and Bessarion of Nicaea declared their agreement.[11] It was, in other words, not a question of 'Latinizing', but rather of following the saints of the Church. The Fathers could not have been mistaken, nor could they have been opposed to each other, because the Holy Spirit had spoken in them.[12]

These ideas gradually came to be accepted and on 12 April Bessarion made his magistral dogmatic pronouncement, which was in fact a full pneumatological treatise.[13] Maximus the Confessor's letter to Marinus was taken as the basis for union (on 17 April 1439), since the holy Fathers of the Church clearly in no way explicitly denied a relationship of eternal existence between the Holy Spirit and the Son. The Greek Fathers and the Patriarch Tarasius, whose work was also cited, used the formula 'through the Son' and a number of other formulae which were quite close to the *Filioque*. They could, it was argued, not be regarded as heretics and the formula 'through the Son' could only point to a contribution from the Son, received from the Father, to the 'procession' of the Spirit. Interpreted in this sense, it was seen as equivalent to *ex Filio*, explained, as the Latins did, *tanquam ab uno principio*.[14]

Union was achieved on this basis, proclaimed on 6 July 1439 and accepted by the emperor and thirty-nine Eastern Christians—bishops, procurators, deacons and superiors of monasteries.[15] The text of this decree on the procession of the Holy Spirit is as follows:

> In the name of the holy Trinity, the Father, the Son and the Holy Spirit, with the approval of this sacred universal Council of Florence, we define that this truth of faith must be believed and received by all Christians and that all must profess, namely, that the Holy Spirit has his being eternally from the Father and the Son, that he has his essence and his subsistence both from the Father and from the Son together, and that he proceeds eternally from both as from a single principle and by a single spiration. We declare that what the holy doctors and Fathers say, that is, that the Holy Spirit proceeds from the Father through the Son, is intended to mean that the Son is also, according to the Greeks, the cause and, according to the Latins, the principle of the subsistence of the Holy Spirit, as the Father is. And since everything that belongs to the Father, the Father gives to his only begotten Son by begetting him, apart from being Father, the Son has it eternally from the Father, by whom he is eternally begotten, that the Holy Spirit proceeds from him. We define, moreover, that the explanation (or explicitation) of those words *Filioque* has been lawfully and reasonably added to the creed in order to declare the truth and because of the urgent need.[16]

The essential aspect of this historic text is that the two formulae, the *Filioque* and the *per Filium*, had come to be regarded as equivalent or at least as possibly equivalent. This was also the basis of later unions, such as that achieved at Brest in 1596.[17] I find it difficult to understand that the formula that the Son is, together with the Father, the *cause* of the procession of the Holy Spirit was attributed to the Greeks, since the latter had always reserved this term for the *Father*.[18] I find it equally difficult to understand why the verb

186

ekporeuesthai was used in the Greek text of the act of union in the sentence 'he proceeds (*procedit*) eternally from both as from a single principle and by a single spiration', whereas this verb was reserved by the Greeks for the procession of the Holy Spirit from the Father as from his first origin.[19] Finally, to affirm that *per Filium* is equivalent to *ex Filio* does not express the shade of meaning that exists between two expressions that go back to two quite different theological constructions of a mystery believed in the same way and confessed in the doxology. As Bessarion pointed out, however, *ex* meant equality and not order, whereas *per* pointed to the order of the Persons and not their equality. In accepting the *per Filium*, on the other hand, the Latins provided a critical gloss on it as tending to suggest that the Son was inferior or impossibly instrumental.[20]

In fact, the Florentine act of union did not simply stop at declaring an agreement of intent between two different expressions stemming from two different theological approaches to the same faith. It reduced the Greek expression to the fundamentally Western meaning of its Latin equivalent: *per Filium* is Catholic if it is interpreted in the sense of *Filioque*. This may be so, but then let us take this equivalence seriously and agree with André de Halleux, who said:[21] 'After having affirmed for such a long time that the *di' Huiou* was the equivalent of the *Filioque*, would it not be possible to agree in return that the *Filioque* goes back to the *di' Huiou*, in other words, to recognize the fundamental authenticity of monopatrism?' After having analysed the advantages and the disadvantages of the two formulae, M. Jugie (*op. cit.* (note 4 below), p. 12), provided a meaningful suggestion: 'Omnibus accurate perpensis formula Graecorum praeponenda videtur, quatenus et principii unitatem subindicat, et ordinem personarum in luce ponit, et Patris monarchiam directe exprimit'—'After having considered everything very carefully, the formula of the Greeks seems preferable, inasmuch as it demonstrates the unity of principle, sheds light on the order of the Persons and directly expresses the monarchy of the Father'.

The formula 'to recognize the fundamental authenticity of monopatrism' has, however, to be defined more precisely. The formula 'through the Son', taken on its own, could express forgetfulness or denial of the part of the Son in the eternal production of the Spirit. The Son would only be, in that case, a transitional stage in the act of spiration of the one Father. Karl Barth rightly objected to this interpretation, but he failed in this to understand and perhaps even to show sufficient knowledge of the Eastern tradition.[22] This was undoubtedly the price that Barth had to pay for taking Jesus Christ as his point of departure in all his theology, for working Christologically. With greater recognition than he had of the value expressed by the *di' Huiou*, we can more easily accept the fact that each formula is the complement of the other.

Florenced was too great a victory for the Latins—and the papacy—for it to be a full council of union.[23] The Orthodox are wrong to reject it so completely, because the debate on the pneumatological question was both free and serious. It is not difficult, however, to understand their dissatisfaction and their reluctance to accept the conclusion *in the form in which it was expressed*.[24] The indefeasible deposit of Florence is twofold: (1) the intention to recognize that the two formulae were compatible and even equivalent—I would willingly say, that they were complementary; (2) the principle on the basis of which this intention was pursued, namely that the Fathers of the Church, inspired by the Holy Spirit, held, in communion, both formulae. Any new attempt to approach this question should take this as a point of departure and as a basis for discussion.

NOTES

1. Mansi, 20, 947–992.
2. *DS* 800; the first decretal, *Firmiter*, a theological reference to the thirteenth century; *DS* 805: the decretal *Damnamus*.
3. The Emperor's profession of faith on 6 June 1274; see *DS* 853; and the Constitution *De summa Trinitate et fide catholica*, sixth session, 17 July 1274: see *DS* 850, with its repeated insistence on the *tanquam ex uno principio*.
4. There have been very many special studies. Among the most useful are W. Norden, *Das Papsttum und Byzanz. Die Trennung der beiden Mächte und das Problem ihrer Wiedervereinigung bis zum Untergang des byzantinischen Reiches (1453)* (Berlin, 1903); M. Viller, 'La question de l'union des Eglises entre Grecs et Latins depuis le concile de Lyon jusqu'à celui de Florence (1274–1438)', *RHE*, 17 (1921), 260–305, 515–532; 18 (1922), 20–60; R. J. Loenertz, 'Autour du traité de Fr. Bartélémy de Constantinople contre les Grecs', *Arch. Fratr. Praed.*, 6 (1936), 361–378; *idem*, 'Les dominicains byzantins Théodore et André Chrysobergès et les négociations pour l'union des Eglises grecque et latine de 1415 à 1430'; M. Jugie, *De Processione Spiritus Sancti ex fontibus Revelationis et secundum Orientales dissidentes* (Rome, 1936); A. Dondaine, ' "Contra Graecos". Premiers écrits polémiques des Dominicains d'Orient', *Arch. Fratr. Praed.*, 21 (1951), 320–446; M. Roncaglia, *Les Frères Mineurs et l'Eglise grecque orthodoxe au XIIIᵉ siècle (1231–1274)* (Cairo, 1954); E. Herman, 'Neuf siècles de schisme entre l'Eglise d'Orient et d'Occident', *NRT*, 76 (1954), 576–610; F. Stegmüller, 'Bonacursius contra Graecos. Ein Beitrag zur Kontroverstheologie des XIII. Jahrhunderts', *Vitae et Veritati. Festschrift für Karl Adam* (Düsseldorf, 1956), pp. 57–82; *1274 année charnière. Mutations et continuités. Colloque Lyon-Paris, 30 Septembre–5 Octobre 1974* (CNRS, 1977); C. Capizzi, 'Fra Bonagrazzia di San Giovanni in Persicato e il concilio unionistico di Lione (1274)', *Arch. Hist. Pont.*, 13 (1975), 141–206.
5. See G. Alberigo, 'L'œcuménisme au Moyen Age', *1274 année charnière, op. cit.* (note 4 above); this essay was also published in *RHE*, 71 (1976), 365–391.
6. Although it was admitted at Florence that the Greeks should not pronounce the *Filioque* formula, since there was agreement concerning the doctrine itself, Pope Nicholas III later wanted to impose the formula on them: see *DTC*, V, cols 2340–2341.
7. Between 1940 and 1971, the Pontifical Oriental Institute published ten volumes of the *Concilium Florentinum: Documenta et Scriptores*. In addition to this, the critical works of Mark Eugenikos were edited by L. Petit in *Patr. Or.*, 17, pp. 307–524, and Sylvester Syropoulos' memoirs were translated and edited by V. Laurent in *Concilium Florentinum*, IX (Rome, 1971). See also J. Gill, *The Council of Florence* (Cambridge, 1959);

idem, *Constance et Bâle-Florence* (*Les conciles œcuméniques*) (Paris, 1965); J. Decarreaux, *Les Grecs au Concile de l'union Ferrare-Florence (1438–1439)* (Paris, 1970); A. Leidl, *Die Einheit der Kirchen auf den spätmittelalterlichen Konzilien von Konstanz bis Florenz* (Paderborn, 1966); H. Mühlen, 'Das Konzil von Florenz (1439) als vorläufiges Modell eines kommenden Unionskonzils', *Theologie und Glaube*, 63 (1973), 184–197; H. J. Marx, *Filioque und Verbot eines anderen Glaubens auf dem Florentinum. Zum Pluralismus in dogmatischen Formeln* (Steyl, 1977).

8. Basil the Great: see above, pp. 30, 44 note 9; see also J. Gill, *The Council of Florence, op. cit.* (note 7), pp. 194ff. For the use of patristic texts, see E. Boulerand, 'L'argument patristique au concile de Florence, dans la question de la procession du Saint-Esprit', *BLE*, 63 (1962), 162–199.

9. See Mansi, 31 A, 971, and the declaration made by the Latins on 1 May, Mansi, 31 A, 974–975; see also 'Florence', *DTC*, V, 1 col. 40.

10. Mansi, 31 A, 877 (Greek) and 878 (Latin); see also J. Gill, *The Council of Florence, op. cit.*, pp. 212f. see also above, pp. 52–53.

11. Mansi, 31, col. 886.

12. See *Concilium Florentinum*, Series B, V/2 (Rome, 1953), p. 426: 'Sancti non discrepant, sed idem Spiritus Sanctus locutus est in omnibus sanctis. . . ; ita comperietur sanctos nunquam dissentire'. This section, 'Quae supersunt Act. Graec.', is ed. by J. Gill.

13. Mansi, 31, cols 893–968; *PG* 161, 543–612; E. Candal, ed., *Concilium Florentinum*, VII/1 (Rome, 1961); J. Gill, *The Council of Florence, op. cit.* (note 7), pp. 240–241.

14. Mansi, 31, col. 1002.

15. J. Gill, *The Council of Florence, op. cit.*, pp. 293f. Mark Eugenikos refused to sign. The Patriarch of Constantinople, Joseph II, died on the very day that had been chosen for the union, 8 June: see Mansi, 31, col. 1007. He left a paper in which he clearly subscribed to this union and recognized the Pope as the 'vicar of Christ': see *Concilum Florentimum, op. cit.*, pp. 444–455; J. Gill, *The Council of Florence, op. cit.*, p. 267. Final consent was delayed for a month by the request made by Eugenius IV that, before union was agreed, the Greeks should accept five points: his primacy, purgatory, unleavened bread, the addition of the *Filioque* clause to the creed and consecration of the Eucharist using the words of institution. These points were hastily discussed.

16. *DS* 1300–1302.

17. *Or. Chr.*, 3 (1924), 150. The procession of the Holy Spirit 'non ex duobus principiis, nec duplici processione, sed ex uno principio velut ex fonte, ex Patre per Filium procedere' (§1).

18. See Gregory of Nyssa, *Adv. Eunom.* I (*PG* 45, 416C); Maximus the Confessor, *Ep. ad Mar.* (*PG* 91, 136); John Damascene, *De fide orthod.* I, 8 and 12 (*PG* 94, 832 and 849).

19. See M. Jugie, *op. cit.* (note 4 above), p. 15. Maximus' text, which is the basis of the agreement, was much more satisfactory. Maximus not only insisted that the Father was the only *aitia*, but also, in speaking of the Spirit's dependence on the Son, used the verb *proïenai*.

20. See Thomas Aquinas, *ST* Ia, q. 36, a. 3 and parallel texts; *Contra Err. Graec.* II, 8. See also J. Gill, *The Council of Florence, op. cit.* (note 7), pp. 240ff. The Greeks also discussed more fully whether *ex* and *dia* were equivalent.

21. A. de Halleux, 'Orthodoxie et Catholicisme: du personnalisme en pneumatologie', *RTL*, 6 (1975), 3–30, especially 30, note.

22. K. Barth, *Church Dogmatics*, I. 1 (Eng. tr.; Edinburgh and New York, 1936), pp. 551–552.

23. This emerges even more clearly when the decree *Pro Armenis* of 22 November 1435 is read: see *DS* 1310ff. This text is taken from Thomas Aquinas, sometimes literally: see his *De art. fid. et Eccl. sacr.* It is not a dogma, but merely theology and, what is more, only one theology.

24. It is important to point to the serious limitations of the Council of Florence, which was not

an ideal council of union. The Orthodox, however, have almost always failed to be fair—and sometimes to be well-informed—with regard to the positive achievements of the Council. The history of the Council by Syropoulos—and this emerges especially clearly from the title of the first edition, prepared by the Anglican scholar R. Creyghton, *Vera Historia Unionis non verae* (The Hague, 1660)—is full of elements that are very valuable from the historical point of view, but at the same time passionate and one-sided. It has, however, continued to be regarded by many as the leading work on the Council. A passionate attack against Florence, written by Ivan N. Ostroumoff in Moscow in 1847, has been translated and published in English by Basil Popoff: *The History of the Council of Florence* (Boston, 1971). This publication concludes with a criticism of attempts made by Patriarch Athenagoras to open the way to ecumenism.

APPENDIX

Mgr Sergey published an article entitled 'What separates us from the Old Catholics?' in 1903 in the Russian-language journal *Tserkovniy Vestnik*. A French translation appeared in 1904 in the *Revue internationale de Théologie*, 12, 159–190. A more complete text of this article will be found in *Istina*, 17 (1972), 290–292. The following extract from the text is of direct interest to our subject:

Like the Old Catholics, we also have to bear in mind, in our mutual relationships, the difference that has existed for a thousand years between our two cultures and our intellectual development. This difference has continued to have an effect on our lives since the time of separation. Many words and terms which are used by both sides in fact have for each side a special meaning, very dear to each, which is not acceptable to the other side. If we are both absolutely convinced of the identity of our faith, we will end our debate about words and terminology and grant each side the right to use the term that it is accustomed to use.

Thus, when we deny the *Filioque*, we defend the 'monarchy' as the unity of the source in the Trinity and as an element that is quite necessary for any definition of the truth of the divine unity. For us, or rather for the Greek mind, to accept that the Son is, together with the Father, the true cause of the Holy Spirit is equivalent to accepting two principles of divinity, something both logically and psychologically impossible. In their defence and preservation of this truth in opposition to the Latins, the Greeks are prepared to add these words to the creed from 'the Father alone', so as to define the dogma decisively and beyond dispute, with no possibility of an interpretation other than their own.

The Old Catholics have inherited quite a different tradition. They have worked out a completely different system in order to understand God. For them, to say that the Son and the Holy Spirit are, in their eternal procession, quite independent of each other and that they are not in contact with each other is equivalent to doing violence to the very 'monarchy' that is so energetically defended in the East. The Eastern and the Western Christian each has his own point of view. Each sees through his own glasses of special and different colours, and cannot in any way understand the other's point of departure and way of thinking, or at least can do so only after making a great effort and renouncing all his own ideas.

That is why, when we are completely certain that the Old Catholics, when they take the *Filioque* out of their creed, are not simply going through a formality and trying to make rough canonical ways smooth but are really expressing a faith in the Trinity that is as orthodox as that of the holy Church, we shall not ask them to sign the formula *a Patre solo*. We shall, on the contrary, leave them their *Filioque* in the certain conviction that this formula is indispensable to the Western mind to express the same idea that we stress by means of our formula *a Patre solo*.

It is interesting to compare this passage by Mgr Sergey with the report made by Mgr Basile Krivocheine in the name of the Russian Orthodox Church to the conference held in Belgrade in 1966 with representatives of the Church of England; see *Istina*, 13 (1968):

Certain essential elements of the doctrine of the *Filioque* can be found in the writings of Church Fathers in the West long before the Roman Church became separated from the Orthodox Church (in St Augustine, for instance). What is more, this question is concerned more with theology than directly with faith itself. For this reason, the Orthodox Church cannot insist on the acceptance by Western Christians of the full teaching of the Fathers about the procession of the Holy Spirit as a precondition for the reunion of the Western with the Eastern Church. In this, Orthodox Christians are simply following the example of St Basil the Great, who did not insist that the divinity of the Holy Spirit should be recognized (only the fact that he was not created) as a precondition for reunion with the Orthodox Church on the part of those who accepted the Nicene creed. Disagreements of this kind, as St Basil the Great wrote, can be easily overcome later, after reunion, in the course of life together over a long period and study together without polemics. If that course were followed, it would have to be understood that there is no place in the creed for the *Filioque* clause; otherwise, the opinion of a Western theologian would be placed at the same level as the teaching of the universal Church.

3

RELATIONSHIPS AND DISCUSSIONS BETWEEN ORTHODOX AND NON-ROMAN CATHOLIC COMMUNIONS

A. ORTHODOX AND OLD CATHOLICS

After breaking away from the Roman Catholic Church in 1871, the Old Catholics tried to establish links, and if possible intercommunion, with other Churches whose structure was basically 'Catholic'. The Orthodox Church was very interested in this group of Western Christians who had emancipated themselves from papal authority.[1] One of the direct outcomes of this contact was a conference held at Cologne and Bonn in 1874–1875. This was attended by twenty-two bishops and priests of the Orthodox Church, American and English representatives of the Anglican Church, and a number of Old Catholics, including Döllinger (who refused to be described as 'Old Catholic'), Reusch and others. Altogether, 120 Christians came to the conference.[2] The question of the *Filioque* was at the heart of the discussions.

The Old Catholics and the Anglicans agreed that the addition had been made to the creed in an illicit and one-sided way and without any prior decision on the part of an ecumenical council. The following conclusions regarding doctrinal questions were reached by those taking part:

1. We agree totally that we should accept ecumenical creeds and decisions made by the early, undivided Church in matters of faith.
2. We agree totally that we should recognize that the addition of the *Filioque* was not made in a way that was in conformity with the rules of the Church.
3. We are in agreement with all the aspects of the representation of the teaching about the Holy Spirit suggested by the Father of the undivided Church.
4. We reject every representation or mode of expression containing any acceptance of the idea of two principles, *archai* or *aitiai* in the Trinity.

We accept the teaching of John Damascene about the Holy Spirit as summarized in the following paragraphs, in the sense of the teaching of the early, undivided Church:

1. The Holy Spirit comes from the Father (*ek tou Patros*), as from the principle (*archē*), the cause (*aitia*) and the source (*pēgē*) of divinity (*De rect. sent.* 1; *Contra Man.* 4).

2. The Holy Spirit does not come from the Son (*ek tou Huiou*), because there is only one principle (*archē*) and one cause (*aitia*) in the divinity through which everything that is in that divinity is produced (see *De fide orthod*.: 'ek tou Huiou de to Pneuma ou legomen, Pneuma di' Huiou onomazomen').

3. The Holy Spirit comes from the Father through the Son (*De fide orthod*. I, 12: 'to de Pneuma to Hagion ekphantorikē tou kruphiou tēs theotētos dunamis tou Patros, ek Patros men di' Huiou ekporeumenē'; *ibid*.: 'Huiou de Pneuma, ouch hōs ex autou, all' hōs di' autou ek tou Patros ekporeuomenon'; *Contra Man*. 5: 'dia tou logou autou ex autou to Pneuma autou ekporeuomenon'; *De hymno Trisag*. 28: 'Pneuma to Hagion ek tou Patros dia tou Huiou kai logou proïon'; *Hom. in Sabb. S*. 4: 'tout' hēmin esti to latreuomenon . . . Pneuma Hagion tou Theou kai Patros, hōs ex autou ekporeuomenon, hoper kai tou Huiou legetai, hōs di' autou phaneroumenon kai tē ktisei metadidomenon, all' ouk ex autou echon tēn huparxin').

4. The Holy Spirit is the image of the Son, who is himself the image of the Father (*De fide orthod*. I, 13: 'eikōn tou Patros ho Huios, kai tou Huiou to Pneuma'), proceeding from the Father and dwelling in the Son as his radiating power (*De fide orthod*. I, 7: 'tou Patros proerchomenēn kai en tō logō anapauomenēn kai autou ousan ekphantikēn dunamin'; *ibid*., I, 12: 'Patēr . . . dia logou proboleus ekphantorikou Pneumatos').

5. The Holy Spirit is the personal procession coming from the Father, who is of the Son, but not coming from the Son, because he is the Spirit from the mouth of the divinity, expressing the word (*De hymno Trisag*. 28: 'to Pneuma enhupostaton ekporeuma kai problēma ek Patros men, Huiou de, kai mē ex Huiou, hōs Pneuma stomatos Theou, logou exaggeltikon').

6. The Holy Spirit is the medium between the Father and the Son and he is connected to the Father through the Son (*De fide orthod*. I, 13: 'meson tou agennētou kai gennētou kai di' Huiou tō Patri sunaptomenon').

This pneumatological teaching is clearly Catholic, but it is only one expression of the mystery of the Spirit; there are others, not only in the West, but also in the East. It can, however, be regarded as a suggested synthesis of the common Greek tradition.

At Florence, the Greeks' *per Filium* was reduced to the *Filioque*. The Old Catholics who attended the Bonn conference did the opposite. The Russian Holy Synod, however, appointed a commission to continue the work and strengthen relationship with the Old Catholic Church in 1892. Two historians were given the task of preparing a report. Each did it in his own way. We shall examine B. Bolotov's work below. The other historian, A. L. Katansky, presented the *a Patre solo* as *the* teaching of the Orthodox Church. The Old Catholics also appointed a commission. Its members unfortunately decided to call the Son the 'secondary cause' of the procession of the Holy Spirit,[3] something that neither Thomas Aquinas nor the theologians at the Council of Florence would ever have allowed themselves to say. B. Bolotov died at the age of forty-six in 1900, after having caused a great controversy in Russia with his theses.[4] Even nowadays, they were accepted categorically by such theologians as Sergey Bulgakov and Paul

Evdokimov,[5] but vehemently rejected by Vladimir Lossky, who has said that it is not the historian's duty 'to judge dogmatic values as such'.[6]

Bolotov distinguished three levels of doctrinal statements—the level of dogma formulated in the creeds and at ecumenical councils, that of individual theologies, and, between these two levels, that of the theologoumena, expressions of faith formulated by one or more Fathers at the time when the Church was undivided and accepted by that undivided Church. Bolotov published a systematic and well-documented study, which concluded with twenty-seven theses. I give below the most important elements of these theses:[7]

(1) The Russian Orthodox Church regards as a dogma that has to be believed only the following truth: the Holy Spirit proceeds from the Father and is consubstantial with the Father and the Son. The other aspects, insofar as they do not have the same meaning, should be regarded as theologoumena.

(2) The fact that the idea that the Holy Spirit proceeds, comes or shines from (*ekporeuetai, proeisi, eklampei*) the Father through the Son is frequently found in patristic texts, its occurrence in the treatise on *Orthodox Faith* by John Damascene, above all its introduction into the synodicon of Tarasius of Constantinople, the orthodoxy of which has been confirmed not only by the East, but also by the orthodox West in the person of the Roman pontiff Hadrian, and even by the Seventh Ecumenical Council, give to this idea of procession such importance that theologians cannot simply regard it as the private opinion of a Father of the Church, but are bound to accord it the value of an ecumenical theologoumenon, so to speak, with authority everywhere in the orthodox East.

(3) The opinion that the expression *dia tou Huiou* implies nothing but a temporal mission of the Holy Spirit in the world leads to violent distortions (*Verdrehungen*) of some patristic texts.

(4) At least we cannot find fault with this interpretation, according to which the expressions frequently found in the teaching of the Fathers of the Church of the Holy Spirit's coming through the Son and his shining or manifestation from the Father through the Son contain an indication of a mysterious aspect in the activity, the life and the eternal relationships of the Holy Spirit with the Father and the Son, an aspect that is also known as the Holy Spirit's dwelling and remaining in the Son (*meson, anapauomenon*).

(5) This aspect is the imaginative expression of the identity of nature (*sumphues*) between the Spirit and the other two Persons and of that incomprehensible truth, revealed in the gospel, that the Holy Spirit is the third and the Son is the second Person of the Holy Trinity.

(6) This doctrine is not identical in meaning with that which is revealed in the words *ek tou Patros ekporeuetai*, if these words are interpreted in the strict sense of the technical terms *ekporeutos* and *ekporeuetai*.

(7) As a result of this, the Holy Spirit proceeds from the Father alone, in the strict sense of the word *ekporeutos*. This thesis, however, is not a dogma, but only a theologoumenon.
. . .

(11) The formula *ex Patre et Filio*, as found in the writings of St Augustine, is not

194

identical in its terminology, nor even in its meaning, with the teaching of the Eastern Fathers.

. . .

(13) The difference in opinion between Western and Eastern Christians is not so much in the words *ex Patre Filioque* as in the Augustinian idea that is connected with it, namely of a single spiration by the Father and the Son, according to which both form the single principle of the Holy Spirit. This idea is unknown to the Eastern Fathers; as we know, none of them ever said that the Son was *spirans* or *sumproboleus*.

(14) Even as a private opinion, we cannot recognize the Western *Filioque* as equivalent in authority to the Eastern *di' Huiou*.

. . .

(19) Within God's unfathomable plan, however, no protest was made by the Eastern Church at the time of St Augustine against the view suggested by him.

(20) Many Western Christians who preached the *Filioque* to their flocks lived and died in communion with the Eastern Church, and no objection was raised on either side.

(21) The Eastern Church honours the Fathers of the early Western Church as it honours its own Fathers. It is therefore quite natural that the West should regard the individual opinions of those Fathers as holy.

. . .

(25) Photius and those who followed him remained in communion with the Western Church without obtaining from that Church an explicit and conciliar denial of the *Filioque*, even, as far as we know, without asking for it.

(26) It was therefore not the question of the *Filioque* which caused the division in the Church.

(27) The *Filioque*, as an individual theological opinion, ought therefore not to constitute an *impedimentum dirimens* for the re-establishment of communion between the Eastern Orthodox and the Old Catholic Churches.

The interchange between Orthodox and Old Catholics in the matter of the Holy Spirit has continued until the present time. During the discussions in September 1966 in Belgrade, the representatives of the Orthodox Church observed that the promise made in 1931 and 1932 to withdraw the *Filioque* clause from the creed had been kept only in part. The Old Catholics had only done so subject to the reservation that the true elements of the doctrine expressed by the clause might always be retained as a free, private opinion, and this did not satisfy the Orthodox. The latter, or at least the Greeks among them, asked for a simple and total denial of the Latin construction of the mystery which, they claimed, could not claim to be regarded as equivalent to the 'through the Son' of the Eastern Fathers.[8]

In their proposal to refer to an earlier state of affairs in which there had not yet been any opposition between the teachings of the Churches, the Old Catholics seem, however, to be weakening their links with the Western tradition that has begotten them and sustains them.[9] Is it possible to go back to a situation preceding the events of history? Do we not have to accept the inheritance of our fathers? The International Conference of Old Catholic

Bishops, which comprises the pastors of the Churches belonging to the Union of Utrecht, made the suppression of the *Filioque* in the creed official for all those Churches in 1969, claiming that the addition of this clause had not been made in a canonical manner, that it had an inadequate theological foundation, and that it had contributed to the disunity of the Churches. At the conference held in August 1975 at Chambésy, the Old Catholics simply adopted the Orthodox position.[10]

B. ORTHODOX AND ANGLICANS

For a long time, the Anglicans have wanted as much as the Old Catholics to enter into relationships and, if possible, into communion with the Orthodox Churches. They have a deep sympathy for the religious spirit of the East and this sympathy goes back far into the past. The *Filioque*, however, forms part of the Catholic inheritance that has been preserved in the Church of England and appears in several official doctrinal texts.[11]

The pneumatological question has been discussed in the course of several approaches made by members of the Church of England to the Orthodox Church. Between 1716 and 1725, for example, the Nonjurors attempted to establish relationships and intercommunion with the Patriarchate of Constantinople.[12] The first article raised for discussion was apparently that of the *Filioque*.[13] After this, there were only personal exchanges for a long time.[14]

Together with the Old Catholics, the Anglicans took part in the Bonn Conference of 1875 and the Conference in Belgrade in 1966. I have already discussed these above. Between the two conferences, F. V. Puller visited and had conversations with Mgr Evlogy in Russia in May 1912. Puller kept to Tarasius' profession of faith (see above, pp. 53 and 57), namely that *Filioque* and *dia tou Huiou* were equivalent, which his Russian Orthodox hosts accepted.[15] Mgr Evlogy told Brilliantov, who was questioning Puller, that he authorized him to say that, despite the different formulae, the teaching was the same. These words were printed in the official bulletin of the Holy Synod.

It is interesting in this context to look at the different positions adopted at the two Lambeth Conferences in 1920 and 1930.[16] Reference was made back to the Bonn Conference of 1875. The Anglicans were still prepared to suppress the *Filioque*, but they insisted that this term, in which their Church had for centuries confessed its faith, was quite open to a true meaning. They encountered resistance on the part of the Orthodox on this point.[17]

Progress is inevitably slow and difficult in a question in which the Churches preserve their faith in the formulae of creeds and their liturgical celebration. In their recent conferences with Eastern Christians, the Anglicans have once again committed themselves to suppress the *Filioque* in the creed, irrespective of the merits or demerits of its doctrinal content.[18]

196

NOTES

1. For one member of the Orthodox hierarchy at least—Mgr Anthony, the Archbishop of Finland, has been quoted—it was a question of 'obtaining a foothold in the middle of the Romano-Germanic world' and of thus 'giving a terrible blow to the heart of Roman Catholicism': see the Old Catholic *Revue internationale de Théologie*, 5 (1897), 111.

2. For the history of this question, see A. Palmieri, 'Filioque', *DTC*, V, cols 2331–2342. For the text of the Bonn Conference, see H. Reusch, *Bericht über die vom 10. bis 16. August 1875 zu Bonn gehaltenen Unionskonferenz* (Bonn, 1875). For the conference itself, see E. B. Pusey, *On the Clause 'And the Son' in regard to the Eastern Church and the Bonn Conference* (Oxford, 1876); E. Michaud, 'L'état de la question du "Filioque" après la Conférence de Bonn de 1875', *Revue internationale de Théologie*, 3 (1895), 89–99.

3. The text will be found in *Revue internationale de Théologie*, 5 (1897), 1 and 2.

4. A. Palmieri, 'Filioque', *op. cit.* (note 2); see also M. Jugie, *Theologia dogmatica Christian. Orient. ab Eccl. cath. diss.*, II (Paris, 1933), pp. 467–478.

5. S. Bulgakov, *Le Paraclet* (Paris, 1946), pp. 99ff., 116, 137; P. Evdokimov, *L'Esprit Saint dans la tradition orthodoxe* (Paris, 1969), pp. 74–75.

6. See V. Lossky, *In the Image and Likeness of God* (Eng. tr.; London and Oxford, 1975), p. 72. This comment is reminiscent of the remark attributed to Cardinal Manning at the First Vatican Council, although it is more moderate.

7. The German text of Bolotov's report will be found in *Revue internationale de Théologie*, 6 (1898), 681–712; Fr. tr. in *Istina*, 17 (1972), 261–289. I give here the same extract that Fr Malvy gave, under the pseudonym of 'Valmy', in his 'Bulletin de Théologie russe', *Etudes*, 101 (1904), 856–879, especially 866–867. See also M. Jugie, *op. cit.* (note 4), p. 460.

8. See the preparatory report by S. Karmiris of Athens in *Istina*, 13 (1968), 404–424, and the Declaration of the Inter-Orthodox Theological Commission, *ibid.*, 425–432, especially 428.

9. This is at least what I have found in an article by U. Küry, 'Die Bedeutung des Filioque-Streites für den Gottesbegriff der abendländischen und der morgenländischen Kirche', *Internationale Kirchliche Zeitschrift*, 33 (1943), 1–19.

10. See *Irénikon*, 47 (1975), 514–515.

11. In the Niceno-Constantinopolitan Creed, the *Quicumque* Creed, the litany, the Ordinal and the fifth of the Thirty-Nine Articles. The Church of England, however, leaves its ministers a great deal of freedom in their interpretation of the doctrines contained in these and other texts.

12. The documentation has been edited by L. Petit in Mansi, 37 (Paris, 1905), cols 369–624.

13. The Nonjurors were prepared to suppress the *Filioque* in the creed. On the doctrinal question, they noted that *dia* and *per* were not equivalent; they justified the procession *a Filio* by using the same texts, both biblical and patristic, that the Scholastic theologians had employed, although they did not make use of Scholastic arguments and syllogisms. In suggesting a basis for union (Mansi 37, cols 387–388) they simply adopted the Orthodox position.

14. The most interesting episode among these personal contacts is provided by William Palmer of Magdalen College, Oxford; for the whole of Palmer's mission, see S. Tyszkiewicz, 'Un épisode du Mouvement d'Oxford, La mission de William Palmer', *Etudes*, 136 (1913), 43–61, 190–210, 329–347. In a letter of exposition to Khomiakov, he expressed astonishment that all that the Orthodox Christians wanted the Catholics to do was to take the word *Filioque* out of the creed, while leaving them free to retain their teaching: see Birkbeck, *op. cit.*, below, p. 49. Khomiakov justified this practice, saying that it was not heretical and had never been condemned as contrary to Scripture by any council, but that it was simply an opinion that the Eastern Church regarded as wrong. The mistake that the Latins had made was to have added a purely human opinion to the truth of the creed: see W. J. Birkbeck, *Russia and the English Church. Containing a Correspondence between M. W. Palmer and*

M. Khomiakoff in the Years 1844–1854 (London, 1895; 2nd ed., 1917), pp. 60ff. It is interesting to note the open attitude of the Russian Orthodox: see, for example, in other contexts, Mgr Sergey, Mgr Evlogy to F. V. Puller, and Mgr Basile Krivocheine. Professor N. O. Lossky, the father of Vladimir Lossky, though that the opposition between the Catholics and the Orthodox in the question of the *Filioque* could be overcome by a further evolution of dogma: see his Russian-language *Questions of Russian Religious Consciousness* (Berlin, 1924), pp. 325ff.; quoted by Clément Lialine, *De la méthode irénique* (Amay, 1938), p. 24 and note. Sergey Bulgakov thought that the difference expressed in the two traditions between the *Filioque* and the *dia tou Huiou* was 'neither a heresy nor a dogmatic error, but a difference between theological opinions'; there was, in his view, 'no dogma concerning the relationship between the Holy Spirit and the Son' and he even went so far as to accept the *Filioque* for the West at least: see *op. cit.* (note 5), pp. 140–141. Finally, see also V. Soloviev's questions in the appendix to this chapter.

15. See *DTC*, V, col. 2336; M. Jugie, *op. cit.* (note 4), II, pp. 479ff.
16. For the 1920 Lambeth Conference, from the Anglican side, see *Terms of Intercommunion suggested between the Church of England and the Churches in Communion with Her and the Eastern Orthodox Church* (London, 1921), especially sections VII and VIII; these details will also be found in G. K. A. Bell, *op. cit.*, below, pp. 80–81. For the Orthodox side, see the report made by their delegation to the Conference in G. K. A. Bell, *Documents on Christian Unity*, I (London, 1924), pp. 64–65. For the 1930 Lambeth Conference, see the *Report of the Joint Commission* (London, 1932), pp. 14, 32–33.
17. See the *Report of the Joint Commission*, *op. cit.*, p. 14.
18. See *Irénikon*, 48 (1975), 362, for the work of the mixed sub-committees, July 1975; *Irénikon*, 49 (1976), 507–508, for the session held at the highest level at Zagorsk in July and August 1976; see also K. Ware and C. Davey, eds, *Anglican-Orthodox Dialogue. The Moscow Agreed Statement* (London, 1977), pp. 87ff.

APPENDIX

Below I give the first four questions of the nine asked by Vladimir Soloviev (†1900): see M. d'Herbigny, *Un Newman russe. Vladimir Soloviev* (Paris, 1911), p. 196:

Do the canons of ecumenical councils that stipulate that the faith of Nicaea should be preserved intact have the meaning or the letter of the Niceno-Constantinopolitan creed in mind?

Does the word *Filioque* added to the early text of the Niceno-Constantinopolitan creed inevitably contain a heresy? If it does, which ecumenical council condemned this heresy?

If this addition, which appeared in the creed of the Western Churches in the sixth century, and which was known in the East in the middle of the seventh century, contains a heresy, how is it that the last two ecumenical councils, the sixth in 680 and the seventh in 787, did not condemn this heresy and did not anathematize those who had accepted it, but, on the contrary, continued in communion with them?

If it is impossible to affirm with certainty that this addition (*Filioque*) is a heresy, is every orthodox Christian not free to follow, in this question, the opinion of Maximus the Confessor, who, in his letter to the priest Marinus, justified this addition and gave it an orthodox meaning?

4
SOME SUGGESTIONS FOR AGREEMENT

All those who have studied the question in the Eastern and the Western traditions have agreed that there is a difference in content in the terms *ekporeuesthai (ekporeusis)* and *procedere (processio)*. The fact that this difference was not observed early enough is at the origin of two parallel but not wholly corresponding movements in the two traditions. *Ekporeuesthai* pointed to the origin and could only be applied to the Father. On the Latin side, the same meaning was approached if Augustine's *principaliter* was added to the *procedere*. This is really contained in the *Filioque tanquam ab uno principio*, since the single principle is that of the Father and it is only in the Son as received from the Father. But *that* is precisely what is not *expressed*. Hence the criticism of the Orthodox Christians that has been repeated until the present time, despite the responses made to that criticism, that the West has sought to affirm two principles of the Holy Spirit. The formula *per Filium* would, in this respect, be more satisfactory. How would it be if Thomas Aquinas' formula in the *Summa*—'duo spirantes, *unus Spirator*—were accepted? More than one Latin Catholic theologian has noted the inherent weakness in the Latin formula and has from time to time, tried to remedy it.[1] How can the different state of the *duo spirantes* be expressed in the one 'spiration'?

Paul Henry, who has specialized in the theology of the Trinity, has made the suggestion that the *Filioque* should be abandoned and replaced by a different formula which might better express the reality, for instance *ex unione Patris et Filii procedit*.[2] This formula, however, expresses neither the *principaliter* nor the monarchy of the Father.

Juan-Miguel Garrigues has suggested a way of agreement which merits the greatest attention.[3] He has shown that the West has, since Tertullian, had a theology of the three consubstantial Persons in terms of procession, or a theology of an order of procession from the Father, in consubstantiality. The problem to which the Cappadocian Fathers had to find a solution against the teaching of Eunomius, that of a theology of subordinate participation, smacking of a hierarchical emanation characteristic of Platonism, was unknown in the West. The Cappadocians were led to make an antinomical distinction in God between the divine essence and the hypostases. This meant that there was a possibility of speaking in a differentiated manner of the procession of the third hypostasis and his participation in the common divine substance. According to Cyril of Alexandria, Gregory of Cyprus, Gregory Palamas and others, the Spirit has his hypostatic existence from the Father alone, but his substantial existence (*huparchein*) from the Father and the Son according to his mode of existence as the third Person in the divine consubstantiality. Garrigues says: 'In their hypostatic name, which cannot be communicated, the Son and the Spirit are only in a relationship with the Father, who is, so to speak, the origin of their own personal originality. To the extent that the hypostasis is manifested in a mode of existence (*tropos tēs huparxeōs*), according to which it enhypostatizes the essence (the Latins and the Alexandrians say: according to which it proceeds in the essence), the divine Persons manifest an order according to which they are for one another the conditions of the consubstantial communion.' Finally, he suggests this formula as one which might satisfy both the Eastern and the Western Churches: 'I believe in the Holy Spirit, the Lord and giver of life, who, issued from the Father (*ek tou Patros ekporeumenon*), proceeds from the Father and the Son (*ex Patre Filioque procedit; ek tou Patros kai tou Huiou proïon*)'.

In the course of my study, I have been struck by the fact that, if I am not mistaken, the Greeks think of the hypostatic being as an absolute and autonomous value, after which they see the consubstantiality acquired through the dependence of origin on the monarchy of the Father and expressing itself in the triadic relationships of circumincession. Does this amount to speaking, in a differentiated manner, of the Father as the only source of the hypostasis of the Spirit and the Son as the condition of his full consubstantiality? Several of the Fathers would seem to support this view. Hilary of Poitiers, for example, wrote during his exile in the East:

> 'Everything that the Father has is mine; that is why I told you: "the Spirit will take what is mine and declare it to you" ' (Jn 16:15). Therefore he who is sent by the Son and proceeds from the Father, receives from the Son. And I wonder whether receiving from the Son and proceeding from the Father are the same. If we believe that there is a difference between receiving from the Son and proceeding from the Father, it is nonetheless certain that receiving from the Son and receiving from the Father are the same.[4]

According to Hilary, then, the Spirit proceeds from the Father and receives from the Son. And what the Father gives to the Son is 'everything', that is, the divine substance or essence. The Spirit therefore completes and manifests the unity of the consubstantial Trinity. Maximus the Confessor, for example, said:

> Just as the Holy Spirit exists by his nature according to the essence of God the Father, so too does he exist by his nature according to the essence of the Son insofar as he proceeds essentially from the Father through the begotten Son.[5]

They (the Latins of Rome) have shown that they have not made the Son the cause of the Spirit. They know, in fact, that the Father is the only cause of the Son and the Spirit, of the first by begetting and of the second by *ekporeusis* (original procession). They have, however, pointed to the procession through him (*to dia autou proïenai*) and have shown in this way the unity and identity of the divine essence.[6]

Both Gregory of Cyprus[7] and Gregory Palamas[8] outlined the terms by which, if this interpretation is correct, the Spirit receives his hypostatic being by *ekporeusis* from the Father and has his consubstantial being from both the Father and the Son.

Is this expression of the mystery acceptable as a suggestion for possible agreement between East and West? It would hardly seem to be acceptable to the Latins. Is there a difference between receiving hypostatic being and receiving consubstantiality? Would it not be more useful to develop the theme of the monarchy of the Father on the basis, for the Latins at least, of Augustine's *principaliter* as accepted and explained by Thomas Aquinas?[9] This idea could perhaps be taken to the point where, with a different terminology, the equivalence with the *dia tou Huiou* might be such that the formula of the Florentine union could be reversed and Monopatrism could be recognized as true at the same time as and to the same extent as Filioquism. This is what André de Halleux suggested.[10]

The ideal solution would be a vocabulary that of itself expressed the fact that, in the *tanquam ab uno principio*, the Father is the original source and the Son is associated or a participant. In the absence of such a vocabulary, however, it is desirable that the Latin formulation should be completed by the Greek. The Greeks express this by the difference between the verbs *ekporeusthai* and *proïenai*. The Latin only has the verb *procedere* to cover the meanings of both Greek verbs. The aspect of the Son that is recognized in the procession of the Spirit is his eternal being. There are many statements of this by the Greek Fathers, tinged, it must be stressed, with an apophatism that refuses to be drawn into more precise definitions, but this is sufficient.

What we have to aim at and what can, in fact, be reached is a recognition both of the unity of faith on both sides of Catholicity and of the legitimate difference between the two dogmatic expressions of this mystery. Each expression is consistent in itself, and each is impossible in the categories and vocabulary of the other side. In the course of ten centuries of discussion, neither side has succeeded in convincing the other or in persuading it to accept its point of view. There is no chance that this goal will be reached in the future. In fact, we may say quite unambiguously that this is not a goal to be pursued.

Both Eastern and Western Christians are baptized in a common faith. For both, 'the Spirit is confessed as the third Person-hypostasis of the one divine nature-essence and consubstantial with the Father and the Son'.[11] Both confess the Father as the Principle without principle or beginning of the whole divinity. Both profess the Son as not unrelated to the Father in the production of the Holy Spirit.

The expressions of this faith, however, are different, especially in the matter of the third of these points. There are two main causes for this:

(1) The Latin vocabulary cannot adequately convey the important shades of meaning contained in the Greek terminology. *Causa* is not exactly *aitia*; *principium* is wider in its use than *archē*; *procedere* does not render *ekporeuesthai* very well. This was not always sufficiently taken into account in the past. Each side was so certain of itself and had so little curiosity about the other's views that it only wanted to reduce those to its own ideas and formulae. More than half a century ago, V. Grumel wrote: 'What was above all required, but no one thought of doing it, was for each side frankly and loyally to explain the terms that it used and for this to be followed by mutual tolerance, leaving each Church free to retain its traditional way of expressing dogma, leaving intact the unity of faith in a diversity of languages and formulae'.[12]

(2) A different principle is used by each to establish the distinction between the Persons. For the Greeks, the difference is found in the modes of procession from the Father, that is, by begetting or generation and by *ekporeusis*. This affirms the distinction between the hypostases. Criticism by the Latins has never seriously disturbed the Eastern Christians, who have always steadfastly refused to regard the application of our rules of logic to the mystery of God as legitimate. In the West, however, we have always been conscious of the principle that, in God, everything is common, apart from what is distinguished by an opposition in relationship. I have already pointed out that this principle is not a defined article of faith. It does, however, express a very acute sense of consubstantiality within the Trinity.

In the debate about the ways in which each tradition is expressed, we must, if we are to deal satisfactorily with the difficulties and respond positively to each other's demands, find out why a given Father or teacher of the Church—who was often a saint inspired by the Spirit—approached a given question in a certain way and why he formulated in precisely that way a datum of a faith that is basically shared by both sides. We then have to recognize that we have in this way achieved an inadequate expression of the mystery, which has not been equally illuminated in all its aspects. We are therefore open to criticism from another teacher in the Church, but our work may in this way be completed.

I would conclude this section with a statement by Mgr Damaskinos of Tranoupolis, who is the Director of the Orthodox Centre at Chambésy. His words may seem fanciful, but they echo my own thoughts: 'It is both possible and necessary to explain, on the one hand, the formulations of the Greek Fathers and, on the other, those of the Latin Fathers, including the *Filioque*, and, while respecting the originality of each, to draw attention to the ways in which they are in agreement. From the fourth century onwards, the *Filioque* came to form part of the Western tradition, but it was never regarded as an obstacle to union until that union was ended for other reasons.'[13]

NOTES

1. One of these theologians was V. de Buck, who was appointed by the Jesuit General to be theologian at the First Vatican Council: see his 'Essai de conciliation sur le dogme de la procession du Saint-Esprit', *Etudes religieuses*, 2 (1857), 305–351, which is based on the agreement between the Orthodox confessions of faith and an assessment of the monarchy of the Father, 'unicum fontem Trinitatis'. M. Jugie, *De Processione Spiritus Sancti* (Rome, 1936), pp. 8–12, agreed that the power of spiration 'non esse eodem titulo eodemque modo in Filio sicut in Patre' and that 'formula Graecorum [per Filium] praeponenda videtur'. See also A. de Halleux, 'Pour un accord œcuménique sur la procession du Saint-Esprit et l'addition du Filioque au Symbole', *Irénikon*, 51 (1978), 451–469.

2. P. Henry, 'Contre le "Filioque" ', *Irénikon*, 47 (1975), 170–177.

3. J.-M. Garrigues, 'Procession et ekporèse du Saint-Esprit. Discernement de la tradition et réception œcuménique', *Istina*, 17 (1972), 345–366, and his earlier essay, 'Le sens de la procession du Saint-Esprit dans la tradition latine du premier millénaire', *Contacts*, 3 (1971), 283–309.

4. Hilary, *De Trin.* VIII, 20 (*PL* 10, 251A).

5. Maximus, *Q. ad Thal.* LXIII (*PG* 90, 972C–D).

6. See Maximus' letter to Marinus (*PG* 91, 136). See also B. Bolotov's seventh thesis, 4: 'the thesis of the *ek monou tou Patros ekporeuetai* should not be used to deny, for example, the thesis *ek monou tou Patros ekporeuetai, di' Huiou de proeisin*'.

7. Cited by O. Clément, 'Grégoire de Chypre, "De l'ekporèse du Saint-Esprit" ', *Istina*, 17 (1972), 442–456.

8. Cited, in J.-M. Garrigues, 'Procession et ekporèse', *op. cit.* (note 3), 365.

9. Thomas Aquinas, *In I Sent.* d. 12, q. 1, a. 2. There is also an excellent passage in T. de Régnon, *Etudes de théologie positive sur la Sainte Trinité*, IV (Paris, 1898), p. 103.

10. A. de Halleux, 'Orthodoxie et Catholicisme . . .', *RTL*, 6 (1975), 3–30, and *op. cit.* (note 1), which ends with these words: 'The Roman Catholic Church will be able to restore the creed (to its original state) and recognize the fundamental truth of Monopatrism as soon as the Orthodox Church also recognizes the authenticity of the *Filioque*, interpreted in the sense of the traditional *di' Huiou*'.

11. A. de Halleux, *op. cit.* (note 1), 458.

12. V. Grumel, 'S. Thomas et la doctrine des Grecs sur la procession du Saint-Esprit', *Echos d'Orient*, 25 (1926), 257–280, explained these questions of terminology very lucidly; my quotation is taken from page 279 of this article.

13. Mgr Damaskinos, 'Réflexions et perspectives au sujet du rétablissement de la communion sacramentelle', *Oriente Cristiano*, 15 (1975), 7–25; quoted in *Irénikon*, 48 (1975), 219.

5

SHOULD THE *FILIOQUE*
BE SUPPRESSED IN THE CREED?

As I have, with the passage of time, come to learn more about this question, my attitude has changed, I admit. It is a question that has been asked for a long time. The Latins' answer to it was easy, perhaps too easy. They were, it would seem, not sufficiently aware of the full gravity of the question. Anselm, Thomas and Bonaventure all declared that when Ephesus forbade any change to be made in the faith that had been formulated at Nicaea,[1] that meant a change that would make belief different or contrary. Every council, however, always defines more precisely a point of faith that is challenged at the time—Chalcedon, for example, justified the addition made to Nicaea by the Fathers of the First Council of Constantinople. If the clause *a Patre et Filio* was true, after all, why should it not be declared? It was when this point of doctrine was denied that the *Filioque* was added to the creed by a certain council in the West, with the authority of a Roman pontiff, as one who convokes and confirms councils.[2] These answers to the question were not without value, even if the last point was based on a principle that was contested by the Greeks.

From the very beginning of the Council of Union at Ferrara, the Greeks declared that they were prepared to accept union, but only on condition that the Latins were equally prepared to suppress the *Filioque* in the creed. Unity of faith would in fact be restored in this way.[3] This shows the great importance of this question. The Orthodox have continued to insist on the same question until the present time, although it is being asked nowadays in a very different climate of opinion and with a very different set of implications from 1438. At Ferrara and Florence, at that time, in the spirit of the chief protagonist of the Greek conditions, Mark Eugenikos of Ephesus, to have agreed to suppress the *Filioque* would, for the Latins, have been to admit a doctrinal error.[4] Nowadays, on the other hand, the suppression of the *Filioque* is discussed in an atmosphere which recognizes that two different expressions of a common faith may be compatible and equivalent to each other.

At Florence, as in the mediaeval treatises,[5] the Latins declared that the *Filioque* made no change in faith, but simply explicitated it more clearly. The prohibition at Ephesus against the introduction of a different faith, *hetera pistis*, implied a prohibition of a contrary faith, not of a more perfect

204

formulation. The Greek reply to this was that when a doctrinal point was made more precise by a council, that council formulated its own definition—it did not introduce it into the creed. Ephesus, for example, did not add *theotokos*, 'Mother of God' to 'born of the Virgin Mary' in the creed.

The Greeks, however, had a view of the creed rather different from that of the Latins. In the Eastern Church, converts were expected to profess their faith in the unchangeable form of the creed, which the Church also proclaimed doxologically in the liturgy. The Latins had a more intellectual and a more external view of the creed as a formula of faith or belief promulgated by a council or the Pope, the decisive point here being the authority promulgating it. If we go back to the prohibition formulated by the Council of Ephesus, for example, we can see how this came about in the history of the council itself. It wanted to avoid accepting as the official profession of faith of the Church one or other of the many creeds that existed at the time, Since this would have opened the door to accepting doubtful or even heretical formulations.[6] Both the Council of Ephesus and the later councils of the Church up to the Second Council of Nicaea thought of *hetera pistis* as a teaching that was contrary to that of Nicaea. From the historical point of view, then, the Latins were right.

The situation is quite different when viewed from the point of view of the Church. The one-sided introduction of the *Filioque*, without consulting the Eastern Church, into a creed of ecumenical value was not only a way of behaving that was canonically illicit, but also an action which devalued the unity of the Christian family. Khomiakov called it 'moral fratricide'. There was also a certain touch of contempt for the Eastern Christians in the Carolingian period. It is true, of course, that the Eastern Christians held the Council in 381 without calling a single Latin bishop, an action which caused Ambrose to complain about the *communio soluta et dissociata*.[7] The West recognized its own faith in the text of Constantinople and 'received' the Council as 'ecumenical', but there are many examples of refusal to accept a decision because of a failure to participate in it. The Monophysites, for example, used the Nicene prohibition against making any new definition of faith as an argument against Chalcedon.[8] I think, however, that the Latins, including Anselm and Thomas Aquinas, have all too lightly shrugged off the Greek criticism that they were neither called nor consulted.

Ecumenism consists to a very great extent of repairing the damage that has been done in the past. If this task is to be done properly, a knowledge of the history of the period is incomparably useful.

As we have already seen, the Old Catholics and the Anglicans have decided to suppress the *Filioque* in the creed.[9] The Theological Commission of the World Council of Churches, 'Faith and Order', organized two meetings on 25–29 October 1978 and on 24–27 May 1979, at Klingenthal in Alsace, with the task of discussing precisely the question with which we are concerned here. There were Roman Catholics among the participants.

There was a unanimous vote in favour of the following resolution, which is clearly not a decision of the Church, but has its own importance: 'The original form of the article of the Niceno-Constantinopolitan creed on the Holy Spirit . . . (the text of this article follows) . . . should be recognized by all as the normative form of the creed and be re-introduced into the liturgy'.[10] Many Catholic theologians have also pronounced in favour of this suppression.[11] The formula is already not obligatory for Eastern-rite Catholics.[12] On 31 May 1973, the Greek Catholic hierarchy decided to suppress the formula in the Greek text of the creed.[13] As far as I personally am concerned. I would say categorically that I am in favour of suppression. To suppress the *Filioque* would be a gesture of humility and brotherhood on the part of the Roman Catholic Church which might have wide-reaching ecumenical implications. I can, however, only see this happening under two conditions, both of which are necessary if the suppression is to have a sound basis:

(1) Together with recognized and authoritative representatives of the Orthodox Churches, the non-heretical character of the *Filioque*, properly understood, should be made clear and recognized, as should the equivalence and complementarity of the two dogmatic expressions, 'from the Father as the absolute Source and from the Son' and 'from the Father through the Son'. This was the path followed at Florence. It is still a valid course, though, if it were retraced today, it would take place in a different climate, one in which the Eastern tradition and its depth would be fully respected. The Orthodox should not, for their part, go beyond the implications in the 'from the Father alone' of the monarchy of the Father and the demands made by the New Testament texts.

(2) The Christian people on both sides should be prepared for this so that it may be done in the light, in patience, with respect for each other's legitimate sensibilities, and in love. We should 'love one another so that we are able to profess with a single heart our faith in the Father, the Son and the Holy Spirit, the one consubstantial and indivisible Trinity'.[14]

NOTES

1. This prohibition will be found in canon VII of Ephesus: see J. Alberigo *et al.*, *Conciliorum Œcumenicorum Decreta*, 3rd ed. (Bologna, 1973), p. 65. For the use of this text in polemics, see M. Jugie, 'Le décret du concile d'Ephèse sur les formules de foi et la polémique anticatholique en Orient', *Echos d'Orient*, 30 (1931), 257–270.
2. See Anselm, *De proc. spir. sanct.* 13 (ed. S. Schmitt, *Opera*, II, pp. 211–212); Bonaventure, *In I Sent.* d. 11, a. un., q. 1 (Quaracchi ed., I, pp. 211–213); Thomas Aquinas, *De Pot.* q. 10, a. 4; *ST* Ia. q. 36, a. 2, ad 2: 'Sed postea insurgente errore quorumdam, in quodam concilio in Occidentalibus partibus congregato expressum fuit auctoritate Romani Pontificis'. This vague comment by Thomas, who was usually so precise, is very surprising.

It comes from a *Contra Graecos* by a Dominican in Constantinople in 1252: see A. Dondaine, *Arch. Fratr. Praed.*, 21 (1951), 390ff. It was commonly believed that every council formulated a confession of faith: see my article 'St Thomas Aquinas and the Infallibility of Papal Magisterium', *The Thomist*, 38 (1974), 87, notes 15 and 16, for references.

3. H. J. Marx has written an exhaustive study: *Filioque und Verbot eines anderen Glaubens auf dem Florentinum. Zum Pluralismus in dogmatischen Formeln* (Steyl, 1977).

4. See J. Gill, *The Council of Florence* (Cambridge, 1959), pp. 261ff. For the dramatic events following the council, see pp. 349ff.

5. Bonaventure, *In I Sent.* prol., a. 2: 'est additio distrahens, et est additio complens . . . in qua additum est consonum' (Quaracchi ed., I, p. 23).

6. See H. J. Marx, *op. cit.*, pp. 203ff. The addition of the *Filioque* seems to be in no way scandalous in itself—with the reservation that it is a one-sided approach—if it is seen in the context of the whole history of the Church's creeds: see the preface by J. Gribomont to G. L. Dossetti, *Il Simbolo di Nicea e di Constantinopoli* (Rome, 1967).

7. Ambrose, *Ep.* 13, 6 (*PL* 16, 953): 'Cohaerere communionem nostram cum Orientalibus non videmus' (No. 5) and 'postulamus ut ubi una communio est, commune velit esse iudicium concordantemque consensum' (No. 8)—these are golden rules!

8. See *Or. Chr. Period.*, 18 (1952), 55.

9. This was the last promise made by the Anglicans to the mixed Commission that met at Pendeli in July 1978: *Episkepis*, 195 (15 September 1978), 13. It was approved by the Lambeth Conference in 1978: see the *Report of the Lambeth Conference, 1978*, pp. 51ff.

10. *SOEPI* (Geneva, June 1979).

11. See H. J. Marx, *op. cit.* (note 3); A. de Halleux, *Irénikon*, 51 (1978), 469, which contains his report to the Klingenthal Commission.

12. This decision was made by Benedict XIV in his bull *Etsi pastoralis* (26 May 1742).

13. This decision can be explained and justified by a knowledge of the fact that the terms *ekporeuesthai* and *procedere* are not identical and by the agreement between the two formulae as confirmed by the declaration made by Maximus the Confessor, and by the dialogue between Anselm of Havelberg and Nicetas of Nicomedia. The text of this pastoral instruction will be found in *Les Quatre Fleuves*, 9 (1979), 75–78, which deals with 'God as revealed in the Spirit'.

14. Invitation and introduction to the recitation of the creed in the liturgy of St John Chrysostom.

6

DID THE *FILIOQUE*
HAVE AN ECCLESIASTICAL
IMPACT?

Vladimir Lossky thought that the *Filioque* was the cause of all the conflicts between Orthodoxy and Roman Catholicism, conflicts amounting, in his view, to as many doctrinal errors in the West. The *Filioque* was especially linked to consequences in the sphere of ecclesiology. André de Halleux has provided a very precise survey of the whole, with references to Lossky's work (here given in brackets):[1]

> The Spirit is here reduced to the function of a link between the two other Persons and one-sidedly subordinated to the Son in his very existence, in contempt of the genuine perichoresis. He thereby loses, together with his hypostatic independence, the personal fullness of his economic activity [Lossky, pp. 243–244]. The latter is henceforth seen as a simple means of serving the economy of the Word, both at the level of the Church and at that of the person. The goal of the Christian way of life therefore becomes the *imitatio Christi*, no longer a deification by the Holy Spirit [Lossky, pp. 166, 192–193]. The people of God are subjected to the body of Christ, the charism is made subordinate to the institution, inner freedom to imposed authority, prophetism to juridicism, mysticism to scholasticism, the laity to the clergy, the universal priesthood to the ministerial hierarchy, and finally the college of bishops to the primacy of the Pope. Creative and renewing source as he is, the Spirit was nevertheless expropriated by the Catholic Church, which made that Spirit the supreme guardian of the dispensation set up by Christ in favour of his Vicar. The Orthodox Church, on the other hand, has preserved the mutual subordination and the fertile tension between the economy of the incarnation and that of Pentecost [Lossky, pp. 156–157, 164, 166–167, 184–185; Clément, pp. 201–204].

Olivier Clément, who was Lossky's friend and disciple, took up the same themes.[2] When I spoke with Lossky some years ago, I made him very happy and even confirmed his teaching by making him acquainted with this Thomistic text: 'Those who maintain that the Vicar of Christ, the Pontiff of the Roman Church, does not enjoy the primacy of the universal Church, are committing an error which is similar to that which consists of saying that the Holy Spirit does not proceed from the Son. In fact, Christ, the Son of God, consecrates *his* Church and places *his* mark on it by his character and his seal, that is, by the Holy Spirit. . . . In the same way, the Vicar of Christ, as a faithful servant, keeps the Church subjected to Christ by the exercise of his primacy and his administration (*providentia*).'[3] It is not difficult to cite other more recent texts with the same import.[4]

It is possible to criticize the Western Church for a certain lack of pneumatology, as I have already done in this work and elsewhere.[5] On the one hand, however, I hope that my second volume to some extent makes up for this lack, while, on the other, I think it accords with the New Testament to protect with the utmost fidelity the reference of pneumatology to Christology. This is a condition of soundness for any life in the Spirit, any Renewal in the Spirit. It is something that we Catholics have in common with our Protestant friends, not simply because they are also Western Christians, but rather because they, like us, also follow the evidence of the Bible. Karl Barth, for example, has said:

> In all its aspects, the message of the New Testament implies, in the most indisputable way, that the Holy Spirit (and with him everything that makes the Church and Christians what they are) proceeds from Christ and from nowhere else. . . .
>
> This brings us to the very root of the theme which, within the framework of the doctrine of the Holy Spirit, led the Church to accept the *Filioque* into the creed (see I. 1, Eng. tr., pp. 546–557). The Church's conviction that the Holy Spirit should be recognized as the Spirit of Jesus Christ was such that it was obliged to affirm this and define it by saying: the Holy Spirit not only exists for us, he also exists from all eternity; he forms part of the hidden being of the Trinitarian God who manifests himself to us through revelation; he is the Spirit of the Father and the Son. Because he is the eternal bond which unites the Father and the Son, the Holy Spirit also creates the bond between the Father and all whom the Son has called in this world to be his brothers. The reason why no one can come to the Father except through the Son has to be found in the eternal mystery of God's being, because the Spirit through whom the Father draws men to himself is from all eternity also the Spirit of the Son, and it is through him that we are able to share in the divine sonship of Christ. If Western Christianity was right to recognize that the Holy Spirit to which revelation bears witness is none other than the Spirit of Christ and if the Western Church has really proclaimed the eternal God in the way in which he is pleased to encounter us, we should unhesitatingly declare our solidarity with that Church in the struggle that it has conducted to have the *Filioque* accepted.
>
> It is therefore possible for us to understand how Western Christian thinking came to be dominated throughout the whole of the Middle Ages by that sacramental and ecclesiastical objectivism which was so stubbornly—and victoriously— defended by the Popes, notably against Franciscan Spiritualism and its proclamation of the 'third age', that of the Spirit.[6]

Barth develops a criticism of spiritualism of the Joachimist type which, while appealing to the Holy Spirit, was to terminate in a humanism of man, expressing merely himself and his feelings. I have already discussed and criticized this in Volume I, pp. 126–133. The Orthodox can, of course, show that their own pneumatology does not in any way encroach on their sacramental and ecclesiastical objectivism and they can provide justifications of the titles 'Spirit of Christ' and 'Spirit of the Son'. Their theology is in this respect consistent and balanced. They are no more proof than we are against various forms of 'spiritual' teaching insufficiently closely linked to the Person of Christ, the Word and Son.[7] I would agree that a theological construction of the Triadic mystery in which the procession of the Spirit is linked to the Person of the Word, the Son, favours a tendency of thought which relates personal inspiration more closely to defined forms, but I am convinced that the whole body of consequences to which Lossky drew attention is too much his own reconstruction to be really precise.

The *Filioque* is contained in several of the Reformers' Confessions of Faith.[8] It is clear that the Reformers were able to keep the *Filioque* without subjecting 'the charism ... to the institution, inner freedom to imposed authority, prophetism to juridicism, mysticism to scholasticism, the laity to the clergy, the universal priesthood to the ministerial hierarchy', as Lossky has maintained.

Once again, we can, in this context, go back to André de Halleux for quotations which I have known for a long time: 'It is valuable to recall, for the sake of those who are very impressed by the anti-Filioquist conclusions of Lossky and his school, the words of an Orthodox theologian who was particularly allergic to juridicism and the Roman Catholic insistence on infallibility, Sergey Bulgakov, who said, in *Le Paraclet* (Paris, 1946), p. 124: "For many years, as far as we have been able, we have looked for traces of this influence (of the dogmatic difference in the life and the teaching of the two Churches) and we have tried to understand what was at stake, what this difference really meant and how and where it was manifested in practice. I have to admit that I have not succeeded in discovering this. In fact, I would go so far as to deny it" '.[9]

This, of course, is precisely why Bulgakov disputed the claim that the *Filioque* constituted a real dogmatic difference between East and West. On p. 141 of his book, we read, for example: 'The two sides ... cannot in practice prove that there is a difference between them in their veneration of the Holy Spirit, despite their disagreement about the procession. It is very strange that a dogmatic difference that is apparently so important should have had no practical repercussions, especially when, in most cases, a dogma has such an influence on practice that it determines the religious life of the community. In the present case, however, even the most extreme presentations of schismatic thought have so far not been able to apply this pseudo-dogma to the life of the Churches or to point to any practical consequences. It is possible to say that no important heresy concerning the Holy Spirit has ever been known in the life of either the Eastern or the Western Church, yet such heresy would have been inevitable if there had been a dogmatic heresy.' Paul Evdokimov has also commented in similar terms.[10]

It is just as possible to deny that the *Filioque* expresses a subordination of the Spirit to the Son or a conditioning of the Spirit by the Word as it is to accept it and be glad of it. At the same time, it is also possible to ask whether the decision to reject it would not lead to consequences which might be regarded either positively or critically, according to the Church community and tradition to which one belonged.[11] In the final analysis, then, the quarrel about the ecclesiological consequences of the *Filioque* is of doubtful value.

NOTES

1. A. de Halleux, 'Orthodoxie et Catholicisme: du personnalisme en pneumatologie', *RTL*, 6 (1975), 13–14. 'Lossky' in this quotation refers to V. Lossky, *The Mystical Theology of the Eastern Church* (Eng. tr.; London, 1957)—pp. 174–175 could be added to de Halleux's references; 'Clément' refers to O. Clément, 'Vladimir Lossky, un theologien de la personne et du Saint-Esprit', *Messager de l'exarchat du patriarche russe en Europe occidentale*, 8 (1959), 137–206.

2. O. Clément, *L'Eglise orthodoxe* (Paris, 1961), p. 50: 'Filioquism, according to which the "fontal" privilege which is peculiar to the Person of the Father alone is also shared by the Son, thus placing the Spirit, in his hypostatic existence, in a position of dependence on the Son, has certainly contributed to an increase in the authoritarian and institutional aspect of the Roman Church. The Trinitarian theology of the Orthodox Church, on the other hand, teaches that procession and begetting condition each other. . . . That is why there is also a mutual conditioning in a reciprocity of service between sacrament and inspiration, the institution and the event, the economy of the Son and that of the Spirit.'

3. *Contra Err. Graec.* II, 32 (Leonine ed., p. 87); cf. II, prol., where Thomas traces heresies back to betrayals in the sphere of Christology; see also Bonaventure, *De perf. evang.* q. 4, a. 3, n. 12 (Quaracchi ed., V, p. 197).

4. See, for example, B. de Margerie, *La Trinité chrétienne dans l'histoire* (Paris, 1975), p. 242.

5. See Volume I, pp. 152–154 and 156–160; see also my 'Pneumatologie ou "Christomonisme" dans la tradition latine?', *Ecclesia a Spiritu Sancto edocta. Mélanges théologiques G. Philips* (*Bibl. ETL*, XXVII) (Gembloux, 1970), pp. 41–63.

6. K. Barth, *Kirchliche Dogmatik*, I/2, pp. 272–273; Eng. tr. [not followed here], *Church Dogmatics*, I. 2 (Edinburgh and New York, 1956), p. 250. See also other Protestant texts cited in my study above (note 5), p. 63, note 90. To these can be added O. Henning Nebè, *Deus Spiritus Sanctus. Untersuchungen zur Lehre vom Heiligen Geist* (Gütersloh, 1939), pp. 60ff. who regarded the *Filioque* as the doctrine that prevented the theology of the Holy Spirit from falling into a kind of immanentism.

7. It is possible to see a parallel to Joachimism in the great Hesychastic movement in the Eastern Church: see L. N. Clucas, 'Eschatological Theory in Byzantine Hesychasm, a Parallel to Joachim da Fiore', *Byzantinische Zeitschrift*, 70 (1977), 324–244.

8. The sixteenth-century Reformers preserved the *Filioque* not only by retaining the Niceno-Constantinopolitan creed in its Western form and the so-called Athanasian creed, but also in the credal documents composed at the time of the Reformation: see, for example, the Lutheran Schmalkaldic Articles of 1537, I and II, the Formula and Book of Concord (1577 and 1580), and the *Solida Declaratio* VIII, 73. See also G. Hoffmann, 'Der Streit um das Filioque in der Sicht lutherischer Theologie', *Luthertum* (1941), 56ff. In the case of the confessions of faith of the other Reformed Churches, it is interesting to note that Zwingli accepted the *Filioque*: see G. W. Locher, *Die Theologie Huldrych Zwinglis im Lichte seiner Christologie* (Zurich, 1952), II, p. 110. Calvin's Confession of Faith of La Rochelle (1559), the Genevan Catechism of 1542, no. 91, and the Scottish Confession

(1560), art. 12, have nothing of interest to contribute to our particular subject. The Belgic and the Second Helvetic Confessions, on the other hand, both express the procession *ab utroque*: see the *Confessio Belgica* (1561), art. IX, and the *Confessio Helvetica Posterior* (1566), art. III. It would obviously not be possible to compile a list here of Protestant theologians who have written about this subject.

9. A. de Halleux, *op. cit.* (note 1), 3–30, especially 15, note 30.

10. P. Evdokimov, *L'Esprit Saint dans la tradition orthodoxe* (Paris, 1969), p. 76.

11. Karl Barth, whose Christological emphasis was dominant, as I have noted, in his theology, suggested a clear defence of the *Filioque*: *Church Dogmatics*, I. 1 (Eng. tr.; Edinburgh and New York, 1936), pp. 546–557. Speaking of the Russian theologians and philosophers, he said: 'It is possible that their way of thinking, in which philosophy and theology, reason and revelation, tradition and direct illumination, Spirit and nature, pistis and gnosis tend to be confused, should be explained by other, more immediate causes. . . . It is, however, not possible to prevent ourselves from making a connection between the stubborn denial of the *Filioque* and the way in which that idea is expressed, the manifestations of which it is all too easy to interpret as a consequence or a sign of that denial' (tr. based on Fr. tr.; cf. *ibid.*, p. 551). These comments are suggestive, but it is possible to question them. On the one hand, the Russians, of all the Orthodox, are the most open to the *Filioque*. On the other hand, the points mentioned by Barth depend, in my opinion, on a theology of the natural and the supernatural, which is in turn linked to an anthropology based on the image of God.

7
NINE THESES IN CONCLUSION

(1) Trinitarian faith is the same in the East and the West. Baptism is the same. The Christian, as Basil the Great pointed out, believes as he was baptized and praises as he believes. The experience of all the saints and all believers is the same, with the special marks that form part of the gifts of God. The action of the Spirit is similar. The Fathers are shared by both groups of Christians.

(2) The Tri-unity of God is a mystery which goes beyond all created understanding and expression. As Hilary of Poitiers said (*De Trin.* XII, 55): 'I possess the Reality although I do not understand it'.

(3) The East has remained closely attached to the terms expressed in Jn 15:26 and 16:14ff. Its theological construction of the mystery is quite consistent, but it also has its limitations.

(4) Several of the Greek Fathers have claimed that the Word, the Son, has a share in the production of the Holy Spirit, which cannot be reduced to the economic order. That share has, however, not been defined more precisely or systematically.

(5) If the Palamite theology of 'energies' is accepted, that function is situated not in the procession, but in the energetic manifestation of the Spirit. In the first place, however, Gregory Palamas accepted that, 'proceeding' from the Father alone, the Spirit also receives his consubstantiality from the Son. In the second place, the energetic manifestation is uncreated; it is God.

(6) The *Filioque* is necessary in the Latin Church's approach to the mystery, so that firstly the hypostatic distinction of the Spirit with regard to the Son, and secondly the Son's consubstantiality with the Father will be safeguarded.

(7) Historically, the *Filioque* was introduced as a measure against Arianism, by Augustine and by the Hispano-Visigothic councils. It was retained and expressed in the West at a time when there was communion between East and West and councils were even held in common.

(8) The *Filioque* did not cause any difficulties. The first evidence that we have of this is contained in Maximus the Confessor's letter to the priest Marinus. Maximus explains and accepts the *Filioque* in this letter in the sense of *dia tou Huiou*, without prejudice to the monarchy of the Father.

(9) It is in that direction that we must go. The Council of Florence, to which intelligent recourse must be had, traced the *per Filium* back to the *Filioque*, in an attempt to avoid making the Son a mere passage through which the Father's power of spiration flowed. It is necessary to combine the truth invested in the two formulae by showing that they are complementary. Conditions are favourable to this at the present time. The ideal solution would be to call a new council to complete the creed, for example, by re-using the terms of Jn 15:16 and 16:14–15, but also by avoiding all ambiguity.

The Roman Catholic Church could, under the conditions that I have outlined, suppress the *Filioque* in the creed, into which it was introduced in a canonically irregular way. That would be an ecumenical action of humility and solidarity which, if it was welcomed in its really 'genuine' sense by the Orthodox Church, could create a new situation which would be favourable to the re-establishment of full communion.

PART TWO

THE HOLY SPIRIT AND THE SACRAMENTS

1

THE 'SEAL OF THE GIFT OF THE SPIRIT'
SOME THOUGHTS ABOUT THE
SACRAMENT
OF 'CONFIRMATION'

In this chapter, I do not intend to discuss the present rite of this sacrament, although I may allude to it, its historical development, which is sufficiently well known,[1] or, apart from a few incidental references, the question of the minister who celebrates it. I intend to reflect on the significance of this sacrament. This chapter of sacramental theology is intended as a chapter of pneumatology. In the Apostolic Constitution *Divinae consortes naturae*, published on 15 August 1971, establishing the renewed rite of confirmation in the Latin part of the Church,[2] we read, for example: 'The sacrament of confirmation is conferred by anointing with sacred chrism on the forehead, by the imposition of the hand and by these words: "Accipe signaculum doni Spiritus Sancti" '. In note 20 of this Constitution, there are several references in ancient Christian tradition, all of them Eastern, to this formula 'the seal of the gift of the Spirit'. Paul VI also wrote about it, saying: 'As far as the words that are pronounced at the time of anointing with chrism are concerned, we have certainly assessed the dignity of the venerable formula used in the Latin Church at its true value. We have, however, concluded that it was necessary to give preference to the early formula of the Byzantine rite, in which the gift of the Spirit himself is expressed and the pouring out of the Spirit on the day of Pentecost is recalled.' This noteworthy declaration by the Pope is very close to my own concerns.

(1) *Uneasiness about Confirmation*

Confirmation is one of the sacraments of Christian initiation and is situated between baptism and the Eucharist. The unity of this initiation with these three stages would even seem to be the object of an ecumenical agreement.[3] Whether they are directly connected with baptism or separated from it by an interval of time, the rites of confirmation make the sacrament itself a simple completion of baptism, its final stage rather than a new and different sacrament. The classical statement that there are seven sacraments[4] can certainly be interpreted in this way.[5] Even those who keep to the distinction between the two sacraments—and the fact that they are administered separately would seem to make this distinction necessary—are anxious to stress the close connection between them. There is, however, also the difference between them, in that the second completes the first. That is why a believer who had only been baptized in an emergency had later to be taken to the bishop so that his initiation would be completed.[6]

The urgent question that arises in this context is: What does confirmation add to the grace of baptism? Christian baptism is, of course, baptism in the Spirit (Mk 1:8; Jn 1:33; 1 Cor 6:11; 12:13; Tit 3:5). It confers regeneration or rebirth and introduces the recipient into the life of Christ himself, that is, into his body (Rom 6:4ff.; 1 Cor 12:13; Gal 3:27). This is certainly stated in the Church's liturgies and the writings of the earliest Fathers.[7]

The Spirit, then, is given in baptism. Why is it therefore necessary to add another sacrament in order to give the Spirit? It is not possible to be confirmed without having been baptized, but it is possible to be baptized, that is, it is possible to receive the gift of the Spirit and of Christian life, without confirmation. What does confirmation bring? An increase in grace? This would not be specific enough. The seal placed on what the baptism has brought about? This is what many early texts and the Church's liturgy itself say. This Spirit has already been given, the grace of the gift is sealed liturgically. There is a single process, the different aspects of which are detailed in the liturgy by its ritual expression of them one after the other, including the baptism with water. It is only in this way that we can answer the difficult question asked by Protestants, namely: does confirmation not violate baptism and simply add a kind of useless repetition to the sacrament already administered?

And what is the situation when, in the Western Church, the two aspects have been separated and the second reserved for the bishop? It causes a certain uneasiness when it is said that children who are confirmed at the age of six, eight or twelve are given the Holy Spirit. Is it possible to measure the enormity of such a statement? It is all the more difficult to make such a claim when, in the vast majority of cases, nothing new seems to take place. It is, of course, said—quite correctly—that the supernatural reality takes place in secret and cannot be experienced immediately, and that in baptism too nothing seems to happen. Nonetheless, a certain dissatisfaction remains, and Christians who are already committed to the Christian way of life are troubled by the sacrament of confirmation. Doubts about the age at which this sacrament can most suitably be given, partly because it has become separated chronologically from baptism, likewise indicate the unstable state in which confirmation is situated.[8] The mere fact that these and other questions are still being asked again and again shows that the suggested replies have not proved satisfactory.

(2) *The meaning of Confirmation is derived from the Mystery of Christ*

This explanation is based on a relationship of analogies, but the fundamental structure which is indicated thereby is a combination of the Christological and the pneumatological aspects of the same mystery. There are two ways of approaching this structure and they are so alike that two authors, L. S. Thornton and J. Lécuyer, develop both of them in turn. The relationship can in fact be set out diagrammatically:

$$\frac{\text{Christ in his Pasch}}{\text{Pentecost}} = \frac{\text{baptism}}{\text{confirmation}}$$

Apart from Thornton and Lécuyer, this is also what P. Fransen and E. Schillebeeckx did.[9] The two sides of the equation are closely connected—Pentecost is the fiftieth day of the feast of Easter and is its fullness and completion. Baptism absorbs us into the death and resurrection of Jesus (Rom 6:3–11), and confirmation means life through the fruit of the Pasch, which is the sending of the Spirit by the Lord. This relationship of the two aspects of the same mystery has undoubtedly inspired the Church's liturgy. It can, for example, be found in the celebration of the Eucharist.

Thornton and, even more emphatically, Lécuyer have also referred to the two comings by which the Spirit firstly made Jesus exist as the Word of God and the son of Mary and secondly made him exist as the Christ, by anointing him at the time of his baptism with his messianic function in mind.[10] In the first case, the Spirit came to Mary to give existence to a son who was the Son of God. In the second case, he came to Jesus so that, when he was baptized and emerged from the water and prayed, he was consecrated for his mission (see Volume I, pp. 17–21). In the same way, baptism makes us be conceived and born as sons of God within the Church, and confirmation enables us to participate in Christ's messianic anointing. God created a body, then gave it breath.[11] 'Christ' means 'anointed'. In the writings of the Fathers and in the liturgy, we cannot be fulfilled as 'Christians' unless our spiritual anointing is expressed visibly and tangibly. Cyril of Jerusalem saw in the anointing of the Christian the antitype of Christ's own anointing.[12]

It has even been suggested—quite rightly—that, at confirmation, it should be stated that the candidate participates in those offices of Christ himself that were so frequently mentioned during the Second Vatican Council—the offices of king, priest and prophet.[13] The last-mentioned office is particularly important in the case of confirmation. In considering this, we are led to reflect about the connection between confirmation and the Church.

(3) *Confirmation in the building up and the mission of the Church*

In its description of the common priesthood of the people of God as expressed in the sacraments, the Second Vatican Council declared: 'Bound more intimately to the Church by the sacrament of confirmation, they (believers) are endowed by the Holy Spirit with special strength. Hence they are more strictly obliged to spread and defend the faith both by word and deed as true witnesses of Christ.'[14] *Perfectius Ecclesiae vinculantur*. This conciliar statement is concerned with individuals and is therefore not explicitly ecclesiological. No one would nowadays try to discover, by sound and critical exegesis, the sacrament of confirmation in the two episodes in the Acts of the Apostles, of the Samaritans who were evangelized and baptized by Philip and on whom Peter and John laid their hands (Acts 8:14–17), and of the Ephesian disciples of John whom Paul had baptized in the name of the Lord and on whom he also laid hands (19:1–6).[15] These texts nonetheless contain a meaningful analogy with the sacrament of confirmation, because what takes place in these episodes is a Christian initiation in two stages, marked by two closely linked rites. The very strong ecclesiological significance of the two episodes therefore rightly enables us to understand the ecclesiological meaning of confirmation itself. What takes place in the sacrament is that the baptized persons who are confirmed are fully fitted into the apostolic community of the Church. They are able to become full members of the Church when those who are called to bear the Church's apostolicity have publicly accepted them.

The fact that, in the West at least, confirmation has normally been administered by a bishop, as writers as early as Hippolytus and Cyprian[16] have attested, can be connected with this aspect of the sacrament. Christian initiation at this stage is so much a part of the Church that it has to be carried out and sealed by a leader of the Church, that is, by one who above all bears the Church's apostolicity, representing its unity and catholicity.[17]

This being vitally fitted into the Church can be understood by means of the Church's sacramental structure. M. D. Koster suggested this mode of understanding when he presented the Church as the corporation of Christians organized according to the sacramental characters of the baptized, the confirmed, deacons, priests and bishops,[18] each of these degrees corresponding to a ministry in the whole people of God. Confirmation pointed to the ministry of bearing witness and to participation in the prophetic nature of Christ, which consisted in particular in proclaiming and confessing faith in Christ, to the point, if necessary, of martyrdom.

There can be no doubt that the Holy Spirit is given especially in order to encourage the witness that should be borne to Jesus Christ in space and time.[19] In the Bible, the Holy Spirit is clearly connected with bearing witness—he provides the power, the dynamism and the continuity for this task.

The consecration and the grace of confirmation have also been characterized as a participation in the prophetic mission for which Christ himself was also consecrated.[20] In the heyday of Catholic Action, many members of the movement believed that the sacramental basis of their 'Action' was to be found in confirmation.[21] Others took a wider view and saw confirmation as a basis and a source for the apostolate of the laity.[22] The latter, however, derives from the fact of a Christian and the state of being a Christian. The Second Vatican Council observed that the lay apostolate results from all the elements that contribute to Christian existence: 'Incorporated into Christ's Mystical Body through baptism and strengthened by the power of the Holy Spirit through confirmation, they (the laity) are assigned to the apostolate by the Lord himself. They are consecrated into a royal priesthood and a holy people.... For the exercise of this apostolate, the Holy Spirit who sanctifies the people of God ... gives to the faithful special gifts as well (cf. 1 Cor 12:7).'[23]

(4) Confirmation in the growth of the baptized person

The baptismal gift is a gift of fullness because, through faith and the anointing of the Holy Spirit, it is a communion in the mystery of Christ with eschatological salvation in mind. It is what Irenaeus called, in a well-known text, the *communicatio Christi*. This fullness must be made present and developed, according to the good pleasure of the Lord indeed, as Irenaeus said, but also according to the degree of development of our conscious understanding and our entry into human society and the history of the world.

It is at this point that we can most suitably look at Thomas Aquinas' very remarkable theology of confirmation.[24] It is firmly situated within the Western practice of reserving the celebration of the sacrament for the bishop and separating it by an interval of time from the baptism conferred universally on infants, locating it *tempore juventutis vel pueritiae*.[25]

Thomas distributes the sacraments according to the stages in the life of man and the needs experienced at certain times. Baptism corresponds to birth, and confirmation to the period at which the child is no longer content to live *quasi singulariter, sibi ipsi* or *secundum seipsum*, in a way in which he is only conscious of himself and refers everything to himself, but *incipit communicare actiones suas ad alios*, in other words, when he begins to communicate with others, to feel part of a society in which others also exist and each person has the task of contributing to the life of that society, in history and, of course, in the Church.

Thomas connected the new aspect of this stage in human life with Pentecost and especially with the life of the apostles that was initiated at that time. It was then that they received the Holy Spirit as the grace of the apostolate—for the mission in which they were to bear witness and to evangelize.[26] It is not difficult to apply these ideas to contemporary data, but if we follow Thomas' own brief note, it also becomes obvious that his thinking goes very far. What he says is: 'sicut episcopus confirmat puerum contra pusillanimitatem'.[27] 'Small-mindedness' has a precise meaning in Thomas' teaching.[28] It can be defined as the fault, possibly even the sin, of acting at a level below one's full potential and not letting one's gifts bear

221

fruit. It is contrasted with 'great-mindedness' (*magnanimitas*), which is the virtue by which man realizes himself by committing himself.[29]

This Thomistic teaching about the place of confirmation in the growth of the baptized Christian is certainly very interesting and can be borne out and developed by modern psychology. There is an age when the child moves from an egocentric stage to a social stage, or at least a pre-social stage. At this point, he goes beyond the limited, protected environment in which he has hitherto lived *quasi singulariter, sibi ipsi* and is able to recognize the other person as different. This also coincides with a growth in personal consciousness and discernment. In Western Europe, this stage would seem to be reached when the child is seven or eight years old.[30]

These data obviously have to be transferred into the framework of ages of faith and of a Christian life open to the influence and impulses of the Holy Spirit. In that case, confirmation can be seen as the sacrament marking responsible entry into the communal and missionary life of the Church, following the *Praxeis tōn Apostolōn* reported by Luke. In this context, it is also possible to quote the Epistle to the Hebrews, according to which, we can, with 'our bodies washed with pure water', 'hold fast to the confession of our hope without wavering' and 'consider how to stir up one another to love and good works' (Heb 10:23–24).

(5) *The two Sacraments of Baptism and Confirmation and the two missions of Christ and the Spirit*

For a long time now,[31] I have thought that both the pair of sacraments, baptism and confirmation, and the twofold aspect of story and epiclesis in the celebration of the Eucharist are an expression, at the level of liturgical symbolism, of the double mission of the incarnate Word and the Spirit, with the aim of achieving the same task of saving communion with the mystery of God or deification. The work in question is the realization of the Body of Christ, his body as communion or Church and his sacramental body, after his physical or natural body. This was the work both of the Word, who assumed an individual human nature, and of the Holy Spirit, who sanctified the fruit that he had brought about in the womb of the Virgin Mary. Since then, we have had two closely combined aspects.

Jesus entered the water, identifying himself with those who repent, and, while he was praying, the Spirit came down on him. In the same way, Christians are plunged into the water as into his death (Rom 6:3) and the Spirit is given. This is a baptism of water and the Spirit, introducing the believer into the body which is the Body of Christ (1 Cor 12:12–13; see also Volume II, pp. 189–195). In the one single process of initiation, which is consummated in the sacrament of the body and blood of the Lord, a symbolic aspect, which completes the act of baptism and seals the gift received in it, the sacrament of the 'seal of the gift of the Spirit', has been distinguished from the baptism strictly so called. I believe that this is the liturgical expression of the two missions of the Word, the Son, and of the Holy Spirit, who are closely associated in the task of accomplishing the same work.

(6) *Suggestions for sacramental practice*

There has been a good deal of controversy about the sacrament of confirmation, as is clear from the discussions about the age at which it should be administered (see above, and note 8 below). It is obvious that two views, each with its own logic and truth, are in conflict with each other and would, moreover, seem to be irreconcilable.

The first is a theoretical or theological view. According to this view, there are three sacraments of initiation, and confirmation is simply the seal of baptism. It is so closely connected with baptism, in fact, that it is given with it, and in the early texts, it is sometimes very difficult to distinguish confirmation from the rite of baptism. In the East and in Spain, for example, practice conforms with this principle, and confirmation is administered to infants. It cannot be denied that the problem with regard to the baptism of infants is a very real one. The theological justifications that have been suggested are perfectly valid, but they do not solve the problems that have arisen in connection with the demands of evangelical truth as regards the present situation and what the facts demonstrate.[32]

The second view is pastoral, combining a concern for the truth of gestures and a knowledge of the possibility of personal commitment according to the age of the baptized person. This view has led to a search for a different way of administering the sacrament. This consideration is justified and indeed is almost a necessary consequence of the Western practice of separating confirmation from baptism and administering it at the age of reason, that is, at about seven years old,[33] and very often after first communion (see R. Levet, note 8 below). It is also frequently linked to completing a stage in religious education (the 'catechism'), itself often linked to requiring sufficient discernment and knowledge. In the present age, increasingly conscious of the individual and of personal responsibility, this view (which formed part of Erasmus' suggestions for reform) is inescapable. Not only in the practice of confirmation, but also in the view that we have of its function, it emerges clearly as a personal ratification of the baptismal commitment that we accepted in the faith of our parents and the Church, although we did not play an active part at the time.

If it is a question of honouring that, it is not enough simply to celebrate confirmation at the age of seven or eight or 'during the first years of school (and therefore before the child has received the Eucharist)'.[34] Should it be later still? The synod of German bishops in 1976, for example, suggested the age of twelve, while the Catechetical Congress at Munich in 1928 suggested fifteen, and A. Exeler, about eighteen.[35] If the logic of this option is to be fully respected, I would say confirmation should undoubtedly take place after puberty, when the young person's ways of feeling and perceiving reality are so fundamentally changed, the way is opened to an autonomous under-standing of himself, and he is on the inevitable threshold of adult life.

In my opinion, both the first and the second views outlined above contain truths that should be respected. Their perspectives are so diverse that they do not contradict each other. Each deals with a different aspect. I have often expressed my own attitude towards this question. It is that both truths should be given a place and the special attributes of each respected.

Confirmation is linked to baptism as its seal. If infants are baptized, the sacramental seal of the gift of the Spirit should also be conferred to them. The problems involved in doing this are no greater than those raised by infant baptism. The essential problem, after all, is that of infant baptism itself. There are very good reasons for administering infant baptism when the child's environment is Christian. Baptism is, of course, the 'sacrament of faith' and it calls for religious education, but catechesis can be given after-wards. I can, however, understand why parents delay the baptism of their children. They do so not for the wrong reason of letting the children choose for themselves when they are older, but because they feel that baptism requires knowledge and personal consciousness on the part of the child. They prefer therefore to present the child to the Church, enrol him as a catechumen and let him come to know and pray to Jesus and the God of Jesus Christ.

There should also be a personal act of commitment to the service of Jesus Christ, in the Church, in the presence of witnesses, made at the beginning of adolescence or on the threshold of adult life. For this to take place properly, there must be a ceremony and a choice of texts. The best arrangement would be for it to take place within the framework of the Eucharist, celebrated within the community. An environment of prayer is absolutely necessary. It calls for careful preparation, either in a course lasting for three weekends or in a retreat lasting for several days and should include exchanges with other, already committed Christians, who are able to manifest what commitment to the service of one's fellow-men in the Church means today. All this could take place in religious centres of various kinds. In this way, a beginning would be made in the training of committed, adult Christians. There would perhaps only be a few of them—those who really believed—but something would be happening.

I would very much like to see the members of the Renewal take part in such days of preparation and in the ceremony of confirmation. They would bring to it their vital conviction that 'Jesus lives' together with a warmth and a feeling of joy. It would be a feast of the Holy Spirit. With or without 'baptism in the Spirit', it would be the making real, to an adult personal consciousness, of the grace received unawares in the sacraments of baptism and confirmation.

NOTES

1. D. L. Greenstock, 'El Problema de la Confirmación', *La Ciencia Tomista*, 80 (1953), 175–228, 539–590; 81 (1954), 201–240; J. Lécuyer, 'La confirmation chez les Pères', *M-D*, 54 (1958), 23–52; E. Llopart, 'Las formulas de la confirmación en el Pontifical romè', *Liturgica*, 2 (Montserrat, 1958), 121–180; P. M. Gy, 'Histoire liturgique du sacrement de confirmation', *M-D*, 58 (1959), 135–145; B. Neunheuser, *Baptism and Confirmation* (Eng. tr.; Freiburg and London, 1964); L. Ligier, *La confirmation. Sens et conjoncture œcuménique hier et aujourd'hui (Théol. hist.*, 23) (Paris, 1973); K. F. Lynch, *The Sacrament of Confirmation in the Early-Middle Scholastic Period*, I (London, 1957).
2. *AAS* 63 (1971), 657–664.
3. I am thinking here of the report made by the 'Faith and Order' Commission of the World Council of Churches on baptism, confirmation and the Eucharist: 'Baptême, Confirmation et Eucharistie', *Istina*, 16 (1971), 337–351.
4. This is affirmed by both the Orthodox and the Roman Catholic Churches. See, for example, the profession of faith made by Michael Palaeologus (6 June 1274) (*DS* 860); the Decree *Pro Armenis* (22 November 1439) (*DS* 1310); the Council of Trent, Session VII (3 March 1547), canons 1 and 3 (*DS* 1601 and 1603); the profession of faith of Pius IV (1564) (*DS* 1864); the profession of faith given to the Eastern-rite Catholics by Benedict XIV (16 March 1743) (*DS* 2536). The weakness of these statements is that they contain nothing concerning the analogical, non-uniform and inadequately equal character of the sacraments.
5. See, for example, K. Rahner, *The Church and the Sacraments* (Eng. tr.; Freiburg, Edinburgh and London, 1963), who has pointed out that baptism and confirmation can be seen as two degrees of the one sacrament, just as the diaconate, the presbyterate and the episcopate are degrees in holy orders. See also S. Amougou-Atangana, *Ein Sakrament des Geistempfangs? Zum Verhältnis von Taufe und Firmung* (Freiburg, 1974), p. 279; Hans Küng, 'La confirmation comme parachèvement du baptême', *L'Expérience de l'Esprit. Mélanges Schillebeeckx (Le point théologique*, 18) (Paris, 1976), pp. 115–150.
6. The Council of Elvira (in 306), canons 38 and 77 (Mansi, 2, 12B and 18C; *DS* 120): by the laying-on of hands; the Council of Laodicea, canon 48 (Mansi, 2, 571): by anointing with chrism.
7. See J. B. Humberg, 'Confirmatione baptismus perficitur', *ETL*, 1 (1924), 505–517; G. W. H. Lampe, *The Seal of the Spirit* (London, 1951); B. Neunheuser, *op. cit.* (note 1); *idem*, 'Taufe im Geist. Der heilige Geist in den Riten der Taufliturgie', *Archiv für Liturgiewissenschaft*, 12 (1970), 268–284; P. T. Camelot, 'Sur la théologie de la confirmation', *RSPT*, 38 (1954), 637–657, especially 643ff.; *idem*, *Spiritualité du baptême (Lex orandi*, 30) (Paris, 1960), pp. 237–256.
8. See R. Levet, 'L'âge de la confirmation dans la législation des diocèses de France depuis le concile de Trente', *M-D*, 54 (1958/2), 118–142, based on an analysis of more than 600 documents; G. Biemer, 'Controversy on the Age of Confirmation as a Typical Example of Conflict between the Criteria of Theology and the Demands of Pastoral Practice', *Concilium*, 112 (1978), 115–125.
9. L. S. Thornton, *Confirmation. Its Place in the Baptismal Mystery* (Westminster, 1954); P. Fransen, 'De gave van de Geest', *Bijdragen*, 21 (1960), 403–424; E. Schillebeeckx, *Christ the Sacrament of Encounter with God* (Eng. tr.; London and New York, 1963), pp. 197–210. See also W. Breuning, 'When to Confirm in the Case of Adult Baptism', *Concilium*, 2, no. 3 (1967), 48–54; *idem*, *op. cit.* below (note 15).
10. J. Lécuyer, 'Le sacerdoce royal des chrétiens selon S. Hilaire de Poitiers', *L'année théologique*, 10 (1949), 302–325; 'Essai sur le sacerdoce des fidèles chez les pères', *M-D*, 27 (1951), 7–50, especially 40ff.; 'La grâce de la consécration épiscopale', *RSPT*, 36 (1952), 380–417, especially 390–391; 'Mystère de la Pentecôte et apostolicité de la mission de l'Eglise', *Etudes sur le sacrement de l'ordre (Lex orandi*, 22) (Paris, 1957),

pp. 167–208; *Le sacerdoce dans le mystère du Christ* (*Lex orandi*, 24) (Paris, 1957), in which Lécuyer relates the incarnation and Easter to baptism in chapters VIII and IX and the Jordan and Pentecost to confirmation in chapters XI and XII; 'Théologie de l'initiation chrétienne chez les Pères', *M-D*, 58 (1959/2), 5–26.

11. Adam (Gen 2:7); the dry bones of Ezekiel (Ezek 37). See Cyprian, *Ep*. 754, 7, 5.

12. Cyril of Jerusalem, *Cat. myst*. III, 1 (*PG* 33, 1088ff.; *SC* 126 (1966), pp. 122 (Greek) and 123).

13. Adolf Adam, *Firmung und Seelsorge* (Düsseldorf, 1959), pp. 52–54; E. J. Lengeling, 'Die Salbung der christlichen Initiation un die dreifache Aufgabe des Christen', *Zeichen des Glaubens. Studien zu Taufe und Firmung. Balthasar Fischer zum 60. Geburtstag* (Freiburg, 1972), pp. 429–453. Lengeling himself summarizes the results of his study in the following words: 'The trilogy of the post-baptismal anointing of "confirmation" can be found in the West Syrian, Jacobite, Byzantine, Armenian, Coptic and Ethiopian liturgies and in the Western non-Roman liturgies (the *Missale Gallicanum* and Peter Chrysologus), but also in the Roman post-baptismal anointing which, both structurally and because of its content, can be compared with the anointings of the "confirmation" type found in other liturgies which are the forerunners of the typically Roman anointing on the forehead in the sacrament. Textual evidence of this trilogy includes the prayer of anointing with chrism, the preface to the consecration of the chrism, texts in the Roman Catechism and in the writings of recent authors and, since 1969, the present form of the anointing. It is therefore not exclusively the work of Vatican II, but there is evidence, in the rite of baptism itself, of a very early and universal tradition.' Among the 'recent authors' to whom Lengeling refers in the above passage on p. 452 of his article, I would count myself, especially in my book *Lay People in the Church* (Eng. tr.; London, 1957).

14. Dogmatic Constitution on the Church, *Lumen gentium*, 11, with a note containing references not only to Thomas Aquinas, but also to Cyril of Jerusalem and Nicholas Cabasilas.

15. Not only H. Conzelmann, *Die Apostelgeschichte* (Tübingen, 1963), pp. 54ff., but also many Catholic authors have insisted on the fact that the Spirit of the charisms is given. References will be found in E. J. Lengeling, *op. cit.* (note 13), p. 128, note 26, and W. Breuning, 'Apostolizität als sakramentale Struktur der Kirche. Heilsökonomische Überlegungen über das Sakrament der Firmung', *Volk Gottes, Festgabe J. Höfer* (Freiburg, 1967), pp. 132–163, especially p. 155, note 57 and, for our theme, pp. 152ff.

16. See Hippolytus, *Trad. apost.* 22, 23 (*SC* 11, pp. 50–53); Cyprian, *Ep*. 73, 9, 2 (*PL* 3, 1115; ed. W. von Hartel, p. 784). See also the Council of Elvira (note 6 above). In the East, the priest gives the sacrament, but uses *myron* consecrated by the bishop (or patriarch). Hence we read in the Dogmatic Constitution on the Church, *Lumen gentium*, 26, 3, that the bishops are the '*original* ministers of confirmation' (*ministri originarii confirmationis*). In the Latin Church, the sacred oils are also blessed by the bishop, and a simple priest administers confirmation only when the bishop commissions him to do so. It is always desirable for the sacrament to be celebrated by a minister who, because of his title, points to the diocesan authority.

17. This aspect was stressed by L. Bouyer, 'La signification de la confirmation', *VS* (Suppl), 29 (15 May 1954), 162–179, especially 175–177; also by J.-P. Bouhot, *La confirmation, sacrement de la communion ecclésiale* (Lyons, 1968).

18. M. D. Koster, *Ekklesiologie im Werden* (Paderborn, 1940); *idem, Die Firmung im Glaubenssinn der Kirche* (Regensburg and Münster, 1948). F. Vandenbroucke also showed, in 'Esprit Saint et structure ecclésiale selon la liturgie', *Questions liturgiques et paroissiales*, 39 (1958), 115–131, that the liturgy speaks of the Holy Spirit above all in connection with the three 'character' sacraments, that is, baptism, confirmation and holy orders.

19. This is clear in Acts: see G. Haya-Prats; and in John. See Volume I, pp. 44–47, 57–59; Volume II, pp. 24–35.

20. See A.-G. Martimort, 'La Confirmation', *Communion solennelle et Profession de foi* (*Lex orandi*, 14) (Paris, 1952), pp. 159–201.

21. V. M. Pollet, 'De Actione Catholica', *Angelicum* (1936), 453, note 1; E. Sauras, 'Fundámento sacramental de la Acción católica', *Revista española de Teología*, 3 (1943), 129–258; Damasus Winzen, 'Anointed with the Spirit', *Orate Fratres*, 20 (1945–1946), 337–343, 389–397, especially 394. Pius XI took note of the connection between Catholic Action and confirmation, but did not make it the sacrament of the movement: see his letter of 10 November 1933 to the Patriarch of Lisbon.

22. See D. Winzen, *op. cit.* (note 21); J. R. Gillis, 'The Case for Confirmation', *The Thomist*, 10 (1947), 159–184; Max Thurian, *La confirmation. Consécration des laïcs* (Neuchâtel and Paris, 1957). There are many more books and articles on this subject.

23. See the Decree on the Apostolate of the Laity, *Apostolicam actuositatem*, 3.

24. Thomas Aquinas, *ST* IIIa, q. 72 and par. For this theology, see J. R. Gillis, *op. cit.* (note 22), 159ff.; P. Ranwez, 'La confirmation, constitutive d'une personnalité au service du Corps mystique du Christ', *Lumen Vitae*, 9 (1954), 17–36; J. Latreille, 'L'adulte chrétien, ou l'effet du sacrement de confirmation chez S. Thomas d'Aquin', *RThom*, 57 (1957), 5–28; 58 (1958), 214–243; Adolf Adam, *Weltoffener Christ* (Düsseldorf, 1960; 2nd ed. 1962), pp. 146ff.; R. Bernier, 'Le sacrement de Confirmation dans la théologie de S. Thomas', *Lumière et Vie*, 51 (1961), 59–72.

25. This is Thomas' phrase: see *ST* IIIa, q. 72, a. 8, c and ad 2. For him, *In IV Sent.* d. 40, expos. textus, *pueritia* extended from seven to fourteen, and *juventus* from twenty-one to fifty! Etienne Gilson has pointed out that he apparently took this idea from Isidore of Seville.

26. *ST* IIIa, q. 72, a. 2, ad 1; *In IV Sent.* d. 7, q. 1, a. 2, sol. 2. The apostles already had 'Spiritum Sanctum in munere gratiae quo perficiebantur ad ea quae ad singulares personas eorum pertinebant, tamen in die Pentecostes acceperunt Spiritum Sanctum in munere gratiae quo perficiebantur ad promulgationem fidei in salutem aliorum'.

27. *Comm. in Ep. ad Eph.* Prol., where Thomas is dealing with children between the ages of seven and fourteen.

28. *ST* IIa IIae, q. 133.

29. *ST* IIa IIae, q. 129ff.; see also R.-A. Gauthier, *Magnanimité. L'idéal de la grandeur dans la philosophie païenne et dans la théologie chrétienne* (*Bibl. thom.*, 28) (Paris, 1954). See also my book, *op. cit.* (note 13), pp. 391ff. The whole of chapter VI of Part Two of that book is a development of what I am merely suggesting here.

30. I am not competent to judge in this case and I lack information. I have therefore consulted Jean Piaget and, in the *Encyclopaedia Universalis*, VI, p. 223, the article 'Enfance'; also P. H. Maucorps and R. Bassoux, *Empathies et connaissance d'autrui* (Paris, 1960); R.-F. Nielsen, *Le développement de la sociabilité chez l'enfant* (Neuchâtel and Paris, 1961); F. Tilmann, 'Um den rechten Zeitpunkt der Firmungspendung', *Diakonia*, 1 (1966), 285–291.

31. I have thought this for a long time, at least since 1949: see *RSPT*, 452.

32. It is useful in this context to read P.-A. Liégé, 'Le baptême des enfants dans le débat pastoral et théologique', *M-D*, 107 (1971), 7–28, and to re-read Pascal, 'Comparaison de chrétiens des premiers temps avec ceux d'aujourd'hui', small Brunschvicg edition, pp. 201–208.

33. See also the *Cordex iuris canonici*, canon 788.

34. See Hans Küng, *op. cit.* (note 5), p. 146.

35. References will be found in G. Biemer, *op. cit.* (note 8), 117–118.

2

THE EUCHARISTIC EPICLESIS

Relatively late in the history of Christianity, a controversy developed concerning the consecration or conversion of the bread and wine into the body and blood of Christ. Although the controversy was apparently about the moment of consecration, it was in reality concerned with the agent of that consecration: the priest as the representative of Christ in the sacramental action in which Christ's words were re-used, or the Holy Spirit as invoked in the epiclesis? This is, however, the wrong way of postulating the problem, since it gives the wrong emphasis to this controversial question.

This controversy dates from the first half of the fourteenth century, the first witness to it being that great and greatly loved master, Nicholas Cabasilas.[1] The Latins had criticized the fact that the Greeks had added prayers for the consecration of the sacred elements after the words of institution, which brought about the consecration. Whenever the question was approached in this way, that is, whenever the question was about the precise moment of the eucharistic transformation, to the exclusion of every other consideration, conflict was inevitable.[2] What the Latins did in the case of the words of institution, the Greeks did in the case of the epiclesis, and the same climate of controversy persisted. It was perpetuated at Florence, with Mark Eugenikos. We must get away from this area of controversy. It is not too difficult to do so.

A list of all the books and articles that have been written on this question of the epiclesis would fill several pages and would include studies of the whole problem, monographs and discussions of various aspects.[3] I shall not provide a history of the question here, since it is not difficult to find that elsewhere. It is, however, necessary to go into details in some respects and to quote a number of texts if we are to understand what is at stake and to appreciate the depth of the issues involved. Paul Evdokimov, for example, wrote: 'It would seem that, in the ecumenical dialogue, the question of the epiclesis is as important at present as that of the *Filioque*, since it is above all in the light of the epiclesis that the *Filioque* can be correctly resituated within the whole problem'.[4]

The Epiclesis cannot be separated from the whole of the Eucharistic Prayer or Anaphora
The meaning of the Anaphora

'Epiclesis' (*epiklēsis*) means 'invocation'. The term has come to have the limited and technical meaning of an invocation for the sending of the Holy Spirit after the account of the institution, but this is too particular a significance that has been attributed to it in the course of the discussions about this subject. Even in the work of those Fathers of the West Syrian tradition who witness to the most formal epicleses, this 'invocation' applies to the whole of the anaphora.[5] It is this anaphora that we have to consider here. Those excellent scholars, Le Quien and Combefis,[6] certainly insisted on this. In his study of the question, Louis Bouyer cited and explained the whole of the eucharistic prayers and in this way broke free of the discussions concentrated on particular elements treated in detail.

Although they are very diverse in their formulation, these eucharistic prayers are homogeneous in their spirit and have a very clear sense of the whole.[7] Their common aim is to realize the Christian mystery, that is, to extend to the Body of Christ, the Church, the salvation, deification and membership as sons that Christ himself has gained for us through his incarnation, his death, his resurrection and glorification through the Spirit, and finally the gift of Pentecost. The Eucharist is the synthesis, communicated sacramentally and spiritually, of what God has done for us in and through Jesus Christ—as we sing in the office of the Feast of Corpus Christi, 'memoriam fecit mirabilium suorum'. This simple yet immense fact is expressed in the five aspects of the eucharistic prayer outlined below:

(1) An analogy, even a continuity, exists between the Eucharist and the incarnation. This is clearly revealed in Justin Martyr's description of the Eucharist[8] and in Irenaeus' repeated statements, against the Gnostics, about the coming of the Lord in the flesh, linking this to the Eucharist, the 'unity of the flesh and the spirit . . . in which the earthly and the heavenly realities are intermingled'.[9] Gregory of Nyssa makes use of this analogy to point to our communion with the immortality of God through the Eucharist.[10] The great teachers of the Eastern Church who supported the veneration of icons, such as Germanus I of Constantinople (†738), insofar as the treatise quoted below was written by him, and the Syrian Christians are particularly categorical. Germanus first draws attention to the anamnesis—Christ's incarnation, suffering and death, resurrection and glorious second coming—and then goes on to say, speaking of the incarnation:

> 'From the womb, before the dawn, I have begotten you' (Ps 110:3). Once again he (the priest) pleads (*parakalei*) that the mystery of the Son may be accomplished (*teleiōsai*) and that the bread and the wine may be begotten (*gennēthēnai*) and transformed into the body and blood of Christ and God and that the 'today I have begotten you' will be accomplished (Ps 2:7). In this way, the Holy Spirit, invisibly present by the pleasure of the Father and the will of the Son, demonstrates the divine energy and, by the hand of the priest, consecrates and converts the holy gifts that are presented into the body and blood of our Lord Jesus Christ, who said: 'For them I consecrate myself, that they may also be consecrated in truth' (Jn 17:19).

How does this happen? 'He who eats my flesh and drinks my blood abides in me, and I in him' (Jn 5:56).[11]

The Eucharist, then, is like a begetting every day of Christ, body and blood. Just as the incarnation came about through the action of the Holy Spirit, so too should the consecration and sanctification of the gifts sanctify believers and incorporate them into Christ. Theodore of Mopsuestia traces the eucharistic epiclesis back to the action of the Spirit in the resurrection of Christ.[12]

(2) As Louis Bouyer emphasized, the epiclesis is closely connected with the anamnesis. In the anaphora, thanks are given ('Eucharist') for the good things of creation and for the history of salvation. In the eucharistic prayer of John Chrysostom, the account of the institution is introduced as follows: 'When he had come and had accomplished the whole economy of salvation which was for us, the night when he handed himself over . . .'. This is followed by the account of the institution, which is in turn followed by the anamnesis: 'Mindful . . . of everything that has been accomplished for us—of the crucifixion, of his burial, of his resurrection on the third day—we offer these things that come from you'. Then, after a brief acclamation by the people, the epiclesis begins, with the words: 'We offer you this spiritual sacrifice'. It is thus inserted into the anamnesis.

The same applies to Hippolytus' *Apostolic Tradition*: 'Mindful of his death and resurrection, we offer you the bread and wine . . . and we ask you to send your Holy Spirit upon the offering of your holy Church'.[13] In the Roman canon, which was established in its essential aspects in the fourth century, we also find, after the account of the institution, 'Unde et memores (the anamnesis), offerimus . . .', a little later, 'Supplices te rogamus', which has frequently been regarded as the equivalent of an epiclesis. It is certainly true to say that the eucharistic prayer forms a single whole. What has to be accomplished in the believers through the action of the Holy Spirit comes from the sacrament-sacrifice, which is the commemoration of the actions and gifts of salvation, for which thanks are given.

(3) It is not possible, even though both may occur, to contrast an epiclesis for the consecration of the eucharistic gifts and an epiclesis asking for those present to be sanctified, that is, that the sacrifice-commemoration may have the fruits of grace. The two are in fact combined in certain formulae, such as the one contained in the *Apostolic Constitutions*. There are also several Greek patristic texts referring to an action of the Spirit with the aim of making the 'eucharisted' gifts something that sanctifies believers.[14] These epicleses follow the anamnesis immediately. What we have here is a movement that extends the mystery of Christ who has died and risen again to the believers—it envisages the people's communion as part of the consecration

230

of the gifts. That is also why several epicleses ask the Spirit to *sanctify* the bread and the wine, as in the liturgy of St James and that of St Mark.[15] Did Paul not already speak of it (see Rom 15:16; 1 Tim 4:5)? What the Eucharist has in mind is our deification through our union with the Spirit-filled flesh of Christ. For his part, Christ blessed, sanctified and filled with his Spirit the bread and the wine at the Last Supper.[16]

(4) It would be quite wrong to isolate the epiclesis which follows the anamnesis. There are in fact epicleses not only in the anaphora, before the account of the institution—as in Egypt[17]—but also before the epiclesis in the anaphora, even in the Roman rite. Avvakum believed that those of the prothesis consecrated the gifts. There is, for example, the dialogue between the priest and the deacon at the end of the 'great entrance' in the Byzantine liturgy. The liturgies of John Chrysostom and Basil the Great present it today in the following way:

> *Priest*: The Holy Spirit will come upon you and the power of the Most High will cover you with his shadow.

> *Deacon*: The Holy Spirit himself will concelebrate with us all the days of our life.[18]

(5) An epiclesis asking for the gifts to be consecrated, even after the account of the institution, was developed when the orthodox teachers of faith insisted, in opposition to Macedonius and the Pneumatomachi, on the personality and the divinity of the Spirit. Gregory Dix thought that the epiclesis was not authentically due to Hippolytus. Whatever may be the case, it is certainly not an epiclesis of consecration. It was apparently added during the second half of the fourth century, in the text of Addai and Mari.[19] J. Quasten has likewise shown that, before the First Council of Constantinople in 381, the descent of Christ into the water of baptism was invoked, whereas, after the Council, it was the coming of the Spirit that was invoked.[20] Louis Bouyer was therefore able to say:

> It is easy then to understand that at a time when it was thought necessary to stress the equal divinity and personality of the Spirit in the second half of the fourth century, and probably, as we shall see, in Syria, there developed what at first was merely a subordinate clause making up the first epiclesis: an express invocation of the descent of the Spirit, today, upon the eucharistic celebration, parallel to the invocation of the Son in the incarnation in order that its effect might be fulfilled in us (*op. cit.* (note 3 below), p. 184).

This was done especially in Western Syria—Antioch and other centres—during the second half or the last third of the fourth century. It is at this time and place that the texts of the so-called 'consecratory' epicleses appear.

231

The Fourth-Century Epicleses
Consecration by them or by the words of institution?

The three essential texts are:

The *Mystagogic Catecheses* of Cyril of Jerusalem (written *c*. 350) or of his successor, John II (*c*. 390 in that case):

> Just as, before the sacred epiclesis of the adorable Trinity, the breed and wine of the Eucharist were ordinary bread and wine, but, after the epiclesis, the bread becomes the body of Christ and the wine the blood of Christ. . . .[21] After having been sanctified ourselves by these spiritual hymns (the Trisagion), we implore the God who loves men to send the Holy Spirit on to the gifts placed here, so as to make the bread the body of Christ and the wine the blood of Christ, since everything that the Holy Spirit touches is sanctified and transformed.[22]

The liturgy of Basil the Great:

> We sinners also . . . dare to approach your holy altar and, bringing forward the symbols (*prosthentes ta antitupa*; S. Salaville: 'the antitypes') of the holy body and blood of your Christ, we implore you and invoke you, Holy of Holies, through the benevolence of your goodness, to make your Holy Spirit come down on us and on these gifts that we present to you; may he bless and sanctify them and present to us (*anadeixai*) (in) this bread the precious body itself of our Lord, God and Saviour Jesus Christ and (in) this cup the precious blood itself of our Lord, God and Saviour Jesus Christ, poured out for the life of the world, *changing them by your Holy Spirit*.[23]

The last words of this text, that I have italicized, do not appear in Brightman's classical edition and, according to H. Engberding, whom Bouyer follows, they were added to Basil's text. The word *antitupos* gives rise to a problem of interpretation. John Damascene (†749), who was writing within the context of the polemics with the iconoclasts, understood it to refer to the bread and wine before they had been sanctified by the epiclesis. This interpretation gave the epiclesis the meaning of a prayer of consecration to the exclusion of the words of institution.[24] Cyril of Jerusalem used the word *antitupos* in his sacramental catechesis in order to express a relationship between the visible sacramental reality and the spiritual reality that is made present by the sacrament. For example, baptism, according to Cyril, represented the passion of Christ (*Cat. myst*. II, 6), the anointing with chrism pointed to the anointing of Christ by the Spirit (*Cat. myst*. III, 1), and the bread and wine consecrated and received in communion pointed to the body and blood of Christ (*Cat. myst*. V, 20). In the seventeenth century, Bossuet translated this as 'the figures of the sacred Body and the sacred Blood'. The word *anadeixai* is also problematical. Bouyer translated it as '(may he) present to us', but S. Salaville said 'may he make of this bread', claiming that it was equivalent to *poiēsai, poiein* and other similar words. The meaning of consecration is therefore quite clear, but it does not necessarily exclude the words of institution. Here now is the third important text, taken from the liturgy of John Chrysostom, in the version that is most used:

> Calling therefore to mind . . . and offering you what is yours from all that is yours, in everything and for everything. . . . We offer you this spiritual and bloodless worship and we invoke you, imploring you to send your Holy Spirit of us and on these gifts that are presented and to make of this bread the precious body of your Christ, changing it by your Holy Spirit (Amen) and of what is in this cup the precious blood of your Christ, changing it by your Holy Spirit (Amen), so that they may be, for those who partake of them, for the soberness (S. Salaville: 'purification') of the soul, the remission of sins, the communication of your Holy Spirit, the fullness of the Kingdom, free access to you (*parrēsia*; S. Salaville: 'the pledge of trust') and not judgement or condemnation.[25]

It is worth noting in this context that the earliest Eucharists always either contain the words of institution or else refer to the words spoken by Jesus; Paul does this in 1 Cor 11:23ff., as do Justin Martyr ('the prayer of the word that comes from him', i.e. Christ), Irenaeus (*Adv. haer*. V, 2, 3) and Tertullian (*Adv. Marc*. IV, 40). These words constitute the Eucharist. It is, to tell the truth, not certain that Jesus himself consecrated the bread by saying 'This is my body'. He may have consecrated it by blessing (God) and have given the *consecrated* bread to his apostles, saying: 'This is my body given up for you'. The Scholastics, beginning with Peter Comestor (see P.-M. Gy, note 39 below), were acquainted with this question, but they said that Christ gave it to his Church to 'do this' in memory of him, using *his words*. The institution, then, is connected with the repetition of the account of the institution itself and the words of that institution. This is already clear from St Paul. The Orthodox, on the other hand, believed that it was no more than an account and that it was therefore necessary to add the epiclesis.[26] The Scholastics agreed that it was no more than an account, and that it was necessary for the celebrant to have the *intention* of speaking *in the name of and as in the person of Christ*.[27]

There was (and there is), in fact, only *one* Eucharist—the one celebrated by Jesus himself the night he was betrayed. Our Eucharists are only Eucharists by the virtue and the making present of *that* Eucharist. John Chrysostom throws a very clear light on this problem: 'The words "Increase and multiply", although they were only said once, continue to have an influence and to give you the power to procreate children. The same applies to the words: "This is my body". Although they were only spoken once, they give, and will continue to give until the end of the world, their existence and their virtue to all sacrifices.'[28]

It is quite correct to speak of the words of *institution*. The real question is: how are we to know by what means and by what mediation the words of institution will be effectively applied, now, to the bread and wine of this particular celebration?[29] This was the question asked by Nicholas Cabasilas in his argument for the epiclesis, after he had quoted John Chrysostom's text.[30] His reply was, of course, that it is through the prayer of the priest, in other words, the epiclesis. The Latins' reply was: it is through the words of institution said by the priest with the intention of doing what Christ instituted and what the Church celebrates. The truth, to which both the liturgies and very many authors testify, precludes maintaining the latter to the exclusion of the former.[31] The consecration of the sacred gifts is the act of Christ, the sovereign high priest who is active through his minister *and* through the Holy Spirit. The clearest evidence is undoubtedly provided by John Chrysostom, who asserts the consecration by the Spirit who was invoked in the epiclesis as vigorously as that by the priest pronouncing the words of Christ, or by John the Sabaite in his seventh-century *Life of Barlaam and Josapha* (see note 31 below). This twofold unity of divine action in the sacrament can be connected without difficulty to certain great constants and, in that sense, certain great laws that are effective in God's work, for example:

—the frequent bond between the word and the Spirit: see Ps 33:6; Is 59:21; see also my observations in Volume I, pp. 57–58, and Volume II, pp. 42–43, on bearing witness; see also Acts 4:19–21; 1 Tim 4:5;

—the fact that, in order to make his work after his departure present, Jesus deploys the joint mission of the apostolic ministry and of the Holy Spirit;[32]

—the existence of the two missions, which nonetheless do the same work; to accomplish this, not only was the incarnation followed by Pentecost, but also Jesus Christ himself, the Word made flesh, was sanctified and guided by the Spirit: see above, p. 165–171;

—the Trinitarian structure of the whole economy of salvation, which is reflected both in the creed, as a summary of faith, or in the anaphoras, most clearly in the liturgy of St James. As Gregory of Nyssa and Cyril of Alexandria pointed out, 'all grace and every perfect gift comes to us from the Father through the Son and they are completed in the Holy Spirit'.[33] Bessarion applied this Trinitarian structure to our eucharistic question.[34] S. Salaville saw it as the key to open the door to an understanding of the meaning of the epiclesis (*DTC*, V, cols 293ff.). There is also a parallelism between the creed and the anaphoras.[35]

The meaning of the celebration in the West
The ordained celebrant is himself a sacramental reality

This is, if not a dogma, at least a commonly accepted and official doctrine in the Catholic Church. In the West, then, the consecration of the bread and wine is accomplished by the words of the account of the institution spoken by a priest with the intention of doing what Jesus himself did. The Church has celebrated this from its very beginning (see below, pp. 239–240). The priest therefore acts not through his personal quality or energies, but *in persona Christi* or *in nomine Christi*, taking the place or playing the part of Christ, in his name.[36] This idea has antecedents of a very firm kind in the biblical notion of the *šalîaḥ*, the messenger commissioned by an authority that he makes present by representing, and also in the idea so well known in the early centuries of Christianity that the bishop (the priest) was the image of the Father or the image of Christ in the midst of the Christian community and over and against the people.[37] The most important value in the earliest texts is one of conformity or *model*; it is an iconic value. Together with this, however, there is a value of authority and power. This is found in the teaching of those excellent and well-loved martyrs Clement of Rome, Ignatius of Antioch, Irenaeus and Cyprian. The power comes from the Spirit (see the prayer for the consecration of a bishop in Hippolytus), but it also includes an authority that comes from that of the apostles and is ultimately received from Christ (see Irenaeus and Cyprian). The bishop (the priest) is therefore, in the community, in a sense the incarnation or at least the sacrament of Christ.[38]

I am aware of the fact that, from the twelfth century onwards, when the theology of the sacraments had been stabilized by the early Scholastic theologians and the sacrament of ordination had been defined as the power to consecrate the Eucharist, but above all as a result of accepting Thomas Aquinas' idea of the instrumental causality of the words spoken by the priest *in persona Christi*, the concept of the priest as the representative of Christ, playing the part of Christ, had become somewhat isolated, hardened and material. Thomas believed that the priest would consecrate the bread if he pronounced only the words 'This is my body', but, of course, on condition that he has the intention of fulfilling the sacrament.[39] The Catholic position cannot be traced back to this thesis, which has been widely disputed and which I, for my part, also reject.

The true perspective of the *in persona Christi* is sacramental. The priest who celebrates the Church's act of worship is himself a sacramental reality, that is to say, he represents, at the level of what can be seen, a spiritual reality. He is that reality in accordance with the fullness that is realized by the Church's worship. That fullness is defined, for example, in the papal encyclical *Mediator Dei* of 20 November 1947 and in the conciliar Constitution on the Liturgy, *Sacrosanctum Concilium*, 7, as the 'full public worship performed by the Mystical Body of Jesus Christ, that is, by the Head and his members'. It is in accordance with this organic reality with its two aspects that the priest represents Christ. He represents not only Christ, the sovereign high priest, in whose person he acts, but also the *ecclesia*, the community of Christians, in whose person he acts also. He therefore acts *in persona Christi* and *in persona Ecclesiae*. One of these aspects cannot be isolated from the other—the one is contained within the other. An insistence on the Christological aspect—this has occurred in the West—means that the *in persona Ecclesiae* is situated within the *in persona Christi*, which is consequently seen as the basis and the reason for the first. *Mediator Dei* presents the teaching in this way. If, on the other hand, the pneumatological aspect is emphasized, as the Eastern tradition loves to do, the *in persona*

Christi is more easily seen as situated within the *in persona Ecclesiae*. There is no denial here of the fact that the priest has received, through his ordination, the 'power' to celebrate the Eucharist and therefore to consecrate the bread and wine. The Eastern tradition teaches as firmly as the Western Church that only the priest can do this, but this does not mean that he can do it alone, that is, when he remains alone. He does not, in other words, consecrate the elements by virtue of a power that is inherent in him and which he has, in this sense, within his control. It is rather by virtue of the grace for which he asks God and which is operative, and even ensured, through him *in the Church*.

It is worth recalling at this point the meaning of the exchange of words between the one who presides over the celebration and the assembled people: 'The Lord be with you'—'And with your Spirit'. This does not mean simply 'and with you'. It means 'with the grace that you received through ordination for the common good; we are asking now for that grace to be made present in this celebration'.[40] The 'power' received at ordination and the making present of the gift of the Spirit, the ordained celebrant and the community or the *ecclesia* are united in the celebration of the Eucharist. In the Eastern rite, the epiclesis is spoken in the plural, indicating clearly that the whole community invokes the Spirit. The Roman canon, however, also has 'Memores offerimus' and 'Supplices te rogamus' in the plural. We are not so very far apart.

Several Orthodox theologians whom I have known and loved have, however, severely criticized the *in persona Christi*. This, for example, is what Paul Evdokimov had to say about this question.

> If the very deep reason for the conflict (which keeps the Eastern tradition apart from that of the West, the essential aspect of which is not the eucharistic epiclesis alone, but rather the epiclesis as an expression of the theology of the Holy Spirit) is to be grasped, it is important to recognize that, for the Greeks, the canon of the liturgy is a whole that is inseparable from the one Mystery. It cannot be broken down into different elements so that one central point can be, as it were, isolated. For the Latins, the *verba substantialia* of the consecration, the institutional words of Christ, are pronounced by the priest *in persona Christi*, which bestows on them a value that is immediately consecratory. For the Greeks, however, a similar definition of the priestly action—*in persona Christi*—which identifies the priest with Christ is absolutely unknown. Indeed, it is quite unthinkable. For them, the priest invokes the Holy Spirit precisely in order that the words of Christ, *reproduced and cited* by the priest, acquire all the effectiveness of the speech-act of God.[41]

It seems to me that we Western Christians have, by certain theological statements that we have made, prepared the way for and even caused a misunderstanding here. Statements, for example, such as *sacerdos alter Christus* have to be understood in their true sense, which is spiritual and functional, not ontological or juridical. What I have said here has been part of an attempt to allay suspicions and to come closer to a truth which is, I believe, common to both East and West. For the rest, many Orthodox also invest the *in persona Christi* with meaning. Here I would like to quote a number of contemporary authors; for earlier writers, I would refer to S. Salaville's article (*DTC*, V, cols. 253ff., 257), though I would cite in addition a text by John Chrysostom and another by Severus of Antioch. I begin with these:

Christ is there. . . . In fact, it is not a man who makes the gifts that are offered become the body and blood of Christ, but Christ himself, who was crucified for us. The priest stands there, *schēma plērōn* (*figuram implens*: 'fulfilling a role as figure') and saying the words, but the power and the grace are God's.[42]

The priest who stands at the altar fulfils the function of a mere minister there. Pronouncing the words as in the person of Christ and taking the action that he is performing back to the time when the Saviour instituted the sacrifice in the presence of his disciples. . . .[43]

I find it difficult to place a statement such as this (made by Paul Evdokimov): unlike what takes place in the Catholic Church, the Orthodox priest does not act *in persona Christi*, but *in nomine Christi*. I wonder whether this is not merely a linguistic quibble. The whole of Paul's writings and the whole of the Orthodox tradition provide evidence that *in persona Christi* and *in nomine Christi* are equivalent to each other. . . . The one who acts *in nomine Christi* acts through the power of the Spirit bestowed at the time of ordination. He acts effectively *in persona Christi* for the fulfilment of the *oikonomia* of the mystery.[44]

Like an icon, the priest must be transparent to the message that he bears without identifying himself with it. He must know how to be there without imposing his presence. If the priest enters the sanctuary, behind the iconostasis, this is neither a right nor a privilege, since only Christ has the right to be there. The priest is there as an icon, *in persona Christi*.[45]

In the Eucharist, the eternal priesthood of Christ is continuously manifested in time. The celebrant, in his liturgical action, has a twofold ministry: as the icon of Christ, acting in the name of Christ for the community, and also as the representative of the community, expressing the priesthood of all believers.[46]

The bishop is not simply the successor of the apostles and Jesus Christ himself, whose vicar he is. He is also the sacramental image (or icon) of the Saviour. That image is most fully revealed in the liturgical celebration and in presiding over the eucharistic assembly. Over and against the Church, then, the bishop has a place that is similar to that occupied by Christ himself.[47]

The liturgical expression of the Mystery in the two original traditions

Finally, we can say that the epiclesis confronts us less with a sacramental question, that is, with a problem as to the 'form' of the sacrament of the Eucharist, and much more with a question of Trinitarian *theo*-logy, or rather with a question of liturgical expression of the economy in which the mystery of the Tri-unity of God is revealed to us and is communicated to us.

The Orthodox rightly tell us that the anaphora forms a whole, from which one element, the account of the institution, for example, or the epiclesis, cannot be isolated and treated separately. No Orthodox would think of the consecration as taking place simply through the epiclesis.[48] It is, however, possible to ask whether consecration would take place if the epiclesis were omitted. . . .

In the West, unfortunately, too much and indeed almost exclusive attention has been given since the High Middle Ages to the words of Christ. This has resulted in the rest of the anaphora being devalued and the sense of the unity of the eucharistic prayer as a whole being endangered.[49] This emphasis undoubtedly came about as a result of Scholastic theology, since the sense of unity seems to have been present in the contemplative monastic communities of the twelfth and thirteenth centuries. Until the Middle Ages, no attempt was made to define the precise moment of consecration and even theologians gave considerable value to other moments than the account of the institution. Peter Lombard, for example, thought that an excommunicated priest could not consecrate the bread and wine because he was placed outside the Church and therefore could not say 'we offer you . . .', and the angel of the *Supplices te rogamus*—the epiclesis!—would not accept the offering of such a priest to take it up to the heavenly altar.[50] Whatever hypotheses may have been suggested in the past, we now tend once more to see the anaphora as a whole. The fact that a prayer is said after the account of the institution does not necessarily mean that the consecration takes place after it. It is interesting to quote Bossuet here:

> The spirit of the liturgies and, in general, of all consecrations does not lead us to concentrate on certain precise moments. On the contrary, it makes us consider the whole of the action in order to understand the entire effect. An example will make what I mean clearer. In the priest's consecration, hardly any scholars doubt any more, since the discovery everywhere of so many ancient sacramentaries, that the most important part is the laying on of hands with the prayer that accompanies it (however, after it, the bishop anoints the priest's hands, then makes him touch the chalice and, even after the new priest has celebrated, passes on to him the power to remit sins). Is it possible for anyone to say that a man is a priest without having received this power, which is so inseparable from this character? After all, what is said to him is: 'Receive it'. . . . Why, unless it is that on these occasions the things that are celebrated are so great, have so many different aspects and so many varied relationships, that the Church cannot say everything . . . in one place, and distributes its activity, however simple it may be in itself. . . . (Bossuet here adds the examples of the celebration of confirmation and the anointing of the sick.) . . . All this is an effect of human language which can only be explained bit by bit. . . .
>
> (XLVII) If this doctrine is applied to the prayer used by the Greeks, there will be no further difficulty. After the words of our Lord, the priest asks God if he will

change the gifts into his Body and Blood. This can be either the application of the thing to be done or the more special expression of the thing done. Nothing else can be concluded from the precise terms of the liturgy. . . . In this mystical language of the liturgies and in general in the sacraments, an expression is often given after what may have been done before, or rather, in order to say everything, an explanation is given in succession of what may have all taken place at the same time, without looking into the precise moments. In that case, we have seen that an expression is given of what may have been done already, as though it was done when it was expressed, with the result that all the words of the sacred mystery are related to each other and the entire activity of the Holy Spirit is visible.[51]

What led to the desire to state exactly when the consecration took place, at least from the time of Innocent III onwards, was the principle according to which the conversion of the bread and wine or their transubstantiation must be instantaneous.[52] A 'progressive', 'gradual' or 'dynamic' change in which the body and blood of the Lord might be there a little, then a little more and finally totally, was not envisaged.

This teaching is beyond dispute when applied to the *res et sacramentum*, the reality itself or the 'presence' of the body and blood. It seems less convincing if it is seen from the point of view of the liturgical rite and the celebration as such. There are several cases in which the precise moment of effectiveness is not adequately stated. These cases include, for example, the consecration of the holy oils on Maundy Thursday, or the laying on of hands as the 'form' of the ordination of priests, in which a number of priests impose their hands after the bishop and the celebration lasts quite a long time. There is also the case of concelebration in the Eucharist itself. Thomas Aquinas raised two objections to the latter.[53] The first was that, if there are several celebrants, there would be several consecrations. His reply to this is that this would not be so, since all the celebrants have the intention of bringing about one consecration. His second objection is this: the words of consecration can never be spoken simultaneously if there are several celebrants; the consecration is complete when some of them finish saying the words, with the result that the others do nothing. We should note in passing how far removed such considerations are from the Orthodox understanding of the situation. In the East, there is concelebration even when one concelebrant only intervenes at one moment of the celebration, or when the concelebrants say nothing at all. Thomas' reply to this was to cite Innocent III: priests concelebrating (on the day of their ordination) must refer their intention (to consecrate the bread and wine) to the moment when the bishop says the words of institution. For Thomas, then, the intention of the celebrant is what determines the matter.

Is it therefore not possible to return now to the question that was asked above (pp. 233–234): how can the words pronounced by Christ himself at the Last Supper be applied to this bread and this wine (see notes 28 and 29 below)? The Scholastic theologians gave a very decisive importance to the intention, as we have seen. Is it consequently not possible to say that it is the

239

intention of the priest celebrating *according to the rite of his Church* that determines the change of the bread and wine into the body and blood of the Lord by the application of the words of institution pronounced once only by Christ? In the Eastern rite, the priest's conviction and intention are closely connected with the saying of the epiclesis, in which the Spirit is asked to make the words of the account of the institution effective. This means that the words are only effective through the coming of the Spirit invoked in the epiclesis.[54] It does not mean that the conversion of the holy things only takes place, as Prince Max of Saxony believed,[55] after the epiclesis has been pronounced. My position is very similar to that of S. Salaville. Not only I, but many others who have studied this question, have had to rely on his learning.

Poor Prince Max's intention at least was right. He wanted to recognize the existence and the legitimacy of two different liturgical ideas, both concerned with the same reality, the celebration of the holy Eucharist as received from the Lord. Since his time, there have been very many remarkable liturgical studies—the lion's share produced in the West—and this notion of two liturgical ideas, two styles of liturgy has become commonplace. It would not be difficult to write a great deal about it, but, so as not to lengthen an already long chapter and to keep to the central theme of our subject, at the risk of appearing excessively schematic, I will summarize my ideas in two columns:

Eastern Rite	*Western Rite*
(1) The Eastern liturgies, which were developed in the controversial climate of the fourth century, are fundamentally Trinitarian.[56]	(1) The West was less affected by the fourth-century debates. Its inspiration is therefore more Christological.[57]
(2) The style is that of an epiclesis; this is noticeable in the celebration of various sacraments:	(2) The formulae used are often not deprecatory in form, although the Holy Spirit is expected in every effect of grace:
baptism: 'N. is baptized';	baptism: 'I baptize you';
anointing with chrism: 'the seal of the gift of the Spirit';	confirmation: the renewed rite has the Eastern form (see above, p. 217);
Eucharist: epiclesis;	Mass: the words of institution;
penance: 'May God forgive you'; 'Heal your servant';	penance: 'I absolve you'; but see the formulae of the renewed rite (Volume I, pp. 169–170, and below, p. 269);
ordination of ministers: 'May the grace of the Holy Spirit raise you to the order of deacon (priest, bishop)';	ordination: the renewed prayers are very close to those in the Eastern rite (see Volume I, p. 169, and below, pp. 268–269);

marriage: 'N. is crowned the servant of God'; the crowning has the character of an epiclesis.[58]

marriage: the bride and bridegroom are regarded as the ministers of the sacrament, which consists of the contract made sacred by God.

(3) The liturgy of the Eucharist is a dynamic whole finalized by deification. The sanctification of the elements by the Spirit therefore takes precedence over interest in a 'real presence' by an ontological transformation of the elements.[59]

(3) Attention has, at least since the end of the twelfth century, been concentrated on the 'real presence' and the cult of the Blessed Sacrament.

(4) The epiclesis is said in the plural, as a prayer of the community. The idea that the whole of the people is consecrated is expressed theologically in the profound doctrine of the *sobornost'*.

(4) Apart from a few additions of private prayers in the Middle Ages, the liturgy also speaks as 'we'. In speculative theology, however, and pastoral practice, the person of the priest (the Pope) is dominant.

(5) Interest is centred on the present descent of good things from the eschatological City, through the Holy Spirit.[60]

(5) Interest is more concerned with the historical continuity since the incarnation of the salvation that originated with Jesus Christ.

It is worth noting that, in very many of the questions that I have discussed here, the Second Vatican Council itself, as well as the attitudes, ways of thinking and explorations that prepared the way for it and the renewal in the liturgy and the Church as a whole that has followed it, have given life—or restored life—in the Catholic Church to a spirit that is in accordance with that of the Fathers and has been preserved in the Orthodox Church. The new eucharistic prayers, in particular, all contain an epiclesis before the account of the institution, asking for the gifts to be sanctified and consecrated, and an epiclesis after the consecration, asking for the fruits of the sacrament through the action of the Holy Spirit.[61] The results of this liturgical fact are already making themselves felt in theology and at the pastoral level.

*   *   *

Symbols of Life peculiar to the East

I believe that the Eastern Church has a more Platonic attitude and that it feels at ease with symbols and with a more organic and holistic approach to the world and faith. Its attitude is in striking contrast to that of the Western Church, with its more Aristotelian and analytical approach. As I commented almost half a century ago: formal and exemplary causality, and efficient and active causality![62] The value accorded to and the part played by images is particularly significant in each case, though the dogmatic pronouncements

241

of the Second Council of Nicaea (787), with its affirmation of the veneration of icons, are common to both East and West. The Eastern Church undoubtedly has an 'iconic' approach to realities, and perceives their deep meaning in religious symbols, which are not, for it, simply objects of knowledge, but imply an intense orientation to life and important practical consequences. The most poetic liturgical texts, the most detailed rites, are living, give inspiration to thought and life—this is very evident in two eucharistic rites—the zeon and the celebration with leavened bread.

The 'Zeon' or the Eucharistic Pentecost

In the Eastern rite, the priest or the deacon pours a little boiling water into the chalice before communion, with the words: 'The fervour of faith, filled with the Holy Spirit. Amen.' Nicholas Cabasilas (†c. 1380) explained, in his treatise on the liturgy, that the liturgy, having unfolded the series of mysteries from the incarnation to the passion and the resurrection of Christ in symbols, now continues with a symbolic representation of Pentecost. 'The Holy Spirit came down after all things pertaining to Christ had been accomplished. In the same way, when the holy offerings have attained their ultimate perfection, this water is added. . . . The Church . . . received the Holy Spirit after our Lord's ascension: now she receives the gift of the Holy Spirit after the offerings have been accepted at the heavenly altar.'[63] This concluding sentence is a good illustration of Bossuet's comments quoted above on the laws governing liturgical expression.

This 'zeon' is also an excellent symbolic expression of what we shall be considering in the next chapter. I myself have experienced that, if it is expressed in this way and if it is given this meaning, the zeon is very significant. It is, however, important to point out in this context that this is Cabasilas' interpretation of the zeon. The zeon itself and its interpretation go back a long way in the history of the Eastern Church.[64] It was introduced about 565 during the reign of Justinian and in the context of Aphthartodocetism. In a thesis that was influenced by Monophysitism, Julian of Halicarnassus maintained that the body of Christ was in itself incorruptible and would not pass away. It had therefore remained warm after his death and had yielded warm blood at the lance thrust. In the eleventh century, Nicetas Stethatos, Cardinal Humbert's opponent, explained the zeon rite by the fact that the living Spirit had remained united with Christ's body after his death. When communion was received from the warm chalice, Christians received the warm blood flowing from the side of Christ (with the water and the Spirit; see 1 Jn 5:8) and they were filled with the Holy Spirit, who is warmth. The same explanation was also provided by the Patriarch of Antioch Theodore Balsamon in the eleventh century. A pneumatological meaning was therefore preserved at the same time as a Christological one.

Unleavened or leavened bread?

It would seem that ordinary, that is, leavened bread, was first used throughout Christendom for the celebration of the Eucharist. The first really clear evidence of the use of unleavened bread is to be found in Rabanus Maurus (†c. 856).[65] The Eastern Church has always used and still uses leavened bread. The difference between the practice in the East and the West did not become an active reason for opposition between them until the dramatic confrontation between the Roman legate, the fiery Cardinal Humbert of Silva Candida, and the Patriarch Michael Cerularius in 1053–1054. The history of the polemics, including letters and scurrilous publications, is quite complex, but recent studies have thrown a great deal of light on it.[66]

It was not Cerularius who began hostilities. Leo of Ochrida wrote a letter to the Pope which Humbert believed had come from Cerularius. The latter had first intervened in opposition to Stylichus, the governor of the Byzantine territories in the south of Italy, who had introduced the practice of unleavened bread there. The quarrel soon became bitter: consecrated hosts of unleavened bread were even profaned. On the Greek side, the fires were immediately fanned by an argument that established a relationship between the rite of the Eucharist and the theology of the incarnation. In argument against the Monophysites and the Armenians, it had been said again and again that bread without leaven was dead bread, which consequently expressed only a Christ without a soul. Peter of Antioch and Nicetas Stethatos, with whom Humbert was engaged in controversy, accused the Latins of crypto-Apollinarianism. This accusation was renewed in comparatively recent polemics.[67]

The Latins based their argument on the fact that Jesus celebrated the Last Supper 'on the first day of the feast of unleavened bread' and that he observed the Mosaic Law. Humbert emphasized the lasting benefits of this. They too had their own symbolism—the bread of the Eucharist had to be pure, white, lasting and imperishable, since the body of Christ could only appear as white and immaculate. The argument, then, was Christological.[68] As we have already seen in Volume I of this work (p. 161), this symbolism still plays an important part in the feelings of many Catholics even today.

The Greeks opposed this argument by pointing to the new covenant, the change in the Law and the priesthood and the symbolism of the resurrection, which were not expressed by 'dead', unleavened bread. The Latins, in other words, were Judaizing.

In my opinion, the debate itself is not unimportant, but I am glad of the great number of declarations, some of them very general, others made specifically in connection with this particular question, which have stated, at the time of the controversy and subsequently, that the Eucharist of the Lord is celebrated equally with leavened or with unleavened bread.[69] Outside certain unprogressive quarters, this kind of controversy is almost unknown today. Alexander Schmemann, for example, wrote: 'Almost all the Byzantine arguments against the Latin rites have lost their importance; all that remains to be discussed now are the dogmatic differences with Rome'.[70] In my opinion, the main divergence is without doubt the *Filioque*. I have tried to deal with this question irenically.

NOTES

1. See Nicholas Cabasilas, *A Commentary on the Divine Liturgy*, tr. J. M. Hussey and P. A. McNulty (London, 1960); Fr. tr. S. Salaville, *SC* 4 (1943; 2nd ed., 1967). For Cabasilas, see M. Lot-Borodine, *Nicolas Cabasilas. Un maître de la spiritualité byzantine au XIVe siècle* (Paris, 1958); W. Völker, *Die Sakramentsmystik des Nikolaus Kabasilas* (Wiesbaden, 1977).

2. See T. Spačil, *Doctrina theologiae Orientis separati de SS. Eucharistia* (*Or. Chr.* XIII and XIV) (Rome, 1928 and 1929). For the debate in Russia in the last quarter of the seventeenth century, see I. Smolitsch, *Russisches Mönchtum* (Würzburg, 1953), pp. 345ff., 541.

3. I would mention only the following: S. Salaville, 'Epiclèse eucharistique', *DTC*, V (1913), cols 194–300; see also the Tables, *DTC*, I, cols 1365–1372; F. Cabrol, *DACL*, V/1 (1922), cols 142–184; G. Dix, *The Shape of the Liturgy* (London, 1945); B. Botte, 'L'épiclèse dans les liturgies syriennes orientales', *Sacris erudiri*, VI (1954), 46–72, and many other articles; L. Bouyer, *Eucharist: Theology and Spirituality of the Eucharistic Prayer* (Eng. tr.; Notre Dame, Ind. and London, 1968); W. Schneemelcher, 'Die Epiklese bei den griechischen Vätern', *Die Aufrufung des Heiligen Geistes im Abendmahl* (*Beiheft zur ökumenischen Rundschau*, 31) (Frankfurt, 1977), pp. 68–94; H. A. J. Wegman, 'Pleidooi voor een tekst. De Anaphora van de apostelen Addai en Mari', *Bijdragen*, 40 (1979), 15–43; M. de la Taille, *Mysterium Fidei*, Elucidatio XXXIV, 2nd ed. (Paris, 1924), includes an impressive list of publications and shows at the same time a distressing lack of understanding of the liturgical and theological meaning of the epiclesis.

4. Paul Evdokimov, *L'Esprit Saint dans la tradition orthodoxe* (*Bibl. Œcumén.*, 10) (Paris, 1969), p. 101, note 42.

5. See J. W. Tyrer, 'The Meaning of *Epiklēsis*', *JTS*, 25 (1923–1924), 139–150; O. Casel, 'Neuere Beiträge zur Epiklesenfrage', *Jahrbuch für Liturgiewissenschaft*, 4 (1924), 173. For Cyril of Jerusalem, see J. Quasten, *Monumenta eucharistica et liturgica vetustissima* (*Florilegium Patristicum*, VII) (Bonn, 1925), p. 77, note 2; *SC* 126, p. 95, note 2. For John Chrysostom, *De sac.* III, 4, see A. Naegele, *Die Eucharistielehre des heiligen Johannes Chrysostomus* (Freiburg, 1900), pp. 136ff. For Basil the Great, see M. Jugie, 'De epiclesi eucharistica secundum Basilium Magnum', *Acta Acad. Velehrad.*, 19 (1948), pp. 202ff.

6. See S. Salaville, *op. cit.* (note 3), col. 202, who also cites contemporary authors (col. 203) who wrote in the same way.

7. This emerges clearly from J. Lécuyer, 'La théologie de l'anaphore selon les Pères de l'école d'Antioche', *L'Orient syrien*, 6 (1961), 385–412. The principal Fathers concerned are Theodore of Mopsuestia, John Chrysostom and Theodoret.

8. *I Apol.* LXVI, 2. Justin first says that the 'president of the brethren' 'eucharists' the bread and wine; he then adds in his text: 'We do not receive these gifts as ordinary food or ordinary drink. But as Jesus Christ our Saviour was made flesh through the word of God, and took flesh and blood for our salvation, in the same way the food over which thanksgiving has been offered (= the "eucharisted bread") through the word of prayer (or 'the

prayer of the Word' *or* 'word') which we have from him—the food by which our blood and flesh are nourished through its transformation—is, we are taught, the flesh and blood of Jesus who was made flesh' (tr. H. Bettenson, *The Early Christian Fathers* (Oxford, 1969), pp. 61–62).

9. Irenaeus, *Adv. haer*. IV, 18, 5; V, 2, 2 (*PG* 7, 1027 and 1124).

10. Gregory of Nyssa, *Orat. cat*. 37 (*PG* 45, 93), written in 385.

11. Germanus, *Historia ekklēsiastikē kai mustagōgikē* (*PG* 98, 436–437). See also John Damascene (†749), *De fide orthod*. IV, 13 (*PG* 94, 1140ff.); Nicephorus of Constantinople (†828), *Antirrheticus secundus*, 3 (*PG* 100, 336); see also the two Syrians, Chosroe Magnus (†c. 972) and Dionysius Bar Salibi (twelfth century), *Expositio liturgiae*, ed. H. Labourt (Louvain, 1955). The *proskomidia* of the Eastern Eucharist is an evocation of the life of the incarnate Word.

12. Theodore of Mopsuestia, *Hom. cat*. 16; ed. and Fr. tr. R. Tonneau and R. Devreesse, *Homélies catéchétiques* (Vatican City, 1949), pp. 551–553.

13. Hippolytus, *Trad. apost*. 4; Fr. tr. B. Botte, *SC* 11, who accepts the original authenticity of this epiclesis.

14. For the Apostolic Constitutions, see F. E. Brightman, *Liturgies Eastern and Western*, I: *Eastern Liturgies* (Oxford, 1896), pp. 20ff.; S. Salaville, *op. cit* (note 3), col. 205; L. Bouyer, *op. cit* (note 3), pp. 264, 266. Cabasilas 'calls the conversion of oblations and the sanctification of the faithful by the same terms (*hagiasmos, hagiazō*)': J. Gouillard in Nicholas Cabasilas, *op. cit*. (note 1), 2nd Fr. ed. (1967), p. 37. See also J. Havet, 'Les sacrements et le rôle de l'Esprit Saint d'après Isidore de Séville,' *ETL*, 16 (1939), 85–91 for quotations from Cyril of Alexandria, John Chrysostom, Gregory of Nyssa, Theodore of Mopsuestia and others; 72–85 for quotations from the Western author Fulgentius of Ruspe; 61–72, for the Mozarabic rite; some of the epicleses seem to aim at the consecration of the bread and wine, but as a whole they aim rather at a sanctification of the elements by the Holy Spirit, insofar as this makes them able to sanctify the believers. See also Boris Bobrinskoy, 'Présence réelle et communion eucharistique', *RSPT*, 53 (1969), 402–420, especially 409.

15. S. Salaville, *op. cit*., cols 205 and 206; L. Bouyer, *op. cit*., p. 274; for the liturgy of St James, see the edition of B. C. Mercier.

16. As a good Thomist, J. M. R. Tillard, 'L'Eucharistie et le Saint-Esprit', *NRT*, 90 (1968), 363–387, considered the function of the Holy Spirit firstly in the context of the *res et sacramentum* of the Eucharist (the presence of the dead and risen Christ) and then as the *res tantum* (the charity of unity in the Mystical Body). At the same time, however, he also saw the second in continuity with the first, as Thomas Aquinas himself did together with other Scholastics. The Fathers and the Scholastics of the High Middle Ages were even more synthetic in their treatment of the question: see H. de Lubac, *Corpus mysticum* (Paris, 1944; 2nd ed., 1949).

17. See S. Salaville, *op. cit*. (note 3), col. 206.

18. E. Mercenier and F. Paris, *La Prière des Eglises de rite byzantin*, I (Amay-sur-Meuse, 1937), p. 235. In the present text, the words of the priest and the deacon are reversed. See A. Raes, 'Le dialogue après la Grande Entrée dans la liturgie byzantin', *Or. Chr. Period*., 18 (1952), 38–51, who attributes the text to the fifteenth or sixteenth centuries; R. F. Taft, *The Great Entrance. A History of the Transfer of Gifts and Other Preanaphoral Rites of the Liturgy of St. John Chrysostom* (*Or. Chr. Anal*., 200) (Rome, 1975), who goes back to tenth-century manuscripts. See also Paul Evdokimov, *op. cit*. (note 4), p. 100, who stresses the fact that there are epicleses that precede the canon.

19. See H. A. J. Wegman, *op. cit*. (note 3); L. Bouyer, *op. cit*. (note 3), pp. 146ff. and, for Hippolytus, pp. 170ff.

20. J. Quasten, 'The Blessing of the Font in the Syrian Rite of the Fourth Century', *ThSt*, 7 (1946), 309–313.

21. Cyril of Jerusalem, *Cat*. I, 7; ed. A. Piédagnel and P. Paris, *SC* 126 (1966), p. 95, who, in a

footnote, observe that the epiclesis should be understood here in the wider sense as designating the whole Canon of the Mass.

22. *Cat.* V, 7; A. Piédagnel and P. Paris, *op. cit.* (note 21), p. 155, who, again in a note, draw attention to the absence of any reference to an account of the institution or of the anamnesis and point to parallels for the epiclesis taken from the theological and geographical context. See also A. Tarby, *La prière eucharistique de l'Eglise de Jérusalem* (*Théol. hist.*, 17) (Paris, 1972).

23. See L. Bouyer, *op. cit.* (note 3), pp. 295–296; S. Salaville, *op. cit.* (note 3), cols 194–195. See also H. Engberding, *Das eucharistische Hochgebet der Basiliusliturgie* (Münster, 1931). In *De spir. sanct.* 23, 65 (*PG* 32, 188B), Basil the Great speaks of the words of the epiclesis 'at the moment of consecration' and Pruche translates *epi* in this way, to avoid the precision of 'following' or 'in view of': see *SC* 17, p. 239.

24. Hence S. Salaville's very severe judgement, *op. cit.*, cols 247–252.

25. See L. Bouyer, *op. cit.*, pp. 287, 288; S. Salaville, *op. cit.*, cols 195–196.

26. Nicholas Cabasilas, *Commentary on the Divine Liturgy*, 29.

27. Duns Scotus, *In IV Sent.* d. 8, q. 2; Durandus, *ibid.*, wrote that, in the account alone, 'non significatur quod corpus *Christi* sit sub speciebus panis quem sacerdos tenet vel coram se habet, sed solum sub speciebus panis quem Christus accepit et benedixit'.

28. John Chrysostom, *De proditione Iudae, Hom.* 1, No. 6 (*PG* 49, 380); see also *Hom.* 2 (*PG* 49, 589–590); tr. based on Fr. tr. by S. Salaville.

29. See A. Chavasse, 'L'épiclèse eucharistique dans les anciennes liturgies orientales. Une hypothèse d'interprétation', *MScRel*, 2 (1946), pp. 197–206. This can be compared with Isidore of Kiev at Florence (Mansi 31, 1686–1687); see also S. Salaville, *op. cit.* (note 3), col. 258.

30. Nicholas Cabasilas, *op. cit.* (note 26); see also J. Lukman, article in Serbian on 'The Doctrine of Nicholas Cabasilas and Simeon of Thessalonica on the Epiclesis', *Bogoslovni Vestnik*, 7 (1927), 1–14, who pointed out that Cabasilas uses the word *epharmozō*, 'to harmonize, put in touch with, make a connection between'.

31. See S. Salaville, *op. cit.*, cols 232–240; for the Eastern texts, see cols 236–238 (John Chrysostom) and col. 240 (John the Sabaite).

32. See Jn 14–17 and my *The Mystery of the Church* (Eng. tr.; London, 1960), pp. 147–186.

33. Gregory of Nyssa, *Ep. ad Ablabium* (*PG* 45, 125); Cyril of Alexandria, *Comm. in Luc.* XXII, 19 (*PG* 72, 908); see also S. Salaville, *op. cit.* (note 3), col. 236.

34. Bessarion, *De sacr. Euch.* (*PG* 161, 516).

35. This suggestion was made by A. Hamman, 'Du symbole de la foi à l'anaphore eucharistique', *Kyriakon, Festschrift J. Quasten* (Münster, 1970), II, pp. 835–843. I am inclined to think that this parallelism justifies the commemoration, in the anamnesis of the Byzantine rite, of the second coming of Christ in the future; in the creed, what concerns the Son is complete before professing faith in the Spirit.

36. Texts will be found in B. Marliangeas, *Clés pour une théologie du ministère. In persona Christi. In persona Ecclesiae*, with a preface by Y. Congar (*Théol. hist.*, 51) (Paris, 1978). These include mediaeval texts, texts from the thirteenth century and from Thomas Aquinas, important theological texts from the fourteenth to the seventeenth century and finally 'magisterial' texts: see pp. 231ff.

37. B. Marliangeas does not draw attention to these aspects, because he limits himself to the themes stated in the title of his book (*op. cit.*). See, however, J. Pascher, 'Die Hierarchie in sakramentaler Symbolik', *Episcopus. Studien über das Bischofsamt. Festschrift für Kardinal M. von Faulhaber* (Regensburg, 1949), pp. 278–295, and especially O. Perler, 'L'évêque, représentant du Christ, selon les documents des premiers siècles', *L'Episcopat et l'Eglise universelle*, ed. Y. Congar and B. D. Dupuy (*Unam Sanctam*, 39) (Paris, 1962), pp. 31–66.

38. O. Perler, *op. cit.* (note 37), p. 65.

39. *ST* IIIa, q. 78, a. 1, ad 4. See, for this question, in which Thomas played a special part,

P.-M. Gy, 'Les paroles de la consécration et l'unité de la Prière eucharistique selon les théologiens de Pierre Lombard à S. Thomas d'Aquin', *Mélanges C. Vagaggini* (Rome, 1980), pp. 189–201.

40. In this context, I quoted, in Volume I, p. 43 notes 33 and 35, W. C. van Unnik, 'Dominus vobiscum: The Background of a Liturgical Formula', *New Testament Essays in Memory of T. W. Manson* (Manchester, 1959), pp. 270–305. I would add, to the references given by the author to John Chrysostom and Theodore of Mopsuestia, A. Piédagnel's note 1 on Cyril of Jerusalem's fifth *Mystagogic Catechesis* (*SC* 126, p. 150), and what J. Lécuyer has said, *op. cit.* (note 7), 390, with reference to Theodore of Mopsuestia, *Hom. cat.* 15, 37–38, in which Rom 1:9 is cited, and to John Chrysostom, *De S. Pent. Hom.* 1, 4 (*PG* 50, 458–459).

41. Paul Evdokimov, *L'Orthodoxie* (*Bibl. théol.*) (Neuchâtel and Paris, 1959), p. 250; *idem*, 'L'Esprit Saint et l'Eglise d'après la tradition liturgique', *L'Esprit Saint et l'Eglise. L'avenir de l'Eglise et l'Œcuménisme* (*Acad. Int. des Sciences Relig.*) (Paris, 1969), pp. 85–111, especially p. 108; see also *idem*, *op. cit.* (note 4), pp. 103–104. See also Cyprien Kern's book in Russian, *The Eucharist* (Paris, 1947), (reviewed by C. R. A. Wenger, *Rev. Et. byz.*, 10 (1952; pub. 1953), 163ff.); *idem*, 'En marge de l'épiclèse', *Irénikon*, 24 (1951), 166–194, especially 182ff. and, for example, 184: 'The priest always acts *in persona Ecclesiae*, imploring in the name of the assembled people and not manifesting his own power'.

42. John Chrysostom, *De prod. Iud., Hom.* 1, 6 (*PG* 49, 380). But the same author also says, *De Pent., Hom.* 1, 4 (*PG* 50, 458–459): 'The priest only places his hand over the gifts after having invoked God's grace. . . . It is not the priest who brings about whatever takes place. . . . It is the grace of the Spirit, coming down and covering it with his wings, who brings about the mystical sacrifice.'

43. See the whole text of Severus of Antioch and the reference in S. Salaville, *op. cit.* (note 3), col. 240.

44. See André Scrima, *L'Esprit Saint et l'Eglise*, *op. cit.* (note 41), p. 115.

45. Anthony Bloom in an interview on 2 January 1977; reported in *Le Monde*, 2–3 January 1977, p. 14.

46. An agreement reached by the Mixed Anglican-Orthodox Doctrinal Commission; Moscow Conference, 26 July–2 August 1976, No. 27: see *Istina*, 24 (1979), 73.

47. Mgr Meletios, in an address to the plenary assembly of the French bishops at Lourdes, 1978: *Unité des Chrétiens*, 34 (April 1979), 57.

48. Cyprien Kern, 'En marge de l'épiclèse', *op. cit.* (note 41), 181.

49. J. R. Geiselmann, *Die Abendmahlslehre an der Wende der christlichen Spätantike zum Frühmittelalter* (Munich, 1933). I will confine myself to one quotation, from Paschasius Radbert, *De corp. et sang. Dom.* 15 (*PL* 120, 1322): 'Reliqua (apart from the *verba Christi*) vero omnia quae sacerdos dicit, aut clerus canit, nihil aliud quam laudes et gratiarum actiones sunt, aut certe obsecrationes fidelium, postulationes, petitiones'. This text was often attributed to Augustine: by Peter Lombard, *IV Sent.* d. 8, for example, and by Thomas Aquinas and others.

50. *IV Sent.* d. 13. Thomas Aquinas here abandons the Master of the Sentences.

51. Bossuet, *Explication de quelques difficultés sur les prières de la Messe, à un nouveau Catholique* (1689), XLVI and XLVII.

52. This is clear from the way in which Albert the Great displays a lack of understanding of the meaning of concelebration: see *De Euch.* d. 6, tract. 4, c. 2, Nos 15 and 16 (ed. A. Borgnet, 38, pp. 428–429). He cites the fact of concelebration at an ordination Mass as an *objection*, whereas Thomas treats this fact as a datum.

53. Thomas Aquinas, *In IV Sent.* d. 13, q. 1, a. 2, q^a 2; cf. *ST* IIIa, q. 82, a. 2.

54. May I quote two Orthodox texts here? The first is from Nicholas Cabasilas, *Commentary on the Divine Liturgy*, 29: 'We believe that the Lord's words do indeed accomplish the mystery, but through the medium of the priest, his invocation, and his prayer'; here

Cabasilas is referring to the application of the words said by Jesus at the Last Supper, words that the priest uses again in the form of an account in order to apply them to the oblations: see section 27. The second quotation is from Paul Evdokimov, *op. cit.* (note 4), pp. 103–104: 'So that the words of Christ that he has memorized may acquire a divine effectiveness, the priest invokes the Holy Spirit in the epiclesis. The Holy Spirit makes the words of the anamnesis: "Taking bread . . . he gives it to his disciples . . saying . . . This is my body" an *epiphanic anamnesis*, pointing to the intervention of Christ himself as identifying the words said by the priest with his own words and identifying the Eucharist celebrated by the priest with his own Last Supper. This is the miracle of the *metabolē*, that is, of the conversion of the gifts.'

55. Prince Max of Saxony, 'Pensées sur l'union des Eglises', *DTC*, V, col. 276, a thesis that was sanctioned by Pius X's letter of 26 December 1910: see *DS* 3556. The mistake that Prince Max made was to separate the two aspects, thus attributing a kind of autonomy to the epiclesis; this was, of course, alien to the Orthodox conception: see above, pp. 238, 247 note 48. Ambrosius Catharinus took up a similar stance in the sixteenth century: see *DTC*, XII, col. 2432. His document was placed on the Index of forbidden books, but has since been withdrawn.

56. All the liturgies are Trinitarian—the Roman and the Eastern liturgies: see C. Vagaggini, *Theological Dimensions of the Liturgy* (Eng. tr.; Collegeville, Minn., 1976), chapter 7, esp. pp. 217ff.; the Eastern liturgies are, however, more full of Trinitarian expressions. On the other hand, their economic and Trinitarian structure called for a formal epiclesis invoking the Spirit after the thanksgiving had been addressed to the Father and the sacrifice in the upper room had been made present by the words of Christ, the sovereign high priest.

57. See my article 'Pneumatologie et "christomonisme" dans la tradition latine', *Ecclesia a Spiritu Sancto edocta. Mélanges G. Philips* (Gembloux, 1970), pp. 41–63.

58. See P. Evdokimov, *Le sacrement de l'amour* (Paris, 1962).

59. The opening sentence of Nicholas Cabasilas' *Commentary on the Divine Liturgy* is very characteristic: 'The essential act in the celebration of the holy sacred mysteries is the transformation of the elements into the divine body and blood; its aim is the sanctification of the faithful, who through these mysteries receive the remission of their sins and the inheritance of the kingdom of heaven'.

60. See J. D. Zizioulas, 'La continuité avec les origines apostoliques dans la conscience théologique des Eglises orthodoxes', *Istina*, 19 (1974), 65–94; see also Volume II, pp. 50–51.

61. See Volume I, p. 170; D. Lallement, 'Le Saint-Esprit dans les prières eucharistiques nouvelles', *Bienfaits spirituels de la nouvelle liturgie romaine de la Messe* (Paris, 1979), pp. 35–46.

62. See my article, first published in May 1935, 'La déification dans la tradition spirituelle de l'Orient d'après une étude récente'; Eng. tr., 'Deification in the Spiritual Tradition of the East', *Dialogue between Christians* (London und Dublin, 1966), pp. 217–231.

63. Nicholas Cabasilas, *Commentary as the Divine Liturgy*, 37.

64. See H. Grondijs, *L'iconographie byzantine du crucifié mort sur la croix* (*Bibl. Byzant. Brux.*, 1) (Brussels, 1941); the author has collected together in this book all the texts relating to the zeon rites.

65. K.-H. Kandler, 'Wann werden die Azyme das Brotelement in der Eucharistie im Abendland?' *Zeitschrift für Kirchengeschichte*, 75 (1964), 153–155; see also J. A. Jungmann, *The Mass of the Roman Rite* (Eng. tr.; New York and London, 1959), pp. 330–331.

66. Mahlon H. Smith III, *And Taking Bread. Cerularius and the Azyme Controversy of 1054* (*Théol. hist.*, 47) (Paris, 1978). It is also worth consulting K.-H. Kandler, *Die Abendmahlslehre des Kardinal Humbert und ihre Bedeutung für das gegenwärtige Abendmahlsgespräch* (Berlin and Hamburg, 1971).

67. See *Revue de l'Orient chrétien* (1901), 98; M. Jugie, *Theologia dogm. Christ. Orient.*, III, p. 244; IV, p. 442.

68. D. N. Egenter, 'La rupture de 1054', *Irénikon*, 27 (1954), 142–156, quoted Peter Damian: 'Christ took out of the leavened mass the azyme of sincerity that had been purified of the infection of decay. From the flesh of the Virgin which was conceived from sin came a flesh that was without sin': *Liber gratissimus*, 19 (*PL* 145, 129).

69. Cardinal Humbert himself wrote, in the name of Leo IX, to Cerularius in September 1053: 'Although you have closed the Latin churches, the Greek liturgy is still celebrated freely in Rome, since the Church knows that a diversity of practices is not an obstacle to the salvation of believers when one faith, acting through charity, recommends all men to God' (*PL* 143, 764): see C. Will, *Acta et Scripta de Contr.* (Leipzig, 1861), p. 181, containing the text as reproduced in the collections of Ivo of Chartres and Gratian. Peter of Antioch's reply to Cerularius was: 'If the Latins agreed to suppress the addition to the creed, I would not ask for anything more. I would even include the question of unleavened bread, with all the rest, among the indifferent things': see C. Will, *op. cit.*, p. 203. See also Gregory VII, *Reg.* VIII, 1: 'ipsorum fermentatum nec vituperamus nec reprobamus': Caspar, p. 513; Anselm, *Ep. de sacrificio azymi et fermentati*, 1 (ed. S. Schmitt, *Opera*, II, p. 223): 'De sacrificio in quo Graeci nobiscum non sentiunt multis rationibus catholicis videtur quia quod agunt non est contra fidem christianam. Nam et azimum et fermentatum sacrificans panem sacrificat'. Thomas Aquinas, *Contra Err. Graec.* II, 39, defended the use of unleavened bread, on the grounds that Christ employed it, and concluded: 'non autem propter hoc intendimus quod ex fermentato hos sacramentum confici non possit'.

70. A. Schmemann, *Historical Road of Eastern Orthodoxy* (New York, 1961), p. 248, quoted by M. H. Smith, *op. cit.* (note 66), p. 26, note 18.

APPENDIX
THE PART PLAYED BY THE
HOLY SPIRIT IN THE EUCHARIST
ACCORDING TO THE WESTERN
TRADITION

The effectiveness of the grace of the sacraments has always been attributed to the effectiveness of the Holy Spirit, the *virtus Spiritus Sancti*, throughout the history of the Church. This means that the sacred action celebrated in the Church's Eucharist calls for the complement of an active coming of the Spirit—though this is a complement that is not in any sense an optional extra.

What is true of all the sacraments is clearly true of the Eucharist. There is ample testimony that the consecration of the bread and wine into the body and blood of Christ is brought about by the Holy Spirit. This testimony does not, however, necessarily have in mind the existence of an epiclesis. The texts that in fact allude to an invocation (of the Spirit) may refer to the whole of the Canon or even to the whole eucharistic celebration, which includes prayers which have the value of an epiclesis. It is well known that the Roman Canon does not include an epiclesis to the Holy Spirit, and it is very doubtful whether it ever included such an epiclesis even originally. Is the prayer *Supplices te rogamus*—'Almighty God, we pray that your angel may take this sacrifice to your altar in heaven—an epiclesis? The significance of this prayer is still being debated. It is obviously a supplication, in which God is asked to accept the Church's offering and that the offering may obtain its spiritual fruit. It is in the place of an epiclesis, but it does not have a consecratory function and it is not indisputably pneumatological.

Here I now cite a number of witnesses and texts showing that the Latin West has always been convinced not only of the consecratory function of the words 'This is my body' and 'This is my blood', but also equally of the part played by the Holy Spirit. I must openly admit that I compiled this list of witnesses before reading S. Salaville's great article to which I have frequently referred in the earlier part of this chapter: 'Epiclèse eucharistique', *DTC*, V, cols 194–300. Had I consulted this article first, I should not have needed to do the work; his list is more complete, and quotes the text more fully. I am, however, also indebted to another author, Kurt Goldammer, whose dissertation *Die eucharistische Epiklese in der mittelalterlichen abendländischen Frömmigkeit* (Bottrop, 1941) has proved very valuable. Goldammer quotes many versions and descriptions of spiritual experiences, which I have not included. Also, his theological position, as a Protestant, is not one that I have wished to follow in this work.

Ambrose (†397) is the most powerful witness to testify to the consecration of the elements by the words of Christ himself, pronounced by Christ, that is, over the bread and wine: *De sacr.* IV, 14–23; V, 24; *De myst.* 52 (Fr. tr. and ed. B. Botte, *SC* 25bis (1966), who produces convincing arguments in favour of the authenticity of the treatise). Ambrose, however, knew that the Holy Spirit was invoked by priests with the Father and the Son *in oblationibus*: *De spir. sanct.* III, 16, 112 (*PL* 16, 803).

The only text of Augustine (†430), who clearly believed in the decisive part played by the *verbum* (*Sermo Denis*, 6 and other texts: see *DTC*, V, cols 241–242 for S. Salaville's comments) that I would quote here is from *De Trin.* III, 4, 10: 'The consecration, which makes it such a great sacrament, comes only from the invisible action of the Spirit of God' (*PL* 42, 874; Fr. tr. M. Mellet and T. Camelot, *Bibl. August.*, XV, p. 291). Augustine might have admitted that there was an epiclesis, but its aim would have been to make the sacred gifts gifts according to Christ and capable of being received by him, not to 'consecrate' them for their conversion into Christ's body and blood: see A. Sage, 'S. Augustin et la prière "Supplices te rogamus" ', *Rev. Et. Byz.*, 11 (1953), 252–265.

The Leonine Sacramentary has this Secret for the third Mass of Christmas Day: 'Lord, look with benevolence upon the offering of your people; on your altars it is not an alien fire or the blood of animals without reason that is poured. By the virtue of the Holy Spirit, our sacrifice is the body and blood of the Priest himself' (ed. C. L. Feltoe, p. 61).

Fulgentius of Ruspe, who was Augustine's disciple, replied *c.* 508 to Monimus, who had asked him why we ask for the mission of the Spirit to sanctify the gift of our oblation (*Ad Mon.* II, 6; *PL* 65, 184), that it is to obtain the gift of charity and unanimity (*Ad Mon.* II, 10; *PL* 65, 188), that is, the holy fruit of the Eucharist, what the Scholastics called the *res* of the Eucharist.

Pope Gelasius I (†496) wrote to Elpidius of Volterra about 'the way in which the heavenly Spirit whom we invoke must come to consecrate the divine mystery'[1] and a little later wrote, against the Christological errors of the period, that the bread and wine 'change into the divine reality and the Holy Spirit brings this about'.[2]

There is no explicit epiclesis invoking the Holy Spirit in the Roman rite from the time of Gregory the Great until our own century, although the *Quam oblationem* before the consecration and the *Supplices te rogamus* after the consecration certainly have the value of an epiclesis. In the practical use of this liturgy, however, this relative gap has been filled by a great number of prayers, which were sufficiently widespread to show that they must have been commonly used: see Joaquim O. Bragança, *op. cit.* (note 5 below), pp. 39–53. From a great number of examples, I have chosen this text: 'Lord, may your Holy Spirit descend on this altar, we beseech you, may he bless and sanctify these gifts offered to your Majesty and may he deign to purify all those who receive them'. Until the present century, the Missal of Pius V contained a prayer, the fourteenth-century version of which was, according to a manuscript of the period: 'Veni, sancte Spiritus invisibilis sanctificator, veni et sanctifica sacrificium istud tibi hodie praeparatum ad laudem et gloriam nominis tui. In nomine Patris et Filii et Spiritus Sancti. Amen.'

The Gregorian Sacramentary, the oldest form of which goes back to Gregory the Great (†604), has this prayer: 'The Host which is offered by several and becomes one body of Christ by the infusion of the Holy Spirit': see C. L. Feltoe, *JTS*, 11 (1910), 578; see also the edition by H. Lietzmann (Münster, 1921), nos. 116, 196.

The Hispano-Visigothic rite, which is sometimes called the Mozarabic rite, is extremely rich and even prolix, lyrical and full of patristic inspirations. Isidore of

Seville (†636)[3] regarded the sacrament as brought about 'operante invisibiliter Spiritu Dei' (*Etym.* VI, 19; *PL* 82, 255). His sixth prayer ensures the 'confirmatio sacramenti, ut oblatio, quae Deo offertur, sanctificata per Spiritum Sanctum, Christi corpori et sanguini conformetur' (*De eccl. officiis* I, 15, 3; *PL* 83, 753). It is not easy to say exactly what this *sexta oratio* included. According to Férotin, Cabrol and Séjourné, it was simply what followed the account of the institution—the *Post pridie*. In the opinion of Geiselmann and Havet, on the other hand, it was everything that came after the *illatio* (the Preface) and the Sanctus. In any case, these *Post pridie* prayers, which changed with each Mass, but had a similar structure, asked for the sanctification of the gifts and their fruit of charity and unity in the hearts of the faithful. They are addressed to the Father, the Son or the Holy Spirit, or else to the Holy Trinity. They pray that the body and blood that are offered may be sanctified by the *virtus* of the Holy Spirit, by his warmth. Colunga, and Havet, *op. cit.* (note 3 below), 61–72, thought that these prayers presupposed the consecration of the gifts by the words of institution, but there are several texts which can be opposed to this. The truth is that in the *Liber ordinum* (ed. M. Férotin, 1904) and Isidore of Seville it would be wrong to isolate a single aspect of the entire prayer that begins with the *Sanctus* and ends with the *Pater noster*, because it forms a single whole. The celebration of the Eucharist is a dynamic process which concludes in the communion of the believer, whom the Holy Spirit, transfiguring the gifts into the body of Christ, incorporated by this means into the same Christ.

Bede (†735) was close to Isidore. He believed that the sacrament was brought about by the 'ineffabili Spiritus sanctificatione' (*Hom.* 14; *PL* 94, 75).

Paul the Deacon (†799) reported a eucharistic miracle which has often been described and discussed, from which Pope Gregory benefited. The Pope apparently said: 'Our creator . . . changed the bread and wine with water, leaving them their own appearance, into his flesh and blood, at the Catholic prayer, through the sanctification of his Spirit' (*Vita Gregorii Papae*, c. 23, *PL* 75, 53).

The prayer of the Roman rite, *Summe Sacerdos*, which is attributed to Ambrose of Milan and used to appear in missals as a prayer of preparation for the celebration of the Eucharist, is in fact the work of John of Fécamp (†1078). Its language is taken from various pre-existing texts which go back to a *Post pridie* in the *Liber ordinum* of the Hispano-Visigothic rite. John of Fécamp simply transferred this prayer to the beginning of the celebration.[4] It begins with the words: 'Supreme Priest and true Pontiff, Jesus Christ, . . . who instituted this mystery in the virtue of the Holy Spirit, saying :"Each time that you do this, you do it in memory of me" '.

Many witnesses can be found in the ninth century. There is Florus of Lyons, *De actione missarum*, c. 59 and 60 (*PL* 119, 51B and 52C; ed. P. Duc, Bellay, 1937). The response to the *Orate fratres* in several missals of this period is: 'The Holy Spirit will come upon you . . .'.[5] Like the incarnation, the Eucharist is also brought about by the coming of the Spirit. Paschasius Radbert (†865) also said this (*Liber de corpore et sanguine Domini*, c. 7; *PL* 120, 1285): 'quod sane corpus, ut vera caro sit Christi, pro mundi vita quotidie per Spiritum Sanctum consecratur'. In the same treatise, c. 3 (*PL* 120, 1275–1276), he says that the consecration is brought about 'per sacerdotem super altare in verbo Christi per Spiritum Sanctum' (*PL* 120, 1279) or 'virtute Spiritus Sancti per verbum Christi' (c. 12; *PL* 120, 1310–1312). Paschasius here combines the Christological and the pneumatological aspects, the Spirit having the task of making the words of Christ effective, while those words bring about the consecration. Gottschalk (†c. 866), in his controversy with Paschasius, was not opposed to the latter in this particular case. He also used the analogy of the incarnation (*Ep.* 3; *PL* 112, 1513),[6] but he spoke more explicitly of a supplication addressed to the Holy Spirit; this was undoubtedly the *Supplices te rogamus*: 'Spiritus Sanctus, per quem ea creat et consecrat, et in quo sacerdos ista fieri supplicat' (*PL* 12, 1516). It was at this time that Pope Nicholas I wrote to the Byzantine Emperor Michael (in 860): 'Post sanctificationem Spiritus sanguis Christi efficitur' (*PL* 119, 778D).

This, then, was the generally accepted teaching. It is worth noting in this context another text that originated at the very interesting Council of Arras (1025), held to combat the first manifestations of anti-sacramental dualism. At that Council, it was said of the Eucharist, 'fit sacramentum operante invisibiliter Spiritus Dei' (Mansi, 16, 431A) and 'quae invisibiliter eodem Spiritu vivificatur quo operante in utero Virginis incarnatus est Dei Filius' (Mansi, 16, 433B).

As we shall see, this was to continue to be the teaching of theology and of the Catholic Church. The importance of that teaching was to some extent lessened by the stress laid on the effectiveness of the words of institution—made necessary by the heretical teaching of Berengar of Tours. In opposition to his one-sidedly spiritual teaching about the Eucharist, the Church insisted on the 'real presence', in other words, that what was found on the altar *after the consecration* was the true body and blood of Jesus Christ. The second profession of faith that Gregory VII obliged Berengar to make, on 11 February 1079, says: 'per mysterium sacrae orationis et verba nostri Redemptoris'.[7] The force of circumstances, however, reinforced by the juridical mentality and by the need felt by the Scholastic theologians to define this teaching precisely, led to special emphasis being placed on the exact moment of the consecration when the words of institution are pronounced by the priest.[8] This is clearly illustrated by two great authors, the classical canon lawyer Gratian in 1140, and the classical theologian of the Church Thomas Aquinas in the thirteenth century.[9] According to the latter, it is the words of institution which consecrate; the rest are not the *substantia*, but *decor sacramenti*. Thomas also believed that the mere fact that there were different liturgies proved that they were not concerned with the essence or form of the sacrament. That essence or form was to be found exclusively in the words of Christ as pronounced by the priest *in persona Christi*. Thomas was aware, however, that the water of baptism and all the sacraments were effective because of the Holy Spirit, who was their first cause (*ST* Ia IIae, q. 112, a. 1, ad 2; IIIa, q. 66, a. 11 and 12) and that, if Paul said that we were 'all made to drink of one Spirit' (1 Cor 12:13), this must also be understood in a second sense of the sacramental drink consecrated by the Holy Spirit (*Comm. in 1 Cor*. c. 12, lect. 3). But we must return to the eleventh century, the period of Berengar of Tours.

His first profession of faith, which was not acceptable, was composed in 1055 by Humbert of Silva Candida (†1061), who had in the previous year, on 16 July 1054, placed the bull excommunicating the Patriarch Michael Cerularius on the altar of the Church of Hagia Sophia. What is remarkable, however, is that, in his dialogue with Nicetas Stethatos, he attributed the change in the elements of bread and wine to the invocation of the whole Trinity.[10] He regarded all the sacraments as gifts and instruments of the Spirit, who, in one way or another, dwelt in them.[11]

Peter Damian (†1072) was even more devoted to the Holy Spirit than Humbert. He attributed the consecration of the elements to the words of institution, but the sanctifying and life-giving virtue to the Spirit (*Liber qui dicitur gratissimus*, c. 9; *PL* 145, 110). Since, he believed, simoniacal priests administered valid sacraments, the *virtus Spiritus Sancti* was able to act through the Eucharists of such priests for the benefit of those who had a good disposition. This teaching was taken up again by Cardinal Deusdedit, who died at the end of the century, although he did not name Peter Damian (*Libelli de Lite*, II, p. 322).

There is a great deal of evidence that theologians in the twelfth century were convinced that the Holy Spirit played a part in the Eucharist. Hildebert of Lavardin (or of Le Mans; †1123) affirmed, in connection with the *Supplices te rogamus*, that the gifts were made into the body and blood of Christ 'virtute Spiritus Sancti . . . per Spiritum Sanctum' (*Liber de expositione missae*; *PL* 171, 1168). Rupert of Deutz (†1135) also thought that the fire of the Spirit changed the bread and wine into the eucharistic body and blood of Christ. The Spirit who did this was the same Spirit who had made the Virgin conceive and who had driven Jesus on to offer himself as a living sacrifice (*De Trin. et operibus eius, in Exod. lib.* II, c. 10, in connection with the paschal Lamb cooked in the fire; *PL* 167, 617).

The mysterious Honorius Augustodunensis stated that the body of Christ was produced 'Spiritu Sancto consecrante' and thought that this was proclaimed in the *Quam oblationem* (*Eucharistion seu de corpore et sanguine Domini*, c. 1; *PL* 172, 1250; and *Gemma animae*, I, 105; *PL* 172, 578) respectively. Hildegard, the visionary of Bingen (†1179), frequently spoke of the priest's prayer or *invocatio* in the action of the Eucharist and claimed that the *verba sacerdotis* which invoked God in his power made the Spirit come as he had come on the Virgin Mary at the incarnation (*Scivias*, lib. II, vis. 6; *PL* 197, 516). At the end of the twelfth century, Adam of Saint-Victor (†1192) wrote, in a sequence to the Holy Spirit:[12]

Tu commutas elementa.	You change the elements.
Per te suam sacramenta	Through you the sacraments
habent efficaciam.	have their effect.

It was at this time that the formula of the profession of faith for the Waldenses, the disciples of Peter Waldo (1179–1181), and later for Bernard Prim and Durandus of Huesca (Osca), which was finally prescribed by Innocent III (1208), was first defined. We should note these significant statements: 'Sacramenta quoque, quae in ea (Ecclesia) celebrantur, inaestimabili atque invisibili virtute Spiritus Sancti cooperante' and 'Sacrificium, id est panem et sanguinem . . . in verbo efficitur Creatoris et in virtute Spiritus Sancti' (*DS* 793 and 794). On the other hand, Innocent was convinced that it was the words of institution that brought about the consecration.

It was this certainty that the Scholastic theologians attempted to express and to justify. Albert the Great, for example, asked: 'An in sacramento Eucharistiae potest dici creari corpus Christi per Spiritum Sanctum? et utrum per spiritum fiat transsubstantiatio?' (*In IV Sent.* d. 10, a. 10; ed. A. Borgnet, 29, p. 262). This question was prompted by a text of Peter Lombard, who quotes a passage by Paschasius Radbert under the name of St Augustine: 'sicut per Spiritum Sanctum vera Christi caro sine coitu creatur, ita per eundem ex substantia panis et vini idem corpus Christi et sanguis consecratur, etc.' (*De corp. et sang. Dom.* c. 4; *PL* 120, 1278). Albert believed that the consecration of the elements was brought about by the words of institution and, in the matter of transubstantiation, he attributed the effect of the love that unifies the mystical Body of Christ, which is the *res* of the sacrament, to the Holy Spirit.

Thomas Aquinas also commented on the same passage of Paschasius, still attributed to Augustine. In his gloss, he maintained that transsubstantiation was appropriated to the Son as the one who brings it about and to the Holy Spirit as the one through whom Christ is active (*In IV Sent.* d. 10, expos. textus; ed. Moos, No. 144). A little earlier in the same treatise, he raised in objection a text by John Damascene: 'the conversion of the bread into the body of Christ takes place only by the virtue of the Holy Spirit' (*De fide orthod.*, IV, 13; *PG* 94, 1139). Thomas keeps to the principle of attributing transubstantiation to the Holy Spirit as the one who is principally active, but insists that this does not exclude the action of an instrument, in this case, the words of the priest (*In IV Sent.* d. 8, q. 2, a. 3, ad 1). There is, then, a lack of complete agreement between these two passages of Thomas, but there is nevertheless agreement that the words of institution and the Holy Spirit have to be taken together. It can be added here that Thomas did not regard the *Supplices te rogamus* as a consecratory epiclesis (*In IV Sent.* d. 13, Expos. textus: ed. Moos, no. 174).

From the beginning of the fourteenth century onwards, the Latins became acquainted, in the East, with the Orthodox view of the rôle of the epiclesis. This led to a series of papal declarations in favour of the words of institution as the form of the sacrament and the moment when the elements were converted into the body and blood of the Lord:

Benedict XII: libellus *Cum dudum*, addressed to the Armenians, August 1341 (*DS* 1017).

Clement VI: letter *Super quibusdam*, addressed to the Catholicos of the Armenians, 29 September 1351 (*DTC*, V, col. 199).

Benedict XIII: instruction to the Melchite Patriarch of Antioch, 31 May 1729 (*DTC*, V, col. 200).

Benedict XIV: brief *Singularis Romanorum*, 1 September 1741 (*Collectio Lacensis*, II, 197).

Pius VII: brief *Adorabile Eucharistiae*, 8 May 1822, addressed to the Melchite Patriarch of Antioch and bishops (*DS* 2718; *DTC*, V, cols 200 and 264).

Pius X: letter *Ex quo, nono*, addressed to the apostolic delegates in the East, 26 December 1910, against the article written by Prince Max of Saxony ('Thoughts on the Union of the Churches') (*DS* 3556; *DTC*, V, col. 276).

These communications did not preclude an acknowledgement of the part played by the Holy Spirit in the bringing about of the sacrament and consecration of the gifts.

Cornelius a Lapide, the Jesuit biblical exegete (†1637), exalted the eucharistic sacrifice above the Levitical rites because of its mode of offering: 'consecration and transubstantiation are brought about by a sublime and mysterious activity of the Holy Spirit'(*Comm. in 1 Pet.* II, 5–9; based on Fr. tr. by P. Dabin).

French scholars in the seventeenth and eighteenth centuries made the Greek patristic texts and Eastern liturgies accessible on a wide scale to the West. The effect of this was apparent in the work of a great number of authors who, without prejudice to the statements made about the words of institution, continued to insist on the part played by the Holy Spirit in the transformation and the sanctification of the sacred elements. S. Salaville provides some useful references: *DTC*, V, col. 273.[13]

The eucharistic prayers introduced since the Second Vatican Council have given the epicleses back their place. Theology will in this case follow Christian practice.

NOTES

1. See A. Thiel, *Epistolae Romanorum Pontificum*, I (1868), p. 484; see also J. Brinktrine, 'Der Vollzieher der Eucharistie nach dem Brief des Papstes Gelasius (†496) an den Bischof Elpidius von Volterra', *Miscellanea C. Mohlberg* (1949), II, pp. 61–69.
2. Thiel, *op. cit.*, I, pp. 541–542. Attempts have been made to appeal to this text as a denial of the change from bread and wine into the body and blood of the Lord.
3. See the remarkable study of J. R. Geiselmann, *Die Abendmahlslehre an der Wende der christlichen Spätantike zum Frühmittelalter. Isidor von Sevilla und das Sakrament der Eucharistie* (Munich, 1933); A. Colunga, 'La epiclesis en la liturgia mozárabe', *Le Ciencia Tomista*, 47 (1933), 145–161, 289–366; J. Havet, 'Les sacrements et le rôle de l'Esprit Saint d'après Isidore de Séville', *ETL*, 16 (1939), 32–98, especially 72: 'For Isidore, the metamorphosis that occurred in the Eucharist was very complex. It did not merely consist in making the body and blood of Christ present—this was only its sacrificial aspect. This body and blood had in addition to be sanctified by the Holy Spirit, in such a way that they would themselves be sanctifying for those who received them. This was, for Isidore, the truly sacramental aspect of the eucharistic change. The whole of this complex transformation was accomplished by the *oratia sexta* or *prex mystica*, which culminated in the *Eucharistia*, the sanctifying body and blood of Christ.'
4. A. Wilmart, 'L'Oratio S. Ambrosii du Missel Romain', *RBén*, 39 (1927), 314–339; repr. in *Auteurs et Textes dévots du Moyen Age* (Paris, 1932), pp. 101–125; B. Fischer, 'Eine ausdrückliche Geistepiklese im bisherigen Missale Romanum', *Mélanges liturgiques offertes à B. Botte* (Louvain, 1973), pp. 139–142.
5. See J. O. Bragança, 'L'Esprit Saint dans l'Euchologie médiévale', *Le Saint-Esprit dans la liturgie. Conférences Saint-Serge, 1969* (Rome, 1977), p. 44; A. Raes, 'La Dialogue après la Grande Entrée', *Or. Chr. Period.*, 18 (1952), 52–88, who thought that this might have influenced the East; from the fifteenth century onwards, the following excellent formula can be found in the above-mentioned dialogue in the Orthodox Church: 'The Holy Spirit will concelebrate with you'.
6. This *Ep. ad Egilem*, printed under the name of Rabanus Maurus, was attributed by G. Morin and later by C. Lambot, *Œuvres de Godescalc d'Orbais* (1945), pp. 324–335, to Gottschalk.
7. *DS* 700. For the decisive influence of the Berengarian controversy on the development of the theology of the Eucharist, see H. de Lubac, *Corpus mysticum. L'Eucharistie et l'Eglise au Moyen Age (Théologie*, 3) (Paris, 1944, 2nd ed., 1949).
8. This is expressed in popular devotion by the 'desire to see the Host': see H. Dumoutet, *Le désir de voir l'hostie et les origines de la dévotion au Saint-Sacrement* (Paris, 1926) and *Le Christ selon la chair et la vie liturgique au Moyen Age* (Paris, 1932). It was also expressed by the institution of the Feast of Corpus Christi by Urban IV in 1264; this feast was extended to the 'whole Church' in 1311.
9. See Gratian, *De cons.* d. II, c. 55 and 61 (ed. E. Friedberg, 1334–1355 and 1337); in c. 72, however, he quotes Paschasius Radbert. See also Thomas Aquinas, *ST* IIIa, q. 78, a. 1, with an ad 4 which must make everyone who is familiar with and devoted to the liturgy feel uneasy! See also his q. 75, a. 7.

10. 'Taliter praeparatus azymus fideli invocatione totius Trinitatis fit verum et singulare corpus Christi': Humbert, *Dial.* c. 31; C. Will, *Acta et Scripta quae de controversiis Ecclesiae Graecae et Latinae saeculo XI composita extant* (Leipzig and Marburg, 1861), p. 108. See also K.-H. Kandler, *Die Abendmahlslehre des Kardinal Humbert* (Berlin and Hamburg, 1971), pp. 78–81.

11. *Adv. Sim.* II, c. 20 (*Libelli de Lite*, I, p. 163); K.-H. Kandler, *op. cit.*, pp. 42–43. It should be borne in mind that this treatise begins with a passionate invocation of the Spirit, who is the most free of all and will therefore defend the *libertas Ecclesiae* and overthrow the simoniacs and their trafficking (p. 102).

12. Adam of Saint-Victor, *Sequentia X de Spiritu Sancto* (*PL* 196, 1455).

13. I do not know what use to make of an excellent text attributed to Charles de Condren (†1641), since the first Paris edition (1677) was by Quesnel and does not contain this text except for a fragment: Part IV, XXVII, pp. 210ff. This is what can be found in *L'idée du sacerdoce et du sacrifice de Jésus-Christ par le R. P. de Condren*, rev. and augmented ed. by a Benedictine of the French Congregation (Paris, 1901), Part III, Chapter VIII, 'In which it is shown how the Holy Spirit is the fire of the sacrifice of Jesus Christ, in whatever state he is regarded', pp. 160–161: 'The liturgies of the Greek Church attribute everything to the Holy Spirit, both the change of the bread and wine into the body and blood of Jesus Christ and the oblation that this adorable victim makes of himself to God through himself, his ministers and the whole of the Church. As Cyril of Jerusalem said, referring to the liturgy of his own time, which was the fourth century: "What the Holy Spirit touches is changed and sanctified". Is it not also apparent that it is in relation to the fire which from time to time descended from heaven on to the sacrifices of our ancestors that the priest prays in this way in the early Latin liturgies: "Lord, may the Spirit of consolation, who is co-eternal with you and therefore also co-operates in your blessing, descend on these sacrifices"? This is also similar to what is said in the Roman Missal in the Secret of the Friday of the octave of Pentecost: "Lord, may this divine fire, which, through the descent of the Holy Spirit, has inflamed the hearts of the disciples of your Son Jesus Christ, consume these sacrifices that are offered in your presence".' The Paris Missal, which contains this Secret of the Friday in the octave of Pentecost, also contains a Secret for the Monday of that week, in which the Church prays that the gifts that are on the altar may be consecrated by the coming of the Holy Spirit: 'Munera nostra Domine, sancti Spiritus sacrentur adventu'. On the Tuesday of the same week, the Secret is as follows: 'Send, Lord, the Holy Spirit, that he may make these gifts into your sacrament for us'.

3

THE HOLY SPIRIT IN OUR
COMMUNION WITH THE BODY
AND BLOOD OF CHRIST

Many epicleses ask for the Spirit to bring about not only the consecration of the gifts into the body and blood of Christ and their sanctification, but also the fruits of the communion received by the believer. I propose to consider in this chapter the part played by the Spirit in communion.

The Fathers and the later theologians discussed this question a great deal, and they did so in such a way as to reflect the careful balance they maintained between their Christology and their pneumatology. That is precisely what is theologically at stake in this question and the response we make to it involves the way we practise communion in the Eucharist. Is the Holy Spirit implicated in communion? Why is he implicated? How?

In any examination of the evidence provided by the Church's Tradition, we are confronted by two, even three different approaches to the problem—the Alexandrian approach, the Augustinian approach, which was taken up and extended by the Scholastic theologians, and the Syrian tradition. Let us try to benefit from them all.

(1) The Alexandrian Fathers Athanasius (†373) and Cyril of Alexandria (†444) spoke about the Eucharist in the context of their struggle against Arius and later against Nestorius. In other words, they were anxious to affirm the divinity of the incarnate Word and the sanctifying and deifying power of his 'flesh'.[1] As Cyril declared, 'The body of the Lord himself was sanctified by the power of the Word who was united to him, but it was made so effective that, in the Eulogy, it can communicate its own sanctification to us'.[2]

This does not mean that these Fathers associated the power of sanctification with the incarnation as such and neglected the facts of Easter, that is, the redeeming passion and resurrection. There are many texts testifying to their concern with the latter.[3] Nor does it mean that they had a purely Christological view of the Eucharist, without any pneumatological emphasis. Cyril, for example, wrote: 'Just as the virtue of the sacred flesh makes those who receive it con-corporeal with each other, so too, it seems to me, does the Spirit, who comes to dwell in all of us, lead them to spiritual (pneumatic) unity'.[4] Athanasius' gloss on the text of 1 Cor 10:3–4 is frequently quoted: 'Made to drink of the Spirit, we drink Christ'.[5] The two are inseparable and the Alexandrian Fathers did not separate them, even though they stressed the Word. They say again and again that the Father brings everything about through the Son in the Holy Spirit.

(2) A great tradition that has flourished for centuries in the West is associated with the sixth chapter of the gospel of John on the bread of life and the exposition of this text by Augustine.[6] This exposition is based on a Pauline text: 'Our fathers . . . all ate the same supernatural (spiritual) food and drank the same supernatural (spiritual) drink. For they drank from the supernatural (spiritual) Rock which followed them and the Rock was Christ' (1 Cor 10:3–4).

Augustine's argument is as follows: We all eat and drink the same Christ in the eucharistic bread and wine. The 'sacraments' as signs are different, but the reality to which they point is the same—it is Christ. The Jews of the exodus did not attain to Christ and are therefore *our* fathers only to the extent that they ate and drank 'spiritually'. This is why Augustine stressed, even for us, the need to 'understand' and, what is more, to understand 'spiritually'. It is necessary to come, in and through the sacrament, to what is signified by the sacrament. This is done through faith (in Christ).[7] That faith is the essential. Hence the famous *crede et manducasti* (*Comm. in ev. Ioan.* XXV, 12)—'Believe and you have then eaten (Christ)'. The man who desires life should approach, believe and be incorporated in order to be given life (XXVI, 13). Considering Christ, Augustine saw him as our Head, he considered the 'whole Christ', that is, Head and members, the whole Body, and the principle that animates it, the Holy Spirit. These ideas follow each other and combine in his thought: the living bread, the Body of Christ (Head and members), the sacrament of the Body that is on the altar. Also, on the altar there is what you are; we are the body and this is what is on the altar, Christ, but a Christ who is not without his Body, the city of saints. It is necessary to belong to that Body to live in the Spirit, which is to that Body what the soul is to our body. The Spirit, who is common to both the Father and the Son, is their love for each other.[8]

There is a constant movement from the sacramental body to the Body of the Church. In order to live from the Spirit, it is necessary to belong to the Body (of the Church). We are of the Body of the Church, firstly if we have the spirit of communion and unity, and then, if we eat the sacrament of the body, if we go beyond the visible sign of bread to reach the Reality to which it points. This is done by eating the bread in a spiritual manner. The expression *manducatio spiritualis* is not used as such by Augustine, but its equivalent is: 'panem coelestem spiritaliter manducate' (XXVI, 11); 'ut carnem Christi et sanguinem Christ non edamus tantum in sacramento sed usque ad Spiritus participationem manducemus et bibamus' (XXVII, 11).

What part, then, does the Holy Spirit play in all this? It refers back to the

Body of Christ which we form: we have to be in that Body if we are to live from the Spirit of Christ (XXXV, 13). The flesh of Christ present sacramentally on its own has nothing to offer in itself. It has to be given life by charity in our eating of it, and that is precisely what the Spirit does (XXVII, 4–6). In a word, the Spirit gives life to those who receive communion. The latter must not simply receive the sacrament, however, but must eat and drink to the point of sharing in the Spirit, through the lively faith that they have in Christ (XXVII, 11).

These Augustinian master texts had a powerful effect on the meditations of the Latins and the reflections of theologians. I do not attempt to trace the history of this influence here—all that I can do is to refer to a number of important authors and texts. The first is Prosper of Aquitaine, who was active only a few years later than Augustine himself.[9] During the early years of the sixth century, Fulgentius of Ruspe[10] saw the intervention of the Spirit in the gift of charity enabling us to preserve unanimity and to be crucified to the world. The Spirit brings about the charity of Easter in the one who receives communion.

The early Scholastic theologians were concerned with the sacrament itself as one of the Church's celebrations. Following Alger of Liège, Peter Lombard adapted a vocabulary inherited from Augustine to suit contemporary needs and distinguished two res in the Eucharist. By res, he did not mean, as Augustine had meant, Christ himself, but also an aspect of the sacrament. The first of these two res is the reality that is at once aimed at and contained. This is the personal body of Jesus Christ. The second is the reality aimed at but not contained. This reality is the unity of the Church in its saints.[11] Thus when Peter Lombard distinguished between 'two modes of eating', he defined these by reference to one or other res acquired in that eating. He spoke of manducatio sacramentalis and of manducatio spiritualis, taking place through faith and enabling the one who receives the sacrament to remain in the unity of Christ and the Church.[12] Its virtue is such that it is possible to eat (the second reality or res) without eating (the sacrament itself), or not to eat (the second reality) when one has eaten (the sacrament), 'quia non manducans sacramentaliter aliquando manducat spiritualiter, et e converso'.

According to H.-R. Schlette's analysis, Bonaventure took the distinction made between the two modes of eating from the point of view of the believer, 'per comparationem ad manducantem', whereas Thomas Aquinas continued in the line followed by Peter Lombard and took it in terms of the structure of the sacrament. He distinguished between a manducatio spiritualis, in which the res tantum was acquired, that is, the spiritual reality to which the sacrament finally pointed, and a manducatio sacramentalis, which reached the res et sacramentum, what we term the 'real presence'.[13] Fundamentally, however, this manducatio is only that of the sacramentum. On the contrary, the manducatio spiritualis, which normally presupposes the *manducatio sacramentalis*, has such a power that it can obtain the effect of the sacrament without the sacrament itself being received.[14]

This teaching about the *manducatio spiritualis* led eventually to what is now known as 'spiritual communion'.[15] This gives us altogether three modes of eating: the first is the purely external eating of the sacrament alone, the second the truly spiritual reception of the sacrament, and the third the purely spiritual eating without the real reception of the sacrament. This is what the Council of Trent and the Roman Catechism taught.[16] As J. Eichinger pointed out, however,[17] a curious inversion of the vocabulary has taken place in this process, so that now, someone who does not receive the Host does not *really* receive communion—but only receives it *spiritually*. In the past, as we have seen, *real* communion, that is, receiving the ultimate reality or *res* of the Eucharist, presupposed a *spiritual* eating.

It is interesting in this context to note the part that Thomas attributes to the Holy Spirit. In the first place, like all the Scholastic theologians, he attributes the effectiveness of all the sacraments in a general sense to the Spirit.[18] At the same time, like Augustine, he also maintains that the spiritual eating of the sacrament is a participation in the Holy Spirit. In the following passage, quoted from Thomas' commentary on the gospel of John, I show this in small capital letters:

That man eats and drinks sacramentally who receives the sacrament, and spiritually if he goes as far as the *res* of the sacrament, which is twofold: the one is contained and signified; that is Christ who is complete, contained in the species of bread and wine; the other is signified and not contained; that is the mystical Body which is found in those who are predestined, called and made righteous. Thus, the man who is united to him through faith and charity so as to be transformed into him and to become his member eats his flesh and drinks his blood spiritually in respect of the Christ who is contained and signified. . . . It is therefore a food that is capable of making man divine and of making him drunk with divinity. In the same way, in respect of the mystical Body which is simply signified, if he participates in the unity of the Church. . . . In this relationship with the mystical Body, he will have life if he perseveres, since the unity of the Church is brought about by the HOLY SPIRIT, according to Eph 4:4: 'one Spirit and one Body', and Eph 1:14: 'the guarantee (earnest-money) of our inheritance'. That food therefore brings a great benefit, that is, the eternal life of the soul—and also of the body.

Paul also adds: 'And I will raise him up on the last day'. The man who eats and drinks spiritually comes to participate in the HOLY SPIRIT, through whom we are united to Christ in a union of faith and charity and through whom we become members of the Church. The HOLY SPIRIT enables us to obtain resurrection, according to Rom 8:1. . . . If what he said: 'Whoever eats my flesh . . .' refers mystically to the body and blood, then the words are clear, since, as has been said, that man eats spiritually so far as the *res* that is merely signified is concerned who is incorporated into the mystical Body by the union of faith and charity. But charity enables God to dwell in us and, according to 1 Jn 4:16, 'he who dwells in charity dwells in God and God dwells in him'. This is precisely what the HOLY SPIRIT does, as we are told in 1 Jn 4:13: 'By this we know that we dwell in God and God in us, because he has given us of his own Spirit'.[19]

Thomas Aquinas, then, attributed the gift of faith and charity to the Holy Spirit in communion. It is through this gift of faith and charity that the believer is united, as their member, to Christ and the Church, which Thomas calls the mystical Body. The action of the Spirit is in this way situated on and in the believer. Even in the details, this is fully within the tradition of Augustine, except for the fact that the category of res had been defined more precisely by Hugh of Saint-Victor and Peter Lombard.

(3) The Syrian tradition is rather different from the Alexandrian and the Augustinian traditions.[20] The image of fire is frequently used in it. According to Ephraem Syrus,

> There is fire and Spirit in Mary's womb;
> there is fire and Spirit in the river in which you were baptized.
> Fire and Spirit in our own baptism,
> in the bread and in the cup, fire and Holy Spirit.[21]

> In your bread is hidden the Spirit who is not eaten;
> in your wine dwells the Fire that cannot be drunk.
> The Spirit in your bread, the Fire in your wine,
> a remarkable miracle that our lips have received.[22]

This image of fire is also found, together with visions of fire, in the West, but there they are both connected with the consecration of the elements of bread and wine through the virtue of the Holy Spirit.[23] It seems to me that the distinctive aspect of the Syrian tradition is that the activity of the Spirit in the Eucharist is linked with his activity in the Christological economy of salvation, that is, in the conception, baptism, Last Supper and resurrection of Christ. The Spirit first came upon Jesus and filled him. Jesus himself filled the bread and the wine of the Eucharist with the Spirit. A number of texts should provide evidence of this:

> In the same way, after supper, he took the cup, made a mixture of wine and water, raised his eyes to heaven, presented it to you, his God and Father, gave thanks, consecrated it and blessed it, filled it with the Holy Spirit and gave it to his holy and blessed disciples, saying. . . .[24]

> He called the bread his living body, filled it with himself and with the Spirit, stretched out his hand and gave them the bread: 'Take and eat with faith and do not doubt that this is my body'. And the one who eats with faith, through it he eats the fire of the Spirit. . . . Eat all of you and eat through it the Holy Spirit.[25]

> Henceforth you will eat a pure and spotless Pasch, a perfect leavened bread that the Holy Spirit has kneaded and baked, a wine mixed with fire and the Spirit.[26]

> He wanted us no longer to see according to their nature those things (the bread and the wine) that had received the grace and the coming of the Holy Spirit, but to

take them as the body and blood of our Lord. For the body of our Lord, it was also not of his own nature that he had immortality and the power to bestow immortality, but it was the Holy Spirit who gave these to him and it was through the resurrection from the dead that he received the combination with divine nature and became immortal and the cause of immortality for others.[27]

According to the *Testament of Our Lord*, a Syrian document dating back to about 475 or even earlier, the one giving communion to his fellow-believers said: 'The Body of Jesus Christ, the Holy Spirit, for the healing of soul and body'.[28] As we have seen, at the zeon in the Byzantine rite, the deacon says: 'The fervour of faith, filled with the Holy Spirit', and the priest, putting a fragment of the bread, the Lamb, into the chalice, says: 'The fullness of the Holy Spirit'. Again and again, the Syrian authors stressed that, when we receive the body and blood of the Lord, we receive the Holy Spirit, his grace and his gift of immortality.[29]

*　　*　　*

To what conclusion can we come? Fervent, but reasonable, reasonable, but fervent, we take our place modestly in the assembly of believers who are celebrating and then in the line of those who are receiving communion.

The 'eucharisted' bread and wine can be taken merely *sacramentaliter* or materially, just as a thing. This attitude may be encouraged by too much insistence on the 'real presence', but in the same way the most beautiful hymns about the fire of the Spirit and the most beautiful words about the Spirit himself can also become purely ritual.

Sacramental communion, if it is to achieve what it aims to achieve, calls for an act on the part of the one receiving it which is an act of living faith and love and at the same time an act which comes from the Holy Spirit as its first cause. Rather like a packet placed in a trough and then carried along by a current of living water, my sacramental communion is taken up by the movement and the warmth with which the Spirit, who is invoked and who opens up a channel for himself in me, invests the presence of Jesus. My communion is therefore a cleaving, in abandonment and love, to what Jesus is, wants and brings about in me.

In his very illuminating study of the Eucharist, Henri de Lubac denounced the disadvantages of a movement 'from symbolism to dialectics'.[30] One of these disadvantages was the distinction that led to what de Lubac called a break in the earlier unity between the *res contenta* or 'real presence' and the *res non contenta*, the unity of the mystical Body. For Augustine, on the other hand, the bread and wine, the body and blood of Christ on the altar, 'represented and contained, in a real and physical way, his mystical Body, since the head without the body was not the head'.[31] In Scholastic theology, a bond was preserved between Christ present or 'contained' in the sacrament and his mystical Body, but this bond was to a reality that was extrinsic to what is found on the altar and to what we eat.

I would like to have what Thomas Aquinas meant by *res non contenta* investigated more closely. Examples concerning other sacraments would lead me to think that it means the effect to which the sacrament points (*res significata*), but what is not obtained or produced by the sacramental act alone.[32] It calls for the intervention of another energy. It is true that the sacrament of the Eucharist 'perficitur in ipsa consecratione materiae', is brought about by the consecration of the bread and wine and their 'conversion' into the body and blood of Christ.[33] In that sense, the spiritual fruit of the sacrament, which takes place in the one who receives communion, is 'extrinsic' to it. Thomas, however, knew that a sacrament was 'the sign of a sacred reality *insofar as it sanctifies men*',[34] in other words, that the spiritual fruit belonged to the sacrament and that it was its *res* or 'thing'. The bond between the Eucharist and the unity of the mystical Body was very carefully preserved in Scholastic theology. I myself have a file on this subject which would fill many pages in a book. Albert the Great would have a privileged place. But—and this brings us back to our point—if the sacrament is to have, in the life of Christians, its 'reality', that is, the fruit to which it points, what is required is an intervention on the part of the Spirit, who is, in us, the author of charity. And that charity is paschal, it is of the Church, and it is orientated towards God's work in the world and towards his kingdom.[35] Jesus is in us, but, if his sacramental presence is to have its effect, the Holy Spirit must add his breath, his fire and his dynamism.

The Eucharist follows the structure of the economy of salvation. It was, in other words, necessary for the Holy Spirit to sanctify, anoint and guide Jesus, the Word made flesh. On pp. 165–171 of this volume, I have provided an outline of what might be called a pneumatological Christology. It was necessary for the Holy Spirit to 'pneumatize' him, according to the teaching of Paul in, for example, Rom 1:4; 1 Cor 15:45; 2 Cor 3:17–18. The Christ whom we receive in sacramental communion is the Christ of Easter who has been 'pneumatized' or penetrated by the Spirit. According to the Decree on the Ministry of Priests promulgated by the Second Vatican Council, 'the most blessed Eucharist contains the Church's entire spiritual wealth, that is, Christ himself, our Passover and living bread. Through his very flesh, made vital and vitalizing by the Holy Spirit, he offers life to men.'[36]

What the Spirit has brought about in Christ in order to make him the Head of the Body, he has also to bring about in us to make us his members and to complete and sanctify his Body. The same Spirit is at work in the three realities that bear the name of the body of Christ and are dynamically linked to each other through the dynamism of the Spirit: Jesus, who was born of Mary and who suffered, died and was raised from the dead and glorified→ the bread and wine that are 'eucharisted'→ the communion or Body of which we are the members. There is only one economy of grace in which the same Spirit sanctifies the body of Christ in its three states that are differentiated but at the same time dynamically linked together and this is to the glory of God the Father: 'Through him, with him, in him, in the unity of the Holy Spirit', as we say at the end of every eucharistic prayer.

NOTES

1. J. M. R. Tillard, *L'Eucharistie Pâque de l'Eglise* (*Unam Sanctam*, 44) (Paris, 1964), pp. 60ff.; A. Houssiau, 'Incarnation et communion selon les Pères grecs', *Irénikon*, 45 (1972), 457–468, especially 466.
2. Cyril of Alexandria, *Comm. in ev. Ioan.* XI, 9 (*PG* 74, 528) for Jn 17:13.
3. J. M. R. Tillard, *op. cit.* J.-P. Jossua has shown that this opposition points to a false alternative for the Latin Fathers as well: see his *Le Salut. Incarnation ou Mystère pascal chez les Pères de l'Eglise de S. Irénée à S. Léon le Grand* (Paris, 1968).
4. Cyril of Alexandria, *Comm. in ev. Ioan.* XI, 11 (*PG* 74, 561). See also *Comm. in Luc.* XXII (*PG* 72, 912): 'Giving life and uniting himself to a flesh that he made his own, the Word of God made that flesh life-giving. It was suitable for him also to unite himself in a certain fashion to our bodies through his sacred flesh and his precious blood which we receive in the bread and wine for a life-giving blessing.' This passage is quoted by Thomas Aquinas in his *Catena aurea, in Luc.* 22 and in *ST* IIIa, q. 79, a. 1.
5. Athanasius, *Ad Ser.* I (*PG* 26, 576A). It is also possible to cite Gregory of Nyssa, *In illud 'Tunc ipse Filius'* (*PG* 44, 1320D); *Antirrhet.* 42 (*PG* 45, 1224B).
6. Augustine, *Comm. in ev. Ioan.* XXVI, 12 to XXVII, 11; see *Œuvres de S. Augustin*, 72: *Homélies sur l'Evangile de S. Jean XVII–XXXIII*, Fr. tr. and notes by M.-F. Berrouard (Paris, 1977). Berrouard's notes are especially valuable. For the commentaries and the exegesis of Jn 6, there are references in J. M. R. Tillard, *op. cit.* (note 1), p. 183, note 3 and in my own study, first pub. in *Parole de Dieu et Sacerdoce. Etudes présentées à Mgr. Weber* (Tournai, 1962), pp. 21–58; Eng. tr., 'The Two Forms of the Bread of Life in the Gospel and Tradition', *Priest and Layman* (London, 1967), pp. 103–138, esp. p. 127, note 2.
7. Hence, in Augustine's teaching, the importance of this idea, which was later used by Thomas Aquinas and which can be summarized as: the ancient world, with its faith in Christ to come, and we ourselves, with our faith in Christ who has come, together make up the same church.
8. For this point, see M.-F. Berrouard, *op. cit.* (note 6), p. 832; see also Volume I, pp. 77–79, 85–90.
9. Prosper, *Sent.* 341 (*PL* 45, 1890).
10. Fulgentius, *Contra Fab.*, fragment 28 (*PL* 65, 789–791).
11. Peter Lombard, *IV Sent.*, d. 8 (Quaracchi ed. (1916), p. 791). For what follows, see H.-R. Schlette, *Die Lehre von der geistlichen Kommunion bei Bonaventura, Albert dem Grossen und Thomas von Aquin* (*Münch. Theol. Stud.*, II, *Syst. Abt.*, 17) (Munich, 1959), pp. 22ff. for Peter Lombard.
12. *Sent.* IV, d. 9 (Quaracchi ed. (1916), pp. 793ff.).
13. Thomas Aquinas, *In IV Sent.* d. 9, a. un. qᵃ 3; *Comm. in ev. Ioan.* c. 6, lect. 7; *ST* IIIa, q. 80, a. 1.
14. *ST* IIIa, q. 80, a. 1, ad 3.
15. There are articles on this subject by H. Moureau, *DTC*, III (1923), cols 572–574, and L. de Bazelaire, *Dictionnaire de Spiritualité*, II (1953), cols 1297–1302.
16. Council of Trent, Sessio XIII, c. 8; *Roman Catechism*, II, c. 4, q. 41, n. 1–3.
17. J. Eichinger, 'Die Lehre vom "sakramentalen" und vom "geistlichen" Empfang Christi', *TQ*, 132 (1952), 87–92.
18. Thomas Aquinas, *ST* Ia IIae, q. 112, a. 1, ad 2; for baptism, see IIIa, q. 66, a. 11, ad 1; a. 12 c and ad 3. See also Albert the Great for the Eucharist: *In ev. Ioan.* c. 6: 'Haec autem

omnia per causam non facit nisi Spiritus divinus operans in sacramento' (ed. A. Borgnet, 24, p. 281); 'Spiritus divinus operatur omne quod in sacramento est operandum' (Borgnet, 24, p. 286).

19. Thomas Aquinas, *Comm. in ev. Ioan.* c. 6, lect. 7, § 3–5; Cai, Nos 972–976.

20. See J. M. R. Tillard, *op. cit.* (note 1), pp. 83ff., and especially E.-P. Siman, *L'expérience de l'Esprit par l'Eglise d'après la tradition syrienne d'Antioche* (*Théol. hist.*, 15) (Paris, 1971); *idem*, 'La dimension pneumatique de l'Eucharistie d'après la tradition syrienne d'Antioche', *L'Expérience de l'Esprit. Mélanges Schillebeeckx* (*Le Point théol.*, 18) (Paris, 1976), pp. 97–114; I. H. Dalmais, 'L'Esprit Saint et le mystère du salut dans les épiclèses eucharistiques syriennes', *Istina*, 18 (1973), 147–154; P. Yousif, 'L'Eucharistie et le Saint-Esprit d'après S. Ephrem de Nisibe', *A Tribute to Arthur Vööbus. Studies in Early Christian Literature* (Chicago, 1977), pp. 235–246.

21. Ephraem Syrus, *De Fide*, VI, 17. I have taken these texts from the authors mentioned in the preceding note.

22. *De Fide*, X, 8.

23. K. Goldammer, *Die eucharistische Epiklese* (Bottrop, 1941), pp. 78–79, quoted Rupert of Deutz, *De Trin. et oper. eius, in Exod.* II, 10 (*PL* 167, 617) and Hugh of Saint-Victor, *Sermo* 27 (*PL* 177, 958), according to whom the fire of the Spirit cooked the Host as the paschal Lamb; on pp. 96ff., Goldammer speaks of visions of a fiery sphere above the altar and the priest at the time of the consecration. The idea of cooking in the fire of the Holy Spirit can also be found in Augustine, in connection with the sacrament of Christian initiation: see *Sermo* 272 (*PL* 38, 1247).

24. Liturgy of St James.

25. Ephraem Syrus, *Sermons for Holy Saturday*, IV, 4; *Hymni et Sermones*, I, ed. T. Lamy (Malines, 1882), pp. 415ff.

26. *Ibid.*, p. 418.

27. Theodore of Mopsuestia, *Hom. cat.* XV, First on the Mass, No. 10 (Fr. tr. R. Tonneau and R. Devreesse (Vatican City, 1949), p. 475); cf. XVI, Second on the Mass, No. 24 (*ibid.*, p. 571).

28. E. P. Siman, *L'expérience de l'Esprit par l'Eglise, op. cit.* (note 20), p. 106.

29. E. P. Siman, *ibid.*, pp. 106ff., 222–242; Theodore of Mopsuestia, *Hom. cat.* XVI, Second on the Mass, Nos 13, 22, 25 (*op. cit.* (note 27), pp. 555, 565, 573).

30. H. de Lubac, *Corpus mysticum* (Paris, 1944; 2nd ed. 1949), chapter X and the end of Part II.

31. O. Perler, *Le pèlerin de la Cité de Dieu* (Paris, 1957), p. 135.

32. Thomas Aquinas, *Comm. in 1 Cor.* c. 12, lect. 1 and c. 15, lect. 1, who says that grace is the *res contenta* of the sacraments and that the *res non contenta* is the resurrection, 'cum non statim habeat eam qui suscipit sacramenta'; *In IV Sent.* d. 26, q. 2, a. 1, ad 4: in marriage, 'unio Christi ad Ecclesiam non est res contenta in hoc sacramento sed res significata'.

33. *ST* IIIa, q. 73, a. 1, ad 3.

34. *ST* IIIa, q. 60, a. 2.

35. It would be possible to comment on each of these words. Apart from J. M. R. Tillard, *op. cit.* (note 1), see my earlier works: *L'Eglise une, sainte, catholique et apostolique* (Paris, 1970), pp. 31–38; 'The Eucharist and the Fulfilment of the World in God' (Eng. tr.), *The Revelation of God* (London and New York, 1968), pp. 189–197; *Lay People in the Church* (Eng. tr.; London, 1957).

36. Decree on the Life of Priests, *Presbyterorum ordinis*, 5, §2.

4

THE LIFE OF THE CHURCH
AS ONE LONG EPICLESIS

Before I try to give an overall view, and in order to do this properly, I would like to look briefly at the other sacraments, all of which refer to the Eucharist.

The three sacraments of initiation—baptism, anointing with chrism, and the Eucharist—are celebrated thanks to an epiclesis which, in the Syrian Church, has a very similar structure in all three.[1] These sacraments, in which the faith of the subject is expressed, lead him, by progressively incorporating him into the glorified Body of Christ, towards eschatological fulfilment. The Holy Spirit is the eschatological gift through and in which we return to the Father.

(1) This initiation begins in the water, over which the Spirit hovers, as at the beginning of the world (Gen 1:2), as though he were hatching it. This connection between the Spirit and water was often stressed by the Fathers.[2] It is also a biblical theme.[3] The Spirit himself is represented by water—living water 'welling up to eternal life' (Jn 4:14). The business of the liturgy is to express in rites accompanied by words the truth of God's activity, and the water of baptism is therefore consecrated in it by invoking the Spirit in a solemn epiclesis. This water is like the womb of our mother the Church, in which the Spirit gives birth to the Body of Christ.[4] Christology and pneumatology are closely associated in the liturgy, as they are in the whole divine economy of salvation. In the Roman liturgy (there is evidence as early as the Gelasian Sacramentary), the celebrant plunges the paschal candle with its flame (representing the risen Christ) three times into the water and at the same time three times invokes the descent of the Holy Spirit, as at the baptism of Jesus himself in the Jordan.[5]

I have already considered, in Volume II, pp. 189–190, the part played by the Spirit in the act of baptism, with reference to the New Testament. It has often been pointed out by theologians that the virtue or power of the Spirit is active in this sacrament.[6] It is not simply a question of divine activity in the neophyte according to the general attribution of the effectiveness of the sacraments to the Holy Spirit. In the case of the baptism of infants, the Holy Spirit intervenes as the principle of communion which transcends the details of space and time and is able to include the infant, who is still unconscious, within the faith of his parents, his sponsors and the whole Church. This presents us with a real problem today and, what is more, one for which psychological, sociological and biological considerations have not been adequate. What is needed is an effective power of communion and a trans-supplementation of one consciousness by another in a unity that transcends human experience. This is supplied by the Spirit: 'If the faith of one person or rather of the whole Church is valuable to the infant, this is thanks to the activity of the Holy Spirit who is the bond of the Church and through whom the treasures of each person are shared by all the others'.[7]

(2) The process by which a minister—a deacon, priest or bishop—is ordained also takes place subject to the invocation of the Spirit. I have called it a process, because it begins before the act of ordination in the strict sense of the term. It begins in fact with the election or the call of the one who can no longer be called a 'candidate' in the modern sense of the word. There are prayers for this election, which is attributed to the Holy Spirit.[8]

In the ordination rite itself, according to the Apostolic Constitution of Pius XII, *Sacramentum Ordinis*, of 30 November 1947, the 'matter' is the laying-on of hands.[9] This is in itself a gesture pointing to the communication of the Spirit, but it has always been accompanied or followed by prayer.[10] It is also a gesture that was practised by the apostles and the first disciples (see Acts 6:6; 13:3; cf. 1 Tim 4:16; 2 Tim 1:6). The 'form' of ordination is the Preface which follows. Its expression is deprecative and for this reason it is clearly an epiclesis. Here is the text of the *Sacramentum Ordinis* for the ordination of deacons, followed by that for the ordination of priests:[11]

> Lord,
> send forth upon them the Holy Spirit,
> that they may be strengthened
> by the gift of your sevenfold grace
> to carry out faithfully the work of the ministry.
>
> Almighty Father,
> grant to these servants of yours
> the dignity of the priesthood.
> Renew within them the Spirit of holiness.
> As co-workers with the order of bishops
> may they be faithful to the ministry
> that they receive from you, Lord God,
> and be to others a model of right conduct.

When a bishop is consecrated, those consecrating lay their hands on the man elected and, while they do this, 'all remain silent, praying in their hearts for the descent of the Spirit. After this, one of the bishops present, at the request of all, laying on his hand on the one who is made a bishop, prays, saying: "Pour out the power that comes from you, (that) of the sovereign

Spirit, (that) which you gave to your beloved Son Jesus Christ and which he granted to his holy apostles who constituted the church in various places as your sanctuary, to the praise and glory of your name".' This is how Hippolytus described the consecration of bishops in his *Apostolic Tradition* (*Trad. apost.* 3). It is also the text which the Apostolic Constitution *Pontificalis Romani* of Paul VI (18 June 1968) established as the form of episcopal ordination. This Constitution refers explicitly to Hippolytus and notes that the text is still in use in the Coptic and West Syrian rites. This renewal by allowing an early source to well up again is something that I find very valuable. I also appreciate very much the allusion to Pentecost, since it is well known that many of the Church Fathers saw in Pentecost the ordination of the apostles.[12]

(3) Several of the Fathers saw a first ordination in what has wrongly been called the 'Johannine Pentecost' (Jn 20:19–23): 'Receive the Holy Spirit. If you forgive the sins of any, they are forgiven; if you retain the sins of any, they are retained.' The so-called 'power of the keys' and the sacrament of penance are entirely under the sign of the Holy Spirit. The Spirit is mentioned more than twenty times in the *Praenotanda* of the new ritual which was promulgated in December 1973. The renewed formula of absolution is not simply a declaration and it is only implicitly in the form of an epiclesis. It is, however, strikingly Trinitarian. The text is as follows:

> God, the Father of mercies,
> through the death and resurrection of his Son,
> has reconciled the world to himself
> and sent the Holy Spirit among us
> for the forgiveness of sins:
> through the ministry of the Church
> may God give you pardon and peace,
> and I absolve you from your sins
> in the name of the Father, and of the Son,
> and of the Holy Spirit.

(4) In the Latin Catholic West, the important moment in the sacramental celebration of marriage is the exchange of consent between the bride and the bridegroom in the presence of witnesses from the Christian community, normally the priest and other witnesses.[13] In the Eastern Churches, the celebration culminates in the crowning of the bride and bridegroom by the priest, his function being parallel that to the part that he plays in the celebration of the Eucharist. The crowns symbolize the descent of the Holy Spirit on the couple. The priest's gesture and the prayer that follows it correspond to the invocation of the Holy Spirit, the epiclesis, in the celebration of the Eucharist.[14]

(5) In the seventeenth and eighteenth centuries, it was suggested by a number of canon lawyers that religious profession should be seen as a contract between the professed religious and his or her institute. This was not very successful, because the reality presented greater spiritual substance.[15] Religious profession is a consecration and it is not difficult to understand why early Christians included it among the *sacramenta*, at a time when that term was less precisely defined than it is today, or even called it *ordinatio*, as Theodore of Canterbury (†698) did. Pseudo-Dionysius described the consecration of monks at the beginning of the sixth century, probably in Syria, in the following way: 'This ritual includes a prayer of consecration (or epiclesis), an oral profession in the form of a renunciation of the world, and the tonsure and clothing'.[16] Whenever the Christian mystery or our *vita in Christo* has to be made present here and now, the Spirit has to be invoked.

(6) This is particularly true of an area of Christian life which is very dear and familiar to me, that of Christian knowledge and the word of God. These also have a sacramental structure of a kind, in that they are meant to go through and beyond a visible and tangible expression, which as such is part of our world, to an insight into the Word of God himself in and through men's minds, which can be assimilated to the *res* of the sacraments.[17] Does, for example, chapter 6 of the gospel of John not present the bread of life in the two forms of faith and the Eucharist? Has the theme of the two tables at which the people of God are fed, that of the Word and that of the Eucharist, not been taken up again and again in the Church's Tradition?[18] If it is necessary, however, to have spiritual fruit to make the mystery of Christ present here and now in our lives, then it is also necessary to invoke the Holy Spirit in epicleses.

It is traditional to invoke the Spirit when the Holy Scriptures are read. It is not for nothing that they have been called *lectio divina*! We always need the Spirit to come when we read the Scriptures, Jerome declared.[19] I have already spoken, in Volume II, pp. 27–29, of the part played by the Spirit in our 'spiritual' understanding of the Scriptures. The Holy Spirit is the principle of all right knowledge.[20]

It is obvious that there is a need for the Spirit to intervene and therefore for an epiclesis in the preaching of the Word as a human activity, which is always a risk, involving the transmission of the absolute Word. God has to open the hearts of the listeners, as he opened the heart of Lydia (Acts 16:14). The anointing by faith mentioned by John (1 Jn 2:20, 27) and Paul (2 Cor 1:21) comes from the Spirit and, if the Word is to be expressed in human words and the mystery of Jesus is to be manifested in them, the Spirit has to act. Without him, there can be no spiritual event. With him, something will happen.[21] The preacher has to beseech him earnestly to come both into his poor words and into the hearts of those who hear them. What is more, he is not the only one who should pray for the Spirit—the community should pray with him: 'Pray for us also', Paul wrote to the Colossians (Col 4:3), 'that God may open to us a door for the word, to declare the mystery of Christ'.[22] The word of God, then, has a kind of sacramental structure.[23] It has its external form, its content of truth and its spiritual fruit or its *res* in our souls. It has in fact often been compared to the Eucharist.

*   *   *

(7) The Church as a whole is sacramental in its nature. It is, *in and through Christ*, the great and primordial sacrament of salvation. I have elaborated this teaching already in another book.[24] The whole Church—its people, its ministers, its treasure of the means of grace and its institution—is that sacrament of salvation. So far from the comings of the Holy Spirit to the Church challenging and questioning its institutional character, they establish it in its truth. The Church is, after all, an institution of a very special kind. It acts in the present on the basis of past events and in the prospect of a future which is nothing less than the kingdom of God, the eschatological City and eternal life in communion with God himself. This is undoubtedly a sacramental structure, containing a memory of the event of foundation, a prophetic sign of the absolute future, and present grace coming from the first and preparing the way for the latter. It is, however, the Holy Spirit who ensures the unity of these three aspects. 'There is a sacramental presence where the Holy Spirit enables, by means of "earthly" elements, men to live here and now from the past, present and future work of Christ, and where he makes them live from salvation.'[25]

In and for the purpose of all these activities, the part played by an intervention of the Holy Spirit and by an epiclesis is to affirm that neither the 'earthly means' nor the institution of the Church produces these by themselves. What we have here is an absolutely supernatural work that is both divine and deifying. The Church can be sure that God works in it, but, because it is God and not the Church that is the principle of this holy activity, the Church has to pray earnestly for his intervention as a grace. As an apostle, Paul was convinced that he was proclaiming the Word of God, yet he still prayed and had others pray for it (see Col 4:3; Eph 6:19). Jesus was sure that he was doing God's work, yet he too prayed before he chose his apostles (see Lk 6:12–13). In the same way, the Church does not in itself have any assurance that it is doing work that will 'well up to eternal life'; it has to pray for the grace of the one who is uncreated Grace, that is, the absolute Gift, the Breath of the Father and the Word.[26] At the level of dogmatic theology, as we have seen already in Volume II, pp. 5–6, 'I believe the holy Church' is conditioned by the absolute 'I believe in the Holy Spirit'. This dogma means that the life and activity of the Church can be seen totally as an epiclesis.

*   *   *

(8) The Spirit is the principle of unity. He is present and active everywhere,[27] but he is that principle in a more formal and intense way in the Christian communions, which, alas, have been disunited for centuries. The ecumenical movement was given life and has been kept alive by him. For many decades now, there has been a growing awareness of and sensitivity to the Holy Spirit in the Christian communions. Even the Lutherans, who have always been so orientated towards the Word that their Lord's Supper does not contain an epiclesis,[28] but who have always at the same time affirmed the bond that connects the Spirit with the Word (see Volume I, pp. 139–140), agree with us now sufficiently to be able to say: 'the eucharistic action of Christ is brought about by the Holy Spirit. Everything that the Lord gives us and everything that makes us ready to appropriate it is given to us by the Holy Spirit. This is expressed in the liturgy and especially in the invocation of the Holy Spirit (the epiclesis).'[29] I would gladly quote the Reformed theologian J. J. von Allmen here (see below, note 25), but the place of the Holy Spirit in Calvinist dogmatic theology is obvious (see Volume I, pp. 138 and 141). There is no need for me to speak of the Orthodox Church in this context, as I have again and again throughout this whole work presented it, quoted its authors and, I hope, walked along with it. Not long ago, Nikos Nissiotis spoke about the Holy Spirit and the Churches in connection with 'Faith and Order' in the World Council of Churches (see below, note 26). It was, moreover, the secretary of the 'Faith and Order' Commission, Lukas Vischer, who recently suggested that the epiclesis should be seen as a sign of unity, the pledge of renewal for the Churches and a new breakthrough for ecumenism.[30]

I hope very much that this long and thankless study that is now completed will contribute to the holy work of restoring Christians to unity—a unity not of uniformity and imperialism, but of communion through the one who, distributing his charisms of every kind, wants to lead everything back to the Father through the Son.

NOTES

1. E.-P. Siman revealed this vividly in his synopsis, given in the form of a table, in *L'Expérience de l'Esprit par l'Eglise* (Paris, 1971), pp. 227–229. Cyril (or was it John?) of Jerusalem compared the epiclesis of post-baptismal anointing with the epiclesis of the eucharistic gifts: *Cat. myst*. III, 3 (*PG* 33, 1092A; *SC* 126, pp. 124 and 125). See also Lufti Laham, 'Der pneumatologische Aspekt der Sakramente der christlichen Mystagogie (oder Initiation)', *Kyrios* (1972), 97–106.

2. See J. Daniélou, *Bible et liturgie* (*Lex orandi*, 11) (Paris, 1951), pp. 100ff., 125ff.; the second reference is to the sea and the Cloud.

3. See Volume I, pp. 49–51; Volume II, pp. 189–190, and 199 note 7. O. Cullmann thought that Jn 3:4 established a connection between the Spirit and water that was reminiscent of the connection between the Word and flesh: *Urchristentum und Gottesdienst* (Zürich, 1944), p. 50.

4. W. M. Bedard, *The Symbolism of the Baptismal Font in Early Christian Thought* (Washington, 1951); J. Daniélou, *op. cit.* (note 2), p. 69.

5. E. Stommel, *Studien zur Epiklese der römischen Taufwasserweihe* (*Theophania*, 10) (Bonn, 1951).

6. Alcuin, *Comm. in Ioan.* I, 2, n. 33 (*PL* 100, 757); Haymo of Auxerre, under the name of Haymo of Haberstadt (*PL* 118, 50); the Council of Arras, 1025, c. 1 (Mansi, 19, 427); Thomas Aquinas, *ST* IIIa, q. 73, a. 1. ad 2 and other references.

7. Thomas Aquinas, *ST* IIIa, q. 68, a. 9, ad 2. For the Holy Spirit as the principle of the communion of saints, see Volume II, pp. 59–61.

8. R. Sohm, *Kirchenrecht* (Munich and Leipzig, 1923), II, p. 264, note 3 and ff.; see also my *Ecclésiologie du Haut Moyen Age* (Paris, 1968), p. 115, note 236.

9. *AAS* 40 (1948), 5–7; *DS* ch 3860.

10. V. E. Fiala, 'L'imposition des mains comme signe de la communication de l'Esprit Saint dans les rites latins', *Le Saint-Esprit dans la Liturgie* (*Conférence Saint-Serge, 1969*) (Rome, 1977), pp. 87–103; German version of the same article, 'Die Handauflegung als Zeichen der Geistmitteilung in den lateinischen Riten', *Mélanges liturgiques offertes à D.B. Botte* (Louvain, 1972), pp. 121–138.

11. It is interesting to quote the epiclesis for the ordination of priests in the Eucology of Serapion in this context (ed. F. X. Funk, II (1905), pp. 188–190): 'We raise our hand, sovereign God of heaven, Father of your only Son, over this man and we pray that the Spirit of truth may fill him. Grant him the understanding and the knowledge of a right heart. May the Holy Spirit be with him so that he may govern your people with you, uncreated God. Through the Spirit of Moses, you have poured out your Holy Spirit over those whom you have chosen. Grant also to this man the Holy Spirit, through the Spirit of your only Son, in the grace of wisdom, growth and right faith, so that he may serve you with a pure conscience through your only Son Jesus Christ. Through him may glory and honour be given to you for ever and ever. Amen.'

12. J. Lécuyer, *Le sacerdoce dans le mystère du Christ* (*Lex orandi*, 24) (Paris, 1957), pp. 316–320.

13. P. Jounel, 'La liturgie romaine du mariage. Etapes de son élaboration', *M-D*, 50 (1957), 30–57.

14. I. H. Dalmais, 'La liturgie du mariage dans les Eglises orientales', *ibid.*, 58–69. See also P. Evdokimov, *Le sacrement de l'amour* (Paris, 1962).

15. See F. Vandenbroucke, *Le moine dans l'Eglise du Christ. Essai théologique* (Louvain, 1947), pp. 83ff.

16. F. Vandenbroucke, *ibid.*, p. 67; Pseudo-Dionysius, *De hier. eccl.* 6.

17. See my ideas in 1946: *M-D*, 16 (1948), 75–87; Eng. tr., 'A "real" Liturgy and "real" Preaching', *Priest and Layman* (London, 1967), pp. 139–150.

18. See my study first pub. in *Parole de Dieu et Sacerdoce. Etudes présentées à Mgr Weber* (Tournai, 1962); Eng. tr., 'The Two Forms of the Bread of Life in the Gospel and Tradition', *Priest and Layman, op. cit.*, pp. 103–138. The theme of the two tables occurs quite often in the documents of Vatican II: see, for example, the Dogmatic Constitutions on Revelation, *Dei Verbum*, 21; on the Liturgy, *Sacrosanctum Concilium*, 48; the Decrees on the Ministry of Priests, *Presbyterorum Ordinis*, 18; on Priestly Formation, *Optatam totius*, 8; on the Religious Life, *Perfectae caritatis*, 6 and 15.

19. Jerome, *In Mich.* 1, 10–15 (*PL* 25, 1215). According to Bonaventure, it is only possible to understand any branch of knowledge when one knows its language. In the case of eternal life, the knowledge of which is the scientia sacra, Bonaventure said: 'lingua eius est Spiritus Sanctus. . . . Non potest homo intelligere eam nisi Spiritus Sanctus loquatur ad cor eius'; *De S. Andrea Sermo*, 1 (Quaracchi ed., IX, p. 463); cf. *De S. Stephano Sermo*, 1 (Quaracchi ed., IX, p. 478b); *De S. Nicolao Sermo* (Quaracchi ed., IX, p. 473a). See also E. Eilers, *Gottes Wort. Eine Theologie der Predigt nach Bonaventura* (Freiburg, 1941), pp. 57ff.

20. There is a reference to this in my *Ecclésiologie du Haut Moyen Age, op. cit.* (note 8),

pp. 114–115. For the councils, see Isidore of Seville's *Adsumus*, composed for the Fourth Council of Toledo (633) and still in use. This prayer is a real epiclesis! See also Volume II, pp. 28–30.

21. See Gregory the Great, *In lib. I Reg. IV*, 122 (*PL* 79, 267): 'Habent ergo electi praedicatores experientiam Spiritus in se loquentis in repentina revelatione veritatis, habent in subito ardore caritatis, habent in plenitudine scientiae, habent facundissima verbi praedicatione: nam et subito instruuntur et repente fervescunt et in momento replentur et mirabili eloquii potestate ditantur'. The text of Bonaventure's *De S. Andrea Sermo*, 1, quoted above (note 19), continues: 'Nihil facimus nos praedicatores nisi Ipse operetur in corde per gratiam suam. Ut igitur possemus istam linguam intelligere et audire, rogabimus Spiritum Sanctum ut iuvat nos per gratiam suam, me ad loquendum, vos ad audiendum'. See also *In Hexaem*. Coll. IX, 7: 'Radiavit Spiritus Sanctus in cordibus praedicatorum ad omnem veritatem praedicandam et scribendam' (Quaracchi ed., V, p. 373b); *Comm. in Luc*. Proem. 3: 'Quod aliquis sit doctor idoneus eorum quae per Christum sunt suggesta, et per Spiritum Sanctum scripta, necesse est quod sit inunctus superna gratia' (Quaracchi ed., VII, p. 3b); I would also refer the reader to what I said about the *gratia praedicationis* in Volume I, p. 128.

22. Preachers have often asked the assembled people to pray at the beginning of their sermons; this could clearly become routine! Or else they ask the congregation to give 'prayerful attention': see A. Olivar, 'Quelques remarques historiques sur la prédication comme action liturgique dans l'Eglise ancienne', *Mélanges liturgiques offertes à D.B. Botte, op. cit.* (note 10), pp. 429–443, especially pp. 432–434. See also Bonaventure, in the quotations in note 21 above; see also E. Eilers, *Gottes Wort, op. cit.* (note 19), pp. 76ff., 78–79.

23. There have been many German studies and, in French, G. Auzon, *La parole de Dieu*, I (Paris, 1963), pp. 167–175.

24. Y. Congar, *Un peuple messianique. L'Eglise, sacrement du salut. Salut et libération* (*Cogitatio fidei*, 85) (Paris, 1975).

25. J.-J. von Allmen, *Prophétisme sacramental. Neuf études pour le renouveau et l'unité de l'Eglise* (Neuchâtel and Paris, 1964), p. 300.

26. See N. Nissiotis, 'Appelés à l'unité. Le sens épiclétique de la communion ecclésiale', *Lausanne 77. 50 ans de Foi et Constitution* (Geneva, 1977), pp. 45–60, especially p. 52.

27. See Volume II, pp. 218–221. Since then, this has also been said by the Pope in his encyclical *Redemptor hominis* of 3 March 1979, Nos 6 and 12.

28. See H. Geisser, 'Das Abendmahl nach den lutherischen Bekenntnisschriften', *Die Anrufung des Heiligen Geistes im Abendmahl* (*Beiheft zur ökumenischen Rundschau*, 31) (Frankfurt, 1977), pp. 119–147, especially p. 142. In the same collection of essays, W. Schneemelcher quotes a declaration made by P. Brunner, 'Zur Lehre vom Gottesdienst der im Namen Jesu versammelten Gemeinde', *Leiturgia*, I (1954), p. 349: 'dass die Epiklese nicht notwendig ist', 'that the epiclesis is not necessary': *op. cit.*, p. 68.

29. The agreement on the Lord's Supper reached by the Mixed Roman Catholic and Lutheran Commission: *Doc. cath.*, 76, No. 1755 (7 January 1979), 22.

30. L. Vischer, *Oekumenische Skizzen. Zwölf Beiträge mit einem Vorwort von Bischof O. Tomkins* (Frankfurt, 1972), pp. 46–57. Just as I was sending my manuscript to the publisher, I received the final document of the Dombes Group, *L'Esprit Saint, l'Eglise et les sacrements*; Nos 113ff., pp. 70ff., are devoted to the epiclesis.